NEW SCIENCE LIBRARY

offers traditional topics from a present perspective. Its aim is the enrichment of both the scientific and the spiritual views of the world through their dialogue and exchange. The series encompasses a wide range of subjects, with special interest in the following three areas:

COGNITIVE SCIENCE. Cognitive Science investigates the mind and mental processes through a blend of disciplines that includes artificial intelligence, neuroscience, linguistics, philosophy, and psychology. To these approaches, New Science Library adds anthropology and meditative techniques.

SCIENCE AND SPIRITUALITY. This area includes comparative or integrative studies relating any of the modern hard sciences with all of the great spiritual and wisdom traditions, rituals, and practices. Of particular interest are contributions from mathematics, the physical sciences, and biology.

ECOLOGY AND GLOBAL CONCERNS. Ecology is inseparable from cultural, political, and economic global concerns since the human species is a part of the complex and interdependent web of life and cannot ultimately dominate it.

New Science Library is an imprint of Shambhala Publications.

EDITORS   Jeremy W. Hayward
            Francisco J. Varela
            Ken Wilber

Charles D. Laughlin, Jr.
John McManus
Eugene G. d'Aquili

BRAIN, SYMBOL & EXPERIENCE

Toward a
Neurophenomenology
of Human Consciousness

NEW SCIENCE LIBRARY
SHAMBHALA
Boston & Shaftesbury
1990

NEW SCIENCE LIBRARY

An imprint of
SHAMBHALA PUBLICATIONS, INC.

Horticultural Hall
300 Massachusetts Avenue
Boston, Massachusetts 02115

The Old School House
The Courtyard, Bell Street
Shaftesbury, Dorset SP7 8BP

9 8 7 6 5 4 3 2 1

First Edition
Printed in the United States of America on acid-free paper
Distributed in the United States by Random House and in
Canada by Random House of Canada Ltd.
Distributed in the United Kingdom by Element Books Ltd.

Library of Congress Cataloging-in-Publication Data
Laughlin, Charles D., 1938–
    Brain, symbol, and experience : toward a neurophenomenology of
human consciousness / Charles D. Laughlin, Jr., John McManus,
Eugene G. D'Aquili.
    p.cm.
    Includes bibliographical references.
    ISBN 0-87773-522-0
    1. Consciousness. 2. Consciousness—Physiological aspects.
3. Symbolism (Psychology) 4. Experience—Psychological aspects.
I. McManus, John, 1942–   II. D'Aquili, Eugene G., 1940–
III. Title.
BF311.L26 1990   89-43324
153—dc20   CIP

This book is dedicated
to the memory of Victor Turner.

CONTENTS

Part Two: Consciousness and the Symbolic Process

Part Three: Consciousness and the Limits of Experience

PREFACE

Who knows what form the forward momentum of life will take in the time ahead or what use it will make of our anguished searching? The most that any one of us can seem to do is to fashion something—an object or ourselves—and drop it into the confusion, make an offering of it, so to speak, to the life force.

—Ernest Becker, *The Denial of Death*

ALL OF SCIENCE, anthropology included, is in a crisis of self-reflection. This disturbance is not merely superficial, narrowly affecting this or that discipline as it shops around for a new paradigm. Rather, it is a crisis of the depths, a movement within the very spirit of science that is in search of expression and meaning. The crisis is thus a hermeneutical process that began long before the advent of science, and that will not end with the emergence of a few new theories, another Nobel Prize winner or two, or some popularly applauded magical formula. It will begin to subside only when science begins to recognize its source within the unfolding tapestry of sentient awareness and consciousness in the universe. In other words, the crisis will become resolved only when science becomes phenomenologically mature (Husserl 1970).

The path leading to the exquisite tea house in which a Japanese tea ceremony is enacted is formed from a series of stones that gently meander through a garden. Each stone represents a stage in the emergence of consciousness symbolized by the tea ceremony itself. From a certain point of view, the tea ceremony begins as one first steps into the garden. In the same sense, this book is offered as a series of touchstones in this quest for meaning. It is not presented as a theoretical *fait accompli*, an elegantly constructed and seamless system that answers all the right questions and avoids the wrong ones. Far from it. In these times no serious theory will prove worthwhile that does not readily admit to its inherent paradoxes. The only view that will nurture science in its depths is one that invites and promotes further reflection, refinement, and exploration; that is, one that urges a repeated return to phenomenological "things in themselves." Husserl was right when he predicted a crisis in science whose resolution would come from the human sciences, not the older, so-called hard sciences. The questions to be resolved are not ones amenable to the definitive experiment, the proper instrumentation, or just the right blend of seminal genius and institutional support. The questions plaguing the roots of science are far more basic than that, and they will be amenable to nothing less than the radical revision of the scientific endeavor so that it becomes aligned with the primal urge to know—what we call the *cognitive imperative*—from which it first arose.

In a real sense, the only science there is or ever has been is psychology: the psychology of humans looking at levers, the psychology of humans looking at stars and ecosystems, the psychology of humans looking at human psychology. This book is a synopsis of an anthropological and neurophenomenological theory of consciousness and suggests an incomplete language for the description of the relationships of brain, symbolic culture, and consciousness that both facilitate and thwart the pursuit of free inquiry. Although the perspective of this book may be incomplete, it has sufficiently matured, and the groundwork has been prepared in other places, so that the views presented can foster the human sciences' search for a foundation of meaning for the scientific enterprise.

The reader should be forewarned that no attempt will be made here to present a simplistic model of consciousness. The human nervous system is the most complex system in the known universe, and no simplistic model can explain its nature and its activities. Oversimplified models of mind are the natural by-product of human cognition, which constructs views of reality in the interests of efficient adaptation (Laughlin and Brady 1978). Although that process may be useful in adapting to a transcendental, simultaneously nurturant and dangerous environment, oversimplification is inappropriate when the object of the cognition is the very system that does the cognizing. When inquiring into the nature of the human brain and consciousness, one must construct theoretical views that are as complex as necessary to bridge the vast gulf that looms between experience and understanding. The view expressed in this work draws upon relevant material from the neurological and cognitive sciences, as well as from anthropology, psychology (both Western and Eastern), transcendental phenomenology, and transpersonalism. Understanding this view will require as much effort and study on the part of the reader as it has of the authors.

This volume is the natural outcome of a venture that began with the publication of *Biogenetic Structuralism* (Laughlin and d'Aquili 1974). At that point there was little interest in what new developments in the neurosciences portended for anthropological and other social science theory. This lack of interest has changed, for activities within the neurosciences have become increasingly relevant to current developments in science generally. In the decade and a half since the publication of our book, the importance of biology, especially neurobiology, to an understanding of human nature has developed rapidly. During the 1970s and early 1980s, the neurosciences (1) have flourished, producing more data and relevant theory on the human brain than in the entire previous century; (2) have become increasingly interdisciplinary in scope, cooperation, and comprehension; and (3) have become increasingly indispensable to the psychological and sociocultural sciences. Furthermore, the same period has seen a renewed interest in phenomenology (see Ihde 1986), and particularly in the writings of Edmund Husserl (1931, 1970, 1977). As we hope to demonstrate, integrating aspects of the neurosciences with anthropology and phenomenology is a potent combination indeed for the generation of creative theory.

The dialogue between Laughlin and d'Aquili that produced *Biogenetic Structuralism* began before the full potential of the neurosciences had begun to reveal itself. The authors met at a small conference called "Theory on the Fringe: New Developments in Theoretical Anthropology," which was held at Oswego, New York, in 1972. They immediately realized that they had a common interest in the relationships of brain and culture, and that a book was in the offing. The collaboration that ensued proved to be as fast-paced as it was smooth. Because the issues that were being addressed in their book were new to mainstream anthropology, the authors became fully aware of the relevance of *Biogenetic Structuralism* to the works of Earl Count, the American neuroanthropologist, and Jean Piaget, the great Swiss genetic epistemologist, just as the manuscript was being readied for press.

Developments in biogenetic structural theory over the past decade and a half have not remained static, but indeed have been both fluid and cooperative. *Biogenetic Structuralism* has gained a small but growing following among anthropologists and other social scientists in North America and abroad (it was published in Japanese in 1985). And the authors have continued their interest in advancing this useful framework for analyzing aspects of the human condition. A major study of a "universal" cultural institution was needed as a practical example to complement the application of the principles set forth in *Biogenetic Structuralism*. The year after the publication of the first volume, d'Aquili and Laughlin teamed up with John McManus and several other colleagues to produce the first book-length application of biogenetic structural theory. This work, *The Spectrum of Ritual* (d'Aquili et al. 1979), traced the evolution of ritual as it occurs throughout the animal kingdom, from early vertebrate behavior through the mammals and primates to its manifestation in the genus *Homo*. The book also considered the neurocognitive and sociocultural role of ceremonial ritual among human societies.

As it turned out, the application of a biogenetic structural analysis to sociocultural phenomena had many implications, not only for conducting research, but also for our understanding of science. Laughlin and McManus joined forces with Robert Rubinstein to write *Science As Cognitive Process* (Rubinstein et al. 1984), a work which explores the neurocognitive foundations of science, its strengths and its limitations. Meanwhile, d'Aquili focused his efforts on applying biogenetic structural theory to the relationship between science and religion, producing a number of papers on the subject. Together with Hans Mol, he is completing a volume entitled *Wholeness and Fragmentation: the Dialogue of the Non-Rational and the Rational*. This book applies the principles first presented in *Biogenetic Structuralism* to the relationship between the philosophy of science and the philosophy of religion.

Brain, Symbol, and Experience will borrow freely from the previous writings of the biogenetic structuralist group. The group has for some years been interested in the relationships between neurocognitive, ethological, and ethnographic factors in universal or widespread cultural phenomena related to consciousness; this interest prompted our investigations of topics such as ritual (d'Aquili, Laughlin, and McManus 1979; d'Aquili and Laughlin 1975), epistemology (Rubinstein, Laughlin, and McManus 1984), alternative phases of consciousness (Laughlin 1985a; Laughlin et al. 1986; Laughlin, McManus, and Shearer 1984), phenomenology (Laughlin 1986, 1988), and meditation practices (Laughlin, McManus, and Webber 1985; Laughlin 1984; Webber, Stephens, and Laughlin 1983). The far-reaching approach of this book does not mean we are posing anything like an apodictic explanation for mind, brain, or culture. Our views—however involved, inclusive, or occasionally elegant they may appear—are never more than fictions developed in the service of what Peirce might have called the "process of ongoing inquiry," the movement from doubt to belief; a process that Husserl taught us is a never-ending dialogue between mind and its own nature.

For reasons we will make clear, the book will be informed first and foremost from the authors' own contemplative experiences of consciousness, and the reports of the many students, clients, and informants who have shared their experiences with the authors. Discussion of certain aspects of consciousness will presume the shared knowledge of "state-specific" scientists of the kind we will term *mature contemplatives* (see chapter 1). Serious insight meditation will be treated as a major source of introspective data available to persons who have trained themselves to access those data. Although an introspective approach to consciousness may be sufficient (under proper guidance) for expanding awareness and self-exploration, it cannot alone provide a complete ground for science. For this reason our work will also take into account information from other perspectives, particularly from neural structures and behavioral concomitants of structures.

In Part One we will develop a view of the organization of the brain that will allow us to discuss consciousness in sensible neurological and phenomenological terms. These terms will require the introduction of several concepts, new to many readers, that will be defined in the biogenetic structural context. Our goal is to be able to talk about "mental" phenomena like percepts, dreams, and ecstasies using the same terms that we use to talk about "physical" phenomena like reflexes and breathing. Realizing that the use of language—particularly a language like English that is a part of materialistic culture—creates a conceptual dualism by the mere act of speaking, we will strive for a unified view that both creates distinct conceptual domains and conceptually bridges those domains. This effort requires a delicate balance between analysis and synthesis so that in the end we all come to see a coherent picture. We choose not to speak about the brain first and consciousness second because brain and consciousness are distinct entities. Rather, analysis and linguistic conventions require that we divide the field of discourse in some way; we could have as easily begun with consciousness as with the brain. It will help immeasurably to keep squarely in mind that when we are speaking about the brain we are looking at one side of a coin; and when we are speaking of consciousness we are looking at the other side of the same coin.

Part Two will present an elaboration of the theory presented in Part One in order to reach a better understanding of the symbolic process. It is our contention that a full understanding of how symbols operate neurocognitively to canalize meaning, and how meaning becomes expressed, even enshrined in symbols, is requisite to an understanding of what anthropologists refer to as "culture." We believe that symbols operate according to a finite set of fundamental and universal principles, which can now be at least partially described. We will show that the symbolic process is a principal operator both in the limiting of the range of human experience and in the transcending of such limits.

Part Three will apply the theory of consciousness and symbolic process to an explanation of dreaming and other alternative phases of consciousness. The neurocognitive processes operating in dreaming will be examined in one chapter and the range of approaches to the interpretation of dreams cross-culturally will be surveyed. Another chapter will examine the neurocognitive principles operating to define and attain higher phases of consciousness as apparent in the various contemplative disciplines practiced today. The discussion of higher stages of consciousness among humans will occur in the framework of developmental neurobiology, and will place the process of development within a greater evolutionary perspective.

The ideas expressed in this book have been worked out over many years and in collaboration with several people, especially with Ivan Brady, Robert Rubinstein, Judi Young-Laughlin, John Cove, Mark Webber, Chris Stephens, Sheila Richardson, and Jon Shearer. They share partial credit for developing the best aspects of this work; but the authors alone take responsibility for any idiosyncratic uses to which our joint efforts are put and, of course, for any errors of substance and understanding found in rendering the biogenetic structuralist group's work. Special thanks are given to Mrs. Else Brock, who efficiently—and with good humor—typed and edited the final manuscript of this book. We would also like to express our gratitude to Jeremy Hayward and David Dietz of Shambhala Publications, and copy editor Elena LePera, who gave us the benefit of their editorial skills. And one of us (JM) would especially like to thank the following people for their help during the writing of this book: Mary Griffin and Andy Rheis for their financial assistance; Dr. Duane Ball, Dr. Roger Harmon, Gwen Gladhorn, Peter Couglin, and Greg Welsh for their tolerant and flexible employment opportunities; and Baila Woloff for her emotional support.

Charles Laughlin
John McManus
Eugene G. d'Aquili

PART ONE

THE STRUCTURES OF CONSCIOUSNESS

1 INTRODUCTION: BIOGENETIC STRUCTURALISM AND MATURE CONTEMPLATION

> Prior to Galileo science thought of Man as the mathematical and moral center of a World composed of spheres turning statically upon themselves. But in terms of our modern neoanthropocentricity, Man, both diminished and enlarged, becomes the *head* (terrestrial) of a Universe that is in the process of psychic transformation—Man, the last-formed, most complex and most conscious of 'molecules.' From which it follows that, borne on the tide of millions of years of psychogenesis, we have the right to consider ourselves the fruit of a progression—the children of progress.
> —Teilhard de Chardin, *The Future of Man*

THIS BOOK IS ABOUT CONSCIOUSNESS and about the role played by symbols in the neurocognitive operations mediating consciousness. We present a theory of consciousness that allows us to explain the relationship between activities of the brain and activities of the mind, and between symbols and experience. We also intend to show how a person's experience comes to be canalized (constrained, limited, focused, preprogrammed) by society, and the role of symbolism in the process of a person's enculturation. Before outlining the book, however, we must clarify a few fundamental philosophical and methodological issues.

THE APPROACH: ANTHROPOLOGY-PLUS

Our approach in this book is largely anthropological: The data we use from numerous sources outside of the confines of anthropology—notably the neurosciences and phenomenology—are always evaluated from an ethnological background covering many of the thousands of societies that exist or have existed on the planet. Two of the authors (CDL and EGd'A) have had anthropological training, Charles Laughlin having done fieldwork among East African pastoralists and more recently among Tibetan Buddhist monks in Nepal and India. The material covered will quite naturally be evaluated from the standpoint of ethnography and anthropological theory. We are speaking of a fundamental grounding in anthropology, not merely the odd inclusion of an anthropological reference. The lack of an in-depth understanding of ethnology can easily lead to pessimism when attempting to relate neurological and sociocultural phenomena (e.g., see Gazzaniga 1985:182ff).

It is our conviction that a reasonably satisfactory account of consciousness by science requires at a minimum the serious consideration of all appropriate data bases and observationally grounded points of view available to our inquiry. This conviction means that we must take a multidisciplinary approach; inclusion of multidisciplinary material is perhaps a bit easier in anthropology because anthropologists have been borrowing conceptual material, often wholesale, from its sister disciplines for generations. Furthermore, this means that we must seriously consider other systems of knowledge developed in societies other than our own. For instance, it would be preposterous from an anthropological point of view to discuss consciousness without some background in the several Eastern psychological disciplines that were studying consciousness long before Western science and philosophy existed. Likewise, it would be ridiculous to discuss dreaming (as psychological sleep researchers often do) without examining the systems of knowledge in societies, unlike our own, for whom dreams are considered routine and important phases of conscious experience. The reader should realize that anthropology, alone among the social and behavioral sciences, and akin to ethology, is a naturalistic discipline. As a naturalistic discipline, it seeks to understand human affairs as they spontaneously occur in the world, and not as contrived in simulated, experimental settings (see Edgerton 1974 on this issue).

We will therefore be examining consciousness from the broadest possible vantage point, utilizing where appropriate the cross-cultural ethnographic literature, and blending material from the neurological, cognitive, and symbolic sciences, as well as material from ethology, transpersonalism, and phenomenology.

Science in Transformation

It is a particularly auspicious time in which to carry out this broad-based project, for science in general, and anthropology in particular, is in a period of radical transformation. Beginning in the fifties and sixties, this transformation has led us away from a mechanistic, positivistic, hyperrational conception of science toward one that is more holistic, reflexive, and creatively intuitive (see Suppe 1977). Previously, scientists were fairly clear about their methods and goals: science was seen as a means of solving problems while remaining of itself largely nonproblematic.

The project of science was the explanation of facts, and facts were almost palpable things that were ascertained by objective public scrutiny and rigorous, replicable methods. As Somerhoff wrote:

> Any exact science must start with objective data. The essence of scientific concepts is that they are definable in terms of public operations and observations. This is the very secret of their power. The exact sciences, therefore, cannot proceed from things of which we have only private awareness. They must start with objective and public events. But there is no reason why it should not be possible at a later stage to interpret subjective events in terms of such objective events. (Quoted from Ackoff and Emery 1972:6)

Yet many authorities in the disciplines of science, as well as in the philosophy of science and mathematics, have come to view scientific inquiry itself as problematic. There have emerged at least two principal themes from this revolutionary readjustment of view: (1) a shift away from a fragmented, mechanical, nonpurposive conception of the world toward a holistic, organic, and purposive conception (see Bertalanffy 1968; Buckley 1968; Bohm 1980; Prigogine 1980; Ackoff and Emery 1972; Hayward 1984; Varela 1979; Maturana and Varela 1987; Wilber 1983, 1984; Piaget 1971a); and (2) a shift away from a concern with objectivity toward a concern with subjectivity—that is, with the role of perception and cognition in the process of scientific inquiry (see Kuhn 1970; Neisser 1976; Rubinstein, Laughlin, and McManus 1984).

Anthropology has not been immune to these developments—far from it. From the turn of the century the discipline has been a bastion of positivist and materialist science. It was only after the structuralist movement began to take hold in the early 1970s that concern with issues such as mentation, cognition, consciousness, and symbolism began to shift from the periphery to center stage. Phenomena relevant to an understanding of consciousness like myth, dreaming, vision quest, healing, trance states, and so forth, that were once thought to be marginal to the ethnographic enterprise have gradually become phenomena of prime concern to anthropologists, both in fieldwork and in construction of theory. This development, combined with an inherent tendency within the discipline to consider societies, cultures, and persons from a holistic point of view, places anthropology in the forefront of disciplines able to give credence to a view of consciousness that is at the same time neurocognitively *processual*, nondualistic, and transpersonal. Let us look briefly at how these three qualities of view, so necessary for a satisfactory account of consciousness, will influence the approach taken in this book.

PROCESS

Ample evidence from various sources affirms that the world of our experience is largely a construct of our nervous system (see e.g., Changeux 1985; Young 1987; Varela 1979). This cognized world and all "things" in "it" are manufactured in the mind. According to modern physics and related sciences, the world "out there"—which, of course, includes our own beings as well—apart from the processes of observation and knowing, is an undifferentiated energy field that is in a continuous process of evolutionary unfoldment (Jantsch 1981). Yet our point of view in this field of energy produces a world of experience that is an erroneously fragmented picture, but is nonetheless cleverly adaptive. This would seem to be an apparent paradox that should prove crucial and central to any account of consciousness.

The cultural tendency to conceptually fragment the world is naturally carried over into the activities of science as well. This tendency is, as Bohm (1980) notes, at the very root of many of the puzzles facing modern science. As regrettable as this tendency may seem, we believe that it is the natural outcome of human cognition at certain levels of conceptual development. Consider the sentence: "It is there." We tend to assume uncritically that there is a "there." Furthermore, we scientists make our observations, compute our data, adopt our theoretical positions, duel with our opponents, and congratulate our colleagues on the basis of whether their "there" is equivalent to our "there." Much time and energy is expended trying to determine what actually is "there," and how "it" may be organized, of what "it" might be composed, and to what "it" may be related. We do this all our lives, in and out of our role as scientists, always assuming that we are *not* assuming there is a "there" out "there."

We are not trying to be frivolous; this is too important a matter to treat lightly. It is an especially serious business when one approaches the issue of consciousness and the role of symbolism in experience, and when one uses language to communicate about these issues. We first have to develop some idea of what *it* might be that we are approaching and the position from which *we* are approaching it. We have to understand the difference between *we* and *it*. In a very fundamental way (that we will explore in some detail later) it seems that we create the world we live in, we create what we see, and what we experience. To create in this manner is a principle function of our brain, and somehow in this process we create a world of *things*. Perhaps it is not too surprising that we turn out to conceive of ourself as one of those things. The manner in which we create the thing that is "us" reflects also the nature of the things we experience outside of "us."

We can come to understand the difference between the "things" we create and the way the world really is by exploring the way we create our "us-ness" and the way we really are. The nature of this creation of things is not random, but generally quite predictable. It is a process highly conditioned by the laws of development peculiar to living organisms, particularly organisms with large brains. As human beings, we all follow the same general course by which we create an identity and come to experience ourselves as distinct from the unified field of which we are an inseparable part. We distinguish ourselves from this field by creating an opposition of sorts between the thing that is "us" and the things that are "not-us." What we take to be other objects or entities apart from "us" (whether these objects or entities are conceived to be within our organism) changes quite radically over the course of cognitive development for each of us.

We manage this creation of self and world over an entire lifetime in part by means of the *noun*. And we seem to use the noun, or something very much like it, long before we actually acquire language. By noun we wish to suggest a certain property of recurrent invariance or permanence—a sense or belief that there is such a thing as a "thing" (see Bohm 1965). A thing is something that will still be there when we look for it again. A thing is something in memory, something we tend to *re-cognize*. Things are essentially solid, touchable, point-to-able. Compare a noun to a verb, the latter being a sort of "process-happening" to and between things. It is difficult for most of us to imagine "run" without a runner, "throw" without a thrower, "think" without either a thinker or thought to think about. Yet this orientation toward a world of nouns with verbs between them is an artifact of the means by which we construct ourselves. It forms the basis for our world and of our experience of our world. In Bateson's words, "We experience not the world but our interactions with the world." And the world with which we interact is a world full of nouns.

To pinpoint when the indication of nouns or things first appears in human cognitive development is still perplexing. Despite recent advances in pre- and perinatal psychology, no one has yet interviewed an infant, much less a neonate. It is known that interactions implying nounlike awareness occur very early in life. There are indications that an infant re-cognizes its mother's face, breast, and voice from birth. But the more research is carried out into the capacities of the pre- and perinatal child, the more likely it seems that this cognitive ability arises in the womb. There is clear evidence that nounness, in the sense of expecting *it* to be *there* when we look for it, begins to emerge around the age of ten to twelve months, even before more advanced semiotic functions develop. The capacity to hold a stable internal image—one that can be interacted with in the absence of the object itself—is present in rudimentary form by eighteen months. Certainly by the end of the first year, some general sense of the permanence of *things* is developed and it is upon this development that we construct the world in which most of us will experience our living. From here on we act upon, interact with, and are acted upon by things that appear to have an existence independent of us and that transcend the immediate moment, the immediate sensation. At that moment the world as we have learned to know it begins. It may be useful to point out the obvious: This "world," as we *assume it to be*, actually does *begin* at some point in cognitive development and is not *given* as ontological fact in the cognized world of our experience. This world is one that we construct, and in that process we construct ourselves and the experience of ourselves. We tend to construct ourselves as nouns in a world of other nouns, a thing in a world of other things.

WORLD AS PROCESS

The tendency to think about and interact with a world of things has even influenced the way we as scientists research "processes." In classical physics we encapsulated reality in tiny "systems"—in beakers and cloud chambers designed to manifest the timeless and immutable laws of nature. We treated time as a constant, and process as reversible. In other words, we imposed thingness onto the world and then presumed to study its thinglike qualities.

> We were seeking general, all-embracing schemes that could be expressed in terms of eternal laws, but we have found time, events, evolving particles. We were also searching for symmetry, and here also we were surprised, since we discovered symmetry-breaking processes on all levels, from elementary particles up to biology and ecology. (Prigogine and Stengers 1984:292)

The same may be said for much of ethnology. Personalities and cultures have been generally treated as either static objects or states, or when change is at issue, a series of transformed static states. This static view was certainly evident during the heyday of structural-functionalism, but is still evident in today's semiotic structuralist formulations as well; that is, myth in Levi-Straussian theory becomes an "ahistorical" structure that somehow "thinks its way through" the mind of the primitive (see Hawkes 1977). This view is also evident in ecological anthropology where human societies are typically portrayed as static adaptors in static environments with little or no provision made for either positive feedback (i.e., "deviation amplifying mutual causality") relations or reversible or irreversible change. There are, of course, *theories* that imply a sophisticated systems view of human adaption (e.g., Geertz 1983), but virtually no human ecological field studies have applied such perspectives.

By contrast, our concern with consciousness, symbolism, and brain is primarily a concern for irreversible processes—processes that change, develop, and evolve. We will be examining processes that more or less exemplify what Ackoff and Emery term a *natural mechanical system:* "a formal system composed of time-slices and a set of laws applicable to these time-slices" (1972:20). The error of attributing thingness to any particular time-slice view of a dynamic system may occur (1) if the time-slice is taken out of its temporal (eventful, developmental, historical, evolutionary) context, or (2) if the time-slice is itself treated as a static entity in an otherwise dynamic context.

We hope to avoid the first pitfall by treating consciousness within its eventful, developmental, and evolutionary frame—indeed, we will later define the problem of consciousness in terms of a phase space model and will also show that the tendency to perceive reality as a sequence of time-slices is, itself, a product of neurocognition. We will try to avoid the second pitfall by treating time-slice views of consciousness, or components of any time-slice view, as dynamic systems in their own right. We will view any such segment, part, or phase as a system of Whiteheadian *actual entities:* "an actual entity endures but an instant— the instant of its becoming, its active process of self-creation out of the elements of the perishing past—and then it, too, perishes and as objectively immortal becomes dead datum for succeeding generations of actual entities" (Sherburne 1981:206; see also Whitehead 1978).

Yet we must still contend with communication via an extremely nominalizing language. We could go to the extent of creating a new language—one of processual and denominalized concepts—much as David Bohm (1980) has done. Short of this we must rely upon the wit of the reader to "see beyond" the categories of language to the reality being described; a reality which is always processual, fluid, and impermanent.

PURPOSE, CAUSE, AND PRODUCTION

Entailed in the view of process we are adopting here is a particular attitude toward the question of causality. Our orientation toward causality may be summarized by two considerations: First, the processes we will be examining should be conceived as purposeful systems. The laws and principles regulating the unfoldment of sequential time-slices determine an emergent order to the system. As Prigogine (1980) has put it, the time-slices comprise the *being* aspect of a system, while the emergent and irreversible order apparent in the sequence of time-slices constitutes the *becoming* aspect of a system.

Second, a crucial distinction must be made between *causation* and *production* of elements within a time-slice. After Ackoff and Emergy, system S_1 may be considered the *cause* of system S_2 "if both time-slices belong to the same natural mechanical system and S_1 precedes S_2 along the time axis . . . [and if S_1] is the *necessary* and *sufficient* condition of S_2—that is, if S_1 occurs, S_2 must follow, but if S_1 fails to occur, S_2 cannot follow" (1972:21). However, we may say that subsystem x in environment $x(-)$ *produces* subsystem y in environment $y(-)$ under the same temporal conditions if x is *necessary* but *insufficient* for y—that is, if x occurs, y may or may not follow, but if x fails to occur, y cannot follow. In our schematic, both subsystem x and environment $x(-)$ are producers of y, and combined are the cause of y and its environment $y(-)$. The distinction between causation and production will become important as we discuss the development of the brain and consciousness: an earlier neural structure can only be a producer, never a cause of a later neural structure. In other words, we will always presume that the cause of a neural structure at time T_2 was a precursory neural structure plus its environment at time T_1. The precursory structure and its environment will each be considered producers of the succeeding structure.

THE MIND-BODY PROBLEM

With the shift toward subjectivity in science has come a renewed interest in the perennial question of the relationship between mind and body. At the very roots of this persistent problem is an inherent tendency toward mind-body dualism in the natural attitude of people in Euro-American cultures. Members of Western cultures tend to be conditioned to think in terms of mental versus physical events and to experience themselves as being distinct, separated, or even alienated from their bodies. Developing a stable epistemology in science and philosophy for moving perceptually and conceptually between the two domains, given this regrettable prescientific enculturation, has never proved an easy matter (see Merleau-Ponty 1962 for a profound analysis of this issue; see also various articles in Eccles 1987).

There have been various solutions posed for the mind-body problem (see Campbell 1984 for a good summary). Some have held that mind is spirit and essentially noncausal in nature, and therefore outside the province of the physical sciences. Others, like many behaviorists in psychology, have virtually denied any existence for mind other than as sets of behavioral dispositions (e.g., Skinner 1974). Of the many philosophical points of view, only two hold sway in contemporary science as serious positions. These have been called by Campbell (1984) *central-state materialism* and the new *epiphenomenalism*. Central-state materialism holds that all mental and physical events are reducible to laws of the physical sciences. The physical sciences are considered complete explanations for all conditions arising either in mentation or in behavior (this view includes many so-called identity theories of mind and brain; e.g., Presley 1967). On the other hand, the new epiphenomenalism holds (along with the "old" epiphenomenalism of the nineteenth century) that mental and physical events exist as two distinct domains, but some (never all) mental events exist in a causal relationship with physical events (e.g., see Charles Taylor's discussion of "functionalism" in Secord 1982:35).

The position of anthropologists is often vague and inexplicit with respect to the mind-body issue. Yet the problem is methodologically important, for how one "gets at what's happening in the native's head" depends a great deal upon how one conceives of the relationship between outer physical events (like physiology, behavior, and speech) and inner mental events (like sensations, perceptions, images, thoughts, and moods). For example, anthropologists will want to argue that cultural practices, like ingesting psychotropic drugs or participating in certain types of dance-drama (physical events affecting the body via biochemical or behavioral means), exist in a causal relationship with the experience of alternative phases of consciousness (mental events that may result in notably different behaviors). Yet, causality in those events is often not clear. Are alternative phases of consciousness merely passive effects of physical causes (like drugs or rituals)? Are such phases epiphenomena that occur separately from, but simultaneously with, physical states? Are out-of-body experiences due to this epiphenomenal relationship, or are such experiences occurring within the "inner space" of the body? And what can we make of claims for extraordinary effects of mind upon physical matter (i.e., psychokinesis)?

Questions like these inevitably arise from a dualistic conception of mind and body (Taylor in Secord 1982), and how one evaluates them depends to a great extent upon how one resolves the mind-body problem. With Michael Polanyi (1965), the present authors reject both central-state materialism and the new epiphenomenalism as inappropriate to a modern and sophisticated science of consciousness. Rather, we embrace a *structural monism*, which holds that mind and body (including experience and behavior) are two imperfect ways of perceiving and knowing the same unknown totality we may call "being." "Spiritual" awareness is one way of knowing the being; "physical" awareness is another way of knowing the being. Neither the more spiritual disciplines (theology, parapsychology, transpersonal psychology, anthropology, etc.), nor the more physical disciplines (physics, chemistry, physiology, etc.), can claim to be complete representations or explanations of reality as required by central-state materialism (we side with Charles Peirce here; see Almeder 1980). Furthermore, consciousness does not neatly divide itself into spiritual (noncausal) and mundane (causal) attributes (as required for the new epiphenomenalism). This type of split is implied, for example, in Levi-Strauss's distinction between causal laws operating in "statistical models" (read *action*) and transformational laws operating in "mechanical models" (read *mentation;* see Levi-Strauss 1967:278 and Ardener 1971, and for our criticism see Laughlin 1973).

Anthropologists were understandably reluctant to buy the behaviorist paradigm,[1] even in its heyday, and so it has had but sporadic effects upon ethnographic fieldwork. However, the materialistic views prevalent among anthropologists have resulted at times in insufficient emphasis being placed upon experientially relevant data. Whole volumes are written about religious ceremonies and mythologies that contain little or no information about the experiences of people involved in those activities. We would suggest that a good measure of this materialist bent becomes understandable if one carefully examines the discipline's prevailing attitudes about the mind-body problem. The reader should understand us clearly here. We will make analytical distinctions and will apply the law of complementarity in polarized relations. But we are quite aware that such distinctions and polarized relations are not real; they are tools with which we hope to know the world better. What we reject are fragmented views, derived from a phenomenologically immature natural thesis and reified upon the world.

BIOGENETIC STRUCTURALISM

The structural monist view that the authors and their colleagues have developed over the years is, as we have said, *biogenetic structuralism* (Laughlin and d'Aquili 1974; Laughlin and Brady 1978; d'Aquili, Laughlin, and McManus 1979; Rubinstein, Laughlin, and McManus 1984). Our views, although structuralist in many of the same ways as are those of semiotic structuralists like Levi-Strauss (1967, 1976), Foucault (1970), and Chomsky (1968), are nevertheless quite different: biogenetic structuralism is grounded in evolutionary biology, and most especially in the neurological sciences. As such, biogenetic structuralism has more in common with evolutionary structuralist views such as Count's (1973) theory of the biogram, Piaget's (1971a) genetic epistemology, Hinde's (1982) ethological perspective, and Pribram's (1971) holographic paradigm (see also Changeux 1985; Churchland 1986; Young 1987; Globus 1976; Granit 1977; and Crook 1980 for equally consonant views).[2] It should, perhaps, be mentioned that some critics of biogenetic structur-alism have treated our perspective as a simplistic reductionist theory—equivalent, say, to sociobiology in that respect (see e.g., Durham 1982:80). Any serious study of this volume or any other of our previous writings will disprove that criticism. To ground one's structuralism in neurobiology is not logically equivalent to reducing all explanations to the biological or genetic.

Biogenetic structuralism specifically holds that "mind" and "brain" are two views of same reality—mind is how brain experiences its own functioning, and brain provides the structure of mind (see Young 1987:11). As we noted above, this is *not* an identity theory, for neither the social and psychological sciences nor the neurosciences can be considered to be complete accounts of consciousness. By implication, we must consider mind to be a characteristic of all animals that have brains, and animals that have brains, we must presume, have minds. The reader will soon see that we are interested in the interrelationships between neurocognitive events, behavioral events, and experiential events within the field of consciousness. For reasons already discussed, our rendering of all three domains is processual, developmental, and evolutionary.

A useful metaphor of the structural monist approach is to think of the theory's intended scope—in this case human consciousness—as existing within a sphere. Access to information about the scope may be gained through three windows: one marked *structural information*, another marked *behavioral information*, and yet another marked *experiential infor-mation*. The view of the scope is never more than partial, even if one looks through all three windows, and the view from any one window has no a priori logical predominance over the view from any other window. Of course, the view from one window may have a practical advantage over the others, because the question being asked may be better addressed through one window rather than another. But it amounts to an epistemological fallacy to claim (1) that the only logical approach to the intended scope is via one window to the exclusion of other windows; (2) that the view from each window is a separate and discrete domain having no causal relationship with the other domains; or (3) that an explanation developed solely from the information accrued from one window forms a complete accounting for all information accrued through the other windows as well. The following is a rather simplistic example: if the intended scope of our theory was the activity of grasping, a structural monist would not be satisfied until he accrued data about the physiology of the hand (the structural window), about the full range of movements of the hand (the behavioral window), and about the experience of grasping from the introspection of a grasper (the experiential window).

Stepping back a bit from our metaphorical sphere, we can see that the reason the views of scope from the three windows are equivalent is that all possible vantage points are grounded in perception and intentionality (in the following pages we will more clearly define "intentionality"). The ground of all scientific enterprise is, as Merleau-Ponty (1964) argues persuasively, the primacy of perception over cognition about the objects of perception. In a very real sense, there is no "brain," no "behavior," and no "experience." Rather, these are but three ways of conceptually breaking up views of the scope, assuring that we assume the broadest possible field of perception from which to draw our information. In science, as in everyday life, there is only perceptual and intentional activity relative to the world. Understanding the perceptual/intentional roots of knowledge not only makes the conceptual integration of the three perspectives imperative, it also allows a more thorough understanding of the relationships of individuals in groups as "societies" and "cultures" (Burridge 1979; Secord 1982). Due to the conditioning of the structures of consciousness, individuals come to "see" and "mean" the same things, and to act occasionally in accordance with the commonweal.

But why, one might well ask, are we concerned to take all possible views of the scope into account if all are equivalent, and all partial? An immediate answer is that multiple views provide a much-needed corrective to the effects of bias operating in any one view. For example, if one is limited to the behavioral view to the exclusion of the neurobiological, one could erroneously conclude that our species is no longer subject to the principles of genetics and ontogenesis that are evidently operating when viewed from the structural vantage point. For another example, serious consideration of experiential reports can lead to adjustment in physiological theory, and vice versa. Physiologists long believed that the body requires a certain minimal quantity of oxygen per unit of tissue at rest. This quantum of oxygen was based upon relaxation experiments and was held to be a fundamental law of human physiology. However, research in the late fifties with yogic meditative trance demonstrated that under certain conditions, basal oxygen requirements can be far lower than previously suspected (see Anand et al. 1961). Information was previously available about this ability in the reports of yogis who would have themselves buried in boxes for hours—too long to be possible under previously held physiological views. Yet these reports were ignored or discounted as so much superstitious nonsense.

But another, and perhaps more important, answer is that by requiring the broadest inclusion of information about the scope of inquiry into our theoretical formulations, we clearly foster the general movement evident in all the sciences toward what Einstein chose to call a *unified field theory*. It seems that the more sources of information one considers in formulating theories, the more the product of theory construction approximates a holistic conception of consciousness and the universe: That is, our understanding of the scope of inquiry better fits a higher, shall we say, cosmological comprehension of the universe—a universe presented to mind in experience and comprehended through the activities of science. As the works of such writers as Bohm (1980), Prigogine (1980), Prigogine and Stengers (1984), Pagels (1982), and Capra (1975) in physics, Jantsch (1981) and Sheldrake (1981) in biology, as well as many others like Young (1987), Maturana and Varela (1987), Pribram (1971), and Wilber (1980) in the neurosciences and psychology exemplify, there is a major movement afoot to reach a single, comprehensive theory of the field of energy relationships that produces the world of experience.

The natural tendency of most scientists when confronted with the vast complexity involved in understanding consciousness is to take refuge in specialization. But, however productive of refined information and insight this strategy has proven in the past, the science of consciousness has now reached the point where a general comprehension of consciousness is not only required, it is *possible*. We cannot know everything about consciousness, for the transcendental nature of its scope renders that goal unreal. What we do have available is a vast fund of information about consciousness collected from the sphere's many windows, which is now begging for comprehension. And comprehension requires theory construction. The data *never* order themselves; they only cohere in relation to theory. The task of this book is to provide the germ of a theory by which the various data bases relevant to the study of consciousness can find coherence. That the time is ripe for such work is confirmed by the long-called-for and rapidly increasing interdisciplinary emphasis in the neurosciences (Changeux 1983; Kirk 1983) as well as other disciplines.

A BIOGENETIC STRUCTURAL ACCOUNT

A biogenetic structural account of consciousness requires three major considerations. In the first place, we must be open to incorporating information about consciousness obtained from the theories and data of all three domains of research in consciousness: the structural aspects of consciousness (neurocognitive, neurophysiological, neuroendocrinological, neuropsychopharmacological, etc.); the behavioral aspects and expressions of consciousness (ethnographic, psychological experimentation, ethological, etc.); and the experiential aspects of consciousness phenomenology (various introspective psychologies, reports from participant observation, transpersonal experimentation, dream psychology, cross-cultural records of experience, etc.).

One strength of this view is that it requires interdisciplinary exchange, cooperation, and pooling of information and ideas—a process that leads naturally to a larger fund of what Karl Pribram (1971) calls "paradoxes" (see also Kuhn 1974; Rubinstein et al. 1984: chap. 4). The pyramiding of paradoxes is further accelerated in biogenetic structural theory by the inclusion of cross-cultural data on consciousness, psychology, and where available, physiology. The advantage of compounding the incidence of paradoxical evidence is that it will encourage not only a more rapid development and turnover of theory, but also a greater emphasis upon what Hanson (1958) called (after Reichenbach) the "context of discovery" and a de-emphasis upon the "context of justification" in science.

The conceptual format that integrates the three domains—structure, behavior, and experience—will be fleshed out more in time; but for the moment we can say that by *structure* we will always mean the organization of the nervous system and other somatic systems, or that portion of these systems subserving the phenomenon under discussion. We may be concerned with the functioning of that organization, with its emergence during evolution, or its development in the individual organism, but we will always be referring to physiological, especially neurophysiological structures. Thus, biogenetic structuralism contrasts sharply with other structuralist perspectives (including theories in psychology, cognitive science, and artificial intelligence research) that either ignore the neurological aspect of structure, or pay lip-service to the neurological locus of structure and thus fail to ground their theories in the neurological sciences. As Pribram notes, there is a tendency for many theorists "to construct 'unrealistic' models of human cognitive processing unless they give serious heed to developments in the neurosciences. In fact, heed is paid, but often there is a lack of seriousness whenever the neurological data become the least bit complex" (1978:113).

By *behavior* we mean the observable activity of neurological and other physiological structures comprising the organism. Behavior may occur within or outside of a social context, and may occur with or without the awareness of the actor. Behavior may be as simple as a twitch or as complex as a ceremony. In any case, behavior will always be conceived of as being subserved or *mediated* by neurological and other physiological structures.

By *experience* we mean direct participation in or observation of events by an individual and the knowledge gleaned from those acts, whether reportable by that individual or not. The concept is specifically *not* limited to ego-bound experience and knowledge, but refers more generally to all experience whether personal or transpersonal. Experience may or may not involve a behavioral component: we can experience and know without behaving, but experience as we conceive it will always be mediated by structure.

A perfect balance between the three domains of structure, behavior, and experience is, of course, an ideal for which we strive. In actual practice, however, we find we have had to come down more heavily on the structural (or neurobiological) and experiential (or phenomenological) than on the behavioral. We feel that heavier weighting in the structural and experiential domains is required to compensate for the relative neglect of these domains of research and theory in orthodox anthropology.

In the second place, a biogenetic structural account requires the minimal inclusion of all levels of systemic organization logically entailed by the problem at hand. As Bohm (1980), Whitehead (1978), and others have noted, there is a tendency for the scientific mind to fragment reality—observed through any of the windows of the sphere—not only into categories, but also into organizational levels. Thus in neurophysiology one may speak of the level of the synapse, the level of the local circuit, the level of the lobe, and so on. Special languages develop to describe, and special theories to account for, the events observed at these several levels (special languages that are not necessary to the growth of knowledge; see Young 1987:12). Arguments ensue, of course, as to which level is "fundamental" to all the others, and to which all the other levels may be reduced.

Biogenetic structuralism agrees with the views of such theorists as Jantsch (1981), Whitehead (1978), and Prigogine (Prigogine and Stengers 1984) that reality is simultaneously composed of many levels, *none* of which is fundamental, and that levels are born of the analytical mind trying to make sense of an essentially undifferentiated field of systemically related processes. For this reason we are opposed to the view that each level requires a discrete explanation (see e.g., Wimsatt 1980, or Johnson-Laird 1983). We thus apply what we call the *rule of minimal inclusion:* An explanation of a scope must encompass any and all levels of organization efficiently present in the interaction between the system under observation and the environment of that system (Rubinstein, Laughlin, and McManus 1984). As the reader will soon see, we attempt to construct a theory that helps us relate events perceived and conceived at the cellular level with those at "higher" levels, up to and including the environment of the organism. And we try to do this without changing our language or appealing to more readily available but empirically incommensurable theories. The reader should not get the idea that the "windows" to which we have referred represent single levels of view or homogeneous bodies of theory. On the contrary, within any of these perspectives may be found theoretical and method-ological schools that are exclusive of each other. One may find in the neurosciences, for example, an ongoing controversy between anatomists and physiologists who may each reach conclusions to the exclusion of the relevant data from the other perspective (Brodal 1975).

We could, of course, have gone further to incorporate the physics of the topic, as any theory must ultimately do in order to expand inclusion relative to scope. Were we to do this—say, include the quantum mechan-ical relationships relevant to our scope (Schumacher n.d.)—our theory would prove far more powerful than it is now. That we do not incorpo-rate the physics of consciousness into the present formulation is a practical decision pertaining to length of the book and the tentative data in the quantum mechanics of perception. The omission should not be interpreted as either affirming that the microanatomy of the nervous system defines the ultimate constituents of reality or claiming that theory and data from physics are incompatible with those from the "windows" we have chosen to utilize. Our three windows are not the only ones possible. And it is very clear that in the future our under-standing of the brain and consciousness must incorporate relativity and particle physics if it is to participate further in the formation of a truly unified field theory.[3]

In the third place, biogenetic structuralism requires the consideration of a transpersonal data base. And because the inclusion of a transper-sonal perspective within the phenomenological domain may be to some readers the most novel and controversial inclusion thus far advocated, we will clarify and examine what is meant by *transpersonal anthropology*.

TRANSPERSONAL ANTHROPOLOGY

Transpersonalism is a movement in science that acknowledges as data the significance of experiences beyond the boundaries of ordinary ego-consciousness (see Tart 1975a, 1975b; Grof 1976; Zinberg 1977; and Laughlin, McManus, and Shearer 1984). Roger Walsh and Frances Vaughan in their book *Beyond Ego* use the term *transpersonal* to "reflect the reports of people practicing various consciousness disciplines who spoke of experiences of an extension of identity beyond both individu-ality and personality" (1980:16). From the range of such experiences, *The Journal of Transpersonal Psychology* lists several in the preface to each issue: "Transpersonal process, values and states, unitive consciousness, meta-needs, peak experiences, ecstasy, mystical experience, being essence, bliss, awe, wonder, transcendence of self, spirit, sacralization of everyday life, oneness, cosmic awareness, cosmic play, individual and species-wide synergy, the theories and practices of meditation, spiritual paths, compassion, transpersonal cooperation, transpersonal realization and actualization; and related concepts, experiences and activities" (quoted from Lee 1980:4; see also Wilber 1980). In a more theoretically succinct way, Kenneth Ring (1974, 1976), working from the research of Stanislav Grof (1972, 1973), developed a typology of experiences, grouping these into ever-expanding concentric rings from normal waking consciousness in the middle (the most narrow field), through what he terms "preconscious, psychodynamic, orthogenetic, transindividual, phylogenetic, extraterrestrial, and superconsciousness, to void consciousness at the periphery" (the most expansive field; 1976:127).

As formal disciplines, transpersonal psychology dates to the latter 1960s (Sutich 1968), and transpersonal anthropology to the mid–1970s (see Lee 1980:2 and Laughlin, McManus, and Shearer 1984:141). Transpersonal anthropology is simply the cross-cultural study of transpersonal experiences (Laughlin, McManus, and Shearer 1984). Campbell and Staniford (1978:28) define transpersonal anthropology as "the investigation of the relationship between consciousness and culture, altered states of mind research, and the inquiry into the integration of mind, culture and personality." Although quite recent as a formal discipline, anthropology has evidenced interest in transpersonal experiences that dates back to the nineteenth century and the work of Tylor (1881), who was interested in dreaming and the experiential origins of religion, and Lang (1894, 1897), who was interested in the psychology of the paranormal (see MacDonald 1981, and Laughlin, McManus, and Shearer 1984). Andrew Lang was in fact one of the founding members of the Society for Psychical Research, an organization that later counted among its members both Jung and Freud (Langstaff 1978).

Anthropologists and explorers have routinely recorded data on extraordinary experiences reported by informants, as well as on religious institutions and ritual practices associated with such experiences (e.g., Evans-Wentz 1966; David-Neel 1932; see also MacDonald 1981 for a survey). Nevertheless, some researchers have noted that Western science does not pay sufficient attention to the importance of such experiences to the study of psychology and culture (e.g., Barnouw 1942; Harner 1973; Greeley 1975; Hufford 1982). For example, many theorists have suggested that there exist universal structures resulting in similar transpersonal experiences among people from all the world's cultures (see Lang 1894 and Barnouw 1942, 1946, on *psi* phenomena; James 1890 on ghosts; Lang 1898 on the universal intuition of a supreme being; Eliade 1965, 1967, on various aspects of religious experience).

A few ethnographers have undergone spontaneous transpersonal experiences while in the field. Geoffrey Gorer, for instance, reported such an experience in his book, *African Dances*. He found himself in a large gathering of people that included a famous Dahomeyan shaman. At one point he met the shaman's gaze:

> I felt that for some reason it was necessary for me to meet his gaze and I continued staring at him across a space of about thirty yards til all the surrounding people and the landscape became an indistinct blur and his face seemed preternaturally distinct and as it were detached from his body and nearer to me physically than it was in reality. I wondered whether I was being hypnotized. (1935:131)

More recently, Bruce Grindal (1983) has reported a profound experience, which occurred to him while attending a Sisala funeral in Ghana in 1967. After undergoing several days of arduous privation involving fasting, loss of sleep, physical ordeal, and the like, Grindal entered a phase of consciousness in which he perceived a corpse come alive, dance, and play drums. He also saw a radiant energy emanating from the corpse and other people attending the rite. According to him, this experience also occurred to some of the Sisala, who recognized that he had undergone the experience.

However, few anthropological fieldworkers have made the effort to seek and to realize alternative phases of consciousness in themselves, despite evidence that many human cultures operate within a cosmology composed of multiple realities (Schutz 1945; Eliade 1964)—the veridicality of which is commonly verified via experiences in alternative phases of consciousness (Bourguignon 1973; Ehrenwald 1978). We have argued elsewhere that this oversight is not accidental, but rather a systematic bias in science born of what we call monophasic consciousness in the enculturation of Western observers (see Laughlin et al. 1986). Despite this bias, many fieldworkers have cultivated alternative phases of consciousness in order to enhance their understanding of the culture or phenomenon being researched: These include Coult (n.d.), who explored LSD and attempted in the 1960s to establish a field he called "psychedelic anthropology"; Harner (1973) who worked on hallucinogens; Chagnon's (1977:154ff) experiment with hallucinogens, shamanic dance, and chanting; Hillman's (1987) work with lucid dreaming; and David-Neel's (1971) work among Tibetan *lamas* that involved extensive meditation. Some fieldworkers, like Katz (1982:6ff), have reported participating in ritual practices intended to evoke such experiences, without however attaining the intended state (or failing to report it if attained).

The relative paucity of attempts by ethnographers to enter alternative phases of consciousness and the current, seemingly paradoxical interest to learn about such matters underscore the importance to anthropology of the epistemological issues raised by the transpersonal movement in science (see Laughlin 1984). Among those issues none is more important than the question: What constitutes a "public event"?

What Is a Public Event?

Prior to the fall of the received view of science, a clear and formularized distinction was possible between what constituted a public event and what constituted a private event. The existence of objective perception was taken for granted and formed the observational basis of all science. An event was public and relevant to science if it could be shared by any and all observers. And an event that could not be shared by all observers was considered subjective and of no relevance whatever to science.

However, with the fall of the received view and an increasingly psychological and sociological perspective in the analysis of science, researchers began to show what phenomenologists like Husserl (1960) and Merleau-Ponty (1962) had all along maintained: a reciprocal feedback relationship exists between cognition and perception, and between theory construction and observation (see Rubinstein, Laughlin, and McManus 1984: chap. 4). Explorations of the scientific enterprise began to include the process of observation itself in the scope of their inquiries. Investigators began to ask, To what extent does theory as ideology have a controlling influence upon what a scientist can or does see, and equally important, what a scientist cannot or does not see?

INTROSPECTION

The preceding issues raised the question anew: How much can we know about consciousness from direct experience—that is, how much can we discover by looking at our own mind through "introspection"? After all, introspection is well known to be fraught with epistemological problems. Jean Piaget notes:

> Introspection alone is not enough, because it is both incomplete (it grasps the results of mental processes and not their intimate mechanisms) and distorting (because the subject who introspects is both judge and party, which plays a considerable part in affective states, and even in the cognitive sphere where one's own philosophy is projected into the introspection). (1973:12)

The common tendency in the history of knowledge has been either to embrace uncritically introspection and exclude the dictates of authority or the exercise of empirical rigor, or to reject the evidence of introspection as false, delusional, or heretical and uncritically endorse the views of authority or empirical observation. During this century the use of introspection as a source of data in science has been virtually forbidden to researchers in psychology while under the influence of Watsonian, Hull-Spence, and Skinnerian behaviorism. As we mentioned when discussing various approaches to the mind-body problem, behaviorism took the extreme position of denying mind altogether. The position was somewhat modified by Skinnerians who came to admit data about experience so long as they were reportable. A report is, after all, behavior! The report itself became the data, and any experiences not reportable were considered out of limits for psychological research. This was quite a change from the psychology of, say, William James, who, writing in the last part of the nineteenth century, found no contradiction at all in combining experimental research with introspective methods, particularly when he was addressing such matters as the psychology of religion (James 1902).

The vestiges of the anti-introspectionist view remain with us, of course (see e.g., Weissman 1987; Lyons 1986)—sometimes under the guise of a form of cognitive psychology. For instance, in the process of launching his four-hundred-plus page book describing his cognitive theory of mind, P. N. Johnson-Laird dispenses with data from direct introspection in a single sentence: "Introspection is not a direct route to understanding the mind and, as far as we know, there is no such route" (1983:2). Incidentally, he also dispenses with the necessity of examining the neurosciences by a disappointing bit of doublethink, which is germane to a consideration of early anthropological theory. Appealing to a kind of psychological functionalism, he claims that "mental phenomena depend not on the particular constitution of the brain but on how it is functionally organized" (ibid.:448). He is thus free to apply various mechanical metaphors via flow charts and equations without reference either to degree of fit between these models or to how we know the brain is organized. It is precisely this kind of fragmentation of research and explanation that we would like to counteract in any biogenetic structural account.

In order to avoid any taint of introspectionism, the behaviorist paradigm prescribed experimentation on others rather than upon one's self. But this stricture turned out to be only partially effective as a barrier to more introspective methods in psychology. Many psychological theorists involved in clinical practice nonetheless retained their concern for the larger issues in the study of consciousness. Sigmund Freud, Carl Jung, Carl Rogers, Karen Horney, and many others were developing theories relevant to the study of consciousness grounded upon their own direct experiences and the experiences reported by their clients. Phenomenological psychologists like Maurice Merleau-Ponty, who were following in the footsteps of Edmund Husserl and Martin Heidegger, also advocated introspective methods. In more recent times the "third force," humanistic psychology, has been finding its way back to a view of psychological methods more commensurate with a sophisticated study of consciousness as evidenced, for example, in the writings of Abraham Maslow (1968; see also Wilson 1972). And the "fourth force," the transpersonal movement, in science is now having its effects upon the methods used in studying the psychology of consciousness through the writings of people like Charles Tart (1975a, 1975b; see also Boucouvalas 1980).

INTROSPECTIONISM AND ANTHROPOLOGY

Anthropologists avoided being drawn into the behaviorist paradigm for the same reasons as did many clinical psychologists—anthropologists are forced by the circumstances of their trade to take people as they are, rather than as they are contrived to be under unnatural laboratory conditions. The central methodology in ethnographic research is called *participant observation,* a sort of catch-all term, which includes a remarkable array of methods from the most rigorous and statistical to the loose and serendipitous. But the emphasis since the time of Malinowski (around the time of the First World War) has been upon the fieldworker's immersion in an alien ethos and learning from direct experience. Over the decades many fieldworkers have compiled life histories of informants, thus providing a documentation that is rich in experiential reports from a variety of cultures.

Anthropology has provided a natural history of the human species and has generated a useful perspective that underscores the more dualistic patterns in Western enculturation and provides a balance of views that can ameliorate the ethnocentric bias in much of Western science. It is easy to sense this bias when we study how other peoples conceive of consciousness. We find that their conceptions are often encoded in their beliefs about dream life, in their understanding of what James once called the "stream of consciousness" aspect of experience, in their mythological depiction of the cosmos, and in their beliefs and practices related to healing. Because of this fundamental grounding in the ethnographic enterprise, the cross-cultural perspective will pervade this book, although it may not become obvious until we discuss alien psychologies, cosmologies, and alternative phases of consciousness in later chapters.

Ours is a structuralist perspective, which endeavors to uncover the underlying structural invariance producing the seeming variance at the levels of behavior, expression, and artifact. And we tend to the view that such invariance is due to the neurocognitive capacities of people everywhere. Thus, when we are dealing with cross-cultural reports of alternative phases of consciousness, our presumption of structural invariance takes on epistemological significance and amounts to a strong form of W. T. Stace's *principle of causal indifference:*

> The principle of causal indifference is this: If X has an alleged mystical experience P_1 and Y has an alleged mystical experience P_2, and if the phenomenological characteristics of P_1 entirely resemble the phenomenological characteristics of P_2 so far as can be ascertained from the descriptions given by X and Y, then the two experiences cannot be regarded as being of two different kinds. (1960:29)

Our methods of cross-cultural comparison must therefore be sensitive to the invariance embedded in the seemingly variant, culture-specific, traditional modes of symbolic expression. In short, there is the immediate perception of events, and there is the interpretation of them vis à vis traditional symbolism and cosmological understanding (Stace 1960:31). A clear understanding of the symbolic process is indispensable to transcending apparent symbolic variance in the essential structures of all experience. As we will argue, achieving this transcendence is methodologically difficult without directly experiencing that which is signified.

STATE-SPECIFIC SCIENCE

The serious examination of the role of conditioned perception in establishing the limits of science has led to the scrutiny of state-specific science. Is it possible that the reality being observed is determined to some extent by the phase of consciousness of the observer (Tart 1975a)? Is it not a function of scientific paradigms to limit the range of reality addressed under a paradigm (Rubinstein, Laughlin, and McManus 1984: chap. 4)? If so, then does it not make sense that science, comprehensively defined, should require scientists to be trained to enter all relevant phases of consciousness in order to observe the breadth of reality?

MATURE CONTEMPLATION

Introspection frequently fails as an accurate data source precisely because the scientist is unskilled as a contemplative. The scientist is not adept at entering the phase of consciousness most conducive to obtaining the data about consciousness that he desires. The immature contemplative is easily deluded by the attitudes, presuppositions, biases, and assumptions he has been enculturated to believe. He is, to put it in Husserlian terms, ensnared by his "natural attitude." So well indoctrinated is he as a culture-bearer that he accepts the apparent world as "natural." We wish to contrast such naive introspection with truly mature contemplation in much the same way as we would contrast a child's toying with a chemistry set and the experiments of a trained, mature chemist. And in so doing we must face squarely the issue of contemplative adequacy. Without putting too fine a point on it, most Western philosophers and scientists are poor contemplatives (see Laughlin, McManus, and Shearer 1984). They are not trained to anything like the introspective sophistication found in certain cultural traditions. For our purposes, a *mature contemplative* may be defined as a "state-specific" scientist, who has undergone training sufficient to examine the internal features of his or her own mentation while exercising an uncommon degree of concentration, tranquillity, inquiry, and vigilance.

In Theravadin Buddhist insight practice, a mature contemplative is a meditator who has realized at least stage four but has not necessarily realized stage twelve of the insight practice known as the *satipatthana* path of meditation (see Buddhaghosa 1976: volume 2; Mahasi Sayadaw 1978). This is roughly equivalent to the level of realization characterizing Brown and Engler's (1980:160) "insight group" or higher. In the Tibetan *mahamudra* tradition (Wang-ch'ug Dorje 1978), this is parallel to the state of "signless concentration" or higher (Brown 1977:256). At this level "the yogi sees subtle cognition in 'fore-clarity' *[gsal-ngar]* that is at a stage *before* it is built up into higher cognitive events. Adjectives such as clarity, brightness, and clear light are commonly used; the mind is seen in terms of light rays" (Brown 1977:256–57).

The contemplative is, in other words, capable of directly apprehending the sensory aspect of the moment of consciousness as distinct from the mapping of cognition upon it. The mature contemplative has completed the fundamental phenomenological training requisite to accruing basic introspective data about the nature of consciousness *prior to any scientific reflection upon that nature.*

THE PHENOMENOLOGICAL REDUCTION

An equivalent discipline for producing mature contemplation in Western philosophical tradition is the transcendental phenomenology of Edmund Husserl (1859–1938). In a variety of works, including *Cartesian Meditations* (1977), *Ideas: General Introduction to Pure Phenomenology* (1931), and *The Crisis of European Sciences and Transcendental Phenomenology* (1970), Husserl described a method for training the mind to perceive and intuit its own essential processes. He called this method the "phenomenological reduction." According to Peter Koestenbaum (Husserl

1967:x–xi), the definitive characteristics of transcendental phenomenology are

1. Phenomenology is a method that presumes to be absolutely presuppositionless.
2. Phenomenology analyzes data and does not speculate about world-hypotheses.
3. Phenomenology is descriptive, and thus leads to specific and cumulative results, as is the case with scientific researches; phenomenology does not make inferences, nor does it lead to metaphysical theories.
4. Phenomenology is an empiricism more adequate than that of Locke, more skeptical than that of Hume, and more radical than that of William James.
5. Phenomenology is a scientific enterprise in the very best sense of that term, without at the same time being strictured by the presuppositions of science and suffering from its limitations. Furthermore, Husserl strongly believed that phenomenology can and does offer essential contributions to the foundations of science.

Husserl repeatedly emphasized that phenomenology is a method of self-discovery. The term *method* is not used here merely in the "small-m" sense of a specific sociological or psychological technique. Rather, the claim of phenomenology to the status of methodology is radical: it is nothing less than a spiritual discipline with all the attendant techniques and intuitive insights requisite for leaving the psyche of the practitioner essentially changed (see Fink in McKenna et al. 1981:24). For this reason, transcendental phenomenology may be evaluated relative to other spiritual disciplines, including the Eastern traditions of contemplation noted earlier. Unfortunately, Husserl left no clear, concise manual on how the phenomenological reduction is to be performed, and the student is more or less left on his own to discover the explicit "small-m" methods (see Kockelmans in Kockelmans 1967:25). Husserl teaches that what is reduced is the so-called "natural thesis" of the world; that is, the presumptive cognized order of affairs is taken for granted by people who then reify that order and perceive it as indeed natural.

> Daily practical living is naive. It is immersion in the already-given world, whether it be experiencing or thinking, or valuing, or acting. Meanwhile all those productive intentional functions of experiencing, because of which physical things are simply there, go on anonymously. The experiencer knows nothing about them, and likewise nothing about his productive thinking. The numbers, the predicative complexes of affairs, the

goods, the ends, the works, present themselves because of the hidden performances; they are built up, member by member; they alone are regarded. Nor is it otherwise in the positive sciences. They are naivetes of a higher level. They are the products of an ingenious theoretical technique; but the intentional performances from which everything ultimately originates remain unexplicated. To be sure, science claims the ability to justify its theoretical steps and is based throughout on criticism. But its criticism is not ultimate criticism of knowledge. The latter criticism is a study and criticism of the original productions, an uncovering of all their intentional horizons; and thus alone can the "range" of evidences be ultimately grasped and, correlatively, the existence-sense of objects, of theoretical formations, of goods and ends, be evaluated. (Husserl 1977:152–53)

But the reduction is not simply dropping this thesis and leaving a residue of "real world," but rather, a graduated process of discovering the constitution of the world leading to the clear reflection required to apprehend the essential phenomena. What are gradually intuited and changed are the many onion layers of delusory views of the foundations upon which the natural thesis is constructed. These are set aside via absolutely certain knowledge of their artificiality. At the same time the mind comes to intuit the principles upon which it constitutes the phenomenal world. And in the process of learning to see clearly the essential nature of mind, the mind liberates itself from the chains of delusory misapprehensions, thus replacing the naive personal ego with knowledge of the transcendental ego: what Buddhists might call "the builder"—that hidden "me" that desires the world and for whom the world is constituted.

How, then, does one go about stripping away the layers of the onion that result in the natural thesis? This task is accomplished in Husserlian phenomenology by introspection about the relationships between the object of perception (which is constituted in the mind by the *noema,* or *noematic* functions of consciousness, including generation of sense impressions, orientation response, and attention) and cognitive operations intending the object (which are the *noesis,* or *noetic* functions, of consciousness; see Husserl 1931:255ff). The object being studied is viewed as a product of mind as are the cognitive associations and principles of organization that attend the object. The object becomes the "transcendental guide" for the contemplative, for all of the processes of consciousness to be uncovered in the work are always intended upon that object. Husserl offers the example of the relationship between an object of perception and our enjoyment of that object:

Let us now pass over to the phenomenological standpoint. . . . We now ask what there is to discover, on essential lines, in the nexus of noetic experiences of perception and pleasure-valuation. Together with the whole physical and psychical world the real subsistence of the objective relation between perception and perceived is suspended; and yet a relation between perception and perceived (as likewise between the pleasure and that which pleases) is obviously left over, a relation which in its essential nature comes before us in "pure immanence," purely, that is, on the ground of phenomenologically reduced experience of perception and pleasure, as it fits into the transcendental stream of experience. (Husserl 1931:259)

The meditation is thus an alternation between the object as object of study (the noematic processes that bring the object before the mind) and noetic cognitive processes as object of study. *Noema* and *noesis* are two active processes that rise to meet each other in the moment-by-moment flow of experience, the former constituting the object before the mind and the latter intending meaning or cognitions about the object. Consciousness then is seen as a dynamic mandala, the entire configuration of which changes with each shift in object of focus, and the noetic operations of mind intend (take as their object) whatever the *noema* currently constitutes before the mind.

These relations may become a bit clearer if imagined as a "two hands clapping" model of consciousness (see figure 1). In this model each moment of consciousness (termed *khanapaccuppanna* in Buddhist phenomenology) is the co-production of simultaneously active cognitive and sensorial operations, the latter providing a meaningful object before the mind, the former integrating various cognitive operations upon that object. The co-producing noetic and noematic operations arise and pass away every moment. Direct awareness of these various operations is not easy to attain. Apprehending the role of the object as transcendental guide implies learning a subtle skill. The goal of a reduction is the *relevation* (Bohm's 1980:35 term for lifting a previously unconscious process into the light of awareness) of these processes, an exercise Husserl termed *intentional analysis:*

In an important sense, exercises in "constitution" are exercises in intentional analysis. They consist in beginning with a "sense" already elaborated in an object that has unity and a permanence before the mind and then separating out the multiple intendings [read cognitive associations] that intersect in the "sense." . . . Thus, one ascends from the indivisible stability of the thing, such as it "appears" visually in the flux of profiles, aspects, outlines, or adumbrations through which consciousness anticipates and claims the unity of the thing. Intentional analysis always takes for its "transcendental guide" an object—a sense—in which the intentive processes . . . of consciousness are united. It never begins directly with the untamed generative power of consciousness. (Ricoeur 1967a:36)

An intentional analysis seems quite similar to Buddhist insight practice *(vipassana bhavana)* leading to the realization of the proliferating

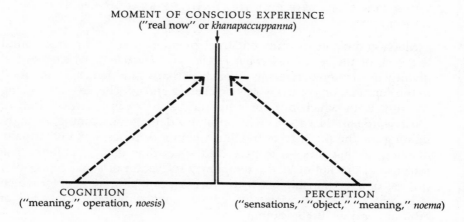

FIGURE 1. A schematic of the roles of cognition (*noesis*) and sensation (*noema*) in unfolding experience within the sensorium.

cognitions about the object (*prapanca sanna sankha;* see Nanananda 1976) that follows lawfully from consciousness grasping any object of perception. One learns from insight practice that investing energy in attending any object results inevitably in recognition (note the advised use of the word *re-cognition*), and following recognition, the relevation of a web of associations intending the object, like iron filings drawn to a magnet.

In either form of contemplation—Husserlian intentional analysis or Buddhist insight practice—the principles inherent in constituting consciousness come to be seen distinctly via an operation of intuitive comprehension (Husserl's *creative intuition*, Buddhism's *vipassana*), an operation that effectively transforms the very consciousness doing the intuiting. What is intuited is not merely the particularistic aspects of perception, but also direct seeing-knowing of universals of mind (Husserl's *eidetic intuition*, Buddhism's *dharmas*). The reader should understand that we are not speaking of logical inference here. We are referring to the capacity of mind to apprehend directly the universal principles upon which it operates and of which its operations are instances. In biogenetic structural terminology, this is consciousness apprehending its own neurognosis (d'Aquili et al. 1979:22; see also below). Jung's exploration of archetypal symbols via *active imagination* is a kind of eidetic (from the Greek root *eidos* or *form* used in the Platonic sense of universal) intuition.

THE REDUCTION, THE EPOCHE, AND THE BRACKETING OF EXISTENCE

Much confusion in transcendental phenomenology centers around the uses of the terms *reduction, epoche,* and *bracketing,* which are frequently used interchangeably. There is perhaps a hidden clue to method in the connotations of the words bracketing and epoche, the latter being the root from which our contemporary word *epoch* derives.[4] Each of these words implies a somewhat arbitrary delimiting, framing, or highlighting for the purpose of treating a chunk of process as individually distinct, be that process in perceived space-time or in cognition. The purpose of bracketing is the temporary relevation of some aspect of a process or a relationship between processes into awareness, after which it is *seen* and *known* within its greater context without the need of arbitrary and willful bracketing.

Whether *the reduction* is a process or an end state is often ambiguous. Husserl clearly uses the term in both senses: the end state and the procedure by which one reaches the end state. As Koestenbaum views it, the *epoche* (Greek for bracketing) is the state of consciousness that arises from:

> focusing on any part or all of my experience, and then observing, analyzing, abstracting, and describing that experience by removing myself from the immediate and lived engagement in it. I must observe the experience in question from a distance, that is, from a state of reflection. (Husserl 1967:xx)

The rub comes in trying to discover the precise means of attaining that end state, the epoche. If there is one point about which all students of Husserl seem to agree, it is that the master never clearly outlined the exact procedures by which the reduction is to be accomplished (see e.g., McIntyre and Smith in Dreyfus 1982:91).

The "transcendental reduction," or the "universal epoche," is thus the goal of all phenomenological psychology in that it produces a mindstate in which the essential order given in the *noema* is seen, undistorted by theories or presumptions about the existence of the object or its order. But this mindstate is attainable only by way of the process of reducing, or bracketing, the distorting influences of various cognitive operations upon the object. One gets the distinct feeling that Husserl's methodology is geared to a stage-developmental process in the unfolding of eidetic intuition; that is, stripping away delusions about the nature of phenomena layer by layer until the ultimate, essential givenness of phenomena stands in pristine purity before the mind (Husserl 1931). And although it is indeed hard to pin him down to precise methodology at times, it is quite clear that Husserl was advocating an unqualified process of self-discovery and ego transcendence that inevitably entailed the transformation of the being as a consequence of bracketing delusions and reconstituting experience on the basis of knowledge thus gained.

> Unlike Descartes, we shall plunge into the task of laying open the infinite field of transcendental experience. The Cartesian evidence—the evidence of the proposition, *ego cogito, ergo sum*—remained barren because Descartes neglected, not only to clarify the pure sense of the method of transcendental epoche, but also to direct his attention to the fact that the ego can explicate himself *ad infinitum* and systematically, by means of transcendental experience, and therefore lies ready as a possible field of work. This field is completely unique and separate, since it indeed relates likewise to all the world and all the Objective science, yet does not presuppose acceptance of their existence, and since thereby it is separated from all these sciences, yet does not in any manner adjoin them. (Husserl 1977:31)

Perhaps it would be useful to offer a concrete example of bracketing so that we have at least one shared experience that makes the term meaningful. May we suggest that you fix your gaze upon some object in the distance. Concentrate your attention upon the object as intensely as you can. Feel the effort such concentration requires. Now, *without moving your gaze from that object,* shift your attention to some sound in your environment, and again intensify your attention upon the new object. Feel the effort this shift of attention requires. Try moving your attention back and forth between the visual object and the auditory object, intensifying concentration upon each in turn. But gradually begin to watch the effort required to shift attention and to intensify attention upon the object. That is, gradually make the attentional effort the principal object of awareness. When you get the hang of this subtle shift in attention, add a third object, say the pressure of your buttocks on the chair or your feet on the floor. Now move attention and concentration around in the sensorial field circumscribed by the three objects from three different sensory modes. Again, gradually pay more attention to the effort required for the change in orientation. Study that effort. Add more sense objects (e.g., breath at the nostrils, other sounds, colors in the peripheral field) if you wish, but keep the gaze fixed upon the original visual object. You may notice that the more you pay attention to the effort—perhaps an aspect of consciousness to which you have never before paid much attention—the more the effort aspect stands out relative to the rest of the context of perception.

Now, in order to carry out successfully this exercise and to study effectively the role of effort in attention, you must not be concerned with the practical aspects of perception. Whether the objects before the mind are real or not is no longer of any consequence. You have momentarily suspended belief or disbelief in the existence of the objects, and they have become guides for carrying out your exploration of one aspect of attention. That is, you have "bracketed existence" relative to the objects. The exercise could be carried out completely even if all or some objects were dreamed, imagined, or hallucinated. Practical concern for the objects, presumptions about their existence, and theories about their relationships to other objects in the world are differentiated from the pure act of perception and are dropped from consideration. This more or less approximates the state of mind Husserl called the *first epoche:*

> We extract only the phenomenon of "bracketing" or "disconnecting," which is obviously not limited to that of the attempt to doubt, although it can be detached from it with special ease, but can appear in other contexts also, and with no less ease independently. In relation to every thesis and wholly uncoerced we can use this peculiar [epoche], a certain refraining from judgement which is compatible with the unshaken and unshakable because self-evidencing conviction of Truth. The thesis is "put out of action," bracketed, it passes off into the modified status of a "bracketed thesis," and the judgement *simpliciter* into "bracketed judgement." (Husserl 1931:109)

In the course of the exercise you have bracketed in another, subtler sense. You have directed attention to an aspect of perception that presumably was previously unconscious to you. Attentional effort has always been there, and it is still there. The difference is that you *relevated* the function to consciousness; that is, you bracketed it or delimited it for study. If you in fact realized attentional effort in carrying out the exercise, then you know that aspect of perception with absolute certainty. There is no question that effort forms an essential part of your perception. This is the so-called apodictic quality of truths discovered via the phenomenological method, a quality that itself remains unquestioned at the level of the first epoche (Husserl 1977:151).

This exercise, however appropriate it might be for clarifying concepts, is trivial and should not reflect any superficiality in the program of self-discovery advocated by Husserl. Husserl was quite aware that even the cognized self does not escape unscathed by the exercise of bracketing. Where once reigned the mundane "empirical" ego of the naive *cogito*, there now reigns the "transcendental" or "pure" ego that has always been there and is characterized as being a spectator to both the essential givenness of perception and the processes of constitution of the world (Ricoeur 1967a:40). The realization of the transcendental ego does not happen overnight. It emerges developmentally as the ego becomes progressively freed from the (previously unconscious, then relevated and bracketed, now reintegrated into awareness) cognitive operations upon which the natural attitude was constituted. Just as the object of consciousness is reduced to its essential nature by bracketing, similarly, the ego is reduced to its essential givenness—the role of undeluded watcher:

> The psychic life that psychology talks about has in fact always been, and still is, meant as psychic life in the world. Obviously the same is true also of one's own psychic life, which is grasped and considered in purely internal experience. But phenomenological epoche . . . inhibits acceptance of the Objective world as existent, and thereby excludes this world completely from the field of judgement. In so doing, it likewise inhibits acceptance of any Objectively apperceived facts, including those of internal experience. Consequently for me, the meditating Ego who, standing and remaining in the attitude of epoche, posits exclusively himself as the acceptance-basis of all Objective acceptances and bases . . . there is no psychology, i.e., as components of psychophysical men.
>
> By phenomenological epoche I reduce my natural human Ego and my psychic life—the realm of my psychological self-experience—to my transcendental-phenomenological self-experience. The Objective world, the world that exists for me, that always has and always will exist for me, the only world that ever can exist for me—this world, with all its Objects, I said, derives its whole sense and its existential status, which it has for me, from me myself, from me as the transcendental Ego, the Ego who comes to the fore only with transcendental-phenomenological epoche. (Husserl 1977:25–26)

Moreover, the changes wrought by the reduction produce knowledge of phenomenal perception that is not only apodictic but is also fundamental to a fully mature science—a status that modern science cannot yet claim. That knowledge of perception is crucial to the evolution of science because without it the scientific endeavor is perpetually doomed to misunderstand the ontological nature of its theories, and the relationships between theory and observation. According to Husserl, that knowledge of perception is unobtainable by any other method than the reduction, the practice of mature contemplation. And for this reason, the approach to consciousness taken in the present book presumes the necessity of a neurophenomenology—a merger of knowledge about consciousness obtained in part by mature contemplation and in part by modern neuroscience.

2 THE NATURE OF NEUROGNOSIS

You may ask whether I am saying that these brain programs think our thoughts. I am indeed saying that, but only "in a certain sense." This is not meant to be evasive. It is important to try to be clear about the relations of mind and brain, but this is not easy! I am proposing that if we look closely at what we wish to convey by using these two words *together* we shall come to a single view of human beings as persons. The brain operates in certain ways that may be described as programs, and the actions of these programs constitute the entity that we call the mind of a person.

—J. Z. Young, *Programs of the Brain*

THOSE WHO STRIVE TO INCREASE the level of their own self-awareness, by whatever method or path, will sooner or later reach at least one inevitable conclusion: the world of experience is somehow a construction of the mind. Whether by dint of practice within some Eastern yogic tradition, or of mastery of modern physics, one comes to question the relationship between the world as experienced and the real world "out there" independent of one's knowing of it. It is our position that the nervous system constructs the world of everyday experience (see Jerison in Eccles 1987), and our task in this chapter is to construe the nervous system in such a way that this basic point makes clear and persuasive sense.

In order to make our point, we must find the means through the topic's dizzying complexity without either simplifying the matter and thus distorting it, or worse yet, causing the reader to give up because of unnecessarily complex language. Ironically we know more about the origin and development of galaxies than we do about, say, sexual differentiation of the brain or the mechanism of pain. This lack of information is a natural outcome of the complex organization of the brain. It is also the result of the brain's trying to understand itself. To make matters worse, a few scientific schools of thought that purport to study brain and consciousness reject the evidence of mature contemplation—a stricture similar to entering a boxing match with one hand tied behind the back.

BEING AS A COMMUNITY OF CELLS

Our body is composed of hundreds of trillions of cells of myriad types and description. Our being is, in fact, a community of cells; a commu-

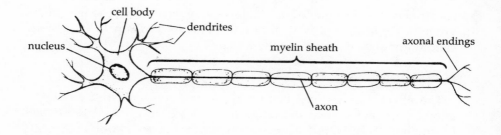

FIGURE 2. The basic map of the neuron showing the cell body, or soma, nucleus, dendrites, axon, myelin sheath and the axonal endings that produce part of the synapses when they interact with other cells. Reprinted from A. M. Schneider and B. Tarshis, *Introduction to Physiological Psychology*, 3rd ed., (New York: Random House, 1986), 76.

nity of discrete organisms that are, themselves, made up of various parts like membranes, mitochondria, organelles, and nuclei (see Varela 1979). Cells develop specializations and organize themselves into systems that in turn form organs, which perform particular functions like pumping blood, filtering waste products, circulating air, and extracting oxygen.

The nervous system is an organ as well. It specializes in the purposeful regulation of vital functions, tracking events in the world and analyzing them, organizing the various systems of the body into adaptively appropriate responses, and most important for our purpose, constructing an internal model of the being and the world within the context of which discrete events are cognitively evaluated (Granit 1977). The brain and the rest of the nervous system is, like all organs, made up of cells of myriad types and descriptions. Some authorities estimate that the nervous system is composed of more than 10 trillion nerve cells, and many times that number of glial and other support cells (Klopf 1982:12)[1]

Nerve cells, or *neurons,* (see figure 2) are made up of the same parts as other types of cells, but they have specialized forms that enable them to send electrochemical pulses to fellow neurons and other types of cells as a form of communication. Neurons develop what are called *processes* that are hairlike projections (two types called *dendrites* and *axons*) that grow outward from the body of the cell to *synapse* ("connect up") with other cells, usually other neurons. Thus few if any neurons are loners. They almost always develop as part of a society of neurons and support cells and other body cells like muscle fibers. Such a society of cells may be called a *network*. The initial growth of any cell is at first largely constrained by the genetic information contained in its ribosomes (deoxyribonucleic acid, or DNA), and later (and in addition to its genetic conditioning) by its interaction within one or more networks.

PENETRATION

The effect that one cell has upon another, one network has upon another, or one system has upon another we have called *penetration* (d'Aquili et al. 1979:354ff). Penetration may be between levels of system, for example, between molar and molecular levels of organization within the same system. For instance, the decision to respond to a stimulus in the environment may involve activation of the autonomic system, which stimulates the activity of the pituitary so that the activity of secretory cells is changed and a chemical (adrenocorticotropic hormone, or ACTH) is released into the blood stream. This mutual interpenetration occurs between nested systems of different levels of organization. Penetration may also be between systems at the same level of organization within the same system. For example, the ACTH released by the secretory cells of the pituitary may effect the internal state of cells within the adrenal glands so that they in turn release a chemical (epinephrine) into the blood stream. As we shall see later on, the concept of penetration is important to understanding how the symbolic process operates in cognition.

THE HEDONISTIC NEURON

A common error committed by those discussing the psychological aspects of the nervous system is to forget that cells are living organisms—that our being is, in fact, a community of cells. In much of the literature, both within the neurosciences and within related disciplines, the basic unit from which the brain is constructed is called a "neuron," but is treated as though it were an inorganic microchip.

A book by A. Harry Klopf, *The Hedonistic Neuron*, presents a theoretical view that will help us avoid this error, particularly when we describe the structure of conscious network and the sensorium in later chapters. Klopf notes that theorists have always presumed that brains are goal-seeking systems made up of *non*goal-seeking components. Because of this presumption, the purposive characteristic of the brain must be conceived of as an emergent property uncharacteristic of individual neurons (ibid.:7). On the other hand, there is reason to suppose that neurons actually are goal-seeking, and goal-seeking in a similar but more primitive way as are the brains of which they are composed. For one thing, most neurons in the brain are involved in *local circuits*, which are tiny systems of cells that are integrated into a series of feedback loops (Uttley 1966; Rakic 1976). That is, much of the information coming into the cell is in immediate response to its own activity. One reason why this feedback relationship has not been given the importance it deserves in neurophysiology is that although most neurons are local circuit neurons, they have been the hardest to study. The most accessible neurons for study—those with long processes called *long axon neurons*—are the least numerous and are relatively less affected by local feedback loops (see Rakic 1976).

Local circuit neurons include the majority of cells constituting the neocortex, the evolutionarily most recent portion of the human brain and the part that mediates all higher cognitive and perceptual functions. According to John Eccles (see Popper and Eccles 1977: chap. E1) each cortical hemisphere averages only three millimeters in thickness, and is comprised of 10 billion or so neurons. To illustrate how tiny neural cells are, a column of cortical tissue measuring 3 mm deep and 0.1–0.5 mm wide may contain as many as 10,000 neurons—most of which are local circuit neurons, interconnected with other cells only within their immediate locality and involved in intricate networks of mutual interaction. It is cells of this sort that carry out most of the cognitive and perceptual functions about which we will be speaking later in this book.

The intricate interaction between local circuit neurons is carried out by the numerous synapses connecting cells in a communicative array. A single neuron may have thousands, even hundreds of thousands of synaptic inputs terminating on its body and processes. If one considers that most of the 10 billion neurons or so making up one half of the cortex are the loci for thousands of synapses, one may get some idea of the dazzling complexity of interconnections involved in making up the working brain. Within the context of the neurons' interaction with countless other members of its networks develops the purposive activity of the individual neuron.

The electrochemical pulse, the neuron's most important means of communicating with other cells, occurs because of activity at its membrane. The cell membrane can *depolarize* and increase the flow of ions between inside and outside the cell, or it can *hyperpolarize* and become even less permeable to ion exchange with its ambience. Whether the neuron's membrane depolarizes or hyperpolarizes depends on the chemical influences upon the membrane of the (possibly thousands of) synaptic inputs from other cells. Those synapses that increase depolarization and the flow of ions are called *excitatory* synapses; those that increase hyperpolarization and block the flow of ions are called *inhibitory* synapses. Klopf's thesis is that neurons purposely seek to maximize excitation (depolarization) and to minimize inhibition (hyperpolariza-

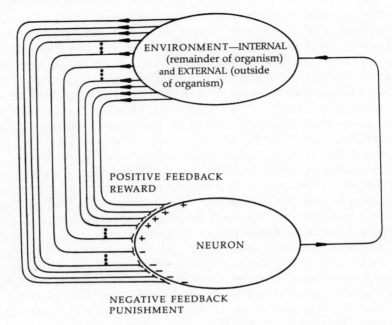

FIGURE 3. The adaptive interaction of the neuron with its environment. The neuron learns to increase pleasure and decrease punishment. Reprinted, by permission, from A. H. Klopf, *The Hedonistic Neuron* (New York: Hemisphere, 1982), 22.

tion). Excitation is equivalent to "pleasure" at the level of the organism and inhibition equivalent to "pain" or "displeasure." The goal of the cell is *not* merely to fire (output), but rather to fire in a way that increases its own excitation (input; ibid.:8). Thus the cell's activity is conditioned by the inputs that result from that activity (see also Powers 1973). That is, a cell continuously strives to "learn" how best to respond to the effects of its synaptic inputs in order to maximize the effects of excitation and minimize the effects of inhibition.

DEVELOPMENT

The complex way that cells link up in the early development of the organism is not a random affair, nor does a particular cell choose what types of inputs it will have. The initial process by which neural cells find the other cells with which to synapse seems to be determined largely by genetic instructions. As far as we know, only later in development, after the initial linkages between cells have been established, does the external environment exercise its influence over synapsing, other than the presence of essential nutriments for growth.

We believe there is far more to the picture than can be accounted for by the simple conditioning of neural cells by the activity of other neural cells. For one thing, Klopf's model fails to take into account the activity of so-called support cells, those enigmatic *glial* cells that surround and far outnumber neural cells. These cells have a great deal to do with the flow of nutriments to and waste materials from the neurons (glial cells always intervene between neurons and their blood supply; see Hatten and Edmonson 1988). Specialized glial cells also lay down myelin, the fatty sheath around the neurons, thus influencing the speed of transmission of the neuron's electrochemical pulse. And the glial cells also facilitate or inhibit the growth of a neuron's processes as they reach out to establish synapses upon other neurons. No one yet knows the full extent of the role played by the glial cells in cognition, but many authorities suspect their role is major. For example, the corpus callosum, the largest axonal tract to be found in the mammalian brain and the major link between the two cerebral hemispheres, first develops in embryogenesis when axons follow a path established by a bridge of glial cells that develop just prior to the growth of callosal neurons (Silver and Ogawa 1983). If something stops the development of the glial bridge, the corpus callosum will fail to develop.

Another problem is that Klopf's model explicitly denies intrinsic activity on the part of the neuron; he seems quite wedded to a stimulus-response view of neuronal activity (ibid.:4). He contrasts his view to that of D. O. Hebb's (1949), which holds that once a pathway has been activated, it is more likely to be activated again because of modifications at the synapse (Klopf 1982:92ff). That is, cells become associated in an array or pathway due to previous activity of that network of cells, and adaptation of the array requires simultaneous adaptation of every component cell. The intrinsic motivation of each cell is to fire (see Bergstrøm 1969; Berridge and Rapp 1979), unless inhibited from doing so by inhibitory cells (a large proportion of all neurons are in fact inhibitory!); Klopf calls this an *association model*, which he contrasts with his own *reinforcement model* (ibid.:92ff).

Unfortunately, although Klopf's model handles well many problems in learning research, it cannot easily account for developmental invariance in learning; that is, universal patterns evidenced in the development of neurocognition over the lifetime of a person. If a neuron acts only to maximize excitatory input and minimize inhibitory input, then it (1) is unlikely to do anything when those inputs are not present, and (2) should manifest a lot more plasticity of form and activity than it in fact does.

Actually, neurons are living organisms, and as such they have an intrinsic tendency to act upon their environment. They reach out and seek the appropriate cells with which to synapse, and this process has not been shown to involve excitatory or inhibitory inputs. The process has been shown to be genetically predisposed to a high degree (Brodal 1975; Dykes and Ruest 1986:25). Other aspects of development follow a similar invariant patterning indicative of genetic predisposition; examples include myelinization (Larroche 1966; Bekoff and Fox 1972), increase in dendritic spines as a consequence of enriched activity (Rosenzweig et al. 1972; Diamond et al. 1964, 1966; Renner and Rosenzweig 1987), and alternation in developmental priority among competing neural systems (Turkewitz and Kenny 1982). If one follows Klopf's strictures too closely, then cognitively and developmentally crucial processes such as play and symbolization must be treated strictly as emergent processes, intrinsic to the development of the organism, but extrinsic to the neurons that make up the organism's brain. To look for the concomitant, intrinsic activity of cells to play in the organism would perhaps be more productive—just as Klopf has done with pleasure and pain (reward and punishment).

The structures mediating consciousness develop, as Piaget (1971a, 1977) has repeatedly argued, within an equilibratory process involving the simultaneous and intrinsic demands of growth and adaptation. Reinforcement models of adaptation all too often slight matters of development and evolution, and paint a picture of completely plastic structures subserving behavior and other physiological functions (see Seligman and Hager 1972; Hinde 1982:188ff for further discussion). On the other hand, it is easy to err in the opposite extreme: to view structures from an evolutionary, or "hard wired," neurological perspective as though their organization were totally implastic and fixed by genetic conditioning. Again, it helps to keep in mind that we are dealing with living cells, cells that adapt to their environments to whatever extent they can. Even functions lost because of serious cortical lesions may be recovered (to some extent at least) by a variety of means including regeneration of damaged tissues, adoption of the function by other uninjured tissues, and reorganization of undamaged tissues into a new network capable of performing the function (Butters, Rosen, and Stein in Stein et al. 1974:459). Some cortical functions may be taken up by tissues immediately proximal to the damaged tissues, and in other cases functions may be recovered by cortical and subcortical tissues distant from the site of damage. The type and extent of functional recovery due to damaged tissue seems to depend upon the age of the child at time of damage, as well as the precise function involved.

An interesting view that explicitly avoids the pitfalls encountered by the total plasticity and implastic, "hard wiring" positions is the "selective stabilization" theory of Jean-Pierre Changeux (1983, 1985; Changeux, Courrege, and Danchin 1973; Changeux and Danchin 1976). Changeux begins from the position that there is too small an evolutionary increment in genetic material to account for the remarkable increase in complexity of human neural organization over that of, say, the chimpanzee. A solution to this apparent paradox is to be found in a process by which patterns of synaptic innervation are stabilized out of a field of potential synapses. Processes develop and synapses are tentatively established during an early "labile" phase of neural development. During the labile phase, the developmental processes have a high redundancy factor and are largely determined by the genetic labeling producing the generalized cell type of which any particular neuron is a member. A period of selection follows the laying down of the field of synapses during which some synapses are reinforced through activity *at both pre- and postsynaptic sites on the membranes of the cell and its target,* and many other synapses are eliminated by irreversible regression and cell death due to inactivity. The distinction between a labile phase and a selection phase concurs with the well-known fact that functional recovery due to tissue damage is more likely in the very young animal than in the adult (Harlow et al. 1970). The reorganization of neural structures would seem to be more plastic if damage occurs during lability than if it occurs after extensive innervation and selection has been completed.

It is important to note that activity of target cells (for example, flexion of muscle fibers) seems necessary for triggering the biochemical processes required to stabilize some synapses and the regression of others (Changeux 1983:469). This triggering provides one neurological mechanism in support of Piaget's claim that development of cognitive structures, *schemes,* requires activity. This view also is in keeping with the suggestion that cells may exercise control over their sensitivity to transmitter substances released by synapses. Cells in both the peripheral and central nervous systems may become "supersensitive" to a transmitter substance after denervation due to lesion of presynaptic fibers, and thus in some cases may allow some recovery of function orginally lost by the lesion (Rosner in Stein et al. 1974:19).

Changeux's solution to the limited genome versus complex elaboration of neural structures paradox is DNA conservative. His solution is thus consonant with the view taken by Simon (1981), and by biogenetic structural theory as well, that the vast complexity of symbolic expression and behavior observed among human beings may be accounted for by considering a relatively simple and finite neurocognitive system in interaction with a rich and ever-changing environment. In this case, it is a simple genotype in interaction with an environment that produces a relatively complex array of phenotypic expressions. Furthermore, Changeux's theory can be considered in accordance with that of Klopf's. As Changeux says, the mechanism of stabilization is "neither unique nor exclusive of other mechanisms of diversification" (1983:475).

The advantage of both Klopf's and Changeux's views to our project is that they offer accounts of cognitive processes based upon the understanding that living *cells*, not some vague sort of inorganic microchips, are interacting to form neural systems within the organism. "The overall conclusion is that intelligent brain function can be understood in terms of nested hierarchies of heterostatic goal-seeking adaptive loops, beginning at the level of the single neuron and extending upward to the level of the whole brain" (Klopf 1982:13). Klopf's view also emphasizes the necessity of positive and negative feedback operating at every level of organization of the nervous system, a crucial factor in explaining how complex organizations develop in adapting to the environment within the general constraints imposed by the genome—incidentally, a point insisted upon by Piaget (see 1971, 1980).

Considering Klopf's model of reinforcement, it is easy to see how penetration may occur at the neuronal level. Any cell or network of cells that has synaptic connections to the target cell or network can potentially penetrate the target and influence its current and future activity by exercising positive or negative feedback. Thus areas like the reticular activating system in the brain stem, an area involved with arousal and attention and widely connected throughout the brain and lower nervous system, exhibit relatively global penetrance into many systems and their component cells and networks. On the other hand, networks such as those monitoring blood pressure may have fairly limited penetrance.

Development is a multileveled affair, involving the growth of each organic level while simultaneously involving adaptation of each level to its own particular environment. The environment of the neuron includes all the cells (neural and support) that affect its activity and growth, and that it in turn affects. Part of the neuron's environment will be the networks in which it becomes involved as a component (see Caianiello 1968 on neural networks and Hebb 1949 on "cell assemblies"). This reciprocal relationship continues up the hierarchy of organization through the entire nervous system and the organism so that the term *environment* begins to take on its more common meaning.

The value of Klopf's position is that it can be easily incorporated into a developmental frame in such a way that the genetic constraints to neural plasticity are kept ever in mind (e.g., Changeux's "categories" of cells). The organization of any particular network of cells will be caused by both intrinsic growth requirements and by communication from its environment (e.g., Changeux's "singularization" of cells; 1983:471). That is, intrinsic growth demands of the cell and the environmental press in the form of synaptic and other inputs to the cell are co-producers of the organization of neural networks. Klopf's argument in favor of the equivalence of depolarization and hyperpolarization with reward and punishment at the psychological level seems sound and persuasive. We will use his view with the reservations previously stated kept clearly in mind.

THE NATURE OF NEUROGNOSIS

Most of us find it very difficult to comprehend that the organization of the nervous system, manifested in its functioning, produces our world of experience (Jerison in Eccles 1987). In other words, our experience at any moment of consciousness is produced by our nervous system, with or without stimulation from events occurring in the external world. The difficulty in grasping this vital connection is fundamental to the Western "natural thesis" about self and world, and is thus very hard to overcome because the schism between experience and body is severely conditioned. Nonetheless, the structure of experience *is* that part of the nervous system mediating experience. And as we have seen, the structure of experience, being living tissue, develops. However, as we have also seen, neural networks never develop in a random or haphazard way. To the layman, the anatomy of the brain may appear as a homogeneous mass of gray and white matter. This is far from the case, for every part of the human nervous system, including the brain, is precisely and uniquely structured down to the tiniest element in the neural network. No two places in the brain exhibit exactly the same anatomical pattern. And yet, the anatomical structure of any one local area is quite similar from brain to brain. This organization is neither random nor chaotic. It is, as far as neuroscientists can ascertain, linked to a specific function of the particular locus (see Brodal 1975; Dykes and Ruest 1986:25). As Alf Brodal notes:

> We may consider the brain as consisting of a multitude of small units, each with its particular morphological (and presumably functional) features. These units collaborate by way of an immensely rich, complicated, and differentiated network of connections, which are very precisely and specifically organized. The anatomical possibilities for (more-or-less direct) cooperation between various parts of the brain must be almost unlimited! (1975:134)

All of these units with their discrete functions and networks develop over time. In fact, the more we know about the early pre- and perinatal development of the nervous system, the more it seems that the entire system emerges according to an exquisitely precise, genetically regulated design. Generally speaking, the earlier a neural network emerges in ontogenesis, the more important will be the role of genetic information, and the less important the role of environmental information via synaptic conditioning of neurons in the formation of the network.

In biogenetic structural theory, the initial organization of a neural network is termed *neurognosis* (Laughlin and d'Aquili 1974: chap. 5). It is the neurognostic structure of experience that accounts for universal attributes of mind (and much of what is generally called "culture") studied cross-culturally (see Young 1987:127). It is in neurognosis that the structures adduced to explain such universals by structuralist theories are realized. This realization is the case whether the observed universals are considered to have a temporal aspect or not—that is, whether the phenomena are viewed synchronically (within a limited time frame), or diachronically (within a longer temporal frame). These two aspects of structure are important and require some further elaboration.

SYNCHRONIC STRUCTURES

Synchronic structural explanations strive to account for universals among observables by reference to real, knowable, but rarely observable structures that are (1) systemic in organization, (2) universal to all human beings, and (3) usually unconscious in activity. A good example of such a structure is that mediating vision. A visual experience is subserved by an incredibly complex system that is the same for all normal human beings, regardless of cultural background. Furthermore, most people are conscious only of the object of perception—that is, the "thing" being seen—and not the functioning of the visual system *per se* that produces the object. We are aware of the coffee cup before us, but are usually unaware that the visual system has moved the eyeballs in order to bring the light reflected from the cup into the fovial region of the retinae (see Searle 1983: chap. 2).

In synchronic structural explanations, observables are conceived of as being variant transformations of the underlying structures. It does not matter whether the object of perception is a coffee cup or a wristwatch; the underlying system that produces the visual experience is the same. For this reason, an explanation of transforms (coffee cup, wristwatch, etc.) in experience is considered incomplete without including the elements, relationships, and principles of operation composing the structures that produce the transforms.

DIACHRONIC STRUCTURES

Diachronic structural explanations, on the other hand, strive to account for universal patterns in the development or evolution of observ-

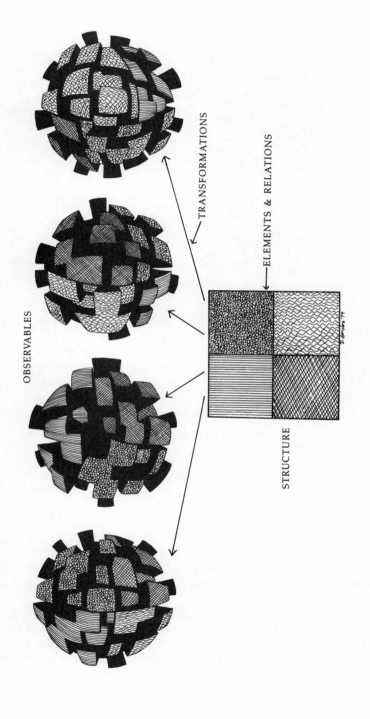

OBSERVABLES

TRANSFORMATIONS

ELEMENTS & RELATIONS

STRUCTURE

FIGURE 4. A synchronic structure. A single structure made up of elements and relations among elements produces various surface transformations that are the observables. Drawing by Donna Gordon.

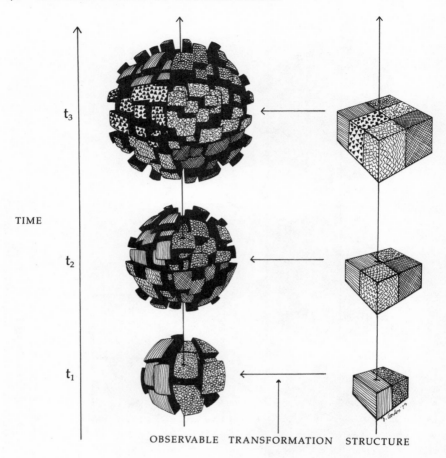

FIGURE 5. A diachronic structure. A structure develops through time and produces surface transformations that appear as maturing observables. Drawing by Donna Gordon.

ables. The characteristics of structure remain the same for any given moment as in synchronic accounts, but here the emphasis shifts to process rather than invariant patterns of form, and to change rather than stasis.

Adding a temporal dimension to structural accounts requires several considerations that are frequently ignored in synchronic structural theories. First, dynamic structures must be conceived to be open to the effects of environmental factors. Diachronic structures are producers of transformations, but not as complete causes; whereas all too often synchronic structural accounts imply causality independent of environmental factors. Orthodox semiotic structuralism, ungrounded in action and synchronically biased, has been open to repeated criticism in its failure to account for structural-environmental relationships (e.g., Wilden 1974:276). The reader might wish to compare the treatment of myth given by a semiotic structuralist such as Levi-Strauss (1964) with a more ecologically structural account like that of Reichel-Dolmatoff (1971).

Second, the addition of temporality and change to structural accounts requires a consideration of the adaptive functions of structures. The question becomes: To what extent do transformations in structure serve the biological adaptation of the organism or species? As Earl Count (1974) has noted, behavior itself does not evolve or develop; rather, it is the structure mediating behavior that evolves. Full understanding of the activities of the human hand requires that we examine the entire process by which the hand participates in exploring and adapting to the world. This investigation would ideally encompass the first gross and clumsy movements of the prenatal child to the highly refined and elegant movements of a concert pianist. But such an investigation would always be centered, not merely on the activities themselves, but on their role in transforming physiological and neurological structures mediating the activities.

Third, and related closely to the second, is that a diachronic perspective conceived in its broadest scope—that is, *considered from the very inception of structures at or near conception or phylogenetic origin*—will recognize the primacy of structural organization over structural activity. Development will be principally directed at forming an initial structure with a minimal or nonexistent behavioral phase, and then later emphasizing behavioral output and perceptual input in the refinement of structural adaptation. On this account, methods limited solely to behavioral observation—information collected from but one of the windows of our sphere—are doomed to error, for they have no means of gleaning data about the structures independent of behavior and no means of defining the initial organization of the structure. Such approaches can easily fall into the trap of treating the nervous system as a *tabula rasa* that becomes structured only with the advent of behavior, when even the most cursory awareness of developmental neurobiology would suffice to contravene that view. Behavior, in our view, is a label for only one (output) phase of the operation of *some types* of structure; perception is a label for yet another (input) phase. Neural structures are inevitably neurognostic in their initial organization, and though many structures may require behavior as a component for optimal development (e.g., the stabilization of the neuromuscular endplate according to Changeux

1983), some will require little and some will require none. In any event, by being neurognostic, structures have developed to some extent with either no behavioral component, or perhaps, with limited motor activity allowable by the fetal environment and the relatively inept motor activities available to the perinatal child.

Fourth, understanding a patterned change of behavior over time requires examination of the structural changes that subserve the behavior, as well as the principles producing or causing the changes at the structural level. In the example of the hand's activities given earlier, we are compelled to understand the principles operating in development that causally link the stages in the development of, say, the cerebellum (the part of the brain involved in regulating fine motor coordination). Are there perhaps sensitive or "critical" periods during which optimal growth of cerebellar networks may occur?

And fifth, concern for process in the development of structure necessitates consideration not only of the operation of structure at various points in its development, but also of the productive and causal principles inherent in the organism that operate to transform structure and function at one point in time to those at other points in time. This concern will often require tracking the relationships between structure at its various stages of development and the environment at each point in time. There is ample evidence, for example, that richness or poverty of environment will produce predictable variations in neural structures at the cellular level (see Renner and Rosenzweig 1987). If we are interested in the operation of a particular structure under a set of environmental conditions, it may well be appropriate to examine the operation of that structure at previous points in its evolution. For instance, for a full understanding of the grasping function in modern humans it might be appropriate to examine the skeletal morphology of our brachiating primate ancestors as represented in the fossil record.

Obviously our position is that the only empirically valid use of the concept of structure as an account of human psychology, consciousness, behavior, or expression in either a synchronic or a diachronic frame is in reference to neural and to other somatic structures. We are also affirming that all neural structures develop from an initial neurognostic organization, which is to a large extent genetically predisposed and developmentally prior to behavior modification. An incidental implication of this view is that the "structures" adduced to explain observables in structuralist formulations, whether synchronic or diachronic, either refer to the organization of the nervous system or simply do not exist. This means that "structures" conceived to explain data outside the confines of the neurosciences are nonetheless open to disconfirmation by data from within the neurosciences. And obviously "structures" developed within the neurosciences are open to disconfirmation from outside the neurosciences as well (cf. Johnson-Laird 1983).

The structures to which we are referring in this book are organizations composed of cells, minimally including neurons and glial and endocrine cells. We further suggest that both cells and networks of cells at every level of hierarchy may be treated as goal-serving, living systems (see Varela 1979, Maturana and Varela 1987). The most difficult and controversial issue relative to these neural structures is precisely their neurognostic properties. For this reason we want to explore neurognosis, as well as attendant concepts like entrainment, equilibration, structure and function, and canalization, in order to clarify further our neurological grounding for such seemingly ethereal questions as dreaming and higher psychic energy experiences.

The Development of Neurognosis

The brain is the organ of behavior. This statement is taken for granted in the neurosciences, but may be meaningless, trivial, or controversial for anthropologists, other social scientists, and philosophers who study behavior, perception, and symbolism in virtual ignorance of well over a century of neuroscientific research. Yet, this statement has profound implications for how one goes about the study of behavioral and other phenomena of interest to social science, not the least of which is the necessity for a developmental frame for research, interpretation, and understanding.

It might be useful, therefore, to note a few facts about the early development of the human brain. For one thing, the brain has developed its full complement of neurons by the end of the eighteenth week of gestation (Dobbing and Smart 1974). This means that by the fifth month of prenatal life the human being has nearly all of the neurons he or she will ever have in their lifetime. The number of nerve cells may actually decrease through attrition from birth to old age (Brody 1955; Cowan 1979). The increase in the brain's size from the end of the eighteenth week on is the result of an increase in the complement of support cells (Dobbing and Smart 1974), an increase in the size of neurons caused by proliferation of processes (dendrites and axons; Diamond et al. 1964, 1966; Rosenzweig et al. 1972), and a progressive myelinization (the fatty sheath that covers the axons of many neural cells; Jacobson 1978).

At birth the human infant's brain (one-seventh of its body weight!) weighs roughly a quarter of its adult weight. At six months of age the child's brain will weigh approximately 50 percent of its adult weight. This period of rapid growth continues for the first few years of postnatal life and then rapidly diminishes as the child approaches adolescence (Norback 1967). Several factors in the child's environment may significantly influence the extent and nature of neural development during the early formative period, including nutrition (L'at 1967; Shneour 1974; Lewin 1975) and richness of environmental stimuli (Diamond et al. 1964, 1966; Rosenzweig et al. 1972).

A word of caution: A common bias exists in our culture that can seriously distort our understanding of the development of the brain and consciousness. We tend as a culture to presume that the psychology of an "infant" or a "child" begins at birth or at some point after birth, and that the environment of the "embryo" and "fetus" is an impervious haven in which the child develops in isolation from an environment outside the womb (note that we have separate words for the prenatal and postnatal child). Not so. Although it is true that the entire mechanism of gestation and perinatal mother-infant bonding is biologically designed to provide the most favorable circumstances for early ontogenesis, the intrauterine and early postuterine environments are anything but impervious to stressful intrusion (Schell 1981; Sontag 1941; DeMause 1981; Stone 1973; Bekoff and Fox 1972; Fries 1977; Liley 1972; Ploye 1973). In fact, the pre- and perinatal child may be stressed to the point of distress (à la Selye 1956), or even death (Verny 1982), and such trauma can mark the entire course of postnatal development (see reviews in DeMause 1981; Verny 1982; Chamberlain 1983; Fries 1977).

We would particularly point to the influence of pre- and perinatal experiences on establishing a characteristic range of autonomic balances relative to perceived objects. The data pertaining to intrauterine autonomic tuning for humans are spotty at best (Richmond and Lustman 1955; Wenger 1941), but much more suggestive data are available for nonhuman subjects (Hofer 1974). It is reasonable to hypothesize that a range of autonomic balance vis-à-vis events in experience is established *in utero*, during birth, and in early infancy, and that responses based upon this range will vary with the individual (see Richmond and Lustman 1955; Grossman and Greenberg in Stone et al. 1973), and among cultures (Brazelton, Kislowski, and Tronich 1977; Liedloff 1975). We disagree with DeMause's contention that the prenatal environment is inevitably distressful and the the pre- and perinatal child is always ambivalent in its response to the world of experience. Rather, we agree with Stave (1978:29) and Liedloff (1975) that a naturally nurturant pre- and postnatal environment, including natural mother-infant bonding, results in a child's positive orientation to experience. The child is innately prepared to be born and to bond with ("imprint" upon) its mother (Sugarman 1977).

The early pre- and perinatal period of the brain's development is a vast elaboration of neural networks—a process that involves the elaboration of dendritic-axonic-synaptic interconnections, differential myelinization of axons and an increment in the structure of support cells. As we have said, this elaboration is exquisitely controlled by the genotype, is never totally plastic, and results in the formation of functional neural networks (1) that provide a set of rudimentary, initial models of the world; (2) that develop sequentially according to a plan encoded in the genotype; and (3) that process information from sensory modes resulting in organizations also controlled by the genotype.

STRUCTURE AND FUNCTION

A word or two should be said about the common distinction between structure and function, for by neurognosis we are referring to both aspects of organization. In common social science parlance, "structure" is what one has left over after "content" has been removed. The relationships between members of a family are arranged to fulfill, to some extent, the structure of family relationships characteristic of the culture. The structure of relationships "does something"—that is, it functions—to organize people into families. In social sciences one can easily speak of structure without reference to function by simply removing the content, namely, the actual interactions among people. In sociology structure is conceived of as a logic of relationships. And, as Campbell (1984) observes, there has been a recent upsurge of "functionalism" in philosophy and psychology that retains a distinction between functional components of mind and their anatomical base.

However, this conception is only partially analogous to the use of these terms in physiology where, in most cases, structure implies function; that is, to demonstrate structure is also to demonstrate function. In physiology, including neurophysiology, structure and function are seen as two ways of talking about the same organization. As Gellhorn and Loofbourrow note, "All functions of the body, mental and emotional as well as the more obviously 'physical' functions, depend upon alterations in the patterns of materials of which the body is built. . . . Mental and emotional phenomena are inconceivable in the absence of a neural substrate, and function without an alteration of substrate pattern is incomprehensible" (1963:3). In this regard, the "functionalism" of which Campbell (1984) speaks is a sophisticated form of dualism that we categorically reject.

One may thus speak of neural networks as structures without content or function only in the sense of *potentiation*. A neural function may lie dormant as in the case of so-called latent processes, structures that do not function unless and until triggered by particular environmental factors (Sade, n.d.; Count 1973), or may be inactive like a hand between episodes of grasping. So when we speak of neurognosis, we are generally referring to structure *and* function, whether or not that structure is functioning at any particular time.

It cannot be overemphasized that we are always speaking of networks of living cells, not inorganic relays or microchips. Cells are organized (that is, structured) organic matter and it is their nature to function. Furthermore, when they form networks, those networks function as living *organ*-izations. The failure to keep the living aspect of neural organization in mind has led to a number of errors, even by neuroscientists. Accordingly, we must clarify two common misconceptions of neural organization before we go on to examine neurognosis in greater detail.

1. *Neural function requires myelinization.* It was long thought that neural structures did not begin to function until their axons had been coated by myelin. It is now known that myelin modifies the speed of transmitting signals in cells that are already functioning (Larroche 1966:273; Bekoff and Fox 1972). Myelinization proceeds from the most archaic parts of the nervous system through the most recent, thus roughly reflecting in ontogenesis the evolutionary stages of the nervous system in phylogenesis (Larroche 1966). The myelinization of the cerebral cortex begins with birth, but it is increasingly evident that the cortex itself is functioning well before birth. Indeed, myelinization has proven to be a poor gauge of cognitive competence in infants (Ellingson 1967). Incidentally, myelinization is one of the more dramatic means by which some types of support cells exercise influence over (penetrate to) the activity of neurons.

2. *Neural function requires complete networks.* As we have seen, nervous systems and networks are erroneously considered goal-seeking, information processing systems made up of nongoal-seeking, noninformation-processing neurons; therefore, neurons cannot begin to function in cognition until networks are fully in place and fundamentally complete. A more realistic view is that each of the nervous system's neurons is a goal-seeking unit that developmentally becomes involved in hierarchy after hierarchy of organization (see Klopf 1982; Brown 1977; Powers 1973). A neuron manifests spontaneous activity (Bergstrøm 1969) and, hence, begins to influence other neurons as soon as synaptic or dendritic contact is made. The initial development of the nerve cell seems to be motivated by an imperative to be active and to "reach out," contact, and communicate with certain other cells. The number of interconnections in which an neuron can become involved is (literally) amazing. A single neuron may come to accrue ten thousand or more synaptic inputs (Haug 1972). This linking up of neurons to form networks, and networks to form even more complex networks and models is a process known as

entrainment. As the term implies, systems become hooked up (much as railroad cars) to form "trains." Entrainments may be relatively enduring or momentary, depending upon the function being performed. As we shall see, the concept of entrainment will take on a complex set of connotations, and will become a pivotal notion in biogenetic structural theory.

NEUROGNOSTIC FUNCTION

An accurate way of portraying the neurognostic aspect of neural functioning is by imagining a set of constraints imposed by the genome (present and active in every cell) on the flexibility of entrainment of cells composing any network, and networks composing more molar systems. Genetic constraints are always present and operating on the growth and activity of cells and the relationships between cells. Changeux (1983:468) calls this constraint the "genetic envelope," within which the free expression of cellular singularity is limited. The constraints will vary from severe to open in different networks, depending on location in the nervous system and on stage of maturation.

One way to clarify the complex relationships among genetics, organization and function of neural systems, and environment is to use C. H. Waddington's (1957:28ff) model of the "epigenetic landscape." Let us imagine for a moment that the entrainment of neural networks forms an undulating landscape and that the functioning of networks is represented by a ball rolling down the contours of the landscape (see figure 6). One can see that on a calm, windless day the ball might roll straight down the central valley with very little effect from environmental press (represented by the wind). Thus environmental press would be "assimilated" (to use Piaget's term) to the structure of the landscape (see figure 7).

On a windy day, the course of the ball would be different. It would probably run down the same valley but exhibit rather an erratic course. Or it might be blown into another valley, or off the landscape entirely. Thus, the course of the ball down the topography of the landscape is a function both of the landscape's contour and of the environmental press at any given moment. That is, the contour and the press are co-producers of the course of the ball (see figure 8).

If the landscape were rigid and unyielding, the path of the ball could easily be blown off course. However, our neurological landscape is not unyielding, but rather is one that alters, or "accommodates" (again Piaget's term), its topography to experience of environmental press. It can do so to the limits allowed by the pegs and wires that underlie its conformation (see figure 9). The flexibility of wires and pegs represents the limits imposed upon the phenotype by the genotype—the "genetic

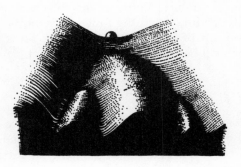

FIGURE 6. The epigenetic landscape. The ball representing the activity of a neural structure is about to roll down the course of the valleys. Extract taken from *Strategy of the Genes* by C. H. Waddington, reproduced by kind permission of Unwin Hyman Ltd. © 1957 by Unwin Hyman Ltd.

envelope"—and in this case upon the organization of neural cells by their genomes. The further down the landscape the ball rolls, the more developed does the landscape become and the broader becomes the range of valleys available to the ball. Neurognosis, then, may be represented by the constraints imposed upon function (the path of the ball) by the initial topography of the landscape, and by the limits (the pegs and wires) to the transformations that may occur in the landscape at any given time (further down the landscape the ball rolls).

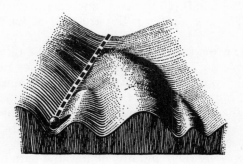

FIGURE 7. The ball in action on a calm and windless day. Extract taken from *Strategy of the Genes* by C. H. Waddington, reproduced by kind permission of Unwin Hyman Ltd. © 1957 by Unwin Hyman Ltd.

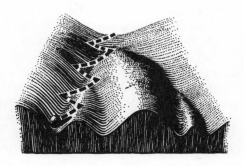

FIGURE 8. The ball in action on a windy day. Extract taken from *Strategy of the Genes* by C. H. Waddington, reproduced by kind permission of Unwin Hyman Ltd. © 1957 by Unwin Hyman Ltd.

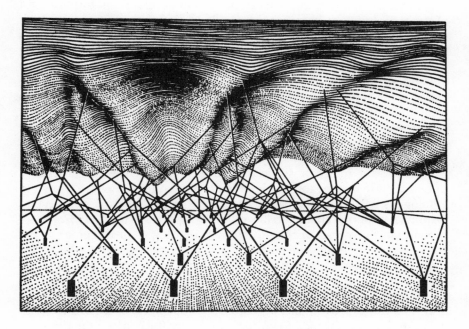

FIGURE 9. The pegs and wires underlying the epigenetic landscape represent the genetic limits of developmental flexibility upon any neural structure. Extract taken from *Strategy of the Genes* by C. H. Waddington, reproduced by kind permission of Unwin Hyman Ltd. © 1957 by Unwin Hyman Ltd.

Again, the model demonstrates that the functioning of a neural structure (the course of the ball) is caused both by its own intrinsic motivation (the gravity that propels the ball) and characteristic entrainment (combined as one co-producer), and by the environmental press (the other co-producer). We can thus define several more concepts that will be of use in understanding the constraints operating upon the functioning of neural networks and, thus, consciousness. The activity of the ball cannot be described as a simple equilibrium system like a thermostat, for after being perturbed by environmental press it returns to a different place on an altered landscape. Rather, the ball *equilibrates* as it moves—returns to a new point, which is a transformation of the old point caused by intrinsic growth and development of the system and adaptation to environmental press (see Piaget 1971a on equilibration; Waddington 1957:32 speaks of "homeorhesis"). This adaptation is what Varela (1979) means by an organism "in-forming" itself.

A series of equilibrating transformations in development forms a kind of canal (a function becomes *canalized*), or pathway of change, which may be called a *creode* (Waddington 1957:32). In our model, the steepness or flatness of the valleys as the ball rolls down the slope represents the rapidity of change of the creode, which may be relatively fast or slow, depending upon its phase of development. Also, the steepness of the valley walls represents the degrees of freedom the ball (function) has from the imperative to return to the equilibration point (ibid.:33–34). *Neurognosis, then, canalizes the developmental entrainment of neural systems into functional creodes that, in a successful organism or species, moderates and integrates the bipolar demands of growth and adaptation.*

Examples of neurognosis as a creode imposing severe constraints upon function may be found in networks mediating behaviors known to ethologists as "fixed action patterns." These are a set of stereotyped response patterns characteristic of every species (Hinde 1982:43ff)— human facial expressions like the frown, the dog's tail-wagging, or the cat's claw-sharpening. The neurognostic loading is evident in the genetically predisposed entrainment of neural and other physiological structures that subserve these responses. However, as living systems, the growth of these closely controlled networks are never closed to adaptation. Thus so-called *fixed* action patterns exhibit variability from individual to individual, episode to episode, and over the course of maturation in the same individual (see Barlow 1977). We seriously doubt there exists anything like a totally fixed neural organization in the nervous systems of higher animals; all networks are open, to some extent, to "learning" and growth in adapting to the environment.

An example of a neurognostic creode having more open constraints is the neuroendocrinal structures mediating "inborn" temperament and later social role among highly social species such as the wolf (Fox 1974, 1975). Here the entrainments are modified considerably in the course of social adjustment during play with peers and later in more serious social encounters as adults. Generally speaking, the higher the network in the hierarchy of neurophysiological functioning, the more open to modification entrainments will be. This is perhaps one reason why the higher cortical functions tend to develop later than do, say, lower limbic functions. One of the functions of higher structures is organizing lower structures into more complex and flexible operations (see Hebb 1949; Powers 1973; Brown 1977).

Highly canalized neurognosis is frequently coded as "inherent content," "instinctual," or "inborn characteristics"; whereas more flexible neurognosis has been distinguished as being "learned," or in the case of human beings, "cultural." Such dichotomous typing of response patterns effectively masks the importance of both the creodic nature of neurocognition, and the evolutionary development of neurognosis. As A. N. Whitehead noted (1978; see also Brown 1977; Powers 1973; Piaget 1971a; Varela 1979), the brain has evolved as a series of levels of control mediating between stimulus input and motor output. Each level of control has developed utilizing the same set of organizational principles that operate at lower levels (Simon 1981 is again relevant here), and each subsequent level of control has, to some extent, subsumed the lower level within its organization (Piaget 1971a). Brown (1977:139) distinguishes between four levels of increasing neurocognitive complexity: the *sensorimotor* is the level of pure sensory input and action output; the *limbic* level distinguishes portions of input for reaction; the *neocortical* level produces a stable world of objects associated with more complex associations; and finally the *symbolic* level (also neocortical) in which self-consciousness is achieved through language. Another example of hierarchical structure is seen in the way the more primitive autonomic and endocrine systems have been partially subordinated within an organization imposed by higher brain stem, limbic, and cortical functions, as suggested by Hess's (1925) model of the ergotropic and trophotropic systems.

NEUROGNOSTIC MODELS

A neurognostic model is composed of an entrained network of neural pathways (dendritic-axonic-synaptic interconnections between neural cells) and attendant cell structures existing within a field of neural processes (Eccles 1973). The functioning of neurognostic models forms an initial, rudimentary form of knowledge about the organism itself and about the world—what Karl Popper (1972:256ff) refers to as inborn hypothetical knowledge:

I assert that every animal is born with expectations or anticipations, which could be framed as hypotheses; a kind of hypothetical knowledge. And I assert that we have, in this sense, some degree of inborn knowledge from which we may begin, even though it may be quite unreliable. This inborn knowledge, these inborn expectations, will, if disappointed, create *our first problems;* and the ensuing growth of our knowledge may therefore be described as consisting throughout of corrections and modifications of previous knowledge. (Ibid.:258–259)

There are a number of generalizations we may make about neurognostic models and the inborn "expectations" and "anticipations" (i.e., inherent creodes) that are the functional activity of models. First, it seems likely that particular sets of sensory stimuli trigger particular neurognostic structures, an operation that activates and perhaps accelerates development in models. The models are lying dormant, so to speak, ready to process information keyed to penetrate them. They are ready to engage with the world. For example, newborn infants seem to prefer particular patterns relative to other patterns, such as faces as opposed to nonfaces (Cohen 1979). Moreover, Meltzoff and Moore (1977) have demonstrated that infants can imitate researchers sticking out their tongues within an hour of birth. Activation of a model physically alters that model by conditioning its component cells and its network of processes and synapses.

Second, activation of one model simultaneously inhibits the activation of alternative models, particularly those closest in function to the model activated. Much of the model's activity is inhibitory, directed at alternative and potentially competing models. This factor causes much confusion in neuropsychological research, for many of the effects of lesioned (damaged) tissue result from the release of inhibitors upon other healthy tissues.

Third, depending upon the complexity of function mediated by a model, the network of neural connections making up the model may involve only local associations or may involve extensive associations over a wide area of the nervous system. A complex model may involve a hierarchically organized pattern of entrainment between afferent, efferent, and interneurones at many levels of the nervous system.

Fourth, neural models function by means of patterned activity over time; that is, they are four-dimensional structures. We might imagine a wave of activity, or *reentrainment,* among the cells making up a model, an activity having a beginning, a series of transformative phases (discrete entrainments, disentrainments, and reentrainments), and an ending. This sustained and patterned activity is called *reverberation.*

Fifth, a model operates as a system. If a part of the model is rendered inoperative due to inhibition, chemical intercession, or lesion, the functioning of the entire model will be impaired or changed—at least until the tissues recuperate.

Sixth, just as the genotype produces (*not* causes; see Waddington 1957) the phenotype, neurognosis is requisite for more mature, developed functioning of a model. Completion of entrainment of a neural network in its rudimentary form causes its characteristic neurognosis— the network is reverberative and, all else being equal, is in a state of readiness (Lenneberg 1967) for development, given the requisite environmental conditions.

Seventh, there are essentially two types of neurognostic models, those having a motor component and those without a motor component. It has long been Piaget's (1971a; Piaget and Inhelder 1969; Inhelder et al. 1974) contention that the latter type of "scheme" is constructed developmentally from the former; that is, models that operate without a sensorimotor feedback loop are a later development in the child. We fundamentally disagree with the Piagetian view in only this respect, for there is now solid evidence that the *conditions of satisfaction*, to use Searle's (1983) term, of the anticipatory operation of a model may not require a motor component, but merely some from of nonmotoric afference. Recent researches into the competence of pre- and perinatal children suggest that the very young child is cognitively far more competent than could be accounted for solely by motor ability as the initiating factor (see Chamberlain 1983; Stone et al. 1973; Verny 1982; Meltzoff and Moore 1977). It is our opinion that Piaget underestimated the importance and the remarkable complexity of neurognosis in the functioning of "schemes." We will return to this issue in the next chapter.

EMPIRICAL MODIFICATION CYCLE

The preeminent function of the brain in all higher species is the cognitive function. It is the brain's job to construct models of the organism's environment that moderate between sensory input and response in order to optimize adaptation (Carver and Scheier 1981; Piaget 1971a, 1977). In the face of an ever-changing stimulus field, the cognitive function requires that its complement of neural models be open to some extent to developmental modification. We have argued elsewhere that neurognosis is inevitably involved to one degree or another in a feedforward or anticipatory-evaluation loop termed an *empirical modification cycle*, or *EMC* (Laughlin and d'Aquili 1974:84), a concept similar to the TOTE cycle (Miller et al. 1960), Whitehead's (1978) notion of "conformation," Piaget's idea of "assimilation-accommodation" (Piaget and Inhelder 1969), and Bruner's (1974) concept of a "constructive process." The EMC is a process by which the functioning

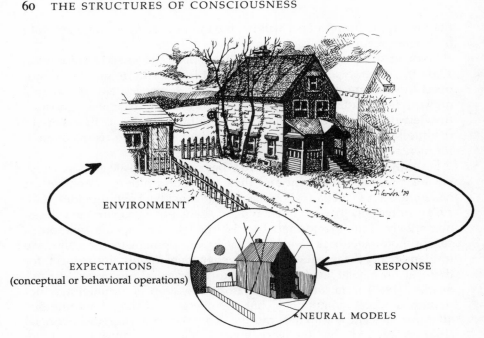

FIGURE 10. The empirical modification cycle. Neural models develop in active interaction with the environment. The world as constituted by models is *never* totally isomorphic with the operational environment. Drawing by Donna Gordon.

of a neural network generates negative and positive feedback from the environment via afference—analagous to the wind influencing the course of the ball and the topography in our tabletop landscape mentioned earlier. The functioning of the model may be seen as a more or less generalized anticipation of environmental conditions, and information from the environment is evaluated for consonance (see figure 10). If a discrepancy between expectation and environmental input is detected, the neural model may transform its structure so that further expectations predicated on that structure become increasingly isomorphic with environmental input (Piaget's "accommodation"). The EMC is highly constrained by the more general principles operating in the development of the nervous system. A model can be reentrained only so much, only so fast, and only when it is developmentally ready.

There are two comments we may make regarding empirical modification of neurognosis. First, EMC activity produces adaptive equilibration of neural models in development. Evidence from sensory deprivation experiments have indicated a number of often bizzare results that arise when normal sensory input is hampered or eliminated (Zubek 1969). At the level of neurophysiology, a number of researchers have shown environmental effects upon the structure of neural systems (Rosenzweig et al. 1962, 1972; Pribram 1971; Changeux 1983). Second, sensory data contradictory to a model will not always result in model reformulation. In fact, the data may be rejected, "assimilated" (again, Piaget's term), or even held in memory without assimilation into the model (see d'Aquili et al. 1979: chap. 1; Kuhn 1970:113; Neisser 1976:84). We have suggested elsewhere that perception is a function of the internal structure of the nervous system, and that if models are not apparently developed or entrained to perceptual structures, anomalous data will not be recognized (see Rubinstein et al. 1984: chap. 4).

Let us emphasize once again that the development of models requires the presence of a living network of cells "in place" and ready to interact with its environment. That environment will involve other networks of cells, as well as information about events in the world. Cognition therefore requires both a complete structure and an activity of that structure relative to environment. It requires input and output functions that are mediated by interconnections between the model and other models in the nervous system. Thus both neurognosis and activity are necessary and sufficient for the development of knowledge.

NEUROGNOSIS IN ACTION

Generally speaking, neurognosis canalizes the processes of perceptual discrimination, motor activity, and conceptual and symbolic differentiation and association. Neurognosis also canalizes both the type and the complexity of cognition of which the individual or the species is capable. Neurognosis determines to a large extent what can be learned, when it can be learned, in what form it can be learned, and how fast and how much of it can be learned. Inasmuch as we have set this study in a processual frame, it will be useful for us to look at neurognosis as a canalizing process in terms of the somewhat arbitrary spatiotemporal domains of ontogenesis, social adaptation, and phylogenesis—namely, a view of neurognosis within an embedded framework from the microcosmic to the macrocosmic perspective.

NEUROGNOSIS IN ONTOGENY

Nature provides any social animal with an apparent paradox: immature members of the society must be socialized into adult patterns of adaptation—must be "cooked" into the social stew, to use Levi-Strauss's metaphor—and yet young members must at every moment of their maturing lives be completely adapted to the environment (Piaget 1971a). The more complex the patterns of adult adaptation, the more complex, costly (in terms of group energy), and lengthy is the process of socialization (Count 1973). In a sense, the process of socialization entails keeping the maturing member alive long enough for the processes of physiological maturation to complete themselves—processes that include the growth and empirical modification of the neural system requisite for adult cognition. Keeping the organism alive requires that the neural development be internally regulated so that reorganization, responding to the twin demands of emergence and adaptation to the environment, occurs smoothly (Piaget 1971a; also Carver and Scheier 1981). Nature has facilitated the coordination of this set of demands by providing genetically transmitted regulation of the type, sequence, and organization of stimulation that may enter and influence neural models (via the EMC) at any particular point in development.

This is a crucial point, as Piaget (1971a) has noted. In order to elaborate the issue, we will look at neurognosis operating as both synchronic and diachronic structure.

Synchronic Neurognosis. We can examine neurognosis synchronically by referring to what Martin Seligman (1970, 1971, 1975; Seligman and Hager 1972) termed the *preparedness paradigm.* Learning may not, notes Seligman, be considered apart from the evolutionarily derived "associative apparatus" (read neurological structures) involved in the process of learning.

> Often forgotten is the fact that in addition to sensory-motor apparatus, the organism brings an associative apparatus which also has a long and specialized evolutionary history. This specialization may make certain contingencies easier to learn about than others, more difficult to forget, more readily generalizable, and so on. (Seligman and Hager 1972:3)

Seligman goes on to argue from a wealth of data that ability to learn may be conceived of as lying on a continuum from prepared at one pole to contraprepared at the other pole:

> We can define the dimension of preparedness operationally. Confront an animal with a CS [conditioned stimulus] paired with a US [unconditioned stimulus] or with a response which produces a reinforcer. Depending on what these are, the animal will be either prepared, unprepared, or contraprepared to learn about the contingency. The relative preparedness of an animal for learning about a contingency is defined by how degraded the input can be before that output reliably occurs which means that learning has taken place. (Seligman and Hager 1972:4)

An animal is prepared to learn if it makes the cognitive association between the conditioned stimulus and the unconditioned stimulus very rapidly with only a few trials. An animal is unprepared to learn if it takes numerous trials or a lengthy time to make the association. And an animal is contraprepared if it never makes the association, regardless of the time spent on the task or the number of trials.

For clarity we will transpose the preparedness paradigm using our terminology: The extent of preparedness or contrapreparedness exhibited by an animal in a learning situation depends upon whether, and to what extent, its nervous system is neurognostically structured both to input and assimilate the environmental contingencies and to mediate the appropriate response. Highly prepared associations have a genetically programmed model that has developed to the point where it can function instantly to mediate the association. This model requires little, if any, modification for appropriate mediation to occur. On the other hand, associations that are highly contraprepared are those for which no neurognostic model is available. In other words, the neurophysiological "wiring," patterned entrainment, or creode, required for the association is not present and may not develop by empirical modification of existing entrainments (at least during discrete phases of development). Learning occurring between the poles of prepared and contraprepared is unprepared because although the requisite neurognosis is present in the entrainment of the nervous system, it must be reentrained or must grow to mediate the appropriate association and response.

Examples of unprepared learning abound in the experimental literature of mainstream learning psychology. Examples of prepared and contraprepared learning are also available, but one frequently must go to the ethological literature for them (see Hinde 1982 for an excellent survey). Extreme preparedness of neurognosis may be seen as subserving so-called fixed or modal action patterns in the responses of animals to environmental stuations (see Eibl-Eibesfeldt 1970:15ff; Hinde 1970:19ff, 1982:43ff). The grasping and sucking reponses are classic examples for humans, as are various forms of psychopathology (see Seligman 1971, 1975; Beck 1967; Laughlin and d'Aquili 1974: chap. 8). Preparedness will usually be modality-specific; that is, it will be evident in the activity of a single sensory, cognitive, or behavioral mode (e.g., lateral asymmetry of function for speech sounds in infants, see Molfese 1976; and the "sauce Béarnaise" phenomenon, see Seligman and Hager 1972:8ff). Generally speaking, the more complex the neural network mediating a phenomenon, the less highly prepared and the more unprepared its neurognosis will be. A tragic example of contrapreparedness may be seen in the seeming incapacity of sperm whales to learn an adaptive avoidance of whaling vessels in the face of centuries-long persecution and predation by humans (Fichtelius and Sjolander 1972). Chimpanzees may be said to be contraprepared to learn complex symbolic communication by means of their auditory system, but are clearly prepared for learning such communication through the visual system (Linden 1974; Crail 1983).

Diachronic Neurognosis. Transposing Seligman's preparedness paradigm into neurognostic terms allows us to apply the view toward an understanding of preparedness in the neurocognitive system's development. It is our opinion that virtually all neurognostic models exhibit periods of relatively greater *sensitivity* to empirical modification, and thus to learning. Such periods of sensitivity are marked by a change in the likelihood that a skill or operation will be learned. In Robert Hinde's words:

> In general, it is a useful working assumption that no particular case of learning would occur with equal facility at all stages of the life cycle. In cases where a learnt modification to behavior occurs most readily in a fairly restricted stage of development, we can refer to that stage as a sensitive period. Viewed in this way, the sensitive period refers not to a sharply defined period during which the learning can occur and outside which it cannot, but to the result of a gradual change in the ease or probability of learning. Furthermore, the period during which any specified type of learning can occur most readily is not rigidly determined but may itself be influenced by experience. (Hinde 1970:564)

The emergence of various neurognostic structures for engagement through the EMC with the environment is anything but a random process. The nervous system does not just develop up to some magical point and then become open to haphazard modification. Far from it; the nervous system is a complex of many subsystems, the development of which are staggered over time—even *in utero*. We suspect that Turkewitz and Kenny (1982) are close to the mark when they hypothesize that the onset of development of the various sensory systems is unequal precisely so as to eliminate wasteful competition between systems in development. We would further hypothesize that the differential development of all neural subsystems is exquisitely orchestrated so as to (1) reduce competition between subsystems for trophic resources, and to (2) facilitate a maximally adaptive organization at each phase of the organism's life.

One need only reflect upon the intricate pre- and postnatal sequence of events requisite for the development of language for the nonrandom, highly orchestrated nature of the process to become evident (see Trevarthan 1983). There is also a great deal of evidence that animals (including humans) cannot learn certain responses prior to the appropriate point in maturation (Hinde 1970:559ff, 1974). Furthermore, development of a complex neural network mediating an advanced response may require completion of a previous series of developments before it becomes

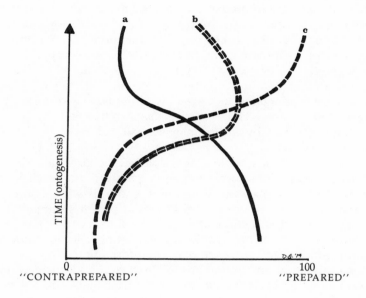

0   100
"CONTRAPREPARED"   "PREPARED"

FIGURE 11. Three different developmental courses that may
be taken by neural structures relative to preparedness. Drawing
by Donna Gordon.

prepared to mediate the advanced response. For example, Emil Menzel
(Menzel et al. 1963, 1970) has shown for the chimpanzee and other
primates that manual skill and curiosity exhibited later in life require
precursory enriching experiences earlier in life. This finding is not in
the least surprising, considering the differential effects of enriched and
deprived environments upon the physical elaboration of neural tissue
(Rosenzweig et al. 1962, 1972; Diamond et al. 1964, 1966).

Combining the synchronic concept of preparedness with the diachronic concept of sensitivity, we have been able to explore two important dimensions of the emergence of neural creodes. In our account
preparedness is the degree to which neural models are at optimal
readiness for adaptive interaction with the environment at some particular point in ontogenesis. The pattern of development of neurognosis
will be highly variable depending upon the nature and complexity of
the environmental stimulus and the progressive sequence of the requisite neural tissue development. As depicted in figure 11, the neural
model may be at optimal preparedness *in utero* or at birth, and decrement to relative unpreparedness thereafter (curve *a*). On the other hand,
the model may not be prepared until later in development, but once

activated, it increases in preparedness throughout the remaining developmental period (curve *c*). Or there might occur a relatively more precise period of optimal readiness before which the model is contraprepared, during which it is prepared, and after which there is a rapid decrement to unpreparedness, or even contrapreparedness (curve *b*). These three types of readiness are offered merely as examples; there will actually be many variations as models and systems of models move through their developmental phases. However, we suspect that a majority of the phenomena examined by anthropologists will look more or less like the progression in curve *b*.

We wish to emphasize again that any view that construes learning as a process of pouring of information into a passive, "floppy disk" brain, where it is then absorbed and stored in memory, is a totally outmoded and erroneous view. The organism brings to the environmental situation a set of neural structures already formed into functional creodes, which may or may not be capable of assimilating relevant information or accommodating themselves to relevant information. Arguments over whether "enculturation" in humans involves cultural transmission, or a transformation, or even innovation of cultural materials are easy to resolve. Learning of cultural material involves both the transmission of information by members of society and the transformation of that information by the equilibratory processes of the recipient's neurocognitive structures (see e.g., "semiosis," page 174). A similar process is probably operating among all higher social mammals, as evidenced by dietary selection among gorillas (Schaller 1963) and the invention and transmission of "cultural" behaviors among macaques (Kawai 1965). Whether the transformation of information among humans appears more like transmission or innovation depends upon the recognition of discrepancy between the material transmitted and the material expressed by the recipient. Obviously, the degree of discrepancy is going to fall on a continuum, and the point at which the discrepancy will fall will be determined by a complex set of variables, such as rapidity of change in the society (e.g., Japan since World War II), change in the environment (e.g., the East African droughts), the ability of people to discern the discrepancy as a discrepancy (e.g., the "generation gap"), and so forth.

NEUROGNOSIS AND SOCIAL ADAPTATION

The primary biological function of neurognosis is to provide initial coherence and continuity to the process of modeling the environment. Neurognosis forms the primitive "cognized" world into which information about the environment is assimilated. At the same time, neurognostic structures are somewhat plastic to accommodate both the exigencies of the environment and the demands of growth. Piaget (1971a) has called these qualities of neurognosis *adaptive intelligence*.

Among highly social vertebrates, the process of empirical modification of neurognosis usually occurs within a social context: that is, adaptation of the individual occurs in the context of and in the facilitation of social adaptation (contrary to some of the views of sociobiology). This adaptation is one of the crucial feedback interactions requisite to society. All else being equal, the longer and more complex the ontogenesis of neural structures, the more flexible will be the range and complexity of adaptive strategies open to the species. Furthermore, the more complex and flexible the adaptive strategies, the longer the group can tolerate dependent members. We can imagine the evolution of social adaptation as an inverted spiral with increase of period of ontogenesis on one axis and with range of adaptive strategies available to the group on the other axis. The gaps between consecutive loops of the spiral represent the feedback relationships between the two dimensions.

To avoid serious theoretical distortions, we must remember that the hallmark of hominid evolution is the emergence of a more complex nervous system. For example, any reconstruction of the socially adaptive strategies of our hominid ancestor *Australopithecus* (e.g., articles in Lee and DeVore 1968) that restricts the range of strategies to fewer than those of nonhuman primate species (see Teleki 1973 on chimpanzees; Kummer 1968 on Hamadryas baboons; Jay 1965; Sugiyama 1967; and Yoshiba 1968 on the Indian langur) is undoubtedly in error. Given what we know about the brain of the australopithecines, we have sound reasons to suppose they had a more advanced range and complexity of socially adaptive strategies than have present-day nonhuman primates (see Laughlin and d'Aquili 1974:70; also see Kurland and Beckerman 1985).

The modification and development of neurognosis into adult structures within a social frame is obviously a complex process and will involve at least three factors: (1) the development of the nervous system proper; (2) the intraorganismic and interorganismic coordination of entrainment patterns and cognitive functions; and (3) the transmission of patterns of cognition, adaptively coordinated with the environment, to subsequent generations. The first of these factors has been addressed earlier, but the latter two must be further elaborated.

We previously noted the apparent paradox between the demands of adaptation and the demands of development as reflected in the modification of neural structures. These conflicting demands become increasingly acute the higher one proceeds up the phylogenetic scale, particularly among the higher social mammals. The task of ontogenesis is to make certain that, at every point in development, physiological systems

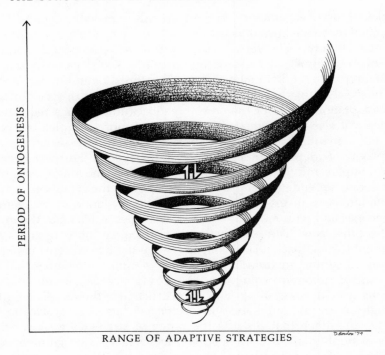

FIGURE 12. The spiral of social adaptation. The longer the period of ontogenesis, the more adaptive strategies become available as the neural structures mature. More mature levels interact with less mature levels to "draw them up" into a more advanced state. Drawing by Donna Gordon.

remain synchronized in a configuration leading to unified action in relation to the environment. The task of social adaptation is to coordinate the physiological systems of members to enable an adaptive, collective response to the environment that is too complex, intense, or effective for an individual to achieve. We would suggest that the neurophysiological mechanism often labeled the "social instinct" is in fact the extreme preparedness of neurognostic structures to input and encode information about the world transmitted by conspecifics and to operate upon that information. An example of possible preparedness of EMC systems is the ease with which the actions of significant conspecifics results in an orientation response (OR) in recipients of information about those actions. An example is the ease and the innate disposition of the young to mimic conspecifics.

For reasons suggested elsewhere (Laughlin and d'Aquili 1974: chap. 4), we reaffirm that the problem of coordinating the cognitive functions of conspecifics reaches a critical stage among human groups. The human brain is capable of modeling an environment sufficiently complex and remote from the immediate stimulus field that the "cognized" world of individuals in a group can potentially become maladaptively discrepant (d'Aquili et al. 1979: chap. 1). If this discrepancy becomes too great, the processes of cognition may become antithetical to adaptive social action. In tacit recognition of the potentially atomizing effects of discrepant cognition, human societies everywhere expend a great deal of effort controlling the development of the "cognized" reality of their members. The role of ritual in enculturation is often directed to that end (see d'Aquili et al. 1979; Laughlin and Stephens 1980).

Higher animals that have successfully adapted using social strategies will generally maintain adaptive coordination by placing social constraints upon the development of neurognosis into adult structures (see Chapple 1970 on this issue). In addition to intrinsic neurognostic constraints, social constraints may in fact operate either to facilitate or hinder optimal development of individual systems in the interests of social patterns of adaptation (see Burridge 1979 on this issue). On the one hand, information transmitted to the succeeding generation will pertain to an environment to which the transmitting generation has adapted. On the other hand, transmitted information will form a part, *and only a part*, of the environment to which the receiving generation must adapt. The information as transmitted and the information as received may easily be transformed and, to some extent at least, become discrepant. The information received by a subsequent generation will never be more than a portion of the information being processed by that generation's neurocognitive systems. Most information arises from the moment-by-moment interaction with the world. Furthermore, the form of information transmitted is a partial function of the neurocognitive structures of the transmitting animal, while the information received is a partial function of the receiver's structures. It is important to understand that neurognosis is an active process that exhibits a plasticity and autonomy far beyond the passive reception of cultural material. Such material, often a vicarious component to the otherwise ongoing, unfolding, and direct experience of the world, provides adaptively significant information, but it is not determinant in any simple way.

The plasticity of transformation of socially derived information is crucial to social change in response to environmental change. Interorganismic coordination of neurognosis will often involve a temporal dimension so that the coordination remains latent until environmental conditions emerge to trigger activity subserved by that coordination. This activity is particularly apparent in the data about adaptation of social animals to recurrent changes in their environments (i.e., fluctuations in the incidence of rainfall, warfare, earthquakes, temperature, etc.), particularly where such changes affect the availability of food and other basic resources. Examining the data on human and nonhuman societies confronted by such recurrent change, Laughlin and Brady (1978:46–47) isolated what they called the *principle of adaptive diaphasis:* "If a decremental shift in basic resources is due to recursivity in the environment of an individual organism or society, then the adaptive infrastructure of that organism or society will at all times be organized to respond and adapt to that eventuality." The society may owe its temporally recursive organization to the neurognostic structures alone (i.e., preparedness relative to recurrent contingencies), or to socially transmitted information encoded in temporally flexible structures. A simple example of the former type of recursivity is to be found in circadian rhythms (Luce 1971; Broughton 1975), while examples of the more complex latter type are described in Laughlin and Brady (1978).

NEUROGNOSIS AND EVOLUTION

Neurognosis provides an evolutionary continuity to cognitive structures in phylogenesis (Jerison in Eccles 1987). It is neurognosis that mediates the *biogram,* to use Earl Count's term; that is, the bundle of adaptations, social relations, and behaviors that are transmitted genetically and are thus characteristic of particular species and phyla. We may speak of a basic mammalian, primate, hominid, or human biogram precisely because of neurognostic structures common to all members of each evolutionary level due to similar genetic coding (see Count 1973). The human biogram may be seen as an evolutionary transformation of the primate biogram, which is in turn a transformation upon the mammalian biogram, and so on down the phylogenetic scale. A major system of transformations for the higher phyla has been the nervous system. One example of an element in the human biogram is neurognostic structuring resulting in a tendency to be attracted to, feel affection for, and cuddle objects and beings with bulging foreheads, big eyes, rounded chins, and so on (Konrad Lorenz cited in Calvin 1983:18). This predisposition to nurture infants and other objects (e.g., E.T. dolls, stuffed animals, cartoon characters like Elmer Fudd, etc.) triggers the neurocognitive structures mediating recognition and response to "babies."

The various parts of the nervous system have not evolved at the same rate. Generally, the lower the structure resides in the functional hierarchy of the nervous system, the older is its organization. In order to make this point clearly, Paul MacLean (1973, 1978) has divided the human nervous system into three evolutionary strata: the new mam-

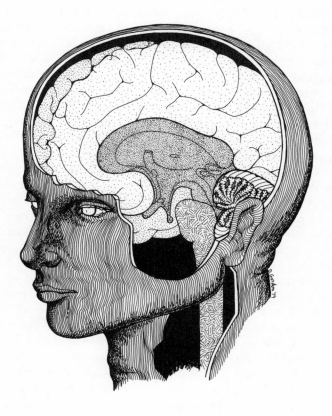

FIGURE 13. Paul MacLean's notion of the triune brain. A cutaway view of the human head showing the new mammalian (lightly dotted), paleomammalian (heavily dotted) and reptilian (cross-hatching) portions of the nervous system. Drawing by Donna Gordon.

malian (telencephalon or neocortical structures), the paleomammalian (rhinencephalon or limbic system), and the reptilian (including the upper spinal cord, portions of the mesencephalon or midbrain, the diencephalon or thalamus-hypothalamus, and the basal ganglia; see also Webber, Stephens, and Laughlin 1983). The organization of the reptilian brain has changed little in the higher animals. In humans this part of the nervous system mediates archaic regulatory functions such as metabolism, digestion, respiration, and the like. The limbic structures were added to the reptilian brain roughly a hundred million years ago to form the primitive mammalian brain, and their models mediate activities such as procreation, eating, searching, fighting, fear, joy, self-defense, drinking, terror, sadness, foreboding, empathy, and hormonal regulation. The brains of the evolutionarily advanced mammals gradually encephalized; that is, developed the thin layer of convoluted cortical tissue that covers the older parts of the brain. The telencephalon (the two cortical hemispheres plus their connecting corpus callosum) is, in fact, the only part of the mammalian brain that has expanded ("encephalized") significantly in higher mammals. The cortical structures extended and refined motor and sensory functions, enhanced memory capacity, reorganized older structures into more complex functional entrainments, and made higher cognitive functions possible. The most dramatic development of the telencephalic structures in the animal kingdom is to be found among the hominids, the group of primate species that are the ancestors of modern humans. We will have reason later on to refer to neurognostic structures at the first two levels of functioning (the reptilian and paleomammalian) as *paleoneurognosis* ("old" neurognosis), and those at the latter level (the neomammalian) as *neoneurognosis* ("new" neurognosis).

We should note that the division of the human nervous system into three strata, while illustrating some basic issues relative to the evolution of the brain, can also lead to gross oversimplification and distortion. The nervous system does *not* divide neatly into three *structural* parts like a Lego toy. We are speaking crudely of a *functional* hierarchy. As we mentioned earlier, the phylogenetically older parts of the nervous system tend to develop first in ontogenesis—one more example of the rule that ontogeny sometimes and in some ways "recapitulates phylogeny" (see Gould 1977). On general principles it would seem that the older models develop and then become reorganized within and subordinated to the control of newer models. The process of reorganization undoubtedly changes the older structures to some extent, so they cannot be considered as exactly the same organization as that in any previous ancestor. On the other hand, nature is notoriously conservative. Once a system has proved itself to be "tried and true" through selection, the tendency is to retain the structure and modify it to new and different purposes (see Simon 1981). In fact the functional hierarchy of the human brain is far more complex than this three-tiered model communicates, for even within each level there are hierarchies of function. However, combining the triune brain concept with the more complex views of hierarchy like those of Powers (1973), Carver and Scheier (1981), and Klopf (1982), it is possible to keep a more complex view of neurocognitive functioning in evolutionary perspective. It will also leave our theory in a position to speak later about direct meditative experience of paleoneurognosis (see page 196).

The principal function of neurognosis is to mediate between sensory input and motor output and thereby increase the probability of the organism's survival. Neurognosis consists of prepared pathways of neural connections specializing in sensory input, information storage, association and retrieval, and motor output, as well as system maintenance and many other functions. The structure and function of neurognosis is genetically produced and modified in interaction with the environment (the environment of any model may be internal and external to the organism). The process of equilibration of model and environment is a physiological process; it is open to the forces of natural selection, and it has therefore evolved.

The most likely origin of neurognosis in phylogenesis is in the most primitive forms of modality-specific neural networks mediating the simple reflex in ancient invertebrates. The evolution of neurognosis from the early neural network has been characterized by a number of developments: First, an increasing proportion of interneurons to afferent-efferent neurons has developed in the nervous system. Higher order neurognostic structures are comprised almost entirely of interneurones, and the increase in their proportion over the course of phylogenesis is one measure of the increasing importance of cognition in adaptation in the emergence of the animal kingdom. Second, an increase in the importance of development of neural structures mediating between stimulus and response has occurred. In other words, the role of the EMC in phylogenesis has become increasingly important. Third, an increasing plasticity in the range and complexity of genetically possible entrainments of neurognostic models has developed. A major role of the emergence of neoneurognostic models has been flexibility in reentrainment of lower-order models relative to different environmental circumstances.

Fourth, the period of ontogenesis has increased. The role of immature phases of development requisite to adult cognition has expanded. Fifth, the nervous system has developed increasingly complex hierarchies of entrainment and control. More primitive models have become subordinated to higher-order models with greater range, complexity, and flexibility of function. Sixth, the range of constraints imposed by neurognosis limiting the functioning of the nervous system has broadened. A greater range of optimal growth exists among individuals of higher phyla than among members of lower phyla. And seventh, neurognosis has become increasingly cross-modal in its associative functions, a principle of organization probably originating in the first multimodal association neurons and progressing evolutionarily toward highly structured multimodal transfer areas like the human inferior parietal lobule (see Laughlin and d'Aquili 1974:52). Cross-model transfer of information

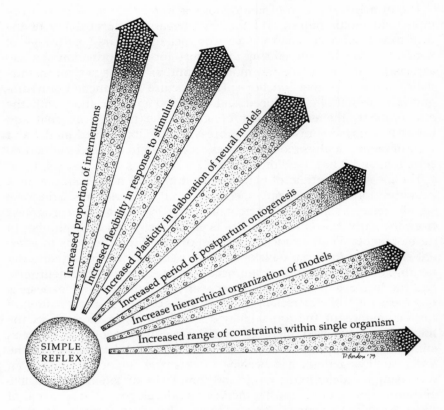

FIGURE 14. Some of the main trends in the evolution of neurognosis from the structures subserving the simple reflex. Drawing by Donna Gordon.

across sensory modalities has been demonstrated for the monkey and chimpanzee, as well as for the human infant (see Davenport 1976; Frampton et al. 1973; Bryant et al. 1972; Cowey and Weiskrantz 1975).

The results of these evolutionary trends in the development of neurognosis are apparent in human cognition. Human cognition would seem to be the most complex on this planet, whether the information being processed is generated from internal or external sources. For example, although the limbic system has changed little in the evolution of the primate order, the human feeling-function would seem to be vastly more complex than, say, that of the chimpanzee. Ample data exists to support the view that the assignation of affect to object is a cognitive process involving higher cortical functions linked to limbic ones. It is higher cortical processing that results in the highly differentiated coding of affect (see Gellhorn and Loffbourrow 1963:40; MacLean 1958; Count in Sebeok and Ramsy 1969; Schacter and Singer 1962; but cf. Mandler 1984).

These evolutionary trends are nowhere more evident than in the remarkable range of conceptual and symbolic coding of knowledge about the world. This range is seen in the development of increasing levels of abstraction of thought in the child (Piaget 1952) and the expansion of complex conceptualization along a broad spectrum of dimensions of experience from the physical environment to the social and moral environment (Piaget 1971b; Piaget and Inhelder 1969; Kohlberg 1969; Harvey, Hunt, and Schroder 1961). This range may also be noted in the variance in the complexity of cognitive functioning in the individual from low to optimal, depending upon environmental circumstances (Schroder, Driver, and Streufert 1967), and in the variance in optimal complexity of cognition between individuals within the group (Schroder, Driver, and Streufert 1967; Dasen 1972; Feldman et al. 1974).

In summary, evolution of neurognosis in hominids has resulted in a neurocognitive system optimally capable of highly complex processing of information derived cross-modally, through multiple associations, and simultaneously structured at multiple levels of control. The hominid neurocognitive system has become sufficiently refined that it can easily associate and model sensory data not apparent by perception alone. Independent of cognitive operations upon them, such data may be unrelated by perceptual criteria alone because they are (1) too distant in space, (2) too distant in time, or 3) too complex (see Laughlin and d'Aquili 1974: chap. 4 on the "cognitive extension of prehension"). The evolution of the human brain took a long time to develop the capacity to associate events and objects not clearly related in perception. Indeed, this capacity seems to be operating primitively among chimpanzees, a fact that has profound implications for reconstructing the cognition characteristic of early hominids (see d'Aquili et al. 1979:98ff). However, as distinctive of human cognition as this would seem to be, we must remember that this capacity is based upon the same principles of neurocognition operating to produce neurognosis in our forebearers (Simon 1981; Sarnat and Netsky 1974). What has occurred is a long period of reorganization and complexification of the hominid brain utilizing these basic principles to new and greater effect than before (Holloway 1972).

3 CONSCIOUSNESS AND THE COGNIZED ENVIRONMENT

Consciousness is the weapon which strengthens the artificiality of an occasion of experience. It raises the importance of the final appearance relatively to that of the initial reality. Thus it is appearance which in consciousness is clear and distinct, and it is reality which lies dimly in the background with its details hardly to be distinguished in consciousness. What leaps into conscious attention is a mass of presuppositions about reality rather than the intuitions of reality itself. It is here that the liability of error arises.

—Alfred North Whitehead, *Adventures of Ideas*

PROBLEMS IN THE STUDY OF CONSCIOUSNESS

A FUNDAMENTAL DIFFICULTY in scientifically approaching consciousness is that the term is largely experiential, belonging to that long list of terms like *sensation, feeling, pain, mind, joy,* and so forth, which denote aspects of direct experience without reference either to the neurocognitive structures mediating experience or to objects outside the being. There are really only two ways to obtain information about consciousness—directly through introspection and indirectly through inferences based upon the experiential reports of others, experimentation on other beings presumed to be conscious, observation of the physical and symbolic concomitants of consciousness (i.e., aspects of the body or artifacts produced by conscious beings), and so forth. We have already noted that data derived from introspection have unfortunately often been rejected or treated as suspect by psychologists. It should not therefore surprise us that the problem of consciousness is troublesome in science. We have also mentioned the many conceptual and experiential barriers that have to be put aside before we can begin to address the issue of brain and consciousness. And we have noted that in coming to comprehend our nervous system, we are attempting to grasp the nature of the most complex of systems. The study of the nervous system is daunting to most researchers, who often take refuge in specialization and usually avoid the far-reaching and interesting questions. Small wonder, then, that discussions of the structures of consciousness are often fraught with error, distortion, apology, even trepidation. Of course, discussions must necessarily remain tentative and incomplete. Any presentation that pretends to be definitive is just that—pretention. What we can do here is characterize the issue of consciousness in such a way that the nature of brain and the nature of consciousness may be discussed using a single language and understood in a unified way.

CONSCIOUSNESS AS A FUNCTIONAL COMPLEX

One reason why consciousness defies easy definition is that the term labels a functional complex and not a discrete "thing" or quality. Any attempt to nominalize such a complex process inevitably becomes simplistic or wrong. Another reason why consciousness is hard to define is that the term typically refers to the immediacy of direct experience with all its richness and ever-changing fluidity. Above all, we wish to develop an understanding of brain and consciousness commensurate with the direct and immediate experience of self and world, rather than cleaving solely to experimental data in psychology and the neurosciences. We will characterize consciousness in such a way that makes inclusion of our three loci of data (experience, neurobiology, and behavior) possible.

DESCRIBING CONSCIOUSNESS

We are all on familiar ground when we characterize consciousness introspectively—that is, if we stick to what we know about our own consciousness, not from books and vicarious descriptions (although these may be useful), but from direct experience. Many people around the world, both now and in the past, have studied the nature of their own minds, and some of them have expressed their insights in their cultural idiom and offered them to others. There are two main types of description of consciousness found cross-culturally: the most common may be called *metaphorical* description and the least common *analytical* description.

METAPHORICAL DESCRIPTIONS OF CONSCIOUSNESS

It is quite common among cultures to use objects and events in the world as symbols to depict knowledge of consciousness. A typical metaphorical description might be phrased, "consciousness is like x." The list of symbols that can take the place of x is of course endless. Consciousness has been likened to a flower atop a murky pond, the moon's reflection in a still pool, a mirror, a rippling stream of water over a rocky bed, a rose in a crystal vase, a garden of raked pebbles, a crystal ball, a magic theater, an eye, a diamond. For example, the essence of

FIGURE 15. The Tibetan Buddhist *vajra* or *dorje*. This is a
symbol that represents the essential nature of consciousness
as discovered in insight meditation. Reprinted from K. Dowman,
"The Nyingma Icons," *Kailash* (Kathmandu, Nepal) 2 (4): 416.

consciousness is often depicted in Tibetan Buddhism by the *vajra*, which
is conceived of as a diamond or a thunderbolt. And, in some versions of
the Tarot, consciousness is depicted as a flowing stream.

Esoteric commonalities run throughout all these metaphors, a full
appreciation of which requires considerable contemplation. Unfortunately, most scientists in the West have not learned with any sophistication how to contemplate symbolism. The predominant Western cultural hermeneutic is toward what has been called in theology
demythologization: the view that religious and other symbolism obscures
the meaning being expressed and requires translation into everyday
language before its meaning becomes clear (see Rasmussen 1971:11 on

this issue in phenomenology, and Hillman 1979:12 in depth psychology). What is often missed or poorly understood by semiologists is that these symbols may arise spontaneously when a person contemplates consciousness and its attributes in a mature manner. Furthermore, these symbols will arise in the expression of people who are perhaps artists and not contemplatives in any formal sense—people who may or may not be aware of the source of their inspiration—but rather as a manifestation of what Levy-Bruhl (1923) called "participation mystique."

Consciousness—or particular aspects of consciousness like will, awareness, or feeling—will be described or expressed by the symbols that emerge from contemplation in some form (whether in drug-induced trance, vision quest, dream, formal meditation, etc.), or more typically by use of mythopoea (myth, drama, poetry, art, etc.) already in place within a cultural repertoire.

Many Western theorists have presumed that such (nondemythologized) expression is somehow more primitive than linguistic-conceptual expression (Levy-Bruhl 1923 is a classic example). In fact, the tendency to dichotomize modes of knowing is very widespread in science (see Bogen 1969, 1977), and the tendency to relegate one of the two modes to an inferior or developmentally prior status seems almost irresistible to many Western intellectuals. Levi-Strauss (1966), for example, distinguishes between the mythic thought of primitive man and the conceptual thought of modern science, the latter being superior to and more advanced than the former. Just as positivism was a predictable intellectual by-product of an extremely materialist culture (see chap. 1), so too is the tendency to relegate nondemythologized symbolism to primitivity or developmental inferiority, a move that may preclude full, adult participation in symbolic systems and thus realization of their rich meaning.

Be that as it may, some of the most revealing descriptions of consciousness and its concomitants available to us can frequently be found in the cosmological and religious symbolism of the many peoples of the world. The nature of consciousness and its relationship to the world is danced, sung, chanted, painted, enacted, and mimed. It is given expression in architecture, mask, ornamentation, dress, story, sculpture, and banner. And as Levi-Strauss (1964), among others, makes clear, such descriptions can be composed of an amazing array of elements and relationships that form a three- and sometimes four-dimensional totality of mind-boggling complexity.

An excellent example is the Tarot. One of the authors (CDL) has used the esoteric Tarot as a contemplation exercise in teaching symbolism to students. The Tarot is essentially a treatise on the nature of consciousness in the form of a deck of cards. The cards are pictures that combine a variety of elements, some repeatedly, to instruct students about the various functions of mind. By combining such basic elements as fire and water, light and dark, cube and sphere, tree and flower, mountain and plain, sun and moon, male and female, and so on, the Tarot is able to manipulate the grammar of symbols in such a way that not only is there coherence among the elements in a single picture, there is coherence at many levels of realization among all the pictures (see Case 1975). As with all complex symbol systems, initiation into, participation in, and contemplation of the Tarot symbolism is required before the meanings being expressed by the system become fully realized.

ANALYTICAL DESCRIPTIONS OF CONSCIOUSNESS

An analytical description tends to resolve the experience of consciousness into its constituent elements. Analytical descriptions range in sophistication from exceedingly crude and naive excursions into introspection to penetrating and insightful portrayals based upon years of intense contemplation. It is very fortunate that the cross-cultural perspective in anthropology encourages us to look beyond our own cultural heritage for material, for much of the Western psychological literature on consciousness is regrettably crude. In fact, the most sophisticated analytical description of consciousness of which we are aware is to be found in the Abhidharma, one of the three Buddhist scriptural sources which together make up what is called the Tripitaka.[1]

> The Abhidharma is not a speculative, but a descriptive philosophy where the description is complete, and is based on scientific method. The description of a thing or phenomenon is made not only by its minute analysis, but also by its synthesis, followed by a combination of analysis and synthesis, and finally the description is completed in accordance with the axiom that "nothing arises from a single cause", with a statement of its relations to other things or phenomena. (Dharmasena 1968:3)

According to the complex analysis presented in the Abhidharma, one may experience some eighty-nine distinct types of consciousness (*cittani*), which are defined by discrete permutations of many concomitant elements (*cetasika*) composing consciousness. There are fifty-two of these elements, of which seven are present in all eighty-nine types of consciousness. In order to give the flavor of an analytical description, we will briefly list and characterize each of the seven universal elements (along with their Sanskrit labels; see Narada 1975:82–89). Because these are empirical categories (not theoretical entities), the reader is invited to reflect upon each element as it manifests in his or her consciousness at this moment:

1. Contact (*phassa*). This is the aspect of "coming together" of

awareness and the object of awareness via the media of one or more senses. You are aware of the words on this page.

2. Feeling (*vedana*). This element refers to affect, be it positive, negative, or neutral. It is the quality of experience associated with the object. For example, one may enjoy the object, or feel fear in its presence, or have no particular affect associated with it. Do you feel positive or negative about what you are reading right now? Most likely you are experiencing neutral feeling.

3. Perception (*sanna*). Perception, always an element in consciousness, is simple recognition based upon qualities of the object such as shape, color, and texture. You are recognizing the words on this page, most likely with ease.

4. Will (*cetana*). This is the element of volition, accumulation, and coordination in consciousness. Will unifies other elements in relation to the object, regulates the functioning of elements relative to each other, and assigns or selects elements and appropriate action in relation to the object. It is will that keeps you concentrating upon what you are reading, and not on the sounds outside or the grumbling of your stomach.

5. Concentration (*ekaggata*). Concentration is the focusing faculty that limits the functioning of other elements to a single object, or to a single point or locus of attention at a time. While you are attending to these words, you cannot be attending to the sounds outside, although the sounds may be detected as background.

6. Psychic energy (*jivitindriya*). This element sustains the other elements of concentration, energizing and revitalizing them. Energy is a limiting factor; hence this element exercises a degree of control over other elements—that is, if the energy is blocked, scattered, or otherwise unavailable, the elements cannot function. Interest and concentration are impossible to sustain in the presence of fatigue.

7. Attention (*manasikare*). This aspect, which has been likened to the rudder of a ship, refers to the orientation of consciousness to the object. It is simple, spontaneous attention to the object. You can move your attention from these words to the color of a book's binding, or to sounds outside, or to the pressure of your bottom on the chair.

Reflection upon the fact that these universal elements are but seven elements of the fifty-two described in the Abhidharma—elements such as decision, effort, joy, jealousy, and tranquillity—will give some idea of the possible complexity attainable in an analytic description of consciousness, particularly if one also considers the various permutations of these elements within the field of consciousness. Simplistic descriptions that point to one or two salient features as definitive of consciousness are uninformative and can lead to the mistaken view that consciousness amounts to a thing or quality, which can be present or absent in a species or a person. It is well to recall that the term *consciousness* derives from the Latin *conscius*, a root that means roughly "experience with knowledge." Thus all of the structures and functions that participate in experience and in the activity of knowing in experience must be considered as elements of consciousness.

CONSCIOUSNESS AND THE BRAIN

It seems ironic that some complex non-Western descriptions of consciousness, whether metaphorical or analytic, seem more congruent with modern neuropsychology than do many Western psychological treatments. Indeed, much of the Abhidharma view coincides with the views expressed in this book of how the brain works. Our nervous system is now conceived of as a complex affair, structured at multiple, hierarchically functioning levels. Our nervous system progressively models and tests models of reality. Establishing reverberative circuits, mixing and entraining circuits into greater networks, the system regulates sensory input, relegation of information processing to appropriate networks, and assignment of appropriate action—all in the interests of adaptation.

COGNIZED AND OPERATIONAL ENVIRONMENTS

As difficult as it is to make neurological sense out of an experiential term like consciousness, the problem is amplified by the need to distinguish clearly between *operational* consciousness and our *cognitive* models of consciousness. As we have seen, the principal function of our nervous system is the construction of models of the world. By processing information about the world through these models, the organism directs adaptive evaluation and action in relation to events in the world. As a matter of shorthand, let us call this set of countless models our *cognized environment*.[2]

In using an abstract concept like cognized environment, we must understand that the same principles of operation (like canalization, goal-seeking activity, etc.), defined for more molecular concepts (like neural model and network), also apply to the more molar concepts. The cognized environment develops in interaction with an ever-changing operational environment, which includes an ever-developing organism. The cognized environment is thus composed of models and networks of models that operate upon the principles of neurognosis, reverberation, reciprocal inhibition, and so on.

In other words, the cognized environment operates under the limitations of neurological principles that more obviously come into play at lower levels of nervous system organization. A moment's reflection will underscore the wisdom of this stipulation. It is precisely this juncture—the leap from a molecular to a molar-level concept—that the insidious dualism we earlier spent considerable time avoiding can creep into our thinking. If we fail to bring the molecular and molar concepts ("neural models" and "cognized environment") into correspondence, we are in danger of generating two conceptual realities, each with its own set of principles and with little in common to bridge the two. If we mention this issue from time to time, we do so to impress on our thinking and on yours the stringent structural monism advocated in chapter 1. When we refer, therefore, to "neurognostic models" in one place and "cognized environment" in another, we are referring to two levels of organization of the same system. Similarly, we will refer to the molar levels of organization of the operational environment as "reality," "the environment," or "the world," and molecular levels as *noumena* (a Kantian term referring to processes in the world as they are, independent of observation or knowledge of them). Our "being" is, of course, a part of our operational environment, and is thus a noumenon.

It is beyond the scope of this study to examine the processes and principles operating in reality, other than as they further our understanding of the brain, consciousness, symbolism, and the structures of experience. Therefore, although we often refer to processes in the world, we specify the physics, chemistry, optics, or other processes required to explain events occurring external to human consciousness and neurophysiology. However, this focus is merely a stylistic ploy and should not be taken to mean that such processes cannot be specified. The Kantian "noumenal world" can in fact be known, but never apart from the neurocognitive processes of knowing.

THE TRANSCENDENTAL NATURE OF THE OPERATIONAL ENVIRONMENT

Perhaps the most important aspect of the operational environment for our purposes is its essentially *transcendental* nature. As Husserl (1970, 1977) taught, there is always more to know about any real noumenon, event, or system than can ever be known. The limitations upon what and how much can be known are inherent in the organization of the nervous system, as well as imposed by culture and personal history. And these limitations apply as much to knowledge of the being as they do to knowledge of the world outside the being. The hallmark of the transcendental nature of the operational environment is the virtual infinity of ways of knowing of any of its aspects. By contrast, the hallmark of the cognized environment is its tendency to close its boundaries to further exploration and knowing.

THE PRIMACY OF THE COGNIZED ENVIRONMENT

Thus, an important point we wish to convey—and yet one of the most difficult to grasp—is that of the *primacy of the cognized environment* over the operational environment. That is, we normally operate upon our cognized models of reality, and not upon reality itself. We quite naturally experience our models of reality as though they are reality. We automatically *reify* models: we construct models in experiential interaction with reality, and then *project* the model into our experience as reality (Bohm 1965; Gibson 1969; Piaget and Inhelder 1969).[3] This is part of our "natural attitude" toward the world (Husserl 1970; Schutz and Luckmann 1973). This primacy of cognized models is our root delusion, the mechanism by which most of us miss the transcendental nature of self and world.

Our nervous system is so proficient at constructing and reifying its cognized environment that we usually become aware of the process of projection only when a model and the noumenon with which it corresponds are perceived to be *dissonant*, or out of phase with each other.[4] Recognition of dissonance in our experience is the realization that a mismatch exists between the anticipatory functioning of our models and the sensory information about corresponding reality. In other words, a perceived discrepancy occurs between the expectation about reality generated by the model and the feedback we get from a reality that is perpetually transcendental. The naive result of dissonance (i.e., dissonance accompanied by minimal awareness) is uncertainty and fear. A more sophisticated use of dissonance (i.e., dissonance associated with an inquisitive, keen awareness) may be as data upon which insights about the nature of our own cognition can be grounded in introspection, particularly relative to the empirical modification cycle. As A. E. Van Vogt notes in one of his novels:

> For the sake of sanity remember: "The map is not the territory, the word is not the thing it describes." Wherever the map is confused with the territory, a "semantic disturbance" is set up in the organism. The disturbance continues until the limitation of the map is recognized. (1970:158)

Examples of dissonance abound. We will share one experience with the reader that is typical of dissonance. One of the authors was having coffee in an upstate New York college cafeteria when, glancing across the room, he noticed a friend, Retta Jay, standing and talking with a student. The trouble was, Retta Jay should not have been standing there as she had no connection with the college and lived in California. For what seemed like minutes, the author's awareness alternated between recognition of his friend and rejection of that recognition. One moment the person across the room perceptually *was* Retta Jay, and the next she was perceptually a perfect stranger. Rejection finally won out and it was then impossible for the author to recollect how he could have been fooled into a false recognition, for by then the person looked nothing like Retta Jay.

Many illusions practiced by conjurers work upon the principle of the primacy of the cognized environment. The magician manipulates sensory input so as to produce dissonant cognition, thus allowing his audience to see a "real" event rather than a mirror, a "real" ball and not a shell, a "real" thumb rather than a flesh-colored cap. In fact, various illusions have been used for generations to study the functions of mind. Take, for example, a typical line drawing depicting an apparently three-dimensional tableau. In actuality, the tableau is made up of only a few lines. The brain's cognized environment provides the rest, transforming a few cues into a landscape, interpreting distance, horizon, and perspective.[5]

POINT OF VIEW

Combining the various considerations already discussed—the competition among neural models, the primacy of the cognized environment, the transcendental nature of being and world, the experience of dissonance and reification—we have amassed sufficient evidence for the existence within our cognized environment of the *point of view*, namely, a set of alternative ways of cognizing a noumenon or other aspect of the operational environment. That multiple views of any aspect of reality are possible is quite easy to demonstrate visually. Merely reflect upon one or another of the ambiguous figures used in psychological research to experience directly transformation of view. One example is the old hag–young woman; another is the chalice–faces. In these cases two ways of viewing the same stimulus are intended, so that if one views the picture one way it is identified as one "thing" and viewed another way it is another. As in the Retta Jay experience, the different views of the same sensory field are provided by the cognized environment. If one works with these figures awhile, one may experience the rapid alternation of view characteristic of dissonance. Given sufficient time, the dissonance may resolve itself and a new view of the figure emerges— one may come to hold both chalice and faces simultaneously, or reduce the drawing without interpretation into its basic perceptual givens.

The point that will be stressed throughout the book is that insofar as

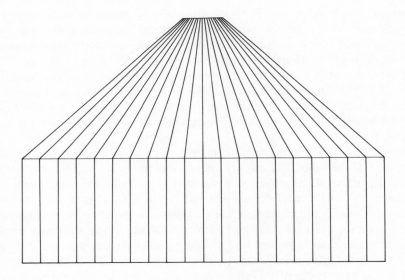

FIGURE 16. The perceptual horizon. A two-dimensional drawing comprised of a few straight lines in the right relation to
each other produces the illusion of a three-dimensional horizon. Drawing by Donna Gordon.

we expend energy to maintain one point of view vis-à-vis other views,
it becomes more and more difficult to perceive alternative views, as well
as transcendental reality. For example, one can easily train oneself to
see one of the two possible views in the ambiguous figures automatically, so that one must expend effort to see the alternative view. In fact,
indicating in various ways and reinforcing the "proper" views of the
world is one of the principal means by which social groups enculturate
their members. For instance, humans everywhere guard against the
dissonance created by the awareness of personal mortality by all sorts
of culturally nurtured fictions. We make "heros" of ourselves, as Becker
(1973) notes, in order to make "objects of primary value" of ourselves
in the face of our finitude, creatureliness, and death.

It is by constructing points of view that we sketch-in the "horizon" of
our knowledge about reality, to use Husserl's (1931:101ff) apt metaphor.
There is an infinity of possible views of any noumenon, but the brain is
conditioned to construct only a few. Thus, most humans do not see
much beyond the horizon formed by their culturally loaded cognized
environment. Only by the application of awareness may the horizon be
expanded in adults:

What is actually perceived, and what is more or less clearly co-present and determinate (to some extent at least), is partly pervaded, partly girt about with a *dimly apprehended depth or fringe of indeterminate reality*. I can pierce it with rays from the illuminating focus of attention with varying success. Determining representations, dim at first, then livelier, fetch me something out, a chain of such recollections takes shape, the circle of determinancy extends ever farther, and eventually so far that the connexion with the actual field of perception as the *immediate* environment is established. But in general the issue is a different one: an empty mist of dim indeterminancy gets studded over with intuitive possibilities or presumptions, and only the "form" of the world as "world" is foretokened. Moreover, the zone of indeterminancy is infinite. The misty horizon that can never be completely outlined remains necessarily there. (Husserl 1931:102)

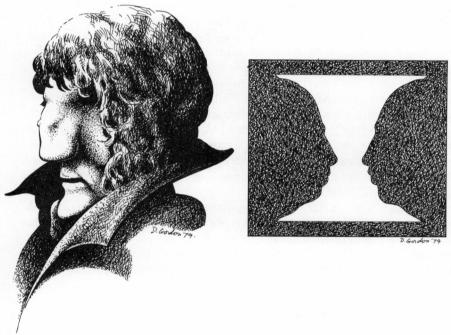

FIGURE 17. Classic ambiguous figures. If you look at them one way they are either an old woman or a chalice, respectively. Seen another way they are a young woman or two faces (silhouettes), respectively. Drawings by Donna Gordon.

This inevitable "zone of indeterminancy" we called (before reading Husserl) the zone of uncertainty (d'Aquili et al. 1979:40). We have argued that questions about the zone of uncertainty are in part responsible for religious systems cross-culturally (ibid.:171).

THE PARADOX OF PERPETUAL ERROR

The modeling function of our nervous system has its own built-in limitations, as we have seen, and these limitations produce systematic errors in our cognized environment. This limitation leaves us open to an apparent paradox: our nervous system, whose function is to "map" reality, constructs models of reality that are perpetually wrong. But consider: our nervous system is constructed to facilitate a good deal of plasticity. Models are being continuously tested for accuracy against reality and when a significant mismatch occurs between model and reality, some form of adaptive reorganization may occur. As previously noted, there are generally three reactions of the nervous system to *perceived* anomaly: First, the model may be physically adjusted so that the view it mediates falls within tolerable limits of accuracy. Second, the nervous system may opt to stick with the model and reject the anomalous input as unreal, irrelevant, or misread. Third, and less frequently, the nervous system may hold the model inviolate while still holding on to the discrepant input ("Yes, I know you saw a purple banana, but all bananas are yellow"; see Rubinstein et al. 1984:67ff on this issue). The third alternative is less obvious to naive introspection but is amply evidenced in clinical literature about the syndrome known as *arosognosia*, the denial or loss of patients' awareness of the symptoms of their disease (see Brown 1977:144ff).

A healthy and maturing cognized environment is one in flux—a system that operates as though it knows, at some level, its models are never more than approximations of reality and its job is the continuous revision of view. Refractory view in the face of anomaly stifles development. Modeling, in other words, is more an ongoing process, and less an existing state.

INNER AND OUTER REALITY

Of course the world does not stop at our skin. For certain purposes it makes sense to speak of an *inner-operational environment* and an *outer-operational environment*. Our cognitive system is not restricted to modeling only the outer reality. Naturally enough, we may also speak of an *inner-cognized environment* and an *outer-cognized environment*. Care must be exercised in wielding these concepts. We must be aware that *both the inner- and the outer-cognized environments are constituted within inner reality*.

That is, the models composing both the inner and outer-cognized environment are structures within the nervous system and are thus part of inner reality. The implications are significant, yet are not fully appreciated by science, which usually reifies outer-cognized events and treats them as if they were outer reality itself. Among other things, if our experience of the outer-cognized environment is actually a function of inner reality, then our experience is ordered by *both* the principles operating upon neural structures (like neurognosis, cognitive development, creodes, reciprocal inhibition of competing models, etc.), and whatever principles in outer reality are operating upon our reception of stimuli.

This term-spitting can get a bit tedious. Let us then call our inner-operational environment our *being* and our inner-cognized reality our *empirical ego*—James (1890) referred to these as the Self and the empirical Me, respectively, and Husserl (1931), to the Transcendental Ego and the empirical, or psychological ego, respectively. We will use the terms being and ego only when specifically referring to the reflexive aspects of modeling—how we construct models of our being. Most of the time we will be talking about the process of modeling, irrespective of whether it is of the being or of the world.

The same principles apply to either type of modeling. That is, our nervous system constructs a set of models of our being in exactly the same way that it does of events in the rest of reality. It uses the same tissues, regulates development, operates upon the principles of antagonism, reverberation, relegation, and so on. And yet, the inner-outer distinction is anything but spurious, as it is founded upon the genetically bifurcated organization of sense receptors into *exteroceptors* (nerve cells like those in the retina of the eye that deliver external information to the system), and *proprioceptors*, or *interoceptors* (cells like those in the arteries that monitor blood pressure and that deliver internal information). The nervous system is neurognostically organized to distinguish stimulation originating within the being from stimulation originating from the world. When we come to model interoceptive and exteroceptive stimuli, the models quite naturally form a dichotomous cognized environment. At the cortical level of neural organization, this dichotomous organization becomes the ego, as opposed to the world—or in common parlance, "me" as opposed to "you," "it," and so forth. Ironically enough, it is likely that this fundamental neurognostic distinction lies at the developmental roots of the type of dualism we were disparaging in chapter 1. It may be argued that an oppositional distinction between ego and world—a world, incidentally, that includes our bodies (Merleau-Ponty 1962: part 1)—carries the adaptive interoceptive-exteroceptive distinction into the realm of erroneous distortion. We are both "beings in the world" and beings reflecting upon our responding to the world. The problem for the contemplative is to distinguish inner and outer reality while realizing their simultaneous totality.

COGNIZED CONSCIOUSNESS

Summarizing a bit, we have said that consciousness is a term referring to the ongoing stream of experience that is mediated by a functional neural complex. This complex is a continuously transforming entrainment and disentrainment of neural networks which, among other things, models the world. The transcendental world that it models commonly includes the being as it operates in the world. We have said that the models that make up our cognized reality include models of the being and models of the world, the ego and the cognized world respectively. The structures of consciousness thus construct a system of creodes that then canalize the functions of consciousness. These creodes, we have said, are inevitably founded upon a neurognostic organization.

We need to dwell a bit more on the distinction between being and world. As always, many of the systemic errors that plague the largely culture-bound Western science of consciousness arise at this juncture. Just what does it mean when we say "I am aware of being conscious"? It could mean that we are cognizing an aspect of the experience of our own consciousness; namely, there is experience arising and an "I" doing the experiencing (the image of the snake devouring its own tail is irresistible here). But this is only one way of knowing. Knowing the experience and the experiencer, the perceived and perceiver is a point of view. Clearly other ways of knowing occur.

Yet there have been those in science who have argued that some kind of self-reflection is requisite to "true" consciousness. By "self-reflection" such writers often mean awareness of an ego, the "I" that is knowing. This awareness is considered by some authorities an evolutionary advance over lower animals who possess rudimentary consciousness at best or no consciousness at all. As we have argued elsewhere (Laughlin and Richardson 1986), ego-consciousness is a stage in the evolution of human consciousness, which will likely be transcended at a later stage in human evolution, just as it is in advanced psychic development among humans today. Hence, to make ego-awareness definitive of consciousness is a preposterous claim for two reasons: It implies that an advanced hominid without ego-awareness would have returned to a state of unconsciousness presumably typical of lower animals; it also argues that ego-awareness is the highest or only true state of consciousness—a contention contradictory to every contemplative tradition on the planet, all of which describe *loss* of ego-awareness as characteristic of advanced states of mind. Even in daily experience the aspect of ego-awareness commonly disappears. When "I" become thoroughly absorbed in reading a book or doing a painting or running, the awareness of "I" falls away and there is only the reading, the painting, or the running—only the unfolding of experience. Buddhist psychology isolates degrees of absorption states (the *jhanas;* see Buddhaghosa 1976:144ff) in the practice of mindfulness and considers them higher states of mind than those in which the "I" is distinguished. Martin Buber (1958), speaking from a more Western theological standpoint, distinguishes between the dualistic I-it relationship characteristic of everyday experience and the nondualistic I-Thou relationship characteristic of all authentic mystical experiences. Thus the abstraction of the knower from the known is but a point of view, useful to some purposes, useless or an outright hindrance to other purposes. The distinction is certainly not definitive of all states of consciousness but rather indicative of a type of cognition occurring within some states of consciousness. We will return to the limitations of ego-centered psychology in a moment.

Those distinctions underscore the importance of conceiving of consciousness as a functional and transcendental complex rather than as a quality that may be present or absent in species. From our perspective, it is easy to see that all species—at least all species with brains—experience, cognize, and are thus conscious. The organization of their consciousness, which is a function of their neural structures, places limitations upon the range and kinds of experience and knowledge that compose their stream of consciousness. Frog consciousness is a function of a frog brain; it is not human consciousness. Accordingly, the consciousness of a five-year-old child is not the same as the consciousness of an adult human, and the consciousness of a mature contemplative is not the same as a noncontemplative.

Furthermore, it should be possible to deduce the kinds of consciousness of which any given species is capable, given a thorough knowledge of its nervous system. For example, knowing that the cortical and subcortical structures subserving visual attention are similar for monkeys and humans (Wurtz et al. 1982), we may reasonably suppose that monkeys pay attention to events in the visual world much as humans do, but they cannot cognize at the human level of complexity because their higher cortical faculties, particularly their frontal lobes, have not evolved to that complexity of organization (Chevalier-Skolnikoff 1975).

BASIC SUBSIDIARY PRINCIPLES

We now expand our analysis of consciousness by reviewing some basic subsidiary neurocognitive principles by which consciousness operates. These principles will flesh out our understanding of consciousness as a functional complex composed of the entrained activity of an immense number of cells organized into networks and models. These principles will also contribute to our analysis of major principles of neurocognition such as intentionality, phases of consciousness, and the symbolic process. Furthermore, by seeing consciousness as a complex function being mediated simultaneously by numerous systems and subsumed by basic principles, we can avoid defining consciousness simplistically as a single polarity, duality, or dialectic.

EXPERIENTIAL-PHYSIOLOGICAL CORRESPONDENCE

Our first principle states that for every event in consciousness there is a corresponding and causally interrelated physiological event. However, the opposite proposition does not hold true. A physiological event may or may not be matched by an event in consciousness. A more technical way of saying this is that, whereas an event in consciousness is a sufficient condition for a physiological event, a physiological event is merely a necessary condition for an experiential event. For example, every conscious visual event is matched by physiological events occurring in the occipital cortex of the brain, but we are not conscious of every physiological event that occurs, say, in the retina or in the superior colliculus of the midbrain. In fact, much of the activity of our nervous system occurs outside the bounds of awareness (see Doty 1975:797–98 for a review). As we shall see in a moment, the role of consciousness in our organism requires intentional selectivity of awareness, and selectivity requires relegation of much information processing to "lower" centers.

EXPERIENTIAL DISCREPANCY

The second principle states that a factual discrepancy may exist between an experiential event and its corresponding physiological event. This discrepancy is particularly apparent in relating everyday perception and the physiology mediating perception. We naively believe that we are conscious of this book "out there," when in fact our awareness is centered upon images, arising neurophysiologically at the retina and reproduced topographically at various locations between retina and cortex. We are conscious, in other words, of the model(s) and not reality itself. We project the activity of models "outward" into the world (or "inward" into our being, for that matter).

We now consider an implication of projecting models that might not be immediately apparent to us. For example, much has been made in some quarters that the so-called *chakras*, or mystical energy centers, of Eastern yoga do not seem to correspond neatly with the autonomic plexes. *Chakra*, like consciousness, is an experiential category. People experience *chakras* when they meditate, but pathologists do not find *chakras* when they do postmortems. One may, for example, experience "energies opening up" at a point two inches or so below the navel, at the *swadhistana chakra*. Plexes, on the other hand, are defined anatomically. One normally thinks of the autonomic plexes in relation to physiological dissections and not yoga sessions. The plexes are rich groupings of autonomic nervous tissue and are responsible for regulating various bodily functions performed by organs. Although there is some evidence that chakric experiences are associated with activity in particular plexes, the place in the cognized body where the experiences arise may not map onto the plexes. For instance, the experience of energy flow from the *swadhistana chakra* would seem to be mediated by the solar plexus, which is the largest of the plexes and located somewhat above and behind the point commonly associated with the *chakra* (Motoyama and Brown 1978).

Another example of the principle of phenomenological discrepancy is provided by the practice of *acupuncture* (an Eastern technique of diagnosis and treatment of disease). In acupuncture theory (again, defined traditionally upon experience and not dissection) the various organs and systems of the body are connected by a complex system of meridians, or channels of psychic energy, upon which lie points especially sensitive to disturbance of associated organs. By monitoring these points, diagnoses and direct treatment of disease in associated organs is possible. The meridians are experientially real. One of the authors (CDL) has informally experimented with them on his own body using an electric probe, and can attest that the meridians can be easily traced by sensations on the surface of the skin. Although the anesthetic effects of acupuncture are being attributed to the release of endorphins, a peptide much like morphene, the meridians and points themselves do not closely correspond to any Western model of neuroanatomy. Yet the system works so well that many Western medical practitioners are turning to acupuncture for both the diagnosis and the treatment of disease, as well as for effective anesthesia during surgery. We would suggest that at least a partial disagreement between our model of neuroanatomy and our experience of meridians may be due to the inherent discrepancy between the cognized body and the operational body itself; that is, between experienced relationships between parts of the body on the one hand, and the neural, endocrine, circulatory, and other somatic interconnections on the other.

CORTICAL REPRESENTATION

A root cause of experiential discrepancy lies in the fact that *conscious-ness is commonly canalized to a cortical representation of the physiological event*. Somatosensory and other information sent into the central nervous system ends up in appropriate areas of the cortex where it is processed. Consciousness may be limited to the processing of that information at the cortical level, although we experience the cortical model of the event as if it were peripheral. A chakric event might entail a complex interaction between activity of autonomic plexes, secretions of endocrine glands, and other organic functions, yet we may be aware of information about the event arising in only the cortex. It has long been known that the body is mapped along several dimensions on the cortex, so that each part of the body has its appropriate areas in cortical topography.

CONSCIOUS NETWORK

All the cells of the nervous system are alive and are thus active to some extent every moment, if for no other reason than to maintain their individual metabolisms. And they are intimately sensitive to neighboring cells. Indeed, much of their electrochemical activity is synchronized with that of neighboring cells, and they will spontaneously fire from time to time, without apparent excitation (Pribram 1971:11ff). But a small fraction of neural cells will be entrained and active at any given moment in some higher-level function like processing visual inputs, exciting the release of hormones, coordinating muscles while running, and so forth.

We have seen that consciousness can be viewed as an integration of neural functions, which are entrained and disentrained from moment to moment. We have also implied that consciousness is mediated by a subset of actively functioning networks, which is in turn a small subset of the total set of potentially functioning networks within the nervous system. Therefore, we may speak of a *conscious network* within our nervous system mediating consciousness. Hence, consciousness refers to function, and conscious network refers to structure: *conscious network is the structure of consciousness, and consciousness is the function of conscious network*.

The actual location of conscious network within the nervous system has been a matter of deep controversy for generations. Penfield (1952) at first placed consciousness in the parts of the brain where information is transmitted and integrated between the cerebral hemispheres, but he later (1975) concluded that consciousness was subserved by the whole nervous system. Others have suggested that consciousness is lodged in the brain stem reticular activating system, which controls arousal and the wake-sleep cycle. A major obstacle to mapping the structures of the nervous system, we believe, has been the (at least implicit) desire of many psychologists to define and "locate" the ego—the subject in the subject-object relation. Western psychologies are predominantly ego-centered; that is, involved in the search for the "ghost in the machine," the little homunculus somewhere in the works that is the audience for the sensorial movie. Such psychologies are hampered by what we earlier called naive introspection: the uncritical but, from a cultural point of view, perfectly natural presumption that the ego is a real, substantial, seamless, and enduring entity located somewhere in the mind or the brain. This naive presumption is grounded upon direct but undisciplined experience of self, and is at the core of what Hebb (in Buchtel 1982:22ff) called the "common-sense view of consciousness" (again, Husserl's "natural attitude"). In contrast, Buddhist psychology recognizes the "pure ego," or *ahamkara*—"that which says 'I' " (Govinda 1974:54)—but repudiates the psychological ego, the "hypertrophic 'I'-consciousness" (ibid.:54), as merely a by-product of ignorance, delusion, and false-seeing (*avijja*). Undisciplined introspection has often led to the absurdity of a reified self-concept and has historically rendered naive introspection properly suspect as a ground for empirical research (see Ryle 1949). Of course, all attempts to locate a psychological ego in the central nervous system have been abject failures (see Pribram 1976 for a more refreshing approach). The weight of more sophisticated opinion in the neurosciences suggests that most of the networks entrained to conscious network are to be found in the cortex, particularly in the frontal lobes (Nebes and Sperry 1971; Sperry 1974; see Doty 1975:796 for a review).

Conscious network is a continously changing pattern of entrainment among the neural networks potentially entrainable to conscious network—a living society of cells and networks of cells whose patterns of organization are never static but are cyclical.

ENTRAINMENT

Conscious network represents the highest level of functional control in our nervous system. As such, it exercises some freedom in entraining and disentraining networks to itself. Conscious network is a system perpetually transforming its internal organization and its engagement with the world. Certain local neural structures will frequently be involved in conscious network; for example, nuclear areas of the thalamus (gating input and output functions), hippocampus (memory and recognition functions), and limbic structures (affective functions) like the septum (fear response) and amygdala (aggression). The most significant areas involved in constituting conscious network are the intentional processes in the prefrontal cortex, but we will speak of this at length in the next chapter.

Models may be entrained and disentrained from the conscious network very rapidly—literally thousands of models at every moment as (say) our visual system scans a vista. This continual change in the organization of our conscious network underlies the remarkable flux we experience as our "stream of consciousness." There is an old mystical aphorism that expresses this flux very well: "No matter how hard you try, you can't step in the same river twice!"

WILL AND REVERBERATION

Control over recurrent patterns of entrainment (i.e., creodes) mediating consciousness is, for most humans, far from complete. To some extent, of course, it makes sense to speak of conscious "will," "freedom," or "volition." But to the extent that control over conscious network entrainment is exercised by networks external to conscious network, we may speak of "reactivity," "unconscious motivation," "nonwill," "lack of freedom," "tyranny of phenomena," and the like. Obviously, the extent of willful entrainment comprising conscious network varies from moment-to-moment in the individual, between individuals in the group, and among groups, depending upon the conditioning of neural systems in development. Again, "will" to some extent refers to the intentional processes of conscious network, which will be discussed in the next chapter.

The matter of will brings us back to the quality of reverberation. Conscious network is a system of reverberative (self-excitatory) networks and models. This quality is in part what provides the sense of continuity to experience. By entraining itself to another model or network, the overall pattern of excitation and reverberation changes. Accordingly, what "willful consciousness" means is that conscious network is significantly auto-reverberative—it remains entrained with a particular array of models, more or less independent of external factors. When we carry out a disciplined program to "strengthen our will" (Assagioli 1965) "like a muscle" (Wilson 1972), what we are doing, in part at least, is increasing the auto-reverberative capacity of our conscious network. Will, then, refers experientially to the degree to which conscious network is auto-reverberative at the moment, whether in the brain of an individual or in the brains of individuals operating as a group.

ENTRAINMENT IN DEVELOPMENT

The whole being is continually adapting to essentially transcendental events occurring in its operational environment—a process that does not cease from conception to death. The most obvious period of development—obvious because of its relative rapidity—is during the early years of life, a period in which the role of consciousness as the great entrainer becomes most evident. During this developmental stage consciousness has the task of constructing adaptively functioning neural networks in response to events arising within the being and in the world. Construction of networks entails a number of subsidiary functions, the more important of which require individual attention. Our view here is consonant with Piaget's conception of consciousness (see Piaget 1976) and Whitehead's cybernetic notions of "regnancy" and "reason" (see Whitehead 1919, 1978; Sherburne 1981:242–43).

ORIENTATION

Cognition presumably evolved as a function of the organization of interneurons intervening between afference (stimulus transmission) and efference (response transmission) among organisms sufficiently advanced to develop networks of nerve cells (Crook 1980). As Pribram (1971:52) notes, simple habituation to a stimulus, one of the simplest of cognitive processes, is often produced by an interaction between interneurons within a stimulus-response circuit. The adaptive function of many components of consciousness—indeed, of consciousness as a whole—seems to be the evaluation of objects and events portrayed within the cognized environment of the organism.

Conscious network is neurologically designed to focus its processes upon single objects and events for evaluation with the rest of experience as context for that evaluation (i.e., it is "intentional"; see chap. 4). This focus-context, or "figure-ground," dialectic is represented in the visual system at its most primitive level in the fovea and periphery of the retina (Barlow and Mollon 1982) and at its most complex level in the attention structure–visual association area interacting in the cortex (Carver and Scheier 1981; Wurtz et al. 1982). Conscious network organizes the totality of its entrained functions oriented upon ("intending") the object, however momentary or sustained the duration of attention. Orientation involves the activity of diverse neural centers from the reticular activating system located in the brain stem and sensory receptors at the periphery to prefrontal and sensory association cortex. Initial orientation may be either willful ("I wonder what that's like?") or responsive ("What was that all about?").

Concentration of consciousness is upon the object, which is to say,

conscious network becomes entrained to the model(s) processing information about the object to the exclusion of other potential objects. Your
consciousness is oriented upon this book at the moment and is probably
not attending the sounds around you—sounds such as birds singing,
air conditioner or furnace humming, people chatting and what have
you. Also, you are likely not viewing television right now or feeling the
pressure of your body on the chair. Yet, as these objects are mentioned
to you, your consciousness may momentarily reorient itself upon them
briefly before returning to the book. The best evidence in support of all
this is your own direct experience, like the experience you had when
we did the exercise in chapter 1.

The orientation function participates in a greater system that concentrates and controls cognitions about the world pervading conscious
network. As such, it has a profound role in development. Concentrated
attention enables consciousness either to call up cognitive and motor
networks already prepared to respond or to entrain and supervise the
development of unprepared networks for future operation. This capacity
is the "programming" function of consciousness (see Young 1978)—
programming in the sense of selecting neurognostically appropriate
models and mediating the development of those models and the adaptive fit between object and response (the EMC). We can see the behavioral concomitants of this process in the infant's repetitive exploration
of an object. The young of humans and of other higher social animals
will spend hours handling and exploring (i.e., "playing" with) a particular object (see Piaget 1952; Laughlin and McManus 1982).

The principal concern of orientation is controlling information being
shunted through attendant networks, plus monitoring the adaptive
response of models to noumena. For consciousness, the processing of
information, either resulting in action (predominating in the early years
of life; see Piaget 1952) or in cognition without an action component,
forms a test of the attendant network. If construction of a network is
incomplete (has not become fully reverberative), or if it requires further
modification (physical change or elaboration of neural networks), consciousness will more likely remain focused on the object.

RELEGATION

When a network has sufficiently developed to mediate an activity
without the concentration and control of information flow provided by
conscious network, the function will be *relegated* to that network; and
the network will tend to be disentrained from conscious network.
Furthermore, the process of relegation most likely continues until *a
particular function is relegated to the lowest functional level of the nervous
system capable of performing that function within the limits of tolerance.* It is

by relegation that many functions carried out by the nervous system, once intimately involved with consciousness, become shunted to relatively unconscious functioning. Deikman (1966) called this loss of conscious involvement in the functions of the nervous system *automatization*.

PENETRATION

The process of relegation may be reversed, of course. Entrainment may be established by shifting attention to the operation of a previously relegated network or to a neurognostic network never previously entrained to conscious network. Again, David Bohm (1980) has called this *relevation*. Relevation is a form of penetration (see page 36) and may occur automatically if, for some reason, a relegated network is not operating within tolerance. For instance, we usually do not pay much attention to the process of walking. However, our attention will immediately return to walking if we suddenly slip on the ice. We become keenly aware and cautious of where we plant our feet for a while. Attention to walking on ice will result in a modification of the networks mediating walking and an "automatic" (that is, relegated) adjustment to the knowledge of ice, which was previously not "built in" to the network.

If there is sufficient interest, consciousness will actively, even persistently search for the requisite network. As a simple example, you might become aware of the tiny bodily movements required in reading this book. If you continue the exploration with sufficient interest, you will discover that the eyes "automatically" move across the page in a series of little jerky movements. These are called *saccades* and are designed to keep the optimal amount of information flowing through the central, or foveal, area of the retinae. You may also notice how the eye "automatically" returns to the beginning of each line of text. If you consciously try to skip a line every time you return to the beginning, you may experience difficulty in overriding this habitual pattern. Should you explore all of the movements involved in reading, you will notice you cannot retain clear awareness of what is being said on the page while doing it. These are subsidiary functions serving the primary function of tracing, perceiving, and interpreting text, and attention to the subsidiary functions conflicts with carrying out the primary function. These subsidiary functions have become relevated, and knowledge about them produces a Husserlian "bracket."

OPTIMIZATION IN DEVELOPMENT

Optimal development of many neural networks requires attention from consciousness. This is especially the case during the early years when layer after layer in the functional hierarchy of our nervous system is developing. Once a network is established and is functioning within tolerance, less attention from consciousness is required. The development of some networks may reach a point when entrainment to conscious network would actually impede the network's functioning. Many of us can remember learning to tie a necktie or a shoelace, tasks that, once learned with abundant, meticulously conscious attention, are thereafter confounded if we pay too much attention to the process. More complex and interesting examples can be found in sports, where a degree of proficiency is attained beyond which conscious attention to the networks mediating the activity could prove disasterous. Many athletes report a form of *flow experience* (see page 299) in which all thought about the activity stops and is replaced by a smooth flow of information through consciousness—information that is used by lower, relegated networks to perform the task. We have heard reports of flow experience from practitioners of motocross racing, grand prix racing, long-distance running, downhill skiing, zen archery, and a number of other endeavors. One motocross racer mentioned that beyond a certain speed, if he ever once thought about what he was doing, he would crash. Optimization of development does *not* mean consciousness is requisite to all learning. In fact, much learning is a task relegated to lower functional levels. Furthermore, relegation of a network does not stop its development. Recall once again that networks are composed of living tissue, not microchips. This will be a crucial point when we discuss contemplation and dreams. Repetition in the functioning of a neural network strengthens and refines the function, regardless of whether it is entrained to conscious network (Eccles 1970).

Generally speaking, the simpler the task, the less likely consciousness will be required in learning that task. This is particularly apparent when the organism is prepared for learning, as in simple conditioning experiments in which a response is paired with a reward desirable to the person (like approval, attention, tactile stimulation, etc.). The person may not be at all aware of the learning. In certain forms of hypnosis, a subject's cognition may be altered without his being aware of it (see Grinder and Bandler 1976). But such experiments are generally performed on adults whose nervous systems are already hierarchically structured, and where the "learning set" (to use experimental psychology jargon) is already established. In other words, adults have "learned to learn" during their infancy and childhood, when the role of consciousness in learning is proportionately greater than in adulthood. However, in order to learn something more complex and, perhaps, antithetical to our habit patterns, or where requisite networks have not undergone sufficient preparatory development, then consciousness is required to initiate and carry forth development. And it is precisely the faculty of intentionality that is the key to understanding the role of consciousness in transforming its own organization.

4 INTENTIONALITY AND THE SENSORIUM

> If the doors of perception were cleansed everything would appear to man
> as it is, infinite. For man has closed himself up, till he sees all things thro'
> narrow chinks of his cavern.
> —William Blake, *The Marriage of Heaven and Hell*

WE MAY BECOME CONSCIOUS of whatever is mediated by models entrained to our conscious network. Consciousness, therefore, forms a
typically vast, ever-changing field of neural activity, often extending
over wide areas of cortex and between cortex and other subcortical areas
of the nervous system. Understanding this nature of consciousness, it
makes no sense whatever to say that consciousness is located in a
particular part of the brain. Rather, consciousness may be likened more
to a 1960s acid-rock light show—first one configuration, then another,
then another, never still and never repeating any configuration exactly.
It is possible now to depict the waves of activity across the cortex by use
of modern video techniques. A person may be "wired-up" to an EEG
machine, and the electrical output from various sensors scattered across
the cortex are transposed into colored lights on a profile of the brain.
The subject is given a stimulus such as a flash of light or a mild shock,
and the resulting activity of the different cortical centers is recorded on
a TV screen. The effect, which is quite dramatic as waves of activity
sweep across the surface topography of the brain, is a depiction of
activity measured merely at the surface of the cortex. Activity is actually
going on throughout the nervous system.

It is very difficult to convey the mind-boggling complexity of neural
entrainment and reentrainment that produces but a single moment of
consciousness, much less the ongoing explosion of activity that is our
"stream of consciousness." Each moment of consciousness is mediated
by a field of neural connections that involves hundreds of thousands,
even millions, of neural cells and their support structures. Furthermore,
any particular neuron may be involved in multiple networks just as the
letter *e* may be involved in countless words. As Sir John Eccles puts it:

> Thus there arises the concept of a wave-front . . . comprising a kind of
> multi-lane traffic in hundreds of neuronal channels, so that the wave-front
> would traverse 100,000 neurons in one second, weaving a kind of pattern

in space and time in a way that Sherington . . ., with his poetic insight, has likened to the operations of an "enchanted loom." Furthermore, when, by means of a micro-electrode, single cerebral neurons are being investigated, it is often found that one can be activated from several different sensory inputs. (Eccles 1970:54)

Yet, as we have seen, the conscious brain may be understood by reference to its fundamental principles—principles that may be known indirectly via neurophysiology and directly via phenomenology.

INTENTIONALITY

The *sine qua non* of consciousness as described in both the Western and Eastern phenomenological traditions is *intentionality:* the fundamental realization that consciousness is always "of something." Intentionality is experienced as a distinction between subject and object, between the phenomenon intended and the "I" doing the intending. It is also experienced as (1) the constellation of cognitive (conceptual, imaginative, intuitive, perceptual, etc.) and sensory (qualities, forms, topological relations, etc.) processes upon and in constitution of the object, and (2) as a unity of phenomenal reality that is both coherent and meaningful. This subject-object polarity, which is apparent to the direct experience of consciousness, was noted in Western philosophical tradition as early as Aristotle, and elaborated by Franz Brentano (1838–1917) in his *Psychologie vom empirischen Standpunkt* (1874), and later by Husserl in a variety of works, including *Cartesian Meditations* (1977) and *Ideas: General Introduction to Pure Phenomenology* (1931; for a useful, but neurophysiologically naive discussion of intentionality, see Searle 1983)

The understanding that consciousness is essentially intentional dates further back in Eastern phenomenological traditions. For example, of the seven universal factors of consciousness mentioned in chapter 3 from the Buddhist Abhidharma, five factors are explicitly intentional by nature: (1) *phassa* or "initial contact" with the object; (2) *manasikara* or "turning the mind" to the object; (3) *cetana* or coordination of mental factors upon the object; (4) *sanna* or "recognition" of the object; and (5) *ekeggata* or "one-pointed" concentration upon the object. What is of significance in the present context is that in both Eastern and Western traditions, the subject is experienced as arising and dissolving with the object. In Abhidharma, as well as other Buddhist teachings, these universal factors arise as a consequence of contact with the object (see e.g., Guenther and Kawamura 1975:11). In Husserlian phenomenology, both the object (*phainomenon*) and the ego (*cogito*) are simultaneously constituted within the stream of consciousness (*cogitationes;* see Funke in McKenna et al. 1981:83).[1]

A significant feature of intentionality is that it normally produces a total (*gestalt*) field of experience as it unfolds each and every moment within consciousness. The cognized environment (Husserl's 1970 "life-world") tends to remain "stuck together" within the sphere of consciousness. And, as we have said, perception operates to differentiate percepts, attentional structure initiates a point of view, and cognition performs associative operations upon percepts—and all of this from the point of view of an ego, an "I" for whom the world arises. This subject and object distinction is produced as a consequence of the interaction of the polarized processes Husserl (1931; see also Gurwitsch in Kockelmans 1967) called the *noematic* and *noetic* aspects of consciousness. Because this intentional polarity is fundamental to the structure of consciousness, it is thus fundamental to social cognition and the "enculturation" (transmission of "culture" from generation to generation) of members of each and every society on the planet (see Schutz and Luckman 1973).

The subject of which we are currently speaking is *not*, of course, the empirical ego, not the ego *cogitons*. The empirical ego is the product of our "natural attitude" directed at naive self-understanding. It is our cognized self about which we will have more to say in chapter 9. Moreover, the delusion of an empirical ego is vulnerable to the phenomenological reduction. Indeed, the mature contemplative from whatever tradition has in a sense "gone beyond" or "behind" the views of self constructed for the culturally and linguistically relative "natural attitude" often reflected in, say, current antitranscendental hermeneutical theories of self and meaning (e.g., Wachterhauser 1986).

During the process of maturation, the contemplative has discovered that there are no phenomenological grounds upon which to lodge any belief in an empirical ego. He or she knows with complete certainty and from direct apperception that there exists no discernible ghost in the machine, no homunculus, no seamless, substantial, enduring "I". This discovery and attendant intuitive knowledge makes it possible both to eliminate the obstacles presented by ego-centered psychologies discussed in the last chapter and to discuss the subjective pole of the intentional polarity in terms more consonant with our knowledge of how the brain works. Nowhere in the Buddhist Abhidharma—that most sophisticated of all phenomenological psychologies of consciousness—is there the slightest reference to an *ego*. Nor is it necessary to ground Husserl's (1970) transcendental phenomenology upon such an ego. Rather, the operational (or "transcendental") ego is discovered to be no more than a "standpoint" related to cognitive operations (the "cogito") performed upon the object of consciousness (Husserl 1931:116ff).

THE PREFRONTOSENSORIAL POLARITY PRINCIPLE

There are three major principles of neural organization that mediate relations characteristic of consciousness. Two of those principles, currently fundamental to thinking about the working of the nervous system, are the hierarchical organization of function and the lateral asymmetry of function. The first principle, discussed in chapter 2, conceives of the nervous system as a functional hierarchy in which networks of cells higher in the order perform more complexly and flexibly by organizing those systems subordinate to them in more complex arrays (see e.g., Pribram 1971; MacLean 1973; Powers 1973; Varela 1979). Discussions of the hierarchical organization of the nervous system, and the correlates of this principle in consciousness, often involve the issues of "top-down" versus "bottom-up" control (e.g., Mandler 1984).

The second principle, discussed in chapter 5, conceives of the nervous system, and especially the cerebral cortex, as operating as a structural dialectic between the left and right hemispheres (TenHouten 1978–79). Left and right hemispheres are understood to function in opposite or complementary ways upon the same object. Thus the left cortical hemisphere specializes in lineal problem-solving and language-related cognitions, while the right hemisphere specializes in *gestalt* spatial relations and imagery (e.g., Dimond and Beaumont 1974; Geschwind and Galaburda 1984). Both of these principles are well documented and are now basic to the consideration of the neural substrate of consciousness, at least among those schooled in the neurosciences.

The third principle, our central concern in the present chapter, is one that we call the *prefrontosensorial polarity principle*. This principle hypothesizes a fundamental dialectical relation between prefrontal and sensorial cortex, a relation, we suggest, that mediates both intentional processes in consciousness and the sense of subject-object distinction when it is present to awareness. This principle distinguishes the conscious network from all other networks in the nervous system. Yet, this principle has been only glimpsed and partially elaborated in science owing to the ego-centeredness of psychological theories discussed earlier and to a combination of factors influencing neuroscientific research until recently—factors which include overspecialization in discrete areas and functions of neural processing, and the lack of technology to map the complex, dispersed processes of interest to those of us asking more global questions. Technological developments (e.g., magnetic resonance, regional blood flow) over the past two decades have made it possible to draw more interesting conclusions about dispersed networks, which have provided some support for our present position (see

Young 1987:51ff for a cogent discussion of intentionality from the neuroscientific viewpoint).

We hypothesize that the essential intentionality of consciousness, characteristic of the structure of conscious network, is mediated specifically by a dialogue between prefrontal cortical structures (more particularly dorsolateral and orbital prefrontal cortex) and sensorial cortex. This dialogue is paramount in integrating the production of the phenomenal world and meaning of, or cognitions about, the phenomenal world both in moment-by-moment experience and in development. As already noted, we agree with Doty (1975:796), citing the work of Obrador (1964), that human consciousness is largely the product of forebrain processes and that afference must reach a threshold of intensity to enter consciousness, even when cortex is directly stimulated (ibid:798).[2] This presumption makes good sense anatomically. Although the cortex is richly interconnected with subcortical structures, the vast majority of connections made by cortical neurons are intracortical; that is, made with other cortical neurons (McCullock 1965:68). And most of these connections are with cortical cells in areas proximal to the area of the cell soma.

Let us briefly characterize both sensorium and prefrontal cortex and their interconnections:

THE SENSORIUM

The *sensorium* is the functional space within the nervous system wherein the phenomenal aspects of the cognized environment are constituted and portrayed in moment-by-moment experience. The sensorium, a time-honored term in science and medicine (Newton used the term in the eighteenth century!), usually refers to the "whole sensory apparatus of the body" (*Dorland's Illustrated Medical Dictionary*, 23rd ed.). *Phenomenal experience* is a construction mediated by the moment-by-moment reentrainment of perceptual and associative structures (see Yates 1985). And, as both perception and association are mediated by living cells within the nervous system (the visual system alone involves the neural networks of the striate, prestriate, parietal, hippocampal, brain stem, and other regions of the brain), the role played by both is active. Phenomenal reality is thus in part an entrainment of cognitive and sensorial networks, which is designed to portray an unfolding world of experience to the organism. The functional space within which association and perception are combined into unitary phenomenal experience is the sensorium (see Young 1987:80). And it is significant that sensorial structures in the cortex are located for the most part in the posterior forebrain.

Both cognitive and sensorial processes are actively involved in constituting the world of experience, as implied by our "two hands clapping" model of experience in chapter 1, because both cognition and sensation are mediated by living cells. The many confusing conceptions of consciousness usually arise from misconstruing the nature of the sensorium. For instance, a naive idealism holds that sensory input about the world is chaotically jumbled until ordered by an active cognition; that is, cognition emerges to order a passive and disorganized world of sensations. On the other hand, a naive materialism holds that sensory input acts to impress the order of the world upon a passive-receptive cognition; that is, the world ("out there") appears to inscribe its order upon the "blank slate" of mind.

Neither of these notions can withstand the evidence derived from either mature contemplation or neuropsychology. First, at no point in performing the phenomenological reduction does the contemplative reach a stratum of "pure" chaotic sensation. Rather, sensation is ever ordered to perception, although that order may not be formal. Second, the systems that mediate the input of sensations into the central nervous system and the structures constituting the brain itself are living systems, and as such are goal-seeking processes. Both sensory and cognitive systems are composed of living cells, each acting selectively upon stimuli at their membranes. Sensory systems operate to transmit veridical, but very selective, information into the cognized environment (Gibson 1969). Cognitive systems operate upon this information in a feedforward, or anticipatory, manner in order to "keep one jump ahead" of noumena in the operational world (Miller et al. 1960, Pribram 1971). This is the adaptive function of the nervous system: to match models and sensations in an adaptively isomorphic way. Behavior, on this account, becomes a means of controlling perception so that sensory order optimizes the order anticipated by models (see Powers 1973; Arbib 1972; Uexkull 1909).

Conscious network is the system of entrainments mediating the entirety of consciousness; the sensorium is the subsystem within conscious network mediating phenomenal experience. Of course, structures other than those mediating direct sensory experience are operative within consciousness: the intentional processes we will discuss shortly, as well as those structures mediating motor activities and intuitive functions, which may or may not be relevant to sensorial operations. Sensorial activities include verbalized thoughts, percepts in all sensory modes, affective feelings, imagination, and the like. The distinction between sensorial and nonsensorial operations of conscious network should not, therefore, be held as absolute or oppositional. Rather, one may speak of structures that are more or less apparent in the organization and presentation of phenomenal reality. The structures mediating form, for example, may be more apparent to casual introspection than, say, attentional structure, but both are integral to the organization of moment-by-moment experience. The structures mediating intuitive associations relative to percepts may be even further removed, yet still experientially salient.

A significant feature of sensorial activity is that it normally forms a totality of experience as it unfolds. Perception does operate to differentiate percepts, and cognition may perform organizational operations upon percepts, but the world of phenomenal experience tends to remain "stuck together" within sensorial space. We have thus far refrained from explicitly defining what we mean by *experience*, but we use the term in a manner similar to Wilhelm Dilthey's *Erlebnis* and Husserl's *Erfahrung*; that is, what the subject "lives through" or that which consciousness is "subjected to." In other words, experience is everything that is constituted within conscious network, everything of which the operational ego may become aware. By orienting our analysis to an understanding of the structures of experience, we are in accord with the advocates of an anthropology of experience (see e.g., Turner and Bruner 1986; Turner 1982). Any difference between our approach and that of more orthodox "performance" or "phenomenological" orientations consists in our concern for the structural underpinnings of experience.

DOTS: THE UNITS OF EXPERIENCE

There is another significant feature of sensorial activity that is elusive and contradictory to naive introspection. This feature is one of the many reasons that evidence derived from introspection by trained, mature contemplatives is essential to a modern theory of consciousness. It is readily apparent to the mature contemplative that experience arising within the sensorium is composed of innumerable, almost infinitesimal, and momentary particles. This field of particles passes through consciousness in epoches ("waves," "frames," "heaps," "chunks," etc.), an intermittence that may correlate with cortical alpha rhythms (see Varela et al. 1981, Laughlin 1988). Most people miss these tides of particles because they are simply not interested in, nor are they trained to concentrate upon, the mechanisms of their own perception—as it were, to perform a "phenomenological reduction." But with training, it is easy to become aware of the activity of these tiny and momentary sensory events, given the requisite calm and concentration. They are directly perceivable in all sensory modes and are readily confirmed as the building blocks of objects and movements in the visual field. Labeling these particles of experience after their visual form, we will call them sensorial *dots*.[3]

The sensorium is a dot-filled "field of perception" (Husserl 1931:101), which is perceptually and cognitively distinguished into sensory modes, and within sensory modes into distinct forms and events. The basic act of perception is the abstraction and reinforcement of invariant features in the unfolding field of dots (see Herrnstein 1982; Gibson 1979). It is the job of the cognized environment to portray an internalized world of phenomena by ordering dots into recognizable configurations. There are, however, phases of consciousness attained in mature contemplation during which the entire sensorium is experienced as a single monad (either bounded or unbounded, finite or infinite), wherein the distinction between the different fields of dots constituting various sensory modalities merge into a unified, singular field (the *coincidentia oppositorum*). During this experience consciousness becomes indistinguishable from the sensorial monad, the sensorial monad indistinguishable from consciousness. This occurrence is the realization of "pure" sensation (*hyle*, "hyletic data," "primordial filling," "sensuous filling," or "primordial givenness") in Husserlian phenomenology (Miller 1984:135) and the realization of the "fullness" of the *plenum void* in Eastern traditions. Conscious experience at this point verges upon totality, a phenomenally undifferentiated, timeless, and infinite monad of awareness in which the unfolding energy events play themselves out without hindrance and with the experience of complete flow. Totality and flow are, in fact, the two qualities *sine qua non* of all higher phases of consciousness (see Goleman 1977).

We will have more to say in later chapters about the interplay between science and higher phases of consciousness. What we want to make clear now is that all phenomena—no matter how intensely experienced, no matter in what phase of consciousness experienced, no matter in what combination of sensory modes experienced, no matter how peripheral or central to awareness, no matter how momentary or enduring, and no matter whether of self or of the world—all phenomena are composites consisting of swarms of dots appearing and disappearing within the sensorium. That is to say, the myriad sensorial dots occur entirely within the nervous system of the perceiver and are produced by networks of neural cells.

It would be well to remind the reader once again that we are *not* saying there is no world "out there," but rather that the phenomenon perceived is not the noumenon that may have given rise to the stimulus penetrating to the models mediating the phenomenon. We do not perceive photons (visual triggers) or molecules of vibrating gas (auditory triggers), but rather patterns of neural activity that provide form, color, motion, frequency, and so forth. These qualities are the result of neurocognitive operations performed upon the field of dots, not upon the photic or sonic triggers, which may or may not have evoked the initial generator potentials leading to perception.[4] Consider that both a flash of light and gentle pressure upon our eyeballs will result in our experiencing "light" owing to the visual receptors' sensitivity not only to photons, but also to the pressure of fluid within the vitreous.

Our concept of dot, although similar to Whitehead's (1978) notion of "actual entity" or "actual occasion," is intended as a descriptive empirical category and not a theoretical one like a black hole or a quark. The dot is directly perceivable to any person who trains to "see" it (i.e., see, hear, feel, taste, think, etc.). In this respect it is analogous to the ancient Sanskrit concept of *bindu* (meaning "dot" or "drop"; see Woodroffe 1974), the elemental particle of *prana*, the fundamental energy comprising the entire universe. Hindu ontology would hold that the entire world, our bodies and minds included, is formed by the interaction of *akasa* (the inherent and imperceptible structure of the world, something like Bohm's 1980 "implicate order") and *prana* ordered by *akasa* (see Vivekananda 1956:34ff). The notions of *bindu* and *prana* are partly empirical in Hindu mysticism: the *bindu* is directly experienceable, at least by yogis, as the building block of phenomena from a gross object such as a table or a planet to the most subtle, like the breath or spirit.

Our construction differs somewhat from the Eastern view: we make few claims here about the constitution of the operational world or noumena in the world, and those claims are confined to our knowledge of the physiology and phenomenology of consciousness. Explaining the dynamics of the world apart from the brain and consciousness is the task of other sciences—incidentally, sciences ideally staffed by people who have become phenomenologically grounded in their own processes of observation (Husserl 1970). What we are affirming is that the entire phenomenal world is a construct of brain, that it arises within the individual sensorium, and that it is composed of dots. *Dot is a phenomenological category*, a Husserlian "essence," the result of what Michael Polyani (1965) would call a *logical disintegration* of form into its constituent fragments. The normally unperceived structures mediating the organization of dots—our equivalent of the Eastern *akasa*—are simply those formed by the organization of the neurocognitive system of the perceiver, a hierarchy of intentional order imposed upon the sensorium by cognition.

We suspect that early atomist theories in Western metaphysics and science, as well as in Eastern ontologies, are examples of projection by inquiring brains of their essential organization upon the world. The notion of the *monad* as the ultimate building block of the world goes back to the early Greeks and is the metaphysical term in the eighteenth century that Leibnitz uses in his *Principles of Nature and Grace*. Many philosophers have developed monadologies over the centuries, including Kant, Husserl, and Whitehead. The term *monad* derives from the

Greek root meaning "one" or "unit," and usually refers to a simple irreducible particle of reality from which all composite things in the universe are constructed. The monad is frequently conceived of as a source of power in its own right, and, as in the case of Whitehead's "actual entity," a point of consciousness. The concept of monad seems closer to a mental particle than, say, the notions of atom or molecule, but it is not clear (and this is the crucial point to us) to what extent those philosophies consider the monad either an empirical, descriptive term, or one applicable only to consciousness mediated by brain.

The accuracy of the projection of dots upon the world seems to be verified to some extent by modern physics, but we must remember that dots are phenomenologically ascertainable and present in every operation of perception. Dots are *not* our version of McCulloch's (1965:37) "psychon," his theoretical basic psychic unit. And dots are *not* being inferred as in physics in order to account for more complex phenomena such as a track in a cloud chamber or the loss of expected energy from a binary star system. Rather, the role of dots in perception is analogous to the particles that make up the image on a television screen or a newspaper photo. We are ordinarily not aware of those particles, but they are there to be seen if we look for them. Although dots are momentarily perceptible as introspective events, they contribute to much more enduring events such as forms, patches of color, and textures. It is apparent to the contemplative mind that all verbalized thoughts, images, percepts, and even perceptual space, the edges of forms, and colors in all hues (including black) are comprised of dots.

Dots are certainly not photons. "There is no light, but we may see light. Light is a sensation and thus has no physical existence" (Baumgardt 1972:32). We know from a whole raft of evidence that although a single quantum of electromagnetic energy may be registered by a rod cell in the retina, it is insufficient to produce a phenomenologically reportable sensation of light (see Baumgardt 1972; Barlow and Mollon 1982). Under special conditions of adaptation to total darkness, between 80 and 100 quanta at 500 nm are required to enter the pupil of the eye in order to generate a sensation 50 percent of the time. The number of effective absorptions in rod cells (scotopic vision) at the periphery of the retina required for reporting 50 percent of the time is between 10 and 15 quanta. And vision at the fovea is a tenth as sensitive, requiring about 600 quanta entering at the pupil and an absorption of 38 quanta by the cone cells for a sensation to be reportable.

We also know that registration of stimuli at the individual receptor cell is spatially indivisible, for its discharge travels along an anatomically distinct pathway (Westheimer 1972). Thus, the absorption of a quantum by a receptor cell places an absolute limit to the resolution of registration of information about noumena, a limit that is only partially overcome at higher levels of neurocognitive processing. These figures are approximate, of course, and are low because of unusual experimental conditions. Many factors actually influence the threshold of energy required for a reportable sensation under normal conditions, including background lighting, light adaptation, ingestion of psychoactive substances like coffee and tobacco, and the level of arousal of the subject. The point is that numerous quanta must impinge upon the retina before the perceptual system will "take notice" and begin to build a picture of the event out of dots.

Our understanding of the neural structure mediating the dot is far from complete, but we concur with Polyani (1965:806) that the neural structures are fairly fixed relative to higher cognitive operations that are mediated by more complex patterns of entrainment. It seems unlikely that the activity of only a single nerve cell is being experienced. Rather, sensorial particles are probably mediated by columns in the sensory cortex, and initially organized via hypercolumns into the primary "given," abstracted order of phenomenal reality (see articles by Marrocco in LeDoux and Hirst 1986 and Sawaguchi and Kubota 1986 for reviews).

Caution should be exercised in conceptualizing the sensorium, for sensorial information was thought to be processed lineally from primary areas to the secondary and then to multimodal areas. It is now known that information processing is far more complex. Prestriate cortex in the visual system, for example, is organized into at least a dozen distinct association areas, all topographically interconnected and receiving afference from, and projecting efference to, subcortical areas (Marrocco in LeDoux and Hirst 1986:46). Striate cortex itself projects back to the thalamus as much efference as it receives afference; and efference may be inhibitory as well as excitatory, suggesting a controlling influence by the sensory cortex over what information it receives. Understanding the functions of such reciprocal innervation is relevant to discussions of "top-down" versus "bottom-up" control in cognitive psychology (e.g., Mandler 1984), as well as the perennial question of the influence of language and culture on perception (e.g., Geertz 1983:147ff; see Rosch 1977).

PREFRONTAL CORTEX

The cortical areas most implicated in intentional functions are the dorsolateral and orbital prefrontal cortex, those parts of the cortex that lie just above our eyes (see Pribram 1971; Pribram and Luria 1973; Fuster 1980; Stuss and Benson 1986). Lateral (or "granular") prefrontal cortex has exhibited allometrically greater development than most other areas of the nervous system in hominid evolution (Nauta 1971, Passingham 1973) and is richly and topographically interconnected with the medi-odorsal nucleus of the thalamus, the parvocellular portions of which are phylogenetically the most recent thalamic area to develop, and, at one time in our evolutionary past, the highest association area in the brain. Granular prefrontal cortex is also the last to myelinate during ontogenesis (Jouandet and Gazzaniga 1979). Orbital prefrontal cortex directly projects to and receives afference from cingulate and other limbic structures (lying underneath the cortex), including the hippocampus (and indirectly the amygdala), the hypothalamus, and brain stem tegmentum (all lying deep inside the brain; Fuster 1980:24ff). No other cortical area is as intimately interconnected with all limbic systems as the prefrontal cortex (Stuss and Benson 1986:25).

The prefrontal cortex is also profusely interconnected with modal and multimodal sensory association cortex, the parts of the cortex that process sensory experiences (Adrianov 1978, Geschwind 1965). Particularly significant to our thesis, only prefrontal cortex receives afference from all sensory modes (including olfaction), as well as from multimodal association areas (areas that handle two or more modes simultaneously; Stuss and Benson 1986:24), and little or none of this afference is from primary sensory cortex where sensory information first enters the cortex (Jones and Powell 1970). There are rich interconnections between the prefrontal cortex and the association cortices in the inferior parietal lobule (mediating concepts) and rostral temporal cortex (mediating imagery). These various interconnections are primarily via cortico-cortical fibers (something like nerves) running along the superior longitudinal fasciculus (connecting prefrontal cortex with association areas of temporal, occipital, and parietal cortex); the inferior longitudinal fasciculus (connecting the same general areas); and the cingulum (connecting cortex along the cingulate gyrus, the isthmus, and the parahippocampal gyrus).

The prefrontal areas in each hemisphere are directly interconnected with homotopical and heterotopical sites in contralateral prefrontal cortex by reciprocal fibers running across the genu and rostrum of the corpus callosum (Stuss and Benson 1986:33). In short, the prefrontal cortex is involved in a three-way dialogue with other parts of the nervous system: via projective fibers to subcortical structures involved in arousal, orientation, and affect, via associative fibers to other cortical areas involved in sensory, as well as motor, language, imaginal, and cognitive functions, and via callosal fibers with prefrontal cortex in the other hemisphere.

Our principal concern here is with the cortico-cortical connections between prefrontal and sensorial areas. Our most accurate view at the moment has sensory information entering cortex at the primary association areas, then being replicated in adjacent "secondary" and "tertiary" association areas in the parietal (somatic), the occipital (visual), and the temporal (auditory) regions, all posterior relative to prefrontal cortex (Fuster 1980:29). Each secondary sensory area sends information not only to the proximal association area(s), but also to (and receives from) prefrontal cortex (Roland 1982). Three major pathways, somatic, auditory, and visual systems, converge on contiguous, but discrete areas of the prefrontal cortex (Fuster 1980:29), but significantly few, if any, afferent fibers are received by prefrontal cortex from the primary sensory areas (Stuss and Benson 1986:22). Thus, part of the function of the prefrontal lobe seems to be a multimodal association area, most likely concerned with "egocentric spatial orientation" toward, and integration of information about, discrete events in sensorial space (Pohl 1973, Mishkin et al. 1977)—sensorial space itself being partially constituted by, and motor activity within sensorial space being integrated in part by, association networks in the posterior parietal cortex (Mountcastle et al. 1975).

The functional picture of the prefrontal lobes is far from clear (see Marrocco in Ledoux and Hirst 1986:80 and Stuss and Benson 1986 for discussion of difficulties in researching human frontal functions), but there are suggestive results from various quarters in the literature. In any event, that the prefrontal cortex is paramount in understanding the evolutionary developments that produced our species and its capacity for culture is clear from the application of the law of proper mass, which states simply that the larger the area of tissue, the more important its function (Jerison 1973). The frontal cortex in humans is estimated to consist of as much as 33 percent of total cortex (Stuss and Benson 1986:1) and is the area that has most dramatically developed in hominid phylogenesis. This leads inevitably to the conclusion that the prefrontal cortex mediates functions, however poorly understood at the moment, that contribute significantly to the unique human capacity for rationality and planning. And, if asymmetries among fossil hominids (indicating left hemisphere analytical and right hemisphere gestalt processing; see Holloway and de la Costa-Lareymondie 1982) are indicative of these unique characteristics, then they have been fundamental to hominid evolution for at least the past three to four million years.

Animals whose frontal lobes have been surgically removed exhibit hyperactivity in purposeful movements, increased spontaneous movements, and considerable trouble suppressing orientation responses. Animals appear to be notably scattered and stimulus-bound (Fuster 1980:61ff). The frontal eye fields in particular are involved in movements associated with anticipation and goal-directed activity (Fuster 1980:91), although visual attention with or without associated movement seems to be mediated by networks in posterior parietal cortex (Wurtz et al. 1982). Pribram (in Pribram and Luria 1973:297ff) notes that temporal ordering of tasks is disrupted in animals with dorsolateral prefrontal lesions, but only if the ordering of activities is cued internally by the animal. This is also the case for spatial ordering when the order is internally generated. In contrast, parietal lesions disrupt spatiotemporal ordering if externally cued, but not if internally cued (ibid.:299). Animals without their prefrontal cortex are easily distracted by spatial events and have marked difficulty attending focal objects and not attending irrelevant cues.

The hallmark of the prefrontal disorder in humans is abnormal attention-related variables. Many symptoms are commensurate with the loss of sufficient interest in problem-solving or objects (Fuster 1980:113ff; Pribram and Juria 1973). Recent memory deficit and loss of ability to concentrate are characteristic features of this syndrome, as are loss of abilities to plan; to carry out complex perceptual and conceptual tasks; to complete a lengthy sequence or complex organization of behavior; integrate supramodally auditory, visual, somaesthetic, and spatial information; and to anticipate novelty. Patients with prefrontal disorders also exhibit flatness of affect and apathy, and occasional euphoria, and have difficulty controlling emotion, especially if frontal-limbic connections are affected (Stuss and Benson 1986:121ff). As Fuster (1980:121) puts it, there seems to be a "profound indifference" to events in the environment and difficulty connecting arousal states selectively to specific objects or purposes. Moreover, the patient shows a "deficiency of an active, intentive element of cognitive function that is essential for pursuing prospective goals" (Fuster 1980:114); there is a loss of will and a notable perseverance despite evidence of error (Fuster 1980:120). Patients cannot alter patterns of response once established, and are usually incapable of accomplishing more complex, especially asymmetrical activities (Gerbner in Pribram and Luria 1973:237). Cognitive disorders of this type are more common as a consequence of lesions of the dorsolateral cortex than with lesions of other areas of the prefrontal lobe (Fuster 1980:117) and seem to indicate a general loss of global sensory integrative capacity with respect to supramodal control, planning, integration, and monitoring of activity and the effects of activity (Nauta 1971). Pribram and McGuinness (1975) and Pribram (1981) have suggested that prefrontal processes may function to produce redundancy in otherwise novel sensorial space, processes that have been shown to exhibit lateral asymmetry and to be associated with dopaminurgic systems; that is, prefrontal systems whose synapses secrete the chemical dopamine (Tucker and Williamson 1984).

Some electroencephalographic research on the prefrontal lobe is relevant to our exploration. EEG theta waves produced by the prefrontal cortex have been shown to be associated with sustained attention in a number of studies (see Schacter 1977:54ff and Pigeau 1985:23ff for reviews). Mizuki and colleagues (1983) demonstrated a correlation between amount of theta and degree of concentration required relative to memorization, retention, and recall of material, with intensity of theta increasing in the presence of distractions. Ishahara and Yoshii (1972) and Mizuki and colleagues (1980) showed frontal midline theta activity during arithmetical problem-solving. And in perhaps the most revealing study to date, Hirai (1978) demonstrated frontal theta among Zen practitioners during meditation. Only advanced masters showed lack of theta-blocking response to a distracting "click" sound, theta waves being intermittent during distraction in less-accomplished meditators.

Related and interesting work has been completed by Roland (1982) measuring the blood flow in various areas of the human cortex while the attention of subjects was directed to a specific sensory mode and away from alternative modes. Subjects were asked to attend to either auditory, visual, or somaesthetic stimuli while stimuli in all three modes were simultaneously presented. Patterns of metabolic activity demonstrated significant enhancement of the appropriate attended mode, and inhibition of the unattended modes. Roland postulates a mechanism of "differential tuning" involving control of attention by the superomesial area of the prefrontal cortex, an area discovered to be active in all three modes of attention.

Summarizing, we have seen that the prefrontal cortex in humans is intimately involved in mediating: (1) superordinate control and monitoring of lower-order, relatively autonomous functions and systems; (2) anticipatory and attentional functions relative to sensory stimuli already constituted by secondary sensory and multimodal association areas; (3) augmentation of intended sensory and cognitive "objects" and inhibition of competitive objects, sense modalities, and cognitive functions; (4) planning, initiating, implementing, and monitoring the effects of complex adaptive behavior; (5) production and imposition of redundancy upon sensorial space; (6) facilitation of memory, but not actually involved in primary sensory memory storage; (7) focusing arousal energy to appropriate objects or goals; (8) construction of temporal cognitive plans, and maintenance of continuous concentration and behavioral response; (9) integration of the sensory world relative to internal states and motor responses, especially when confronted with novelty in the environment; (10) initiation of and motor control of speech, and comprehension of textual material; and (11) control of affect, emotion, and mood relative to sensorial events.

In short, the general function of frontal cortex is the integration of its own functions, and those of other areas of cortical and subcortical tissue intended upon an object, be that object a sensory form, thought, image, or cognitive function. Intention involves anticipation, selection, focusing attention, entraining appropriate cognitions and actions, and monitoring their effects on the environment. The latter function should not be overlooked, for it is evident that much of the motoric activity of organisms controls the perceptual processes going on in the sensorium—that organisms behave in the world so that the sensorial world they desire in fact arises (see Powers 1973; Arbib 1972, Richards and von Glasersfeld 1979).

We suspect that the intentional role of prefrontal cortex in ontogenesis is, as with behavioral systems, primary: the role involves focusing development of subordinate systems upon the object until sufficient neurocognitive growth has occurred, and then relegating those systems to relative autonomy, or later reentrainment for frontal lobe purposive processing and projection of redundancy (see Luria 1973a; Stuss and Benson 1986; Pribram and McGuinness 1975). This crucial role in development includes controlling and monitoring the construction of self-concepts and images, which are thus vulnerable to influence by culture.

THE PREFRONTOSENSORIAL POLARITY PRINCIPLE

It is becoming obvious that the role of the prefrontal cortex is not only to implement "executive" programs when events in the environment become too complex for lower-order networks (Pribram in Pribram and Luria 1973:306ff), but also to mediate the Husserlian "pure ego" in its relationships with the phenomenal world as constituted by sensorial structures within the conscious network entrained between the two. As we have seen, the principal characteristic of prefrontal activity is the mediation of intentional functions: that is, (1) the anticipation of (Teuber in Warren and Akert 1964; Pribram 1971), selection of, orientation toward, concentration upon, cognitive operations upon, and motoric activity relative to the phenomenal object abstracted from its sensorial context (Norman and Shallice 1986); (2) the inhibition of irrelevant sensorial objects and events, as well as affective and other neural activities competitive with the object of the intentional process (Fuster 1980); and (3) the establishment of a point of view relative to sensorial events, and under certain conditions of a cognized distinction between self and other, or subject and object (Nauta 1973).

Numbers one and two above involve, on the one hand, production of abstracted, stabilized patterns of redundancy within the cognized environment by various areas of association cortex under the direction of prefrontal processes complementing, on the other hand, the production of ordered and novel events by the sensorium (Pribram and McGuinness 1975; Pribram 1981; Tucker and Williamson 1984). With respect to number three, we suggest that the sense of distinction between subject and object may be lost under two conditions: when prefrontal involvement in the conscious network drops below a threshold of intensity so that its intentional functions become relatively dormant (we will call this *hypointentionality:* experienced as lack of interest, scattered attention, relatively unaware, "dulled-out"; a mindstate termed *thina-middha* in Buddhist psychology); and at the other extreme, when involvement of concentration of intentional processes rises above a higher threshold of intensity (*hyperintentionality:* experienced as absorption in the object of interest, a mindstate termed *jhana* or *samadhi* in Buddhist psychology).

The prefrontosensorial polarity principle implies that there occurs within the confines of conscious network an ostensible sensorial production of a field of continuously novel phenomenal reality, on the one hand, and the willful, redundancy-producing, intentional associative processes organized by the prefrontal cortex and constellated upon objects within the sensorial field, on the other hand (see Teuber 1972, Pribram 1971, 1976, 1981). Once again, it would be a gross error to imagine this polarity simplistically as a prefrontal homunculus passively watching a sensorially produced movie—although an individual may conceive oneself in that way. Rather, the phenomenal world as experienced is an active co-production of entrained prefrontal, associative, motor, sensorial, and other processes distributed over wide areas of both cortical and subcortical tissues. There is sound evidence (Fuster 1980) that prefrontal intentional processes single out objects by actively augmenting and arousing the sensorial network mediating the object (or the entire sensory mode) of interest, and by actively inhibiting alternative objects (and sensory modes).

We are addressing here only one of several principles of organization that may be operating simultaneously in the organization of the conscious network and the mediation of experience. The more accurate view is that, when prefrontal intentional processes are operating relative to environmentally stimulated sensorial processes, we should expect to find a characteristic pattern of reciprocal entrainment of neural structures distributed between primary sensory cortex and prefrontal cortex. This entrainment may incorporate such widely dispersed systems as feature-processing networks in secondary and tertiary sensory cortex; recognition processes in hippocampal nuclei; selective arousal by brain stem reticular activating systems; multimodal spatial-integration processes in the parietal association cortex; motor processes in the motor cortex, premotor cortex, and cerebellar cortex, and so on. On the sensorial side the impetus will be toward the portrayal of a topographically veridical but fundamentally abstract model of reality; on the prefrontal side the impetus will be toward generating a feedforward-anticipation of, orientation toward, and organization of cognitive processes about sensorial objects and events. The sensorial processes constitute the world; the prefrontal processes constitute the subject rising to anticipate, meet, and cope with the world-object in intentional focus within its sensorial context. Within the field produced by the tension between these impetuses is generated the moment-by-moment reentrainments, which are the momentary resolutions of that tension, and which contribute to the ontogenetic development of structures mediating experience over a lifetime.

Further, within this field of co-production consciousness arises in the uniquely human sense involving potentially profound self-awareness and reflection. The total pattern of neural entrainment arising in the moment-by-moment, polar dialogue between prefrontal and sensorial processes is the conscious network mediating consciousness. Self-awareness may be relatively naive (attention to and awareness of self-concepts, self-images, and habit patterns) or relatively enlightened (attention to and awareness of the watcher, or "pure ego"). The exact role of prefrontal cortex in self-awareness will depend upon how "pure" and conceptually-imagistically loaded are the operations of awareness.

5 PHASES OF CONSCIOUSNESS

> The word *Buddha* may be translated as "awakened." Those who merely know about things, or only think they know, live in a state of self-conditioned and culturally conditioned somnambulism. Those who understand given reality as it presents itself, moment by moment, are wide awake.
>
> —Aldous Huxley, *Tomorrow and Tomorrow and Tomorrow*

UNDERSTANDING THE RELATIONSHIP between brain and consciousness depends in part upon comprehending the patterned changes in neural structure and function through time. Given the advances in modern biology and anthropology, it is an auspicious time to address this matter, for the best approach seems to be a combination of a phylogenetic and an ontogenetic perspective. From the point of view of modern biology, ontogenesis in a sense *is* phylogenesis (see e.g., Gould 1977). That is, the evolution of the hominid brain has favored enhanced flexibility in the development of the neural structures mediating the cognized environment, and thus the range of adaptations available to individuals and the species. A major indicator of this enhancement is the degree of fragmentation evident in the operations, behaviors, and artifacts of human cognition. Cognition varies in its surface manifestations from society to society, and from member to member within the same society. Furthermore, there exists potential and actual fragmentation within individual cognition evidenced in the various modes of consciousness experienced.

We wish to show that fragmentation of consciousness is a natural result of the evolution of the human brain, and that much of what we call ritual in human society is a process that functions to synchronize potentially divergent cognition. We take the view that optimal human adaptation depends upon both the relative freedom of divergent cognition of which the brain is capable, and the ability of the collective brains of group members to be coordinated in the interests of the commonweal. In order to develop this view fully, we must look first at the emergence of the complex hominid brain over evolutionary time, with special reference to the elaboration of conscious network, and then look at some of the more dramatic forms of fragmentation of consciousness among humans today as indicators of the basic underlying principles operating in consciousness to produce both fragmentation and integration. Finally, we will examine the more common forms of fragmentation and integration found by anthropologists cross-culturally. We will be particularly interested in the role of ritual in the control of experience, and we wish to extend the theory already constructed to an explanation of transformations in consciousness.

EVOLUTION OF BRAIN AND CONSCIOUSNESS

In a sense, consciousness does not evolve. Strictly speaking, it is structure that evolves, and not function. This is not mere nit-picking for the sake of drama, but rather a distinction that, like the one between the cognized and operational environments, will carry us far in understanding the structures of experience and how they become conditioned and controlled by biological and cultural factors. The crux of the matter may be put in two ways: (1) it is not consciousness, but rather the nervous system that has evolved; and (2) it is not consciousness per se, but rather the intentional organization of consciousness that has evolved.

As always, we are trying here to avoid an insidious dualism. The distinction we are making is, again, that between consciousness and conscious network. We cannot afford any fuzziness here any more than we could before, for if we talk about consciousness evolving—which everyone seems to want to do these days—without considering the neurobiological substrate of consciousness, then why bother to merge the experiential and physiological domains? We could just as easily ignore the evidence of experience, or the evidence pertaining to the brain (depending upon our point of view) in addressing questions about evolution.

And we could thereby go very easily and seriously awry. An exclusively experiential treatment might, for example, conclude that consciousness sort of popped into existence at some point at an advanced stage in the evolution of the hominids. On the other hand, a biologically grounded treatment would, at the very least, look into the physiological mechanisms of evolution and development, and would more likely view the emergence of consciousness as a gradual process extending over many millions of years, punctuated by occasional spurts of development. The biologically grounded theorist would be required to consider the effects of such factors as the law of proper mass, Cope's law, Gause's law, selective pressures, and the paleoneurological fossil record on his view of the emergence of consciousness.

Speculations about the emergence of human consciousness ungrounded in evolutionary biology have sometimes led theorists to the questionable conclusion that *Homo sapiens* is the only really conscious organism on the planet (see e.g., Jaynes 1976). This notion, seemingly irresistible to some, appears to arise because we are the only animal whose experience we can directly access. "I am conscious, and I infer that you are conscious because you are just like me. But how about the chimpanzee? He is not at all like me, much less the bottlenose dolphin!" This kind of anthropocentric, species-specific solipsism is the bane of evolutionary biology because it sidesteps questions of mechanism and typically posits sudden, saltative "leaps" in human evolution. Such views, furthermore, play havoc with attempts to develop a unitary theory of emergent evolution of, and within, the universe. They can have the conceptual effect of segregating humanity from its inextricable ecological and evolutionary setting, to be treated separately from all other phenomena in reality. It is understandable that we are fascinated with our own being, but abstracting our being from the rest of reality in order to study ourselves is unnecessary. Such abstraction tends to create a conceptually unbridgeable gulf between our direct experience of being-in-the-world, and the received cosmology that emerges from science— an epistemological problem that Whitehead called the "fallacy of the bifurcation of nature." Moreover, that abstraction has the ultimate effect of truncating inquiry and diverting it from the great and interesting questions such as purpose in the emergence of sentience in the universe, and the possible relationships between the evolution of galaxies and the evolution of humanity (see Jantsch 1981).

EVOLUTION OF CONSCIOUSNESS

Consciousness, as we have used the term, is undoubtedly a fundamental property of all organisms with nervous systems and, properly construed, is probably fundamental to all organisms. As Bernhard Rensch notes:

> One important point is that phylogenetic evolution in the animal kingdom has been shown to be a *continuous, gradually progressing process*. Man and animals all belong to an uninterrupted branched stream of life, consisting of unbroken chains of immature and mature reproductive cells . . . leading from one generation to the next. . . . This suggests that psychical processes too have gradually grown more specialized and complex, and have developed progressively in the same way as the psychophysical substratum to whose functions they correspond. . . . [I]t seems most unlikely that at some stage in the three million years or more of phylogenetic development, a psychic element should suddenly have come into being as something fundamentally new, and subject to quite different laws from those affecting matter. This would mean postulating an entirely novel system of psychical laws for which there had been no foundation hitherto. These laws would have arisen at some time in the "eternity" during which our

solar system was undergoing its material development, which had so far been solely governed by the universal causal and logical laws. Besides, it seems difficult to imagine why conscious phenomena should appear, point-like in the universe, in the brains of living organisms alone. . . . [I]f we take an idealistic and panpsychistic view which identifies "mind" and "matter" and only recognizes causally and logically determined relationships within an "ultimate something," then the emergence and further development of psychic phenomena fit without contradiction into a biophilosophical picture of universal evolution. (1971:239–240)

We will not argue this point, for Rensch and others do it very well (see also Doty 1975:801). Besides, we have presented substantial, relevant material elsewhere (Laughlin and d'Aquili 1974; d'Aquili et al. 1979). The point to be made here is that if consideration of the presence or absence of consciousness in animals is restricted to solely experiential investigation, then there is no way to resolve the issue. Those who are intimately involved with dolphin research and who claim complex consciousness for those species can easily be charged with merely projecting their anthropocentric knowledge of their own consciousness upon the behavior of other species. However, if the present program is accepted and the consideration of consciousness in animals necessitates the combination of experiential, behavioral, and physiological evidence in an integrated fashion, then the issue becomes far clearer. If we show that consciousness is a function of the nervous system, mediated by certain structures partially mapped and understood by science, then by application of the law of homology,[1] we may reason that other species with those neural structures are conscious as well. After all, we did not have to be present 14 million years or more ago to know that *Dryopithecus* (a now extinct species of primate) climbed trees. We are able to infer that fact from the fossilized skeletal remains available—in other words, in a general way, as goes structure, so goes function. And, by the same token, we do not require introspective reports from a cat or other mammal with functioning frontal and sensorial cortexes to reason that it is capable of some degree of intentional consciousness.

This, of course, is the position taken here with respect to the evolution of human consciousness. The crucial evidence used in anthropology for grounding speculations about the evolution of hominid consciousness derives largely from paleoneurology, much of which is summarized in Laughlin and d'Aquili (1974: chaps. 2 and 3; see also Jerison 1973; Tobias 1971, Holloway 1972; Blumenberg 1983; Beals et al. 1984). These works assume that patterned changes in structure over time represent patterned changes in function. It will thus be understood that when we speak loosely of "the evolution of human consciousness," we are technically referring to the evolutionary development of the neural structures mediating consciousness as evidenced in comparative neuro-physiology and paleoneurology.

EVOLUTION OF THE BRAIN

We agree with Simon (1981) that all mammalian nervous systems seem to operate on the same, finite set of basic principles, and that this finite set of principles is recombined in a vast number of ways in adaptation to the vicissitudes of environmental press. We have already noted some of these principles: reciprocal inhibition, hierarchical structuring, relegation, entrainment, intentionality, prefrontosensorial polarity, and so on. All of these are as applicable to the brains of dolphins and rats and elephants as they are to our own. Furthermore, they are equally applicable by inference to our now extinct ancestors: humanlike animals such as *Australopithecus* (who lived as long ago as 3 million years), *Homo habilis* (as long ago as 2 million years), as well as *Homo erectus* (going back as much as 2 million years), and early *Homo sapiens* (who existed by at least a hundred thousand years ago). There is nothing fundamentally unique about our brains when compared with the fossilized remains of these earlier forms. At the same time, the hominid brain certainly has evolved, and in significant ways relative to the emergence of human consciousness.

ENCEPHALIZATION

As controversial and indeterminate as the interpretation of the hominid fossil record currently seems to be, the hominid brain has obviously become larger over time. The australopithecines had much smaller bodies than modern-day humans on the average, and had a brain size of roughly between just over 400 to about 500 cubic centimeters with an average of about 450 cc (Blumenberg 1983:590). *Homo habilis* had a brain size ranging from approximately 500 cc to 750 cc with an average of about 660 cc (Blumenberg 1983:590). *Homo erectus* had a body size intermediate between *Australopithecus* and the modern human and had a brain size that ranged between 750 cc and 1200 cc (Blumenberg 1983:590 gives an average for early *Homo erectus* of 942 cc). Humans today range in brain size between roughly 900 cc and 2100 cc (Holloway 1972), with an average of roughly 1350 cc (Beals et al. 1984).

But increase in brain size alone is very misleading. The temptation is to say we become more intelligent because our brains become bigger. However, one would expect the size of the brain to increase along with an overall increase in the size of the body, just as we would expect the size of the hands and feet to increase. A more important indicator of evolutionary progression is the change in the ratio of the brain to body weight, and indeed we find in this measure an indication of significant increase in neural development. *Australopithecus* exhibits a small, but notable, increase in brain size to body weight over that of, say, a chimpanzee, our closest living primate relative. More dramatic is the increase evident among the *Homo habilis* and *Homo erectus* forms. And, of course, modern humans exhibit the largest increase of all (see Granit 1977:52ff). Furthermore, the proportional increase in brain size is evident in the evolution of most orders of animal species (see figure 18; see also Jerison 1973; Laughlin and d'Aquili 1974; Armstrong and Falk 1982), especially among primates that seem to allocate significantly more metabolic energy to their brains relative to the rest of the body (Armstrong 1983).

Most of this dramatic increase is due to the process known as *encephalization;* that is, the tendency toward allometrically greater development of the cerebral cortex in relation to other parts of the nervous system. The cortex, a fairly new development in neural evolution, as evolutionary processes go, is the thin layer of tissue on top of the brain, which forms the undulating washboard texture to the surface of the brain. This is the part of the brain that mediates the higher cognitive functions, as well as the highest and most complex level of control over lower-order neural networks. One can easily see from drawings of the brains of *Australopithecus, Homo erectus,* and the modern human that the cortex has burgeoned outward like the cap of a mushroom. This development provides a rough indicator of the evolutionary enhancement of the higher cognitive functions of the brain, an emergence of cognitive operators that is the true hallmark of human evolution (Blumenberg 1983). The hominids have become progressively more intelligent in the way they adapt to their ever-changing environments. By intelligence we are not referring to the narrow psychological testing notion; that is, "intelligence is that which intelligence tests measure." Rather, we are referring to a gradual increment in the abilities of the cognitive operators that organize the cognized environment, factors such as serial planning of action relative to goal, the formation of ever more complex concepts and images mapped onto sensorial events, the complexity and abstraction of operations performed upon concepts and images, and complexity of communication about the cognized environment between conspecifics (see Laughlin and d'Aquili 1974; d'Aquili 1983; Piaget 1971a).

CORTICAL EVOLUTION

Evolutionary development of the cortex has been greater in some parts of the brain than in others. This differential development reflects to some extent the increased importance of the functions served by those parts in human cognition and adaptation (Granit 1977; Armstrong

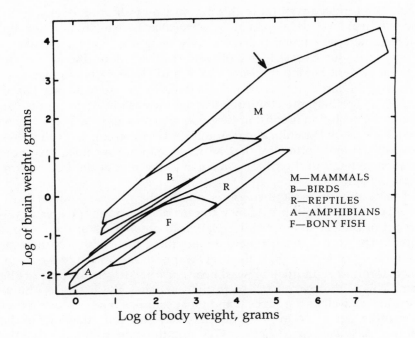

FIGURE 18. Brain/body relations in living species from five vertebrate classes. The polygons are minimum convex hulls drawn around the data of each class. For example the human datum and the dolphin *(Tursiops truncatus)* datum, together at the arrow, form one vertex of the mammalian polygon, and a large alligator provides the datum for the highest point on the reptilian polygon. Reprinted, with permission, from H. J. Jerison, "Animal intelligence as encephalization," *Philosophical Transactions of the Royal Society of London B* 308:28, 1985.

1984). One of the areas that shows increased development is the *parietal* region of both hemispheres—a part of the brain in which various sensory association areas tend to overlap (localized near the angular gyrus). This area has been shown to mediate the construction of concepts in the left lobe (Geschwind 1965; Basso et al. 1973; Friederici and Schoenle 1980; Luria 1966, 1973) and images (Ratcliff 1979; Franco and Sperry 1977; Butlers, Barton, and Brody 1970) in the right lobe. The area on the left side has been called the "inferior parietal lobule." Closely associated with the parietal region in the left lobe is the inferior frontal convolution known as *Broca's area*, which is involved in both speech production (Geschwind 1965) and constructing nested or hierarchical cognitive structures (Grossman 1980).

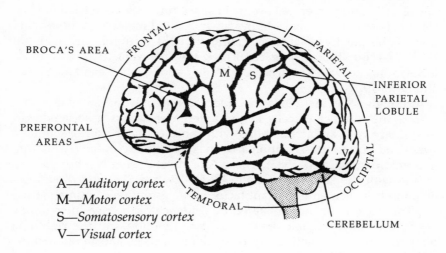

BROCA'S AREA

PREFRONTAL
AREAS

INFERIOR
PARIETAL
LOBULE

CEREBELLUM

A—*Auditory cortex*
M—*Motor cortex*
S—*Somatosensory cortex*
V—*Visual cortex*

FIGURE 19. The left cerebral cortex of the human brain divided into its various lobes. The frontal, parietal, occipital, and temporal lobes are shown, as well as four of the brain's functional areas. Part of the brainstem, spinal cord, and cerebellum are shown in dots. Reprinted, with permission, from D. A. Oakley, *Brain and Mind* (New York: Methuen and Co., 1985), xiii.

Another area of interest is the *temporal* lobe, the region of cortex involved with long-term memory storage. Of particular interest is a system involving an area near the temporal-occipital junction, which is connected to the amygdala in the limbic system, and seems specialized for the recognition of faces—a capacity apparently present and active from birth (Cohen 1979; also Cassel and Sander 1975) and noted as an important factor in the evolution of hominid social organization (Allman in Armstrong and Falk 1982).

As we indicated in the last chapter, the *frontal* lobe has shown remarkable evolutionary advance in the hominid line. It is the remarkable expansion of the frontal lobes that accounts for the prominent foreheads of humans as compared with the other primates. In addition to general prefrontal intentional processes, there is ample evidence that the sequencing of events in cognized time involves a complex interaction between networks of cells in the anterior convexity of the left frontal lobe and networks in the inferior parietal lobule (Luria 1966; Pribram and Luria 1973; Mills and Rollman 1980; Swisher and Hirsch 1971). The left anterior part of the frontal lobes seems to be intimately involved in mediating not only the sequencing of movement, but also the ordering of cognitive and perceptual events in space-time. We have tried to show elsewhere that temporal ordering of conceptual material is the foundation of the faculty of abstract causal thought (d'Aquili and Laughlin 1975). Several studies have confirmed the involvement of the frontal lobes in this activity (see articles by Walter and Livanov et al. in Pribram and Luria 1973).

Although not evident in brain endocasts and only indirectly involving cortex, the number of cells in the anterior thalamus associated with integrating core limbic functions with those of the posterior cingulate gyrus and posterior association areas has notably expanded (Armstrong in Armstrong and Falk 1982). These data are still tentative, but they are in line with the suggestion made by Holloway (1975) and others that emotion has been an important factor in the evolution of human sociality. This view is further bolstered by evidence of the rich interconnections between the limbic areas mediating emotion and the right-lobe temporal cortex mediating the recognition of faces and facial gestures (Fried et al. 1982). But more relevant to our project, these data shed light on the possible organization of neural networks, which mediate the intimate interaction between emotion, perception, and cognition.

The *occipital* lobe at the back of the brain has also expanded notably. This is the area mediating vision, our most highly developed sense. The expansion of the *cerebellum* is also significant, for networks of cells in this area are responsible for refined motor activity. This area was integral to the evolution of tool manufacture and use, as well as other behavior such as playing musical instruments and dance.

It is necessary to emphasize that the brain, like any other organ of the body, evolves and develops as a unit. Implying that one part of the nervous system evolved and another did not is not accurate. The nervous system is a totality, which is formed by its various subsystems and which develops in functional unity in the service of adaptation. So when we stress the differential development of several areas of the brain, we are saying that certain aspects of neurocognitive functioning have been dramatically important in the course of human evolution. It is precisely those aspects that provide the functional ingredients of adaptive intelligence—that is, the ability of the human brain to construct a spatiotemporal cognized environment, test it in relation to the world, assure its "fit" to data about the world, and communicate information about cognized events between conspecifics.[2]

LATERAL ASYMMETRY

We mentioned in the last chapter that there is much discussion these days about the asymmetries in the structure of the human brain, particularly about the different functions of the two cerebral hemispheres. Considerable evidence has emerged from the research of Roger Sperry and others (1979). Patients suffering from certain forms of epilepsy have had their corpus callosum and anterior commissure sectioned in order to stop interhemispheric propagation of seizures. These researches have implicated the left, or "dominant," hemisphere in mediating language production and sequential analytic thought (see Sperry et al. 1979; Nebes and Sperry 1971; Gazzaniga 1970; Bogen 1961; Levy-Agresti and Sperry 1968; and Trevarthen 1969). The right, or "nondominant," hemisphere has been implicated in the production of gestalt perceptions, imagery, and, in general, the construction of sensorial events as wholes, and wholes-within-wholes. The two hemispheres seem to be organized in such a fashion that each side specializes in one of a set of complementary functions that come into play in an alternating fashion, depending on the information being processed, and operating on the basic mechanism of reciprocal inhibition; that is, while one side is operating it is inhibiting the other side (Trevarthen 1969).

We will be particularly concerned with the alternation of conceptual (left lobe) and imaginal (right lobe) modes of knowing later on, but suffice to say here that the two hemispheres operate upon sensory data in different ways (see e.g., Bevilacqua et al. 1979). It is interesting that the cerebral hemispheres are already anatomically asymmetrical both in early fossil hominids (Holloway and de la Costa-Lareymondie 1982) and in the prenatal child (Teszner et al. 1972). In development, the right visual field (projecting to the left hemisphere) recognizes words better than the left field, whereas the left field recognizes faces better than the right field. In general, the right hemisphere predominates in the performance of visual-spatial perceptions (Leehey and Cahn 1981; Hilliard 1973; Sperry 1974; Yin 1970; Benton and Allen 1968), and in associating objects, especially faces, with emotion (Ladavas 1980; Ley and Bryden 1979; Suberi and McKeever 1977; Buchtel et al. 1978; Landes et al. 1979).[3]

HANDEDNESS

Whereas many animals, including primates, exhibit individual hand (or paw) preference when manipulating objects, only humans show a strong statistical preference for right-handedness (Annet 1970; also Laughlin and d'Aquili 1974:64). The large majority of humans prefer the use of their right hands, both for gesturing during speech and for manipulation of objects. The exact factors resulting in the selection for right-handedness (mediated by the left lobe) is a matter of speculation. Currently the most sophisticated and intriguing theory about the evolution of right-hand preference has been suggested by William Calvin (1983), who develops his idea based upon a fundamental physical asymmetry presumably present among protohominids, the asymmetry of the heart. Calvin argues that infants are known to be quieted by the sound of the human heart (see Salk 1973) and that it is easier for an infant to hear the mother's heart if she carries the baby in her left arm rather than in the right arm. And as it is known, much of the hunting of small game in hunting and gathering societies was carried out by women while moving through the bush, often carrying babies; there existed a slight but sufficient selective advantage for women who carried their babies in their left arms because the children would have been quieter. This behavior, of course, freed the right hand for carrying weapons like stones and for throwing them at the game.

Calvin's explanation has at least two advantages over other explanations. In the first place, it rests solely upon the presence of a clearly demonstrable asymmetry, and one that was undoubtedly present in the protohominid population among whom hand preference presumably distributed equally left and right. Thus one need not struggle to find some preadaptive advantage inherent in right-hand, as opposed to left-hand, manual manipulation. Whereas there is evidence of lateral asymmetries for certain neural functions for nonhuman primates and other mammals (see Denenberg et al. 1978; Dewson 1977; LeMay, Billig, and Geschwind in Armstrong and Falk 1982), no such evidence exists for handedness. In the second place, the theory is informed from an intimate knowledge of physiology, and particularly neurophysiology, unlike many of the speculations that have been put forward over the years by anthropologists.

FRAGMENTATION OF CONSCIOUSNESS

Thus far we have emphasized the gross forms of fragmentation resulting from the overall course of encephalization, including enhanced cortical processing, prefrontosensorial polarity in intentionality, and lateral asymmetries in neural functioning. Now we wish to turn our attention to the experiences of fragmentation for clues to the finer structures of experience. We want first to examine several unusual manifestations of fragmentation and then direct our attention to the cross-culturally more common forms.

DUAL CONSCIOUSNESS

Split-brain patients indicate that their two hemispheres operate much like two personalities (Gazzaniga 1970). But Bogen (1961) and Pucetti (1973) have presented evidence for the existence of a duality of consciousness even in the normal brain (see also statements by Sperry et al. 1979). The pioneering work of Wilder Penfield (1975) is of relevance here. The great Canadian neuropsychologist stumbled across the capacity for dual consciousness while making tests during the course of brain operations. His patients were awake and conscious at the time, according to standard procedure for this type of surgery. As Penfield brushed certain areas of the cortex of exposed brain with an electrode, distinctive "dreamy states" were elicited in the patient. During these episodes the patients seemed to relive past experiences while conscious of being in the operating room:

> On the first occasion, when one of these "flashbacks" was reported to me by a patient . . . I was incredulous. On each subsequent occasion, I marvelled. For example, when a mother told me she was suddenly aware, as my electrode touched the cortex, of being in her kitchen listening to the voice of her little boy who was playing outside in the yard. She was aware of the neighborhood noises, such as passing motor cars, that might mean danger to him. . . . A young man stated he was sitting at a baseball game in a small town and watching a little boy crawl under the fence to join the audience. Another was in a concert hall listening to music. "An orchestration," he explained. He could hear the different instruments. All these were unimportant events, but recalled with complete detail. (Penfield 1975:21–22)

And again, when he probed various numbered areas of right-lobe cortex, Penfield elicited the following descriptions from a young patient:

> 11—"I heard something, I do not know what it was."

> 11—". . . Yes, Sir, I think I heard a mother calling her little boy somewhere. It seemed to be something that happened years ago." When asked to explain, she said, "It was somebody in the neighborhood where I live." Then she added that she herself "was somewhere close enough to hear."

> 12—"Yes, I heard voices down along the river somewhere—a man's voice and a woman's voice calling . . . I think I saw the river."

> 15—"just a tiny flash of a feeling of familiarity and a feeling that I knew everything that was going to happen in the near future."

> 17c—"Oh! I had the same very, very familiar memory, in an office somewhere. I could see the desks. I was there and someone was calling to me, a man leaning on a desk with a pencil in his hand."

> 18a—". . . I had a little memory—a scene in a play—they were talking and I could see it—I was just seeing it in my memory." (Penfield 1975:24–27)

These flashbacks were very vivid experiences for the patients, and are quite similar to many kinds of transpersonal experiences that spontaneously occur during meditation, other spiritual exercises, and rituals. It does not take long in intensive insight meditation to learn that the apparent continuity of consciousness is a construct of cognition and is also an illusion wrought by amalgamating memory of events and anticipation of future events with sensory material presently arising in the sensorium. The stream of consciousness continues, but the flotsam of phenomenal reality appears in chunks. This experience is important, for much of the difficulty we have as scientists in comprehending dual consciousness derives partly from our adhering to the illusion that our ego is permanent and that the world of appearances forms a logically continuous stable pattern.

Although the discontinuity of ego and consciousness is, in general, readily apparent to the mature contemplative (Walsh 1977, 1978), most people are not meditators; it may require a radical shift in consciousness before the illusion of continuity comes into question. A student we know once reported sitting on the shore by a river on a fine spring day. She described herself as being at great peace with herself and with the world, concentrating on nothing in particular—just letting her mind wander. Then, suddenly, she experienced herself as swimming in the middle of the river. Just as suddenly she was back upon the bank, and the first thought that arose was, "If my dress is wet, I'm mad!" Her dress was dry as a bone. One minute she was in one place, the next in another, and both experiences were palpably real. Although the experience lasted only a few seconds, it eventually led her to a radical shift in self-view and understanding of the nature of consciousness—a typical response to transpersonal experience.

ENTRAINMENT, LATERAL ASYMMETRY, AND FRAGMENTATION

What sense can we make of this fragmentation of consciousness, and what does it tell us about the evolution and development of the brain and consciousness? First, memory is not restricted to one hemisphere; rather, memories, possibly colored by the discrete capacities of each hemisphere, are lodged on both sides of the brain. This information is derived from the memory material that is elicited from both hemispheres of split-brain patients (Sperry et al. 1979). Thus each hemisphere constructs its portions or aspects of the cognized environment, portions that are available to the alternate hemisphere in the normal intact brain.

Second, there is evidence that our dream life goes on twenty-four hours a day in cycles lasting from 90 to 120 minutes. This activity, which has been linked to the parietal area of the right lobe, continues to operate whether or not we are aware of it. Third, there are only two routes by which one cerebral hemisphere can communicate with the other hemisphere. One route is via the corpus callosum and posterial and anterior commissures, precisely those tracts that are severed in split-brain patients; the other route is via rich interconnections with the limbic system. Thus, although the commissures are severed, the right lobe can still produce a rush of emotion perceived by the left lobe, even when the left lobe does not obtain direct information about the spatio-temporal gestalt that was associated with the emotion for the right lobe.

Fourth, there exists no clear evidence of such extreme lateral asymmetries for any other mammals than humans. It is difficult to imagine in the absence of such data any way to support a preadaptation theory of lateral asymmetries. Rather, it seems more likely that laterality developed as a consequence of some process of selection such as that suggested by Calvin (1983:33ff) for proficiency in manipulating, aiming, and throwing weapons.

Putting all of these pieces together, we might suggest that much of the fragmentation of consciousness experienced by humans, both transpersonally and pathologically, is a by-product of both the evolutionary specialization of the left lobe for language and serial sequencing of movement, and the capacity of conscious network to be canalized via its essentially intentional structure to conditioned entrainments. Taken together, one obtains a picture of a brain that in the course of development specializes in a set of adaptive cognitions and activities that effectively excludes vast areas of cortical and subcortical tissues from active entrainment within conscious network. The major principle operating here is that of intentional canalization of entrainments constellated upon the (usually sensorial) object of consciousness. As we have seen, intentionality not only involves selection of networks for enhancement, but also active exclusion and inhibition of competing networks. Further, excluded networks do not vanish or lay inert like unused computer hardware, but rather remain alive and active in the course of events at a level unconscious to conscious network.

COMPLEXES

The conscious experiences of an otherwise unconsciously active neural organization tend to constellate around a central image and a set of activities, and has been called by Jung a *complex:*

> A complex is an agglomeration of associations—a sort of picture of a more or less complicated psychological nature—sometimes of traumatic character, sometimes simply of a painful and highly toned character. . . . A complex with its given tension or energy has the tendency to form a little personality of itself. It has a sort of body, a certain amount of its own physiology. It can upset the stomach. It upsets the breathing, it disturbs the heart—in short, it behaves like a partial personality. . . . Under these conditions we really are forced to speak of the tendencies of complexes to act as if they were characterized by a certain amount of will-power. . . . Where then is the ego that belongs to the will-power of the complexes?

We know our own ego-complex, which is supposed to be in full possession of the body. It is not, but let us assume that it is a centre in full possession of the body, that there is a focus which we call the ego, and that the ego has a will and can do something with its components. The ego also is an agglomeration of highly toned contents, so that in principle there is no difference between the ego-complex and any other complex. (Jung 1968a:79–80)

What Jung is revealing in his own psychodynamic terms is that several neural networks are operating in the being, more-or-less autonomously and more-or-less entrainable to conscious network. Conscious network exhibits a "normal," fairly canalized, range of entrainment within a subset of potentially available networks. Our set of cognitions (again, including percepts, concepts, images, and affects) about that "normal" range of entrainments is part of our cognized self, of our empirical ego—William James's "me." We tend to become aware of networks ("complexes") excluded from entrainment with conscious network only after a lengthy period of ego consolidation; in Jung's theory, only after the healthy psyche has reached its midlife. Our empirical ego is the way we cognize our principal adaptive structures, structures having their roots in neurognostic organizations and having undergone considerable growth and modification in development. The subset of networks whose operations we perceive and cognize as our ego is typically energetically bounded by intensive neurological inhibitions. Such boundaries assure a relatively free access of conscious network to networks within established "tried-and-true" creodes and relatively little or no access to networks outside those boundaries. The construction of an ego, in neurocognitive terms, is the development of neural networks throughout the body by way of mediation of conscious network and its essential intentional processes, processes that structurally involve the active inhibition of, and resulting relative lack of development of, alternative and competing networks. And, as Jung implies, the excluded networks drop out of sight only from the standpoint of conscious network. They are nonetheless composed of goal-seeking cells, which form networks that continue to function and develop over time to some extent, and may even exercise volition to attain their ends in ways that are unconscious to conscious network.

FRAGMENTATION AND ALTERATION OF CONSCIOUSNESS

In light of what has been said, it is now possible to venture a hypothetical explanation for the student's sudden swimming adventure described earlier. Current evidence suggests that our dream and fantasy cycle continues through the day, whether or not we are conscious of it. Moreover, Jacobs (1976) has suggested that certain types of schizophrenia may be caused by intense leakage of dreamed phenomena into waking consciousness. It is possible that the student while in her peaceful reverie at time T_1 slipped into a momentary entrainment of conscious network with right parietal structures mediating a lucid dream of swimming at time T_2, and then back to the original entrainment of "normal waking consciousness" at time T_3.

The student's experience occurred in a sequential manner, and is therefore easier for us to understand than the simultaneous dual consciousness described by Penfield's patients. When the latter type of experience occurs spontaneously, it may manifest a distinctly numinous quality, often having profound religious significance for the person having the experience. We will have more to say about this in a future chapter.

However, it may also be noted that such experiences, particularly if chronic and uncontrollable, may cause great difficulties in adaptation. Dr. Morton Schatzman, a psychiatrist, has written a book entitled *The Story of Ruth* (1980) in which he describes the case of a woman who was severely troubled by a lucid phantasm of her father that would surface during tea parties and other untoward situations. She could see him and hear him speak as if he were really there, but others could not. In the course of therapy, Ruth learned to control the coming and going of these paternal apparitions, as well as those of her therapist and others.

But Dr. Schatzman did not stop here. He went on to ask, "Was there a way of verifying her apparitional experiences?" (ibid.:366). His answer was to record the EEG patterns from Ruth's visual cortex in response to visual stimuli used in research with normal subjects. Ruth was able to alter these recordings by producing an apparition in exactly the same way as though a real person were intervening between her and the stimulus. Further tests showed that the apparition did not originate at Ruth's retinae, for readings remained unchanged when she caused an apparition to appear before her, blocking a light source. In a similar manner, apparitions could interfere with her perception of sound. It would appear that Ruth is now able to construct, probably largely within cortex, the hallucinated alterations of perception she desires (see also Slade and Bentall 1988). This ability is not unlike the demands of certain visualization practices that form the heart of Tibetan tantric yoga, about which we will take note later in the book.

Another extreme form of fragmented consciousness of relevance to us is multiple personalities, a fascinating syndrome, as much for its diagnostic history as for its actual manifestations (see Crabtree 1985; Hilgard 1977). The syndrome went out of fashion as a diagnostic category for many years, only to be rediscovered in more recent times and dumped under the unfortunate category of "borderline schizophrenia" (see

FIGURE 20. The curious case of the swimming student. The student in peaceful reverie at time T_1 lapses into a radical reentrainment with dream structures at time T_2, and then back to normal at time T_3. Drawing by Donna Gordon.

Grinker 1968). While the syndrome was out of favor, few cases were recorded in the literature (persons manifesting symptoms previously classed as "multiple personality" presumably found their way into other diagnostic niches), but when the syndrome was rediscovered, several cases subsequently appeared. Of particular interest to the layman is a book-length description of a case written by Daniel Keyes, an English professor (Keyes 1981). Keyes describes the multiple personalities (as many as twenty-four!) of a man named Billy Milligan, the first person in the United States to be acquitted of a major crime on the grounds of insanity caused by multiple personality syndrome. Two other partially fictionalized accounts of multiple personalities may be found in the books *Three Faces of Eve* (Thigpen and Checkley 1957) and *Sybil* (Schreiber 1974). Several cases are described by Hilgard (1977:17ff).

The hallmark of this psychopathology is the existence of a number of discrete personalities inhabiting a single psyche, each with its characteristic perceptions and cognitions, activities and motivations, wants and feelings. Some of the personalities may be unaware of the existence of the other personalities. Often the personalities are of different psychological ages and manifest contradictory motivations and affects. They may come into severe conflict with one another in their attempt to inhabit the same psychic "space." These personalities would appear to be the more common complexes blown, as it were, into full empirical ego status. As a consequence, the various personalities interfere with the long-range adaptation of the being. We suspect that the difficulty many scientists and others have had in accepting the existence of this syndrome and of empathizing with its consequences derives ultimately from a lack of experience of themselves as fragmented consciousnesses. That is, most people—and scientists included—do not question the reality of their cognized selves, their empirical egos. It is the rare observer who directly experiences his pure ego and cognizes himself as a multiplicity of consciousness. Yet, as we have implied, such experience is the inevitable consequence of intensive, long-term, mature contemplation, be that by any route to self-knowledge that results in personal involvement in one's own individuation in the Jungian sense.

In terms of the present theory, individuals manifesting multiple personality syndrome are those whose neurocognitive systems most likely exhibit the following characteristics:

1. The boundaries of the subset of networks entrainable to conscious network during waking consciousness are not well established—in common parlance, they have "weak egos." There is unusual "leakage" from networks outside the subset into consciousness.
2. The alternative subsets entrainable to conscious network are

numerous, each a complex, hierarchical network of living cells, and each with its own course of development, sometimes antagonistic to other subsystems. There exists little or no integration between competing subsets of networks, no superordinate conscious network whose task it is to command and supervise such an integration.

3. The alternative subsets may become entrained to conscious network sequentially, thus causing an individual to experience profound discontinuity in consciousness and exhibit a series of different personality configurations.

4. Alternative subsets may also become entrained to conscious network simultaneously, but with no integration of functions, so that the person experiences profound fragmentation of consciousness and may exhibit conflicting personality characteristics.

5. Transfer of information from one subset of networks to another may be selectively blocked. One personality may or may not be aware of the existence of others, or may be unaware of what others are experiencing.

The major point to be drawn here is that the extreme fragmentation and even antagonism between competing conscious network entrainments effectively precludes a functional integration of networks into a primary adaptive system, one that is experienced as a *primary* waking ego. Yet the principles of neural organization and function operating in development to produce such unfortunate fragmentation of consciousness are exactly the same as those operating in each and every one of us. We see those principles reflected in the culturally recognized multiple personalities among many of the world's societies. For example, Robert Mitchell notes that belief in multiple selves is ubiquitous among African traditional religions:

> Central to the African view of personality is the concept of the "multiple self," each aspect of which is believed to have an external character. In Africa the various components of the self are pictured as separate entities rather loosely held together, each having a different source and a different function. (1977:47)

Such conceptions of fragmented consciousness are hardly fortuitous. Rather, they are grounded to a certain extent in the direct experience of consciousness. In one culture experiences of fragmentation may be considered pathological, in another cosmologically appropriate, and even fortunate. Ruth hallucinates her father and is moved to seek therapy, while Alexandra David-Neel (1932:308ff) hallucinates her famous "phantoms" (Tib: *sprulpa*) on a journey to Tibet and publishes accounts of them to illustrate exceptional religious experiences. We see perhaps the same principles of consciousness at work in either case, leading to similar experiences, but accompanied by assuredly different interpretations.

Clearly, the existence of networks actively excluded from conscious network is not remarkable. Consciousness is essentially intentional, and intentionality produces exclusion. Indeed, the crux of maturation in later life, according to Jung, involves the discovery and integration of those networks that have remained unconscious but active in our beings. Rather, it is the failure of the nervous system to allow a single subset of neural networks to predominate in development that is remarkable about these cases.

EVOLUTION AND FRAGMENTATION

The picture of the human nervous system that we have been creating is one of a vast community of cells organized hierarchically into networks, specializing in various functions and developing at their own rate. The goal of much of development, as Piaget (1971a) has repeatedly emphasized, is integrating particular functions in adaptation to particular situations confronted in the world. This selective process involves the construction of one response out of alternative responses, one cognition from the range of possible cognitions, and ultimately one organization of neural structures as opposed to an alternative organization. The task of development, up to a point at least, is the construction of creodes, which are already rudimentarily present in the neurognostic structure of the pre- and perinatal nervous system.

As far as we know, the potential for both good adaptive integration and for severe fragmentation is present in all normal human brains owing to a principal adaptive advantage of encephalization in the hominid line: the enhanced capacity to entrain ever more complex and selective operating structures in response to operational environmental press. As Piaget points out, development favors both the growth and integration of biological structures while favoring selectively adaptive responses (Piaget and Inhelder 1969). The inevitable result of these bipolar demands of development is some degree of fragmentation in the service of moment-to-moment adaptation.

Fragmentation of consciousness may be considered in its serial aspect, that is, over time, resulting from entrainment and reentrainment of alternative networks to conscious network. Fragmentation may also be considered in its simultaneous aspect, that is, occurring in parallel processes, resulting from the inevitable exclusion (inhibition) of competing networks from entrainment to conscious network. In either case, the capacity for fragmentation is inherent in the evolution of hominid encephalization and may reflect a wide range of forms in keeping with the remarkable flexibility of entrainment, which is its *sine qua non*. Put in other words, the nervous system operates both as a totality and an intentional selectivity to orient some, but never all, of its faculties upon the object of consciousness.

As we have said, the prime function of the brain in adaptation is the construction of a cognized environment within which neurocognitive operations may be carried out so that the activity of the organism assures its survival and reproduction. The construction of a cognized environment is the process of developing models of objects, events, and relations from models already in place in the neurognostic structure of the nervous system (Laughlin and d'Aquili 1974:100ff). This process inevitably involves anastomosing some cells and nuclei and excluding others. Much tissue is left out of whatever organization is being established to adapt to discrete objects and events that arise in the sensorium. Yet those tissues are still present in the nervous system and continue to live and function. And some of those tissues will anastomose into organizations that may well incorporate some limbic and motor functions within their sphere of operation, while remaining unconscious to conscious network. Development of a fully integrated nervous system is also possible in principle and potentially attainable in all normal human beings, but in practice is rare. To cite such cases now would take us prematurely into a discussion of higher phases of consciousness. We must first take a closer look at the structures of experience as they manifest in the flux of the stream of consciousness. It is there that the true heritage of complexity and flexibility, as well as canalization and rigidification, of which the human brain is capable reveals itself.

PHASES AND WARPS

As we have seen, experience as it arises within the sensorium is a complex functional integration of information about the operational environment stored in models provided by various senses (see Pribram 1971, 1977). Experience is constituted and mediated by the nervous system, is a function of entrainment of conscious network, and arises afresh with each moment of consciousness. Moreover, the operations occurring within the brain may be exceedingly fragmented, both serially and simultaneously and may be explained in terms of multiple entrainments of neural networks. We wish now to turn to the more common and subtle kinds of fragmentation experienced to some extent by everyone.

Experience appears to be phasically organized; the shifting reentrainment of neural components making up the ever-changing conscious network seems to be organized into temporally recursive configurations (Tart 1975a). Episodes of experience may be as momentary as the rapid shift of sensory focus as the system scans the environment for interesting objects, or may be of relatively long duration and involving circadian and circannual "biorhythms" (see Broughton 1975).

The *awareness* of experience involves cognition about self and world. The root meaning of "awareness" is the same as "wary" and connotes careful attention to the world and detection of danger. Because the definitive characteristic of awareness is *re*collection, *re*membering, or *re*cognition of invariant and recurrent patterns in experience, awareness obviously implies a role played by knowledge in experience (Gibson 1969). Furthermore, since the recursive quality of segments of experience may be cognized as such, awareness itself is organized into different "states" of consciousness. If an experiential episode is perceived both as a unit and as salient, then the episode may be cognized as distinct from other units of experience. It may also be lexically coded, as for example: I am "awake," "stoned," "depressed," "asleep," or "out of my body." The cognized episodes of experience and their mediating neural networks are *phases*, and the points of experiential and neural transformation between phases are *warps* (Laughlin et al. 1986).

PHASE ATTRIBUTES AND BOUNDARIES

In normal human experience phases of consciousness are rarely defined by their formal properties (such as level of structural organization à la Piaget, or the full compliment of constituent cognitive functions à la the Buddhist Abhidharma), even though those formal properties may co-produce the structure and function of phases. Furthermore, phases are rarely cognized by reference to the full range of ever-shifting information present in the sensorium at any moment, but rather, they seem to be commonly recognized by a finite set of recurrent attributes selected from the far greater range of available attributes. For example, in Pukapuka (Beaglehole and Beaglehole 1938:307), the dream phase is conceived as the time during which the soul may move about in the world independently of the body.

Phase attributes may be bodily sensations ("I am hungry"), feelings ("I am in love"), various kinds of sensory cues ("I am listening to music") or actions ("I am running"), or they may involve characteristic relations between perceived objects ("I dreamed I was swimming at the bottom of the ocean"). Recognizable functional organizations or operations in cognition may also be used to define phases; for instance, my thoughts are "discursive," "scattered," "profound," "lucid," or "clever."

The important point is that in any society a finite set of possible phases of consciousness is declared normal. Members of that society are socialized to recognize the appropriate attributes of these phases and to consider them definitive of their own and of other's mindstates (see Bourguignon 1973; Tart 1975b). This recognition operates to set boundaries on phases of consciousness typically experienced in a culture by establishing a conditioned, internalized control of attention (see Burridge 1979). Because many of the structural features composing conscious network are causally entrained by intentionality, the recognition of phase attributes (to the exclusion of, or habituation to, other possible attributes) effects powerful control over other unconscious, but experientially efficacious, formal properties. As we will see, ritual is used in many societies to manipulate perception of phase attributes, thereby transforming the operating structures mediating phases of consciousness. Such manipulation makes new experiences possible.

In addition to being recursively organized, phases are commonly embedded one within another. Embedded phases may form a hierarchy of episodes resembling the "plan" structure modeled by Miller and colleagues (1960), the "differentials" of the calculus, the simple components of artificial complexity (Simon 1981), or to some extent at least the n-dimensional aspect of "phase-space" (Laughlin and Stephens 1980:339ff; Count 1976). Thus, we can speak of embedded phases: one can experience "excitement" while "skiing," "today." The experience of "excitement" is embedded within the phase "skiing," which is in turn embedded in the phase "today."

EMPHASIS UPON WARPS

We wish to pay special attention to the warps between experiential phases. This emphasis is useful, for as a phase is a discrete, cognized strip of unfolding experience dominating (for however long) the sensorium, a warp has a productive influence both on the organization of the phase succeeding it and on the cessation of the phase preceding it. A warp is what Turner (1974:237) calls a *liminal* event; an event that stands between two cognized strips of experience, much as a doorway stands between two rooms (see also Gennep 1960). For example, if one is "happy" one moment and "sad" the next, then somewhere between these two phases of consciousness is a warp, involving the cessation of the "happy" phase and producing the "sad" phase. The liminal aspect of the warp metaphorically implies a threshold through which the stream of consciousness must pass when it "leaves" one phase behind and "enters" another phase.

THE NATURE OF WARPS

Four aspects of warps need to be examined before considering the question of how warps are controlled by society. First, warps are often momentary to the point of evanescence, despite their productive importance for the organization of phases. In fact, so swiftly do they pass, that they are usually unconscious to the perceiver. We are typically aware only of a sequence of phases and not of the warps intervening between phases. To understand how rapid and unconscious are warps, and at the same time to recognize their causal prominence over phases of consciousness, is to comprehend the sense of helplessness many people feel when learning to control their phases of consciousness.

Second, a warp is the intersection of two relatively durable neural configurations mediating two cognitively salient episodes of experience. Warps are, in fact, excellent examples of the points of transformation between systemic states modeled in catastrophe theory, which is an approach to understanding how systems change (see Thom 1975). Warps have both structural and functional aspects just as do phases. However, the functional aspect of a warp is typically *not* cognitively salient, and hence is not consciously experienced.

Third, warps also exhibit embedding. Thus, expanding on the example given above, when one feels "excited" and then feels "tired" while "skiing," we may conclude there is a warp embedded within the phase "skiing" and producing the transformation between "excited" and "tired."

Fourth, a transformation of the operating neural structures composing a warp may be induced by internal or external factors, which include various chemicals, events in external reality, events triggered by the biological clock, metabolic changes, and so on. Although an individual may be aware of the stimulus inducing a warp, its effects upon consciousness may be missed because of lack of awareness of the intermediate warp. In general, the closer in time the trigger, the more likely is a person aware of its causal association with a phase of consciousness. A marihuana smoker obviously is aware of the causal relationship between "toking" and "getting high," but a person suffering from allergic reaction may not be aware that chemicals emitted from the new building through which they walked an hour before produced the irritation they now feel. In the latter case, the person is aware of the stimulus ("walking through the building") and the response ("depression" or "irritation") but is unaware of the warp between.

CONTROL OF PHASES THROUGH AWARENESS
AND EXPANSION OF WARPS

In order for individuals and groups to control phases of consciousness, control must be exercised over the factors inducing warps. In other words, control must be exercised over the structural aspects of experience *about which the experiencer is normally least aware*. The simplest and most direct means of controlling a phase of consciousness is by directing the attention of the experiencer to the warp preceding it. Directing and enhancing awareness of a warp by a perceiver results in the warp "opening up" to conscious inquiry (see Goleman 1977 on insight meditation). If that inquiry is continued, the warp will itself be transformed into a cognized phase. Becoming aware of a warp involves minimally discovering and learning a set of phase attributes, which then become markers recognizable in recurrent experience. Returning once again to our skiing example, exercise of awareness at the warp between "excited" and "tired" might result in discovering various bodily cues that signal depletion of energy and fatigue, a set of sensations that may become cognized as "low blood sugar." If this expanded awareness takes place, the skier experiences *three* phases (and two warps), "excited," "low blood sugar," and "tired," instead of two phases (and one warp). The advantage for the skier is that at the onset of the "low blood sugar" phase, he can take some nutriment and eliminate or reduce the "tiredness" phase by discovering and expanding the preceding warp into a conscious phase.

The psychology of sleep and dreaming offers a less trivial example of warp control. The warp between the waking phase and the dream phase of consciousness has been termed the *hypnagogic* by Maury (1848), and the warp between the dream phase and the waking phase the *hypnopompic* by Myers (1904). There is evidence that mediation of these warps is carried out by neural systems over a wide expanse of the nervous system (see Mavromatis 1987), and involves, among other areas, the serotonergic system in the brain stem (Jacobs 1976). These warps are extremely brief and few people in Western culture are aware of them. Indeed, only a minority of Westerners are aware of very much of their dream life. People can of course learn to recall their dreams (Reed 1973, 1976), and they commonly do so by ritually transforming the hypnagogic and hypnopompic warps so that they no longer remain barriers to recall. Dream "incubation" and ritualization of warps is a common theme in cultures that consider incorporating knowledge and "power" derived from dream experience important to life (see Lincoln 1935; O'Nell 1976; Grunebaum and Caillois 1966). Tibetan yogis work with their dream experiences as a meditation and learn to control events in the dream cycle by first increasing awareness of the two warps and transforming their awareness into a form that can be transferred over the warp and into dreaming (see Chang 1963:88ff; Evans-Wentz 1958).

Warp expansion and control is also found in the techniques of modern cognitive therapy (see Beck 1967; Burns 1980). It is recognized that between a perceived stimulus event and a resulting mood there lies a warp called an "automatic thought" (Burns 1980). The automatic thought is triggered by the stimulus and in turn produces a shift in mood, which occurs rapidly and is usually unconscious to the perceiver. Cognitive therapists use various techniques to bring the awareness of clients to bear on the warp and to discover and evaluate rationally automatic thoughts that have typically been learned and repressed early in childhood (Burns 1980). Via the process of discovery, expansion into awareness, and evaluation, the now cognized automatic thought is transformed into a phase of consciousness, and the client thereafter gains a greater measure of control over mood-states.

RITUAL AND THE TRANSFORMATION OF EXPERIENCE

Anthropology has long recognized the importance of ritual as a marker and mediator of social and psychological change (e.g., Turner 1979, 1974; Gennep 1960; Firth 1967; Goffman 1967; Wallace 1966; Eliade 1964; Lewis 1971). Eliade (1964), for example, has noted the role of ritual in structuring the experiences of an initiate shaman. By learning ritualized control of the warp between the normal phase of consciousness and the "transindividual" phase (as Ring 1974 calls it), the young shaman gradually learns to integrate alternate phases into a single personality. Likewise, by practicing various rituals, tantric adepts learn to transform their ego-centered consciousness into phases of consciousness symbolized by various deities (Walker 1982:17).

The connection between ritual and the control and transformation of consciousness has been central to the biogenetic structural program as well (see d'Aquili and Laughlin 1975; d'Aquili et al. 1979; Laughlin and Stephens 1980:337; Laughlin and McManus 1982:53; Laughlin et al. 1981:226; Rubinstein et al. 1984: chap. 5). We have demonstrated that ritual evolved as a concomitant to encephalization as the principal mechanism by which the collective cognized environment of the group is synchronized for concerted social action (see d'Aquili et al. 1979; also Chapple 1970). But at that stage in the development of biogenetic structural theory, we had yet to integrate the experiential domain and were concerned principally with cognition and adaptive social behavior. We now wish to examine some of the principles that may account for the efficacy of ritual in controlling experience.

ORIENTATION AND ENHANCEMENT OF AWARENESS

Ritual is well known to direct the attention of participants to objects and events of cultural significance. This direction amounts to social manipulation of intentionality. Participants in ritual commonly come to see aspects of their society, cosmology, environment, conditions, even themselves in a new light (see Wallace 1966). The therapeutic effects of enhanced awareness, apart from any ritual manipulation of awareness, is a cornerstone of many forms of modern psychotherapy. An excellent example is to be found in Hans Selye's discussion of factors leading one to transform a "distressed" (negative, life-destroying) lifestyle into a "eustressed" (positive, growth-oriented) lifestyle (1978:74ff).

Awareness is essentially remembering; it is "seeing" and recognizing what one is "seeing." Certainly all ceremonial ritual operates in part by manipulating awareness of symbols. We will discuss symbolism *per se* in the next chapter, but it must be noted that discrete neural networks and models mediate the perception of symbols, and by controlling awareness of certain symbols, a group may easily control the neural systems brought into play. The society may not merely direct attention, it may *determine* to a great extent what is experienced. Directing one's orientation to objects associated with awe and fear (such as some of the characters like Witch and Mudhead in Hopi *katchina* ceremonies), will result in an experience different from one in which attention is directed to objects associated with love and nurturance (such as a Buddhist "longlife" ceremony).

RETUNING THE AUTONOMIC NERVOUS SYSTEM

Events arising in the sensorium are influenced greatly by the activity of the *autonomic nervous system* (ANS). The ANS is divided into two complementary subsystems: the *sympathetic system* and the *parasympathetic system* (see Gellhorn and Loofbourrow 1963; Gellhorn 1967; Gellhorn and Kiely 1972; Lex 1979; Laughlin 1983). The former energizes adaptive ("fight-flight") responses to conditions arising in the cognized environment (within the sensorium) and is experienced as bodily arousal or stress (either positive "eustress," or negative "distress," à la Selye 1978). The latter energizes vegetation, repair, growth, and development and is experienced as relative bodily relaxation, calm, and tranquillity (see especially Benson et al. 1974).

These two sources of sensorial energy operate complementarily and exhibit a characteristic balance with regard to specific events in the world. The particular balance of excitation-relaxation activity of the ANS with respect to environmental conditions can be learned (Thomas 1968; Hofer 1974). This learning is called *tuning* (Gellhorn 1967:110ff). Some evidence indicates that the general level of balance (i.e., basal level and range of flexibility of response) is established in pre- and perinatal life (Grof 1976; Verny 1982). Many of the common attributes of ritual (e.g., chanting, dancing, ingesting psychotropic drugs, fasting, and other forms of privation) may be understood as *driving mechanisms* for retuning the ANS activity in participants (Lex 1979).

Retuning the balance of ANS functions may operate as a warp leading to alternate phases of consciousness. A significant, progressive retuning in favor of an enhanced relaxation response, as is common in formal meditation practice, may lead to transformations of experience within the sensorium. Such changes will be away from the clearly defined conceptual and perceptual distinctions among "objects" in the sensory field, and between "perceiver" as subject and "perceived" as object. There also may occur the experience of *flow* (see page 299).

Simultaneous discharge of *both* the excitation and relaxation systems may lead to profound alterations in consciousness (Gellhorn and Kiely 1972), and even to a reorganization of personality (see page 135). The most common phase resulting from simultaneous discharge of both systems is the orgasm. Because it facilitates rapid cognitive reassignment of affect to object, this mechanism may also be central to the notable success of shamanic healing techniques cross-culturally. The range of driving mechanisms that may result in simultaneous discharge is wide and includes drumming, chanting, dancing, and other rhythmic stimuli, as well as various privations, ordeals, harassments, social isolation, sensory deprivation, and drugs (see Jilek 1982).

TYPES OF TRANSFORMATION

Because a transformation in consciousness implies a change in the organization of the conscious network mediating consciousness, three types of transformation characteristic of warps may be distinguished, each defined by the level of transformation occurring in structures (see McManus 1979; Laughlin et al. 1981:225). A *developmental transformation* refers either to an ontogenetic or a momentary adaptive shift in the complexity of cognition (Piaget 1952; Harvey et al. 1961). There is evidence that an increase in organizational complexity of operating structures is associated with an enhanced information-processing capacity and adaptability of cognition (see Schroder et al. 1967). Research findings also suggest a direct causal connection between complexity of cognition and complexity of perception (Piaget 1971b, 1973). Thus both knowledge and perception may be effected by a change in the complexity of operating structures. A range of organizational structures with respect to complexity of entrainment may produce either an increment or a regression in the complexity of events arising in the sensorium. This view is consonant with those of Western phenomenology (e.g., Merleau-Ponty 1962) and Eastern Buddhist psychology (e.g., Nananda 1976): perception and cognition are conceived to be inextricably and causally interconnected with respect to moment-by-moment functioning and to ontogenesis. By application of this view, the *actual* entrainment of structures need not be as complex as it *potentially* could be. Thus, a shift in the complexity of entrainment of operating neural structures may result in a warp in consciousness.

Within any given level of cognitive complexity, a vast range of surface structures exist that may become entrained to conscious network. These surface structures mediate the content of cognition. Changes in surface structure, although leaving the underlying developmental pattern unchanged, may still result in a *surface transformation* in consciousness.

Developmental and surface transformations influence both perception and behavior in a determinant way. A shift in the sensory qualities of perception or in the organization of behavior (both perception and behavior are seen as equivalent "operations" in Piagetian psychology; see Piaget 1977) may result in a *sensory transformation* in consciousness. It should be emphasized that the three types of transformation (developmental, surface, and sensory) amount to warps only if they result in an alteration of phase. That is, a shift in entrainment at whatever level will constitute a warp only if the individual perceiver cognizes a change in experience (see Rubinstein et al. 1984: chap. 5 and d'Aquili et al. 1979: chaps. 7 and 9). Significantly, the phase attributes by which the perceiver defines a phase of consciousness *are* a form of knowledge and are determined by all levels of structure mediating them. This is true whether the perceiver is actually aware of such structures. In most cases, the perceiver is unaware of the levels of structure underlying their cognized experience, but when an individual does become aware of them, such knowledge may then become a phase attribute, although still mixed with content (e.g., "I am under stress and my thoughts have become scattered").

STAGES OF TRANSFORMATION

Because conscious network is a living system, it is in an active state of equilibration most of the time (Bertallanffy 1968; Piaget 1971a; Waddington 1957; Miller 1978). Equilibration is maintained by active compensation for actual or anticipated intrusions from the operational environment. Thus, the flow of experience arising within the sensorium usually manifests a continuity, especially within the boundaries of any particular phase of consciousness. Yet experience is in flux, mediated by activity within conscious network. When a reentrainment of conscious network occurs sufficient to constitute a warp, it exhibits three stages of transformation. Most such retrainments are usually unconscious to the individual and first entails *discrimination* among all of the intrusive information about the world in an effort to assimilate that information to the presently entrained network. There follows a stage of relatively *differentiated* structures in which activity is oriented toward accommodation of operating neural structures to new intrusive information about the world entering the sensorium. Finally, there occurs a *functional reintegration* of neural structures into a different and again relatively equilibrated, reentrained conscious network. This three-stage view of transformation—discrimination, differentiation, and reintegration—is consonant with the views of Piaget (1971a:216) on cognitive coordinations and of Charles Tart (1975a) on the transition from one state of consciousness to another. It is also somewhat relevant to Chapple and Coon's (1942) description of transformations occurring in ceremonial ritual and Turner's (1974:38ff) stages of social drama.

These three stages are involved in all warps of consciousness and may be further elaborated into the following five steps:

1. Interruption of the ongoing functioning of conscious networks, or intrusion into the operating neural structures mediating experience
2. A comparison process between the intrusive information and the information contained within the operating structures
3. Alternations of attention, affect, or behavior indicating an attempt to reconcile discrepancy
4. Resolution of discrepancy leading to a developmental, surface, or sensory transformation
5. A consolidation or incorporation of new or modified networks into the overall operating conscious network

The interruption of the functioning of conscious network signals the beginning of the end of the preceding phenomenological phase, and the consolidation of the new entrainment signals the beginning of the succeeding phase (see McManus 1979:194ff for further discussion of this model).

We wish to emphasize again that few individuals are aware of this five-step process of transformation, but are only aware of a shift in phase attributes—attributes that are themselves functions of the operating structures mediating the perceptual, affective, imaginal, and conceptual aspects of experience. And yet an extreme decrease in the complexity of structure can pose a severe handicap to an individual and a danger to the group, for it might prohibit the processing of information at an optimal level of conceptual complexity relative to the adaptive needs of the individual or group. For this reason, many ceremonial rituals operate to stabilize and synchronize the operating level of complexity of information processing among participants (see d'Aquili et al. 1979: chap. 7 for further discussion).

SHAMANIC PRINCIPLE

From the transpersonal perspective, the many discussions of shamanism (like those which focus on social status, initiation rites, healing techniques, cosmological sources of power, historical change, and cross-cultural influences upon traits), frequently overlook a fundamental experiential and structural principle: there is an almost universal drive among humans to seek and explore alternate phases of consciousness (Bourguignon 1973), and those who become adept at attaining valued phases of consciousness are expected to help others attain such experiences (Halifax 1979, 1982; Eliade 1964; Lewis 1971; see also John-Steiner 1985:37ff for a related discussion). The master, as one sage put it, is someone who started out on the path before the student did. The healing shaman is quite often the person who was, himself, successfully healed (e.g., Wallace 1969; Jilek 1982). "The shaman and the yogi, the sorceress and the priestess, all derive their strength from an initiatory death and rebirth experience they must each undergo before they can truly be themselves. It is this transfigurative experience that endows them with their unique vision. In traditional societies this experience was highly valued, and the right to undergo it was safeguarded religiously" (Arguelles 1975:288). A primary means for safeguarding this valued experience is by shamanic control of the ritualized conditions used to induce the experience it initiates.

The shamanic principle may be further understood structurally as an intersection of two subsidiary principles. First, inherent in biological systems is a drive toward wholeness (*health, heal, holy,* and *whole*—all having essentially the same root meaning; see Bohm 1980, Piaget 1971a). This *holistic imperative* toward growth in the neural structures mediating consciousness may be reflected in experience as levels of successively more integrated consciousness (Maslow 1968) and will progress as an alternation between differentiation and reorganization of neural structures in ontogeny (Piaget 1971a, 1977; Jung 1971). The universal drive to explore alternative phases of consciousness may thus be interpreted as an experiential manifestation of the structural drive toward differentiation and reintegration of the neural systems mediating consciousness.

Second, an individual whose consciousness is strongly activated by the holistic imperative will frequently recognize a state of advanced development in, or positively project one upon, another individual (Freud 1950). This *shamanic projection* is represented in Western culture by the phenomenon of "transference" between patient and doctor (see Jung 1966). Shamanic projection is also exemplified by the *guru-chela* relationship in Eastern mystical tradition. This mechanism involves the (usually unconscious) "transference" of control over one's intentional processes to the master.

CROSS-PHASE TRANSFERENCE

The induction and control of alternate phases of consciousness depends ultimately upon the transfer of information across warps between phases. We call this *cross-phasing*. Cross-phasing may be facilitated or inhibited by ritual, as well as other factors, and has a determinant effect upon the extent of fragmentation manifested in the consciousness of the individual or of members of a group. We will reexamine some aspects of warp control in relation to the process of cross-phase transference of information.

CROSS-PHASING AS REENTRAINMENT

For cognitive material, or information, to be transferred from one phase to another it must "move" across a warp. We must exercise extreme caution now, for heretofore we have used the term "information" quite loosely as though something were actually transferred from one side of a barrier to another. Actually, nothing moves from one side of a warp to the other (see Varela 1979). The "movement" we speak of loosely is actually a change of state or organization of the system mediating experience. As Hui Neng, the legendary Sixth Patriarch of China, is reported to have said, "It's the mind that moves, not the flag or the wind." In order for apparent "movement" of material to occur across a warp, there must occur a *minimal reentrainment* with conscious network in the succeeding phase of the neural structures mediating that material in the preceding phase. The material literally must be "re-membered" ("re-collected," "re-called"); it is reconstituted in the succeeding phase. Re-membering, or "bringing back together," is the definitive characteristic of awareness. Indeed, awareness *is* a type of re-membering.

During the warp the most rapid, abrupt, and causally efficacious reentrainment of neural networks mediating consciousness occurs. If there is a minimal reentrainment, there will be an experience of continuity of consciousness within the sensorium. If not, the perceiver will experience a discontinuity in consciousness. "Becoming aware of" the warp often implies an intentional enforcement by prefrontal processes of minimal reentrainment throughout the warp so that reentrainment occurs in the succeeding phase.

We have already given an example of discontinuous, dual consciousness with the episode of the swimming student. The shift in consciousness was radical and abrupt with little integration until later reflection upon the experience. However, reentrainment may occur smoothly so that little or no discontinuity is experienced. Take for example the case of the Papago woman who, tired of working her field, lay down on the ground to rest:

> In front of me was a hole in the earth made by the rains, and there hung a gray spider, going up and down, up and down, on its long thread. I

began to go to sleep and I said to it: "Won't you fall?" Then the spider sang to me:

> Gray spider
> Magic making
> At the cave entrance hanging
> Do not think I shall fall
> Twice I go up and down
> And I return again
> Therefore I am hanging, hanging here.
> (Underhill 1936:42)

The transformation from "awake" to "asleep" (the hypnagogic warp) occurs so smoothly that it warrants only vague mention: "I began to go to sleep." Furthermore, recall upon awaking is rich and complete. Rather than being exceptional, this smoothness of continuity across the waking-sleeping warp is characteristic of those who routinely are aware in their dream life. Individuals raised in Euro-American culture tend to be poor dream recallers, but the anthropological literature is replete with cross-cultural evidence of people's experiencing well-integrated dream lives (see O'Nell 1976).

CROSS-PHASING AND INTEGRATION OF PHASES

Minimal reentrainment across warps is all that is required for integration of phases into some semblance, however segmented, of a cognizable continuity. The ethnographic literature reveals many examples of successfully integrating experiences arising in waking, trance, and dream life with little discontinuity (Tart 1975b, Bourguignon 1973, Eliade 1964). The role of the shaman in the integration of experiences derived from various phases of consciousness is also quite apparent from the ethnographic literature: an initiate is told in symbolic terms what will be experienced; he is placed in circumstances conducive to generating a transpersonal experience, and after an experience arises, he is then told in symbolic terms what was experienced. Experiences that emerge are often interpreted in a manner consonant with the normative view of self and cosmos (see O'Nell 1976 on dream interpretation in various cultures). The transformations of consciousness resulting in transpersonal experiences will usually involve the five-step process of transformation outlined earlier. During this process (at the fifth, or consolidation, step) the memory of a transpersonal experience, associated as it is with the highly controlled initiation procedure, is in turn integrated by interpretation into the individual's cosmological worldview (see Ricoeur 1962). For example, in the Sun Dance ceremony the Buffalo (or Eagle, etc.), initially a symbol used only by the shamans to express aspects of the cosmological order, may come alive, become very real and a source of ecstatic power for the initiate and his society (Jorgensen 1972:213ff).

CROSS-PHASING AND RITUAL DRAMA

Ritual drama may produce experience by means of the cross-phase transference of information. In order for the drama enacted in the waking phase to "come alive" in dream or trance, the focus of consciousness will tend to remain upon, or return to, some central aspect of the information crossing the warp. In Tibetan dream yoga, for example, a yogi is taught to transform himself into an imaginal energy form (*yidam*), which incorporates his consciousness and in which he remains conscious across the hypnagogic warp, throughout the dream phase(s), and returns through the hypnopompic warp where he transforms himself back into his worldly form (Evans-Wentz 1958:215ff). The yogi is taught this and other methods in the context of the ritual drama noted earlier, or possibly in a dramatic dance ceremony (*cham*). We are speaking here of the simplest and most direct application of intentional processes to cross-phase transference: awareness fixed (perhaps hyperintentionally) on a single object, which continues to be minimally reentrained throughout the sequence of transformations that constitute the warp. Because the object remains relatively constant, many of the noematic and noetic (perceptual and cognitive) networks initially constellated upon the object also remain constant.

CROSS-PHASING AND ANS TUNING

Too great a discrepancy in the autonomic tuning characteristic of the prewarp and postwarp phases tends to inhibit cross-phase transference. It is far easier, for instance, to maintain awareness entering the dream phase if the hypnagogic warp is entered while in *samadhi*, a phase of consciousness marked by profound bodily relaxation, not unlike that of sleep (see Kasamatsu and Hirai in Ornstein 1973). Each phase of consciousness bears a characteristic autonomic balance. The hyperexcitation of the Sun Dance (Jorgensen 1972), the Balinese Kris Dance,[4] or a West African spirit ceremony (see Rouch 1960) will lead to experiences phenomenologically different from those induced by the hyperrelaxation of the Zen adept (Naranjo and Ornstein 1971). The ANS balance requisite to a phase of consciousness may be driven by rhythmic photic, sonic, or somaesthetic stimuli. These drivers may be augmented by enhanced concentration either upon the driver or upon some associated "symbolic" percept. Also, psychotropic drugs, both ancient and modern, can act to retune the ANS in favor of a desired phase of consciousness (e.g., the natural tranquilizer *rauwolfia* used in India and the "uppers" and "downers" used in modern society).

It is quite common in religious ritual for drivers to be paired with symbols. The pairing of driver and symbol is an efficacious means of cross-phasing information from a phase mediated by one ANS tuning to another. As noted earlier, in some schools of Buddhism visualization of a deity is paired with chanting, resulting (if successful) in the "coming alive" of the deity, once requisite relaxation and "centeredness" has been achieved (Laughlin et al. 1986).

CROSS-PHASING AND TYPES OF TRANSFORMATION

A radical change in the complexity of organization (of the "logic") of phases across a warp may have the effect of dramatically altering the perceptual array and its "meaning." A warp that involves merely a shift in sensory information within the same developmental structure may not be sufficient for a radical shift in intentionality. It is important to note that the relationship between developmental complexity and experience holds not only for waking consciousness, but also for dream and other alternative phases of consciousness. For example, David Foulkes (1982) has shown that developmental structure is involved in dream experience among children.

The greater the disparity in the organization of neural structures mediating two phases separated by a warp, the more difficult will be the problem of cross-phasing information. And the greater the disparity between these structures, the harder it will be to recollect experience from the preceding phase in the succeeding phase. This disparity of structure accounts for the experience that some material can be recalled only in a specific phase of consciousness (Tart 1975a calls this "state-specific memory").

Effective cross-phase transference may be accomplished by at least two methods: (1) by gradual transformation of structures prior to the appropriate warp so that shift in cognitive organization from preceding to succeeding phases is minimized; and (2) by maintaining concentration of awareness upon the material across the warp, despite the degree of disparity in organization of operating structures. These and other methods may be combined, of course, and, in fact, often are in ritual. This importance of ritual does not mean that those adept at attaining a phase of consciousness need remain dependent upon the ritual to perform such transformations. In some traditions, for example, in Tibetan Buddhist meditation, the objective is to internalize the procedures introduced in initiation rituals so that the phase of consciousness dramatized in the ceremony can be realized in individual practice.

BLOCKING CROSS-PHASE TRANSFERENCE

Cross-phasing may be blocked. Any factor that operates to reduce reentrainment below the minimum requisite for cross-phase transference of material can be considered a *blocking factor*. Blocking factors can originate in the individual, the environment, or both. As we have seen, human consciousness is typically fragmented, and may be mediated by mutually antagonistic networks, or "complexes." If the shift in consciousness is from one such configuration to another, as between a waking "ego" and a dream "ego," then the organization of networks on either side of the warp may not be too discrepant for cross-phasing; the one network may actively inhibit the other. We might say that the network mediating the alternative phase of consciousness was "unconscious" from the standpoint of the waking "ego." The active inhibition of one "complex" by another would then constitute a blocking factor.

North Americans are generally enculturated to disattend their dream life, even to cognize dream life as being associated with "evil," "death," and "madness," hence something to fear. Small wonder that few North Americans can approach integrating dream and waking experiences, a process considered routine among many of the planet's peoples. The ethnographic literature amply demonstrates that people in most societies operate psychologically within the context of a cosmos composed of multiple realities (see Schutz 1945). And these realities are frequently coded as experiential. Such people experience *polyphasic consciousness*, and consequently their cognized view of self constitutes a polyphasic integration.

The experience of North Americans, on the other hand, typically tends toward *monophasic consciousness*; namely, ego-identification with experience derived from a single range of phases that excludes other alternative phases (see Laughlin et al. 1985). For North American culture, the only "real world" experienced is that unfolding in the sensorium during the "normal" waking phase (which includes many subsidiary phases like "high," "sleepy," "drunk," and the like), and is thus the only phase appropriate to the accrual of information about self and world. About the only time our attention is directed to alternate phases is either in drug-induced experiences sought as entertainment, or when required in therapy, thus reinforcing the association of alternate phases with pathology (i.e., "My shrink has me writing down my dreams!"). The failure of modern Western culture to prepare individuals for an easy, fearless exploration of alternate phases of consciousness has the unfortunate consequence for science of not equipping most ethnographers with the experiential and conceptual material requisite for sophisticated research into the religious practices of other cultures (see Evans-Pritchard 1965:17, 87). The tendency to associate alternative phases with pathology all too frequently seeps into anthropological theory where "trance," "possession," "ecstasies," and "visions" have been explained by some authorities in terms of the Western medical model (e.g., see

Devereux 1956 on the shaman as a "half-healed man," but cf. Lewis 1971:178ff). Furst (1972:vii) makes the point that even if all psychotropic drugs were suddenly declared legal and perfectly safe, our Western industrial culture would still not accept them or their attendant experiences, for to do so would counter the underlying assumptions about consciousness requisite to a materialist worldview.

Blocked transference, with a resulting discontinuity of experience, may also be a consequence of ritual. This transference seems to be the case among various so-called possession cults in which individuals enter trance as a result of ritualized drivers and manifest "possession" by spirits (see Rouch 1960, as well as the excellent film *Les Maîtres Fous*; also see Deren 1953; Bourguignon 1976). Although one must be cautious of cultural fictions, it is not uncommon for persons thus possessed not to remember the experience later on.

Blocking factors can take many forms and may be any variable contributing to a decrement in minimal reentrainment. They may in fact be the converse mechanisms to those already discussed. Conditions might prevail that block awareness of information so that the neural structures mediating awareness are never entrained to those mediating relevant cognitive material. This obstruction does not necessarily mean the transference of information has not taken place; but if it has, the transference is at a subconscious level. A particularly powerful blocking factor is a rapid and extreme retuning of ANS activity. Again, the easiest example is the transformation that occurs between "awake" and "asleep." Because the hypnagogic warp commonly occurs within a few seconds, and the alteration in ANS tuning involved is profound, awareness in most North Americans is insufficient to maintain cross-phase transference.

Another blocking factor may be a severe discrepancy in developmental transformation across the warp. Such a transformation will involve massive reentrainment of neural structures mediating experience, and will be occurring in a relatively short period of time. Again, unless the structures mediating awareness of symbolic material remain sufficiently entrained during the warp, recall may well be blocked in the next phase.

Ingestion of psychotropic drugs can, of course, cause a massive reentrainment resulting in a transference block. Those drugs that trigger neural networks involving discrete neural transmitter substances may well result in blockage, as may drugs causing a rapid alteration in ANS tuning. The key element in all forms of blocked transference is loss of awareness. By implication, any activity that increases awareness of the warp will also increase the likelihood of minimal reentrainment in the succeeding phase, and thus counteract the effect of blocking factors.

PART TWO

CONSCIOUSNESS AND THE SYMBOLIC PROCESS

6 THE SYMBOLIC PROCESS

> In a state of radical ego-centrism there is complete lack of differentiation between the ego and the external world, and consequently a state of non-consciousness of the ego, or projection of internal impressions into the forms provided by the external world, which is the same thing. The origin of the unconscious symbol is to be found in the suppression of consciousness of the ego by complete absorption in, and identification with, the external world, and it therefore constitutes merely a limited case of assimilation of reality to the ego, i.e., of ludic symbolism.
> —Jean Piaget, *Play, Dreams and Imitation in Childhood*

WE HAVE PURPOSELY FORESTALLED our discussion of the nature and functions of symbolism until we had sufficiently developed the phenomenological and neurological aspects of our theory in order to delimit clearly many of the basic principles operating in the symbolic process. Because the symbolic process is central to our project, it will now be a relatively straightforward matter to show how the symbolic process works, how it has evolved in the course of hominid phylogenesis, and how it functions in the ontogenesis of the cognized environment. Furthermore, we are now prepared to confront some of the seemingly intractable problems that have plagued semiotic studies from their inception; for example, the locus of intentionality, the relationship between symbol and action, the archetypal origins of symbols, the relationship between ego-awareness and unconscious symbolism, the relationship between iconic (symbolic) and noniconic (signal) intentionality, and the understanding of cultures as symbolic systems. While we will be touching on those issues, our main concern will continue to be the central role of the symbolic process in neural organization and experience. For it is in explaining the symbolic process in relation to experience that the full value of a biogenetic structural perspective for anthropology may be appreciated.

SYMBOLIC ANTHROPOLOGY

It is noteworthy that the field of anthropology has become increasingly a semiotic science (see reviews by Turner 1975; Umiker-Sebeok 1977; Dow 1986). Prior to the 1960s anthropology was chiefly concerned with the description and explanation of sociocultural institutions and artifacts. Those concerns were hardly fortuitous, as they were the predictable concomitants of a largely positivist-materialist science.

However, under the joint influence of Levi-Straussian structuralism and American cognitive anthropology, the orientation of an increasing number of anthropologists has shifted away from these earlier positivistic perspectives and toward questions of structure, meaning, interpretation, and communication in the ethos of the native. By the mid-1970s, this reorientation had produced a veritable flood of studies (see e.g., Geertz 1973; Turner 1974; Basso and Selby 1976; Peacock 1975; Schneider et al. 1977), all in one way or another reinterpreting the anthropological project as a semiotic enterprise. Even with this reorientation, few theorists have seen fit to address the neurobiological implications of semiotic processes (see Laughlin, McManus, and Stephens 1981 [orig. written in 1977], Turner 1983; Count 1976), although some have taken an avowedly cognitive perspective (e.g., Sperber 1975). A semiotic anthropology uninformed by the neuropsychology of the symbolic process is, and will continue to be, incapable of constructing a theory that can persuasively bridge from symbol to either action or experience. Because that theory is concerned primarily with creating relationships (causal connections, "dialectics," or what have you) between merely analytical categories, it lacks the unifying organic perspective that can mitigate against the dualistic tendency to conceive of "symbols" and "meanings" as fundamentally different from "behaviors." The theorist becomes trapped in a no-man's-land between two planes of conceptualized reality—between notions of "competence" and "performance," between "mechanical" and "statistical" models, between "iconic" and "noniconic" intentionalities. All of this ebb and flow is expressed without fully grasping the fact that the two planes have only analytic status and that an organic perspective, already in place, can dissolves the problematic before it arises.

THE PROBLEM WITH SEMIOTIC STRUCTURALISM

By contrast, our own account aims at understanding the process by which knowledge and experience are constructed, organized, and transformed by the human nervous system. We have already discussed the ills of mind/brain dualism and many of the principles producing the structures mediating consciousness. We will now show that the symbolic process is integral to the construction of the cognized environment and to experience as it unfolds in consciousness. As should be clear by now, our treatment of the symbolic process is couched in the structural monist terms of biogenetic structural theory, and as such is inclined to consider the relationship between action and cognition. A theory of meaningful action must, in order to unpack the collocation of meanings given symbolic form in events, explain how such events are structured. An explanation of structure, in turn, must factor out the principles of cognition operating to produce structure, a task that is rendered impossible without taking the human brain as the main locus of causality.

Any recourse to semiotic structuralism is futile in this respect, for being essentially dualistic, semiotic structuralism effectively denies the role of action (associated, of course, with the body and the physical) in the ontogenesis of structures. Semiotic structuralists utilize methods that entail an explanation of symbolism by means of *ad hoc* typologies of symbols and *post hoc* models of structure. A preoccupation with the fundamentals of thought without consideration of operations internal to the neurocognitive system—that is, consideration of how they evolved, how they develop, how they are involved in adaptation, how they are related to the organism's genotype—has led several theorists to emphasize the "muted" and "unchanging" nature of "primary" structures of human thought.

Semiotic structuralist tactics may well be useful in constructing heuristics, but they fail as explanations to acknowledge the remarkable interplay between cognition and action in constructing the cognized environment. Typologies remain *ad hoc,* and models *post hoc,* as long as they are minted from the debitage of past events. But such theories let us down precisely at the point where we seek a prolonged look at the processes underlying meaningful action, processes that become inevitably transformed as a result of cognitive operations in intimate interaction with the world.

Semiotic structuralist theory simply cannot help us understand the condition of humans as "beings in the world." Because they are concerned with uncovering the structures of "pure" mind, untainted by the "contingencies" that arise from being a part of, and interacting with, the operational environment, the semiotic structuralist has great difficulty in applying his notions of structure to an explanation of real social action and events. It may be recalled that it was Claude Levi-Strauss who seriously took Victor Turner to task for placing ritual, rather than myth, at stage-center of his theory of symbolism (Levi-Strauss 1971:597). Of course, the only way to uncover the "pure" structures of mind for the semiotic structuralist is to infer structures in those artifacts of mentation exhibiting the *least* environment influence—obviously myth rather than ritual, symbolic text rather then horticultural practice, cosmology rather than experience. The domain of structure is somehow ontologically removed from the realm of action, and observations of the latter domain effectively obscure our understanding of the former. Unfortunately this deductive strategy is but a tantalizing tactic at best, for it leads inevitably to exegetical exercises, which bear little or no relationship to what we actually know about the development of biological structures (Piaget 1970:97ff), or what we can phenomenologically ascertain about human experience and communication in the world (Ricoeur 1967b, 1968).

An alternative tactic, and the one adopted here, circumvents these obstacles and examines the relationship between cognition and action through an understanding of the symbolic process as it occurs in actual nervous systems. Biogenetic structural theory has been augmented to account for the intervention of the symbolic process in the development of cognitive structure and the organization of action to further the dual demands of neurocognitive equilibration; adaptation and growth (Piaget 1971a, 1977). The theory is applicable to an understanding of the symbolic process in both phylogenesis and ontogenesis. In either case, we treat brain-mind consciousness neither as a black-box (i.e., the internal operations of mind are incomprehensible and only input and output are considered), nor as divisible into discrete realms (i.e., a realm of symbols and a realm of actions). We approach the issue from a unitary perspective, which models the symbolic process as incorporating events in the world, perception, cognition, and action as interdependent aspects of a single whole. From this vantage point, only those approaches that consider the neuropsychological principles underlying symbolic thought (Pribram 1971), expression (Ricoeur 1974), and action (Premack 1976) in evolution (Waddington 1972), ontogenesis (Piaget 1962), and adaptation (Ardener 1977) can succeed in giving us a clear view of the conditions that shape human knowledge and experience, as well as an evaluation of the contribution of symbolism to the unique nature of humanity.

THE SYMBOLIC PROCESS

Some authorities on symbolism have argued that simply labeling something as a symbol or symbolic process establishes nothing of interest (see Count 1960; Geertz 1973:87ff; Leach 1976). Rather, a formula is required specifying the kind of event in which the symbol takes form, and through which its many properties are exposed. Such a formula should ideally propose the principles generating all types of symbols. In point of fact, the absence of that formula abrogates whatever explanatory power was intended by most theories of the symbolic process (Spiro 1969). We want to initiate the creation of the requisite formula— one that is in accord with the general neurophenomenological principles discussed. It is our view that only by such a formula will the paradigmatic "anthropological theory of meaning" demanded by Basso and Selby (1976:2) emerge.

THE SYMBOLIC PROCESS DEFINED

The symbolic process is that function of the nervous system by which the neural network mediating the whole is entrained by and to the network mediating the part; that is, the mechanism by which the neurocognitive model(s) of a noumenon is evoked by partial sensory information stimulated by the noumenon. A model may be evoked by a stimulus originating either in the outer operational environment, which excites sensory receptors at the periphery of the nervous system, or in another model within the organism's cognized environment. It is customary to call the stimulus a *symbol* ("signifier," "vehicle") and the model or models evoked by that symbol its *meaning* ("signified," "designatum"). The relationship between symbol and meaning is one of part to whole.

It is crucial to understand that a symbol evokes a neurocognitive model whose meaning may or may not be isomorphic with the event in reality that evoked the model; that is, *a symbol does not evoke the noumenon itself.* Put another way, a symbol evokes knowledge about the evoking stimulus, not the process in reality that provided the stimulus. Failure to maintain this distinction lies behind much of the confusion surrounding the actual operations of the symbolic process (see Schutz 1964; Husserl 1931; and Piaget and Inhelder 1969 for support of this contention). As Polanyi (1965) has argued, the relationship between the symbol and its intended meaning is one of "tacit knowing," an inexplicit movement from the aspects of symbol as clues to intentionality. Polanyi says, "The fusion of the clues to the image on which they bear is *not a deduction* but an *integration*" (1965:800).

The symbolic process operates through all sensory modalities. Any sense receptors may deliver evocative information from the operational environment into the cognized environment. Most discussions of symbolism seem to be restricted to visual and auditory modes and eschew the other senses (see Sperber 1975 for discussion of olfactory symbolism). Quite literally any sensory stimulus may evoke intentionality, via intentionality integrated with its meaning, and thus operate as a symbol—for instance, a heart-flutter, sore throat, green light, gesture, body odor, rough surface, affect, bell, or pain.

TOPOGRAPHIC PROJECTION

The symbolic process depends upon intentionality and the other principles discussed in previous chapters. In addition it operates on two principles: The first of these is *topographic projection* (see Geldard 1972;

Pribram 1971; Barlow and Mollon 1982). Topographic projection refers to the point-to-point conduction of abstracted pattern about a stimulus from the periphery into central neurocognitive models. Sensory input tracts are organized in such a way that a minimal veridicality of pattern imposed by peripheral excitation is maintained at every point along the path of conduction. Veridicality is maintained along the dimensions characteristic of each sense, but for each sensory mode for which there is sufficient evidence, the topographical projection of veridical patterns seems to be a major aspect of functioning.

To appreciate more fully the importance of this principle, we will briefly review the dimensions of topographic projection for each of the sensory modes for which there are data. Projection in the visual system is termed *retinotopic* organization. As the term implies, the abstracted spatial relations among stimuli impinging upon the retinae of the eyes is maintained along the entire pathway from each retina, through the lateral geniculate body of the thalamus, to the occipital lobe on each cerebral hemisphere (Geldard 1972; Lashley 1942; Browuer 1934; Browuer and Zeeman 1926; Talbot and Marshall 1941; Hubel and Wiesel 1962). Topographical relations are then maintained from striate cortex, through prestriate cortical association areas to those areas in the frontal lobes. This organization means that the spatial relations obtaining between features, forms, and elements in the visual field are reproduced at various points on the cortex and provide cognition with the patterned relational information required for object recognition, spatial relational contexts, and so forth.

Projection in the auditory system is termed *tonotopic*, or *cochleotopic*, organization. Position of auditory receptors on the basilar membrane of the cochlea in the inner ear determines the frequency of sound to which they will respond. This organization is represented in the medial geniculate body of the thalamus. Each cochlea is bilaterally represented on the auditory cortex, and some, if not all, of the cortical projection areas are tonotopically organized (Woolsey and Walzl 1942; Rose and Woolsey 1949; Evans in Barlow and Mollon 1982:297). This organization means that the cortex is provided with, among other useful information, veridical patterns pertaining to discrete frequencies and relations among frequencies.

Similarly, a map of the body is projected via the ventroposterior nucleus of the thalamus and onto the cortex in the form of *somatotopic* organization. Information is thus provided to central cognitive processes about the spatial relations among proximal cutaneous and visceral stimuli (Geldard 1972; Werner 1970; Mountcastle 1957; Iggo in Barlow and Mallon 1982:400). Point-to-point projection is also maintained in the olfactory system from the receptor surface to the olfactory bulb (Adrian

1951; Clarke 1957), but the significance of topographic projection in coding information for this sensory system is still poorly understood. Position on the receptor surface may be related to the type of chemical stimulus exciting the field (Adrian 1951). Tracts from the pyriform cortex of the olfactory bulb are now known to project to the orbito-frontal cortex of the frontal lobes via the medialis dorsalis of the thalamus, but little is known about the organization and coding functions of these tracts (see Keverne in Barlow and Mollon 1982:418).

We would suggest that topographic projection in the sensory systems provides not only veridical information along discrete dimensions, *but also a portion of the code for penetration into the models composing cognized reality*. Along with other principles of processing like periodicity of impulse generated by the receptors, topographic projection provides a temporally shifting series of sensory patterns, organized hierarchically into temporal "chunks" (Miller et al. 1960), which are recognized by pattern detector cells (Hubel and Wiesel 1962; Evans 1974) that are themselves organized into keying patterns. Thus, a response to a stimulus consists, in part, of establishing a key to the code represented by the stimulus pattern. But because neural models are provided with veridical information pertaining to phenomenal patterns in development through the empirical modification cycle, the mechanism would require that input, that is insufficient to key models, be stored until a pattern allowing further entree into the models is recognized (Pribram and McGuiness 1975). This consideration implies that there is not only a threshold for detection of stimuli at the periphery, but there is also a threshold of information about stimuli requisite for keying models. Therefore, we may define *a minimal symbol as any stimulus that provides sufficient patterning for entree into a model that contains more information than that provided by the stimulus*. It is remarkable, for example, how little information need be provided in a line drawing for a person to recognize a famous face like that of Marilyn Monroe or John F. Kennedy.

RECIPROCAL INHIBITION

The second important neural principle underlying the symbolic process is *reciprocal inhibition*. As noted in a previous chapter, this is the mechanism by which a model, once evoked, actively inhibits other models from competitive evocation. The rudimentary neurophysiological basis for this principle is the phenomenon known as *inhibitory surround*. Many cortical neurons actively inhibit cells immediately proximal to them when they are excited (Geldard 1972). This is a principle of information processing easily detected and researched in receptor cells at the periphery (see Barlow in Barlow and Mollon 1982:22) where a great deal of feature specificity is to be found, not only in the visual system, but also in the systems mediating hearing and touch. This mechanism mediates the overemphasis of edges and borders of "things" by differential brightness and color contrast. The organization of boundary-imposing pattern detector cells provides the bounded "objectness" or "thingness" by which the totality of phenomenal reality arising in the sensorial field of dots is differentiated into distinct elements. Inhibitory surround may also participate in forming the discrete pathway through neural networks we have termed a *model*.

MEANING AND INTENTIONALITY

Several things should be said about meaning, intentionality, and the symbolic process at this juncture. First, a single stimulus may potentially evoke more than one model, depending upon the sensory frame in which the stimulus is embedded. For instance, the words "to," "two," and "too," when spoken, require a lexical context for removing ambiguity. The meaning of the Christian cross may vary depending upon whether it is suspended around a woman's neck, above a papal altar, or before the eyes of a vampire. Ambiguous stimuli without determining contexts may be experienced as dissonance (Pribram 1971).

Second, two or more stimuli may evoke the same model. This ability is the quintessential adaptive advantage of the symbolic process in evolution, for the organism can impute the same object for a variety of stimuli. The flash of yellow in the bush, the paw-print in the mud, the cough in the night may all trigger the model of tiger, and adaptively appropriate action taken as a consequence. Much of the explanatory power of Piagetian theory is in showing how models (he called them "schemes") are constructed and elaborated as a result of physical exploration of objects in the world (Piaget and Inhelder 1969).

Third, there exists a fundamental drive in the functioning of neurocognition to complete the cycle from stimulus input to evocation of models and appropriate attribution or action relative to stimulus. This process is occurring during every moment of consciousness and is so exceedingly rapid and automatic that one is rarely aware of the process. We have called this drive the *cognitive imperative* (d'Aquili 1972; Laughlin and d'Aquili 1974). The cognitive imperative is an active process by which the "mind rises to meet the phenomenal world," to put it in Buddhist psychological terms (see Nanananda 1976). This matching of models and stimuli goes on continuously and is typically noticed only when it becomes interrupted or thwarted in some way, as with ambiguous stimuli or novelty.

All of which brings us back to intentionality. Readers familiar with the literature in either the philosophy of mind or semiotics will be aware of the virtual quagmire of controversy surrounding the concept of intentionality. Since Brentano's (1924) original formulation, authorities have argued over a dazzling array of issues, including whether animals and infants without language can be said to have intentional states; whether consciousness is unitary relative to object and intentionality; whether the object and experience of the object are the same or to be distinguished; whether we are aware of the object or the intentionality; whether all or only some experiences are intentional; or whether consciousness is essentially intentional, reflexive, or both (see Mohanty 1972; Brown 1977). We have no desire to become enmeshed in this web of controversy, particularly as it seems to be largely a by-product of overintellectualization poorly informed by good phenomenology, good physics, or good neuropsychology. But we will touch on several issues relevant to those controversies as they appear to be integral to our general thesis.

The intentionality of a symbol may be conceived as simply the functioning of the models evoked by and entrained to that symbol, or the functioning of the models that produce that symbol. The same symbol may have different intentionalities (different "meanings") depending upon a variety of factors, including the context in which the symbol is embedded and the intensity of evocation of the symbol. The latter requires some discussion. The *intensity of evocation* may vary depending upon many factors external and internal to the cognized environment. First, intensity depends upon the extent to which the stimulus information penetrates into the models (Hebb 1968). That is, the degree to which excitation from the periphery propagates into central processing structures may vary from object to object. Second, the extent of affective and attentional involvement in penetration will influence the extent of augmentation and elaboration of central neurocognitive involvement. If intentionality includes intense affect, for example, the experience associated with the symbol may be "traumatic," or "numinous." Third, intensity of evocation may be influenced by the level of developmental structure operating upon the stimulus information (Harvey et al. 1961). Great interest in (hyperintentionality) and complex processing of symbolic information may produce greater intensity than, say, bored inattention and habituation (hypointentionality). And fourth, the context in reality from which the symbolic stimulus emerges will condition reception of the stimulus; whether, for example, the stimulus is dramatic or novel (occasional visit of a comet, a full eclipse of the sun, an unexpected earthquake).

We may conceive of *memory* as involving the intentionality of models. When we say we remember something, or we recall something, we are describing an experience of entrainment of a model with conscious network that was previously either latent or functioning unconsciously.

The functioning of the model *is* the memory. If we say we recognize a stimulus in the world, we are experiencing the simultaneous entrainment of the network mediating the "something," and the network that is the model of the something *re*-cognized. As we shall see when we turn later to the question of contemplation in science, it is possible under certain conditions to perceive the difference between the "something" (a field of dots) arising in the sensorium and its recognition (a perceptual order upon the field of dots), for there is a minuscule but distinct time lag between the two events. This lag is usually perceivable only by a mature contemplative.

Any stimulus that elicits a model is functioning as a symbol evoking intentionality, memory, or "meaning." Hebb (1968), as well as Merleau-Ponty (1962), pointed to the significance of the bizarre phenomenon of the "phantom limb," in which individuals whose arms or legs were removed continue to "feel" the limbs for weeks and even years after amputation. What is being evoked to entrainment with conscious network is not the long-gone receptors of the missing limb, but the somaesthetic model of that limb still intact in the brain. And, as we have said, a model may be evoked from nerve endings in the stump of the limb, or from within the cognized body itself.

In other words, any stimulus from within or without the person's cognized environment that succeeds in evoking the phantom limb is operating as a symbol. And, as Whitehead (1927), Bergson (1907), and Husserl (1931) indicated, the symbolic function is the source both of efficient, adaptive inference of whole from part, and of potential error in attribution of whole to part. Whitehead (1927) notes that this source of error is the basis for many of the stage magician's tricks. By using lights and mirrors, the illusionist fools our senses into attributing intentionality to a stimulus event that supplies only partial information, but sufficient information for entree into the appropriate models. When the right models are evoked, voila! we "see" the elephant disappear.

Apparently the symbolic process constitutes a fundamental principle by which neural organization is developed, elaborated, and maintained. It is an organizational function that serves to purvey both economy and quality in cognitive adaptation to the world. By attributing intentional significance to events in the world, the symbolic process enables cognized reality to contain and order its information (economy) and maintain optimal integration (quality) of the several dimensions (space, time, form, etc.) constituting salient aspects of events in the world. Along the spatial dimension, the symbolic process facilitates the embedding of cognitively salient zones projected upon the world ("My farm is near Kempville, which is in Ontario, which is in . . ."). The evocative field of any symbol may be extensive in the range of models entrained (i.e., merely differentiated), or it may be hierarchically organized into different levels of integration (i.e., at different levels of cognitive complexity).

PROBLEMS WITH INTENTIONALITY

There are several difficulties that arise in the literature on intentionality, which can be attributed to lack of knowledge about neuropsychology and to the limits of naive introspection. Few philosophers or anthropologists have made use of either the psychology of perception or the advanced contemplative methods of Eastern psychologies. This lack is immediately apparent in the wealth of unresolved controversies that have busied philosophers of mind for generations. Yet there have been some insightful discussions of intentionality from time to time. An excellent work is that of Merleau-Ponty, a phenomenologist who has written extensively on perception (1962, 1964, 1968). Merleau-Ponty notes that the structures underlying initial perception are well ordered by physiological structures and that perceptual order is primary and fundamental to all observation. Another excellent set of discussions is to be found in Lewis (1977) on the issue of affect and intentionality. These authors point to the error of overintellectualizing our view of intentionality. This assessment is consonant with a symbol's potential to evoke any neural network that becomes entrained to the network mediating the percept. Entrainment may include lower autonomic and endocrine structures mediating arousal and metabolic functions; core brain and limbic structures mediating sentiment, emotion, or feeling; and cortical structures mediating conceptual organization, imaginal organization, logico-mathematical functions, cross-modal sensory transfer, and other functions. Restricting an analysis of intentionality to higher intellectual functions, as has been done in much of semiotic structuralism and American cognitive anthropology, falls short of the mark from a neuropsychological point of view.

An outstanding work on intentionality is John Searle's (1983) book in which he has developed a fairly sophisticated view of the subject within the philosophy of mind—a perspective largely commensurate with our knowledge of the neurocognitive and perceptual systems. He notes, for example, that:

> Intentional states are both caused by and realized in the structure of the brain. And the important thing . . . is to see *both* the fact that Intentional states stand in *causal* relations to the neurophysiological (as well as, of course, standing in causal relations to other Intentional states), and the fact that Intentional states are *realized in* the neurophysiology of the brain. Dualists, who correctly perceive the causal role of the mental, think for that very reason they must postulate a separate ontological category. Many physicalists who correctly perceive that all we have in our upper

skulls is a brain think for that reason they must deny the causal efficacy of the mental aspects of the brain or even the existence of such irreducible mental aspects. I believe that both of these views are mistaken. They both attempt to *solve* the mind-body problem when the correct approach is to see that there is no such problem. The "mind-body problem" is no more a real problem than the "stomach-digestion problem." (1983:15)

In viewing intentionality as lodged in neurophysiological processes, Searle is able to overcome many of the obstacles to understanding current in linguistics and philosophy. He sees, for instance, that the cognition of animals and prelinguistic children operate upon intentionality (ibid.:5), that intentionality is involved in an adaptive interaction with the world (ibid.:49) and is a feedforward process (ibid.:76–83). He also sees that intentionality does not necessarily entail action (ibid.:79), that all intentionality is contextual (ibid.:143), and, with Sperber (1975), that the crucial issue is how intentionality comes to be constructed in development (ibid.:27).

Searle runs into difficulty by relying too heavily upon what he self-consciously calls "'naive' (direct, common sense) realism" with respect to the relationship between intentionality and the object of experience (ibid.:57) He addresses the problem of relating intentionality, which he correctly lodges in neurophysiology, to the object of experience, which he *incorrectly* lodges out in the world. He creates insurmountable problems for his approach by conceiving of, say, the visual experience as incorporating intentionality inside the perceiver and an object outside the perceiver. He is forced, thereby, to the neuropsychologically unsatisfying conclusion that when we see a hallucination (as in the case of Ruth described above) we are having a visual experience, but we are not seeing anything (ibid.:58). Jason Brown (1977) has persuasively argued that it is a fundamental error to conceive of consciousness as "seizing" content from outside itself. Rather, consciousness produces its content.

A useful view of the role of intentionality in perception—and, as we have argued above, one more consonant with modern neurophysiology—is to treat the object of perception as beginning either at the sense receptors or in the imaginal cortex, and treat the relationship between stimulus in the world and receptor activity as a distinct phase in the interaction of the nervous system and the world. In other words, it makes sense for certain purposes to place the visual object inside the perceiver and ask two sets of questions: how does the object interact with intentionality; and how does the noumenon in the world interact with the internal object and its intentionality?

If one sees clearly that intentionality is the functioning of prefrontal and other cortical tissues mediating experience, then to say that the functioning of the networks mediating cognition is intentional and the functioning of the networks mediating sensory input is nonintentional contradicts what we know about the neural processing of experience in the sensorium. Information is not passively collected at the periphery and delivered unchanged to areas of central processing in the brain. Rather, there are neural cells and networks at many levels from peripheral receptors to cortical processors that operate upon and transform the information for various purposes as it passes up the neural hierarchy into the brain. For example, there are ganglion cells in the retina of the eye that will operate only upon selected photic variables, such as speed of movement, direction of movement, or lightness or darkness of stimulus. Of course, all receptor cells manifest a threshold of stimulation below which they will not fire. As John and his colleagues (1967) have shown, evoked potentials measured at the cortex tend to vary with the shape of a visual stimulus, and not with the actual size of the image striking the retina. In other words, the higher neurocognitive centers are operating more upon information about the sensory stimulus supplied by processors at various hierarchical levels than upon the raw sensory data (see Gray 1982 relative to septal-hypocampal functions relative to this point). The form of the object is more a construction of neural networks than it is of the world, and higher cognition seems more interested in the percept than the sensation.

In our opinion, modern neurophysiology can be interpreted as supporting the views of Husserl and other classical phenomenologists to the extent that perception at its most fundamental level is ordered and meaningful along essential dimensions prior to further ordering by higher centers. Perception considered apart from higher cognition is hardly chaotic, but rather, primitively ordered from its very inception as sensory information (compare Merleau-Ponty 1964 and various articles in Barlow and Mollon 1982). More to the point, however, the neural systems mediating perception and cognition are intimately integrated and operate on the same basic principles. To a great extent, dividing this complex integration into a simple duality consisting of "perception" and "conception" is as outmoded as the notion of there being only "five senses." Moreover, the division leads to the very "naive commonsense" conceptions that have hampered Searle; namely, that "cognition" is located in the head, and the "object of perception" is out in the world somewhere.

The object of perception is constructed wholly within the nervous system. Its form and other qualities are canalized by neurobiological creodes and are highly selective relative to the kinds of information that go into constructing objects. We do not have visual receptor cells sensitive to pigments in the ultraviolet range, but bees do. Therefore, bees operate upon ultraviolet qualities of objects and we do not. Likewise, we do not have advanced echolocation structures like the bat or kangaroo rat, or electroreceptors like sharks and certain fish, and thus we do not operate upon objects similar to ones used by those species. Our cognized environment is a distinctly human one, conditioned not only by human cognitive structures, but also by perceptual ones.

COGNIZED SYMBOLS

The symbolic process operates in cognition largely at an unconscious level. It is, of course, possible to become more aware of the symbolic process through contemplation. However, most human beings are only dimly aware of this process in experience, and can only remain so without carefully examining the relationships that obtain between the various factors making up meaningful experience. Yet, for any individual or group there exist many symbols that are consciously cognized to one degree or another as symbolic, for example, stimuli in the world or internalized in ritually delineated bundles. Although cognized symbols are the products of the symbolic process, additional principles come into play for this type of symbol. Furthermore, it may be argued that cognized symbols are an evolutionary advance over simple symbols. For these reasons it is useful to maintain a distinction between the ubiquitous stimulus-as-object of the symbolic process and the relatively less frequent cognized (big-S) SYMBOL.

A person's or society's SYMBOLS are typically those that may evoke models of the most extensive and profound intentionality (e.g., flags, totems, shamanic regalia, religious icons, commercial logos, personal costumary, etc.). SYMBOLS also tend to be hierarchically organized within systemic bundles concentrated upon a few primary ("dominant," "core," "key") SYMBOLS, the evocative fields of which contain the intentionalities of other secondary SYMBOLS (see Ortner 1973; Marshack 1976; Turner 1967). Ritually delimited SYMBOLS provide material of the greatest interest to ethnographers, most of whom come from SYMBOLICALLY impoverished postindustrial cultures. A society's repertoire of SYMBOLS is never more than a small subset of the symbols operating within and between its members' cognized environments (Mead 1934; see also Schneider 1968 on Americans; Munn 1973a on the Walbiri; Ortner 1970 on the Sherpas; Turner 1967 on the Ndembu).

Several authorities have noted the difficulty of dealing with the communal and idiosyncratic aspects of symbolism (Sperber 1975:102, Firth 1973). The distinction between "public" and "private" symbolism or intentionality has only minimal analytic significance and is untenable from the vantage point of ontogenesis. In ontogenesis, the degree of symbolic communality—that is, the degree of overlap between intentionalities in the cognition of various group members evoked by a single stimulus—depends upon the extent to which the object-intentionality relationship has been canalized by (1) genetically predisposed neurognostic ("archetypal") structure; for example, mandala symbolism (Jung 1969), phobia (Seligman and Hager 1972), parenting, and other social cognition (Count 1973); (2) common experience and socially conditioned interpretation; or (3) a combination of factors 1 and 2 as co-producers. In any case, genetic predistribution and social conditioning will combine to provide only sets of constraints to the intentionality evoked by a symbol (recall our structural landscape model above; see page 53ff). There will always be a degree of variance among the evocative fields in different individuals within any social group regarding the range of experiences recorded in memory and triggered by symbols, and the level of cognitive complexity at which the intentionality has been organized. Thus, any symbol will be more or less "public," more or less "private" in its evocation.

Naturally enough, SYMBOLS evidence a great deal of standardization of intentionality among group members. This is because the inculcation of intentionality during ontogenesis ("enculturation," "socialization") is typically focused upon, and ritually structured about, those very SYMBOLS. Standardization of intentionality minimizes the possibility of social dysfunctional meaning, particularly in response to SYMBOLS used to elicit social action. And, as Firth (1973) points out, those in the society who control these SYMBOLS control the intentionality, and thereby social power.

SYMBOLIC PROCESS IN ACTION

As we have seen, the symbolic process is fundamental to the construction of and access to knowledge about the world among all higher animals (Whitehead 1927; Piaget 1952, 1962; Count 1973; Sperber 1975). The impetus behind this process is cybernetic (Granit 1977; Powers 1973). By combining the principles of object and pattern recognition, the process operates as a control mechanism enabling the neurocognitive system to reentrain a total intentionality from partial information about the world as the cognized environment unfolds in the sensorium. The process, thereby, is exceedingly efficient in liberating the organism from *adaptively* inefficient (or redundant) investigation of noumena. We stress "adaptive" in this context because there can well be other motivations for continuing exploration of noumena (remember, *noumena* means unspecified processes in the world that are essentially transcendental relative to the cognized environment; see page 83) than the primeval, "get food without becoming food" cognitive imperative. As Jacques Ellul (1964) has made painfully clear, there is more to human existence than the maximization of efficiency, and there are transcendent reasons for consciously intervening in the automatic closure of intentionality. Premature "hardening of the categories" may assure biological survival in the short haul, but may also produce an overly concrete, spiritually deadened consciousness, which may stultify advanced development.

The consideration of the symbolic process apart from consideration of action in the world is theoretically and empirically untenable. Again, such thinking is a manifestation of the mind-brain (mind-body) dualism that insidiously infests Western sociocultural theory. Peacock (1975:4), while recognizing that the same object or event may be both "symbolic" and "technical in function," insists that the former aspect is produced from a "logico-meaningful" mode of consciousness and the latter from a "causal-functional" mode. These two tendencies in society produce a tension that must be reconciled, particularly in modern society. In all fairness, Peacock does attempt a synthesis of sorts between "symbolic" and "techno-social" systems (ibid.:213) by applying an evolutionary, ideal analysis of the interactions between these systems. Yet he, like so many dualists, is seemingly unaware that the distinction he is making is fundamentally and analytically unreal and is creating a problem in theory that does not exist in the world.

SEMIOSIS

As Piaget (1962) has repeatedly emphasized, a large part of the development of symbolism involves the development of the structures mediating action, especially during the first six or seven years of human life during which most of our neural models and their functional intentionalities are formed. If a symbol-model entrainment is to be effective in completing intentionality so that it facilitates an adaptive response to the world, then the model must be formulated in active dialogue with the world. We term this dialogue *semiosis:* The EMC process by which a symbol develops its intentionality. Intentionality must be constructed during semiosis to accommodate various salient features of the noumenon so that all adaptively relevant information about the noumenon will trigger the model. In order for salient information about the noumenon to penetrate the model it must take a form requisite to pattern-recognition internal to the nervous system. The construction of models requires prior integration of information about the world and regulation by the neurocognitive system of its activities in the world. In other words, models having no motor component, but ontogenetically derived from models that incorporate a motor component, will nonetheless possess pattern keys structured around the early organization of action in the world (Piaget 1952, 1971b; Bruner 1972, 1974; Gazzaniga 1985:103ff).

In Bruner's (1971) view the crucial feature in the early organization of action in the child is the construction process itself. We see that a child's execution of an act involves an orchestration of constituent acts in a way that meets (feedforward) expectations. That is, sequences of action are organized in temporal plans (Miller et al. 1960). A plan to meet expectations is evoked by partial information about a present state of affairs in the child's perceptual world. Acts are executed to bring about a situation in the perceived world in tune with those expectations. Modification of action—perhaps the substitution of constituent acts, alteration of intention, or the like—may thus constitute a test by which the evoked intentionality is evaluated relative to information about the results of activity (Gray 1982).

Empirical modification is set in motion by a preliminary action of the infant, usually an act that has been completed. The act involves intentionality, performance, and feedback. Completed actions in turn become the intentions that precede, direct, and provide a set of conditions (predominantly sensory and motor) for initiating and terminating further activities. However, the structures mediating such activities modify their organization and control functions, not merely by repetition, but through regulation of means and ends objectives (see Piaget 1952; Piaget and Inhelder 1969:52; Bruner 1972, 1974). The component acts, which make up the activities, are modulated and thereby the extent of variation in constituent acts relative to objectives is reduced. Modulation is achieved by the infant through redefining tasks: varying either the means or the ends.

This modulation is the very essence of play. The result of intentional production/environmental feedback is a predictable spatiotemporal patterning, the modular action. The process reaches full circle and exhibits the primitive ingredients of the symbolic process (Piaget 1952, 1962). The next step is simply the provision of a reference, a pattern-detection component to the cycle, in order to make it possible for the neurocognitive system to match patterns in memory and patterns of sensory input. Thus the neural model becomes keyed to any aspect of the action sequence.

Early neurocognitive growth involves mainly the emergence of the symbolic process in play, an intercausal connection between semiosis, action in the world, and exploration of the world that predominates throughout the earliest stages of child development (Piaget 1962). These are the stages of development prior to the emergence of relatively abstract thought and the symbolism characteristic of these stages is limited to small-s symbols. With the advent of operational thought, cognized SYMBOLS begin to take on a central role in the organization of experience. Operations have become internalized so that they may be carried out independent of action in the world, and may become clustered or concentrated upon SYMBOLS.

SEMIOTROPISM

The evocation of these internalized constellations is typically controlled by society to some degree by embedding SYMBOLS in ritual. The society not only controls semiosis in enculturation, but also controls orientation of consciousness to SYMBOLS (e.g., a cross), SYMBOLIC arrays (e.g., a cross in the context of a church), and SYMBOLIC sequences (e.g., a mass or pilgrimage). An orientation of attention upon any symbol to the exclusion of other potentially perceivable objects we term *semiotropism*. Semiotropic responses are particularly dramatic and evident when they are upon SYMBOLS within the context of ritual. The role of prefrontal cortical structures in both augmenting associations configured about the SYMBOL, and inhibiting alternative objects of attention, is paramount.

The problem of social control of consciousness and experience becomes increasingly acute the more the cognition of group members transcends the necessity of an action component and a dependence upon the immediate sensory surround. Interpersonal synchronization of cognition and action, which requires socially canalized semiosis and semiotropism, becomes inherently more difficult to mount in a species that is capable of such advanced cognition while continuing to opt for a social adaptation (see d'Aquili et al. 1979). The problem is in part solved by maintaining a field of action in which SYMBOLS remain embedded. This field has the effect of reinforcing a SYMBOL-action connection, thereby controlling the presentation of SYMBOLS within a socially prescribed context (Geertz 1973). Moreover, it assures some degree of adaptive overlap among competing intentionalities (within and among members), and the organization of those intentionalities in action.

The social control of semiosis with respect to SYMBOL-intentionality becomes even more problematic in abstract cognitive development, a stage Piaget called "formal operational thought" (Piaget and Inhelder 1969:130). At this stage cognition becomes freed from concrete attachment to objects and categories of objects, and may perform cognitive acts upon the systems of logical relations it has previously generated to organize objects within the cognized environment. Prior to this point SYMBOLS represent objects or classes perceived or imagined in the world. With the advent of fully abstract thought, the cognitive system is free to perform transformations ("combinations," "permutations"; see Piaget and Inhelder 1969:133) upon the structures of organization themselves without concern for representation in a concrete perceptual world.

The more cognitive operations become free of sensorimotor grounding, the more potentially difficult becomes social control of semiosis, and the greater becomes the risk of a decrement in socially adaptive activity. Thus, even in abstract thought, the group member's cognitive operations are canalized by socialization so that abstract operations tend to occur in socially prescribed circumstances, upon socially prescribed themes and domains, utilizing socially provided SYMBOLIC materials. Abstract thought is never carried out by more than a small percentage of the population (Dasen 1972) and then is usually within discrete domains of application. Such thought will likely be carried out upon elements and relations already in place in the society's cosmology and will be expressed within the society's mythopoea. No matter how abstract the transformations carried out on such materials, they remain grounded through the inextricable link socially fostered between mythopoeic SYMBOLISM (say, in art and myth) and social action (in the form of ritual). The entire mythopoeic field within which abstract operations may be carried out must be considered a totality, which at the level of social process inevitably involves action. It is common among the world's societies, for instance, for art to be highly stylized and limited to mythopoeic and ritual circumstances. Thus, a transformation of abstract thought, with any social ramifications, will tend to produce a transformation in the entire mythopoeic system (Eliade 1963; Leach 1964; Count 1960; Sperber 1975; Mead 1934; Munn 1973b, Reichel-Dolmatoff 1971; contrast those sources with Levi-Strauss 1971). This transformation may well be one of the main mechanisms of Wallace's (1966) "revitalization" process, which has undeniable application to the sociocultural conditioning of scientists in Euro-American societies (see Rubinstein et al. 1984: chap. 4).

Only through an analysis of symbol, action, *and* adaptation can we fully appreciate the significance of changes in symbolic systems transgenerationally (Foster 1974; Preston 1975; Schmidt 1976). Moreover, only by taking a developmental perspective can we see the relationship between (1) the growth of symbol-intentionality on the one hand, and (2) the range of symbolic processing on a continuum from highly univalent, unidimensional, concrete intentionality to highly plurivalent, multidimensional, abstract intentionality on the other hand. By incorporating these facts into our study of symbolism we come to see how the same symbolic activity (say, a religious ceremony) or mythopoeic text (say, a myth) may be simultaneously meaningful for all hearers in the society, be they child or adult, male or female, or cognitively simple or complex. The key to understanding this phenomenon is in understanding the means by which symbols penetrate to the structures mediating knowledge and experience—a process that is particularly apparent in the role of play in semiosis and the conditioning of semiotropic responses.

PLAY AND SEMIOSIS

A major thrust of neurocognitive development, as we have seen, is the construction, refinement, elaboration, and completion of a system of internalized models of the world. These models intervene between stimulus input and motor output to increase the organism's chances of survival in the world. This is a lifelong process, for neural models are never more than partially isomorphic with noumena in the world, and the world is forever changing. The initial course of modeling is assured by the neurognostic structure of nervous system tissues, a structure that is vulnerable to natural selection and other forces shaping genetic information in the gametes. The adaptibility of models is encouraged in development through active exploration of the world—a kind of natural experimentation with noumena involving EMC feedforward and feedback into the gradually maturing neurocognitive systems. The optimal adaptability of models in higher animals is assured by play in the world, and this includes play with conspecifics as well as other noumena.

Maturation of neural models through active exploration allows the construction of intentionality based upon information about various aspects of the noumenon, as well as about the variety of contexts in which the noumenon is encountered in the world. Anyone who has explored some activity or study (e.g., skiing, stamp collecting, anatomy, cooking, or what have you) with sufficient self-awareness will know that in the begining the object of study appeared unfamiliar, recalcitrant, undifferentiated, unpredictable, and homogeneous; and later as familiar, fully differentiated, pliant, and multifaceted. This learning experience is mediated by matured models. Play facilitates a greater breadth of experience and range of information about objects, tasks, and events in the world.

For our purposes, play may be defined as a special case of the EMC by which an organism acts to complexify its world in order to optimize development of its cognized environment (see Laughlin and McManus 1982; Turner 1983). Play is an activity mediated by a subset of intrinsically motivated, cognitive, and motor components of the EMC. Play specifically functions neurophysiologically to optimize the development of intentionality and is thus an important factor in semiosis and semiotropism. Models of the world are complexified through action in the world either by increasing the complexity of sensory information about domains already modeled, or by increasing the spatiotemporal range of the world modeled. The former mode seems to predominate in the more mature play of organisms, whereas the latter seems to predominate in early play, and particularly in solitary play. Complexity in this developmental context means that models become more ramified by increased information storage, more cognitive associations, greater completeness, and autonomy. The models are also able to anticipate events in the world more precisely and under a greater range of circumstances, and become more differentiated and complex in their organization. For example, models may grow from unimodal models into multimodel ones through development via cross-modal transfer of information from sense-specific associations.

Play facilitates the loosening of context specificity. Adaptation to the noumenon is mediated by intentionality that applies in a greater range of contexts, thus allowing a greater figure-to-ground contrast. For example, you have come to know a person in a particular context such as the office, on the ski slopes, or behind the counter at the bank. Later you see that person in a novel context (say, eating at a restaurant) and for the life of you, you cannot remember from where you know that person. This experience is common, and creates a dissonance betwen a sense of familiarity and a sense of nonrecognition. The model of that person has been previously very context specific. The intentionality that forms that person in your brain is tied concretely to the routine context in which the person's face is encountered. But let us suppose that after a few moments the person in the restaurant is recognized. Not only has recognition occurred in a new context, very likely any future encounter you have with that person in novel contexts (say, at the shore) will not produce dissonance. The intentionality that forms that person for you has become to a greater extent context-free.

The intrinsic motivation of the maturing neurocognitive system is both to complete and elaborate intentionality—to optimize growth of the neural networks mediating intentionality. This motivation seems to be what Ernst Cassirer (1957) means by his notion of "symbolic pregnance," which is an urge to flesh out the meaning of things to their fullest extent. For the most part, intentionality is causally linked to object. That is, intentionality tends to be organized around central images and concepts, much as iron filings are organized about a magnet. The memories associated with the intentionality may span a lifetime and link sensory, cognitive, affective, and motor components into a single system of response to events in the world. This may be what Stanislav Graf is driving at with his "systems of condensed experience," or "COEX" systems (1975:46):

A COEX system can be defined as a specific constellation of memories consisting of condensed experiences (and related fantasies) from different life periods of the individual. The memories belonging to a particular COEX system have a similar basic theme or contain similar elements and are associated with a strong emotional charge of the same quality. . . . [T]he excessive emotional charge which is attached to COEX systems . . . seems to be a summation of the emotions belonging to all the constituent memories of a particular kind. (Ibid.:46–47).

COEX systems would seem to be integrated intentionalities intermediate between full complexes in the Jungian sense (see page 133) and the simpler intentionalities associated with most symbols, and which are not constellated under the provocation of intense emotional discharge. However, intentionalities of any sort are mediated by neural networks organized by the same set of principles.

Evocation of a "meaning" constellation is frequently by way of evocation of the image or concept with which it is associated, and it is easily comprehensible from the standpoint of entrainment. A stimulus pertaining to a noumenon in the world is recognized, and the recognition itself becomes the key to entrance into models mediating intentionality about that noumenon. The recognized form—commonly an image or concept—is the object of intentionality and may be triggered by sensations from inside or outside the being. That is, the noumenon giving rise to sensation may be within or without the organism.

In any event, the growth of this organization of intentionality about an object is the essence of the process of semiosis. The integration of intentionality and perceptual form is typically so complete, and the evocation so rapid, that few people are able to distinguish sensation from percept, or percept from intentionality. Rather, the activation of perception and cognition—symbol and intentionality—is a unitary process, which recurs spontaneously during every moment of consciousness. As we have said, one normally becomes aware of the process only in the encounter with novelty, or when there is dissonant attribution of intentionality to object. Otherwise symbol is experienced as intentionality, and the world and the noumena comprising it are experienced as meaningful and to a large extent redundant. Play operates behaviorally to replace redundancy with novelty and meaningfulness with inquiry. Play is therefore at the very evolutionary foundations of both science and mysticism. Neither a true scientist nor a true mystic may be produced by mere passive socialization or by the institutionalized transmission of technique, for science and mysticism emerge from an intensive and intrinsic urge to explore, to inquire, to "play in the fields of the Lord," so to speak.

THE EVOLUTION OF SYMBOLISM

Not surprising, the evolutionary development of the symbolic process reflects the development of the entire neurocognitive system. Over the course of phylogenesis, the nervous system has increased in anatomical elaboration and complexity along a number of dimensions (see above page 73; also Sarnat and Netsky 1974). The increased functional complexity mediated by the nervous system may be noted in the increased complexity of the symbolic process. Indicators of this evolutionary advance in semiosis include: (1) increased spatiotemporal distance between a noumenon and reception of information about the noumenon leading to evoked intentionality; (2) increased complexity of cognitive associations (or models) entrained as intentionality; (3) increased expansiveness of spatiotemporal extension modeled within intentionality; (4) increased capacity for cross-modal transference and integration of intentionality; (5) increased hierarchicalization of models mediating intentionality; (6) increased autonomy of higher cognitive functions from lower affective ones; and (7) increased complexity of formalized behavior as an expression of intentionality.

In short, the symbolic process has become more ramified and complex along precisely those dimensions that have characterized the allometric elaboration of prefrontal, parietal, and temporal association cortex. For example, the development of cross-modal transfer meant that a symbolic stimulus presented to one sensory mode could potentially evoke models in more than one sensory mode. Obviously, then, we may speak of the evolution of the symbolic process reflecting the evolution of consciousness, for symbolic processing incorporates many of the structures that are routinely entrained to conscious network and that mediate consciousness.

SYMBOLIC INTEGRATION AND EXPRESSION

With reference to the evolution and the development of the symbolic process, it is useful to distinguish between the process of *symbolic integration*, the primary process by which direct experience is given coherence through intentional organization within the cognized environment, and *symbolic expression*, the ancillary process by which experience may be communicated vicariously among different individuals' cognized environments. The evolution and development of expression is clearly a function of integration. For one thing, complexity of integration is a necessary, but not a sufficient condition for complexity of expression. That is, expresson may be, but rarely is, equal in complexity to integrative processes, or it may be simpler in organization than integration, but expression may not exceed the complexity of integrative processes.

Further, an evolutionary increment in complexity of symbolic integration in a species for which selection favors social adaptive strategy will inevitably cause an evolutionary advance in symbolic expression. Our reasoning here is quite simple. A major problem for any evolving social species is the coordination of cognized environments among group members so that corporate action results from a common ground of perceptual, affective, and cognitive intentionality. The primary biological function of expression is to maintain this adaptive coordination (see d'Aquili et al. 1979). Were the cognized environments of group members to become too complex along the dimensions mentioned earlier, without a concomitant development of the expressive mode, then the species would gradually lose its capacity for adaptive social action and would become increasingly solitary in its relations with the world.

SIGNS

The failure to consider symbolism in an evolutionary context has led to confusion about the relationship between *symbol* and *sign*. These two terms are often distinguished along a variety of dimensions, such as iconicity, range of vocality, range of semantic field, arbitrariness of meaning, and openness to associations (see Lewis 1977:1; Turner 1975; Piaget and Inhelder 1969; Leach 1976; Schutz 1964; Ricoeur 1967b; Altmann 1967; Sperber 1975). But such distinctions tend to be analytical and synchronic and often lead to simplistic typological theories, which are insensitive to either the evolutionary processes or neurophysiological structures relating various manifestations of the symbolic process.

From the present perspective, a *sign* is an evolutionarily advanced and specialized SYMBOL. A sign is specialized for participation as a unit in a greater SYMBOLIC system. The evolutionary sequence has been from the primitive symbolic process to cognized SYMBOLS. Coinciding with the development of SYMBOLS, the cognized environment became less stimulus-bound, an occurrence indicating that cognitive associations and intentionality of models could be, to some extent, removed from the pressure of immediate perception. As the cognized environment became less stimulus-bound, the relationship between SYMBOL and intentionality in expression reciprocated. This reciprocation produced (was the necessary condition for) a greater semantic arbitrariness in the intentionality of SYMBOLS over and above symbols.

Arbitrariness of intentionality ("noniconicity") became complete in the next evolutionary phase, the development of *sign systems*. The most important forms of sign systems are spoken and written natural languages. Loss of stimulus-boundness in SYMBOLIC expression produced the problem of providing a context or "frame" (Fillmore 1976) for transmitting the information. A sign system, by combining the primitive symbolic process with a structural hierarchy of plans, provides to a large extent (but not completely) its own frame. The evolutionary course has been from reliance on the perceptual field as frame, to reliance upon intentionality as frame. More properly, as perception is a lower-order intentionality, the move has been from perceptual intentionality, which is highly influenced by sensory input, to conceptual-imaginal intentionality, which is progressively less influenced by sensory input.

But a seeming paradox arose in the development of signs. On the one hand, signs are SYMBOLS with highly constrained intentionality and conditions of evocation. Because their intentionalities are highly arbitrary, their exact "meaning" depends largely upon their symbolic context. For example, the lexemes "mass" and "spend" already have highly constrained intentionalities when standing alone; they become severely constrained when they are embedded in a text; as in, "I am going to *spend* the morning at *mass*." On the other hand, signs are not the SYMBOLS of intent in communcation, but merely the medium for the communication of conceptual and imaginal intentionalities operating in the depths of cognition (see Schmidt 1976; Harman 1971). The development from primitive symbol through SYMBOL to sign is reflected in microcosm by the development of sign elements in American Sign Language (Bellugi and Klima 1976) and by the history of ancient alphabets (Moran and Kelley 1969). In these cases, signs originated from relatively iconic gestures and pictures, but later lost their iconicity in their refinement within their respective sign systems. Because of the loss of stimulus-boundness as requisite for intentionality, sign systems are amenable to far more fluid manipulation of intentionality (since symbolic expression via sign systems provides its own frame, which is relatively free of the perceptual field), and much finer symbolic differentiation (due to the range of symbolic intentionality available within embedded plans, or hierarchical arrangement of constituent elements within the "language game"; see Schmidt 1976).

LANGUAGE AS A SYSTEM OF SIGNS

As Jakobson (1971:556), among many others, has noted, natural language is the fundamental mode of communication among our species. It is the locus par excellance of human semiotic activity. Yet there is a considerable confusion about the nature of meaning, or of semantics, in language (see e.g., Basso and Selby 1976:9). This turbulence is too vast an issue to go into here, but we would like to note several relevant points from our present theory regarding meaning in language.

First, we make many of the same criticisms of Chomskian (1980) structural linguistics as we have of other forms of semiotic structuralism (see Laughlin and d'Aquili 1974:149ff). In short, it is nondevelopmental and—aside from giving a nod toward the ultimate realization of universal grammar in the structure of the brain (Chomsky in Rieber 1976)—takes little real account of the neurobiology of language (compare with Selnes and Whitaker, same volume; Whitaker 1971). Rather, it tends, like Levi-Straussian structuralism, to be logico-deductive and *ad hoc* in its methods, tautological and *post hoc* in its explanatory formulations. Universal rules or structures of language are deduced from the analysis of texts and then tendered as explanations of the texts. These universal structures are presumed to be innate in the brain and operating without development; moreover, the possibility that many logic-deductive schemes could be adduced in a similar manner to account for the same observed regularities in the texts is discounted. In other words, different neural organizations may produce the same behavior, linguistic or otherwise. It is always difficult to imagine a way of falsifying a generative account of language. This is not to say that generative accounts are useless, but rather that they must be evaluated from the broadest possible vantage point, one that includes everything we know about the genetics and development of the brain.

Second, and more to the point, speech and language cannot be usefully annexed from general neurocognitive activity. The development of language comprehension, speech production, reading, and writing are all functions of the development of, and the activity of, the brain (Lenneberg 1967; Arbib et al. 1982; Whitaker 1971; Geschwind 1970). Language activity is the product of complex entrainment of perceptual, neurocognitive, and motor operations involving numerous cortical and subcortical centers, which become integrated into a single process. Damage to any particular area involved in language processing will have its distinct effects upon production (Luria 1947; Whitaker 1971).

Third, as Chomsky (1980) has seen so well, language involves interaction between "surface structural" production operations and "deep structural" comprehension operations, and the deep structures that may occur in the individual or in the group are constrained by the limits placed upon possible grammars by the genetics involved in the biology of the brain. However, because generative models are logico-deductive formulations, they do not conform to what is known about the neurological structures mediating these operations. Thus, as Caplan and Marshall (1975) have noted, generative grammar cannot be mapped onto neurocognitive organization.

What is required is a close study of all types of language-related deficits and their concomitant structures for the purpose of constructing a complex, integrated working map of the structures and functions composing language activity.

Approaches to [this] question have led to the development of process models in which the production of a variety of behaviors is played across a number of interacting neural systems, with no subsystem constituting a complete "mental faculty," but with each subsystem having a well-defined functional role, the result, presumably, of specific circuitry which transforms and is transformed by that of other neural systems. (Arbib et al. 1982:21)

Fourth, we hypothesize (with Lenneberg 1967:302) that a neurocognitively grounded theory of language will recognize that the deepest structures of lexical intentionality are not to be found in discrete linguistic structures, but throughout the neurocognitive system and its perceptual, conceptual, imaginal, affective, and attentional structures. In other words, penetration of intentionality by speech (auditory stimuli), gesture, or written words (visual stimuli) does not stop at some analytically definable boundary on one side of which are to be found linguistic structures and on the other nonlinguistic structures. Rather, penetration is canalized by the same constraints that are imposed upon all symbolic material, and may penetrate to all networks within the nervous system. We need recourse only to common experience to see that linguistic utterances may evoke thoughts, images, scenes, feelings, states of arousal, and autonomic and metabolic responses.

And fifth, language as the primary sign system obtains its notable adaptive power because it is the manifestation of a neurocognitive system relatively freed from a perceptual frame. Speech events are texts; that is, they provide both symbol and context in a way that allows the brain of the listener to construct accurate meanings from the information provided by utterances combined with material stored in memory. In practice the text of a speech event may be embedded in a larger perceptual frame, as when we are being told the history of the ancient building we are actually seeing on a tour. But just as easily we can be told a story around the campfire at night, which has no reference to either the sensory environment of the moment or memories of our experiences during the day. In fact, natural language may be used to transmit information having no perceptual referents at all, as in a discourse on mathematics. At such times language verges upon a formal sign system, the next stage in the evolution of the symbolic process.

FORMAL SIGNS

Complete independence of symbolic expression from stimulus-boundness and actual events in the world became possible only with the evolutionary emergence of *formal sign systems*. For various reasons we suspect formal signs first occurred at the stage of hominid evolution during the fourth major glacial of the Quaternary Period commonly referred to as the Middle to Upper Paleolithic. Among other things, this seems to be the period when symbolic artifacts begin to show evidence of advanced, abstract thought (cf. James 1962 and Marshack 1972, 1976). Formal sign systems are now best represented in Western culture by mathematics, geometry, and symbolic logic (see Inhelder and Piaget 1958; and Beth and Piaget 1966 on the relationship between abstract cognition and formal signs), and in other cultures by certain forms of myth, poetry, and other symbolic performances (Radin 1927; Dasen 1977a, 1977b). Associated with the evolution of concrete and formal operational thought, such systems facilitate not only stimulus-free communication about the world, but the creation of and communication about alternative orders of reality, some of which bear no reference whatever to phenomenal perceptions (Marshack 1972). For example, mathematical logic provides a set of symbols that represent pure classes and relations between classes, which are totally free of content. Boolean algebra presents a system of only two values and the relations that can obtain between those values, again independent of any perceptual content about the world. These formal systems may, of course, be applied to problems about the world. Boolean algebra has provided the basic logic upon which computers are based.

The most obvious use of formal sign systems in the process of symbolic integration of the cognized environment is to be found in science. As many scholars have noted, the relative freedom of intentional and contextual manipulation allows far greater acuity and flexibility of modeling in theory construction than the more primitive levels of the symbolic process. Signs and formal sign systems in science facilitate transmission not only of vicarious experience, but also of vicariously experienced alternative cognized environments. These cognized environments in turn may operate as hermeneutical systems by which experience may be interpreted at the highest cognitive complexity of which the species is capable (Beth and Piaget 1966).

Yet even in science, which is, after all, a human neurocognitive pursuit, all four levels of evolutionary development of the symbolic process—primitive symbol, SYMBOL, sign, and formal sign—are manifested in the integration and expression of the structures of consciousness. The same may be said for any system of thought and expression among any of the world's peoples, presuming that abstract operations emerge in the development of some of the society's members. We explicitly reject the arbitrary distinction between "primitive" and "civilized" modes of thought inherent in a Levy-Bruhlian (1923) view of mentality (see Horton and Finnegan 1973 on this issue). In order to hold such a view, one would have to claim that the neurocognitive systems of "primitive" and "peasant" peoples is somehow different from those of "civilized" peoples, and there exists no such evidence. On the other hand, evidence does exist that some cultures and environments encourage advanced cognitive development and others do not (see Dasen 1972; Feldman et al. 1974). A superb example of transmission of abstract material using sign and SYMBOL by a non-Western culture is to be found in M. Griaule's (1965) book about Dogon cosmology.

7 SYMBOLIC PENETRATION

> On the basis of a phenomenal analysis of human behavior, it seems to me that a primary drive of human beings is towards order, that is, to perceive the environment as comprehensible and to make successful predictions about the future. I am convinced that to every situation a human being brings an orientation which is not derived from that situation but already exists in his perceptual powers before he comes to that situation. Such an orientation works only because it filters out from the situation any data which is not relevant to the needs of the moment. This orientation is the manifestation of the drive to order.
>
> —Moise Peckham, *Man's Rage for Chaos*

EXPERIENCE, WE HAVE SAID, is the ongoing unfoldment of phenomenal reality within the sensorium, that part of conscious network designed to portray a cognized environment for the organism.[1] Experience is reconstituted every moment within the field of dots that is the functioning sensorium and may be cognized as relatively continuous or discontinuous, depending upon all of the intentional and other factors influencing the entrainment of phases and warps. The exact entrainment mediating experience in the moment depends particularly upon orientation and attention within a greater symbolic field (Neisser in Pick 1979). What objects, qualities, or relations are attended will depend a great deal upon the phase of consciousness in which a particular semiotropism occurs. Each phase of consciousness is characterized by its own range of entrainment, as well as its own "logics," which direct attention and assemble "meanings" selectively. Only in certain higher contemplative phases can attention be fixed so that it no longer participates in the calling forth of endlessly changing intentionalities—that is, in which the intentional processes are no longer drawn hither and thither by the spontaneous expression of subordinate sensorial networks.

In a sense, symbols order experience. They attract and focus our attention, modulate the interplay between events of the moment and events of the past, and canalize our experience into accord with that of our fellows. As we have seen, bringing the range of experience of group members into synchronous accord requires a complex personal history of development of each member, at least among the higher animals for whom the extent of disparity in experience, intentionality, and volition is potentially great. Indeed, Whitehead (1927), among others (see Chapple 1970; Burridge 1979), noted that development in higher social beings involves a tricky balance between the evolutionarily emerging freedom of the individual and maintenance of social adaptation.

Part of the problem of bringing intentionality and experience into social accord is solved by the neurognostic origins of models mediating perception, cognition, and other processes mediating consciousness. The nervous system is already predisposed in pre- and perinatal life to attend certain stimuli over other stimuli in the environment, such as faces, edges and patterns of things, breasts, and voices. The young brain knows to seek these patterns and explore them, to play with them, and thus to modify and elaborate intentionality in adaptive ways as the cells and social relations among the community of cells intrinsically develop.

Elaboration of and interrelations among models may become extremely complex in time so that the role of the symbol is much like that of the tip of the proverbial iceberg. The organism is aware of only a fraction of the intentionality entrained by, and to, the symbol. We may only be aware of the percept (perhaps a familiar face), but not of the entire range of intentionality evoked by the percept ("unconscious" associations, affects, metabolic responses, etc.). During semiosis, then, symbols accrue an expanding evocative field within the cognized environment as meaning develops in the dialogue between the intentional processes and the sensorial model mediating the symbol. Symbols become polysemic, "pregnant" with meaning. Meanings elaborate and multiply via continuous integration of information about noumena in the world as the organism explores its cognized environment and responds to events arising in the sensorium (see Changeux 1985:126ff). As Ricoeur (1962:192) notes, "symbols invite thought." Paraphrasing him a bit, symbols invite entrainment—the evocation of thought and other functions of consciousness in the ordering of experience. They thus invite experience by attracting our attention (semiotropism) and by evoking multiple associations configured upon them as cores (semiosis). In other words, symbols invite experience by penetrating to the neurocognitive systems mediating the organization of the field of dots that is our phenomenal experience as it unfolds moment-by-moment in the sensorium.

SYMBOLIC PENETRATION

Penetration, as previously defined (page 36), means the effect exercised by the activities of one neural system upon another neural system. By *symbolic penetration* we wish to refer specifically to the effects exercised by the neural system mediating a symbolic percept (or the entire perceptual field) upon other neural, endocrine, and physiological systems within the being. We are speaking of the pattern of evocation and entrainment of neural and other physiological systems produced in the wake of activating a perceptual network (Changeux 1985:140ff). Generally speaking, penetration is an activity occurring over a duration beginning with the initial activation of the perceptual network either spontaneously or by exteroception or proprioception at the periphery. We have already discussed many of the fundamental principles upon which symbolic penetration is based in the last chapter. Here we wish to address some of the possible applications of our view to understanding how the symbolic process operates to facilitate adaptation to the world, as well as integration or fragmentation of systems within the organism.

EVOKING THE OBJECT

Much of neurocognitive processing of information about the world occurs as a consequence of recognizing objects and relations among objects already encoded in neural models. The first state of penetrance from the world is to neural pathways that operate to recognize invariant patterns neurognostically present in the immanent structure of models, or that may have been encountered and coded in memory. We are able to recognize the same chords or words regardless of pitch and the same shapes regardless of size (see Pitts and McCulloch in McCulloch 1965:46ff, John 1967; John et al. 1967; Pick in Pick 1979:145ff; Gibson 1969). Recognition of pattern would seem to be the first order of the day (Bohm 1965), followed rapidly by entrainment of associated neural networks mediating available information, affect, higher cognitive processing, and perhaps motor and metabolic activity.

All such entrainments are keyed to recognized patterns, often experienced as perceptual objects and activities, or relations among objects. Objects, of course, have their experiential concrescence in the sensorium as dynamic fields of dots, whose organization is produced in part by topographic projection, inhibitory surround, and other principles of neurocognitive operation variously applied in the hierarchical organization mediating the perceptual field. Once constituted in a concrescence of dots, the brain will maintain the stable object-pattern until the operations upon it have been completed. In other words, the model mediating the percept will reverberate.

Reverberation is an active process. The brain expends metabolic energy actively constituting its cognized environment and maintaining attendant entrainments by which operations are carried out upon the cognized environment. The percept may or may not continue in the absence of stimuli from the initiating *noumenon*, which may have produced the initial percept. In the absence of the initiatory stimulus, or where activation of the percept is spontaneous, the model mediating the percept may be said to be autoreverberating. This mechanism underlies what Piaget termed *object permanence* (see Piaget and Inhelder 1969:14) and has much to do with symbolic penetration techniques like Tibetan arising yoga (see page 198f). It is fundamental as well to the processes of object (or "visual") knowledge, which is frequently contrasted with linguistic (or "verbal") knowledge, and about which a great deal has been written (see e.g., John-Steiner 1985:205ff).

PENETRATION TO INTENTIONALITY

In theory at least, any neural network within the nervous system may be entrained to the models mediating percepts with or without intervention of conscious network. Thus any network may potentially participate in the field of intentionality entrained to a percept-as-symbol. Recognition of an object or pattern can produce the experience of love or terror, voiding of the bladder, movement of the hands, salivation, increased blood pressure, fantasies and thoughts, and reminiscenses. The extent of penetrance from a symbol to its intentional network will be determined by various factors, including whether the process is conscious (occurs within and as a part of conscious network), the perceptual frame of reference in which the symbol is embedded, the intensity of evocation, the state of arousal of the organism, the duration of peripheral stimulation, the degree of novelty involved, and so on (see Changeux 1985).

Symbolic penetration does not, of course, require mediation of conscious network. Symbols penetrate directly to unconscious intentionalities, and far from being impossible or unlikely, this process is common and characteristic of the ongoing functioning of the nervous system. Habituation is one form unconscious penetrance may take: the process by which events in the world are monitored for salience at lower levels of cognitive processing. Also, Grinder and Bandler (1976) explore the methods of hypnotherapist Milton Erikson by which symbolic material is introduced to a client at an unconscious level. And Jung (1968b) notes the role of symbolism in orchestrating events in the unconscious (see also Sperber 1975:17ff).

In addition to operating both in and out of consciousness, symbolic penetration may evoke intentionalities that are formed at different stages both in phylogenesis and ontogenesis. For instance, intentionality may be mediated by neoneurognostic models or paleoneurognostic models, or a combination of these. Furthermore, intentionality may develop very early in life, as in pre- or perinatal life, or later in life, such as during university studies. The range of intentionality to which a symbol or symbolic field may penetrate is vast and multileveled. In order to give credence to the enormous complexity of the symbolic process, we must examine the two main aspects of its communicative role: first, the facilitation of intraorganismic coordination of somatic systems; and second, the facilitation of interorganismic coordination of cognized environments among group members.

HOMEOMORPHOGENESIS

The symbolic process may be completely internal to the physiology of an organism, for example, the Jungian "active imagination." The being is a community of cells organized into multiple somatic systems and into multiple levels of hierarchical control functions. These various somatic systems must communicate with each other so that their discrete functions remain adaptively and harmoniously organized within the context of the activities of the being as a whole. It should be remembered that the nervous system, only one of many systems in the body, carries out its activities in intimate concert with other physiological systems. The brain controls the activity of the body relative to the operational environment by moving muscles; it is fed by controlling metabolic activities and by receiving nutrients from the circulatory system; it controls many other nonneural vital functions by regulating endocrine activities and hormone levels in the body.

This intimate interaction among the nervous system and other somatic systems, and between one neural system and another, entails penetration: the activities of one system affects other systems. For example, a disorder in the colon may produce generator potentials in nociceptors in that organ, which in turn penetrate into central nervous system networks mediating the cognized body, causing one to experience abdominal pain. The effect produced by one system upon another will not be the same as the change of state in the original system. The effect elicited in system B will be only partially isomorphic with the change that produced it in system A. Each system must manifest its responses to inputs through its own unique organization. A change of state in some somatic system penetrating to, say, the visual cortex can produce only a visual effect. Thus, although the systems of the body completely interpenetrate, their effects upon each other vary with the particular functional organization of the systems involved. We can say, therefore, that a morphogenesis occurring in one somatic system may produce a morphogenesis in other somatic systems but that the various changes of state are only partially isomorphic with each other. In other words, morphogeneses in various interactive somatic systems are lawfully related to each other, but only similar to (never exactly the same as) each other. Penetration between the various parts and levels of the body may therefore be said to result in *homeomorphogenesis*.[2]

SYMBOLISM AND HOMEOMORPHOGENESIS

Homeomorphogenic interactions among neurocognitive systems, or among neurocognitive systems and other somatic systems, can assume a symbolic status when any of the neurocognitive systems involved mediate sensorial events. A common situation is one in which a transformation in a somatic system that does not mediate experience produces a transformation in a neural network that does mediate experience. In this case the sensorial effect may be understood as a symbolic expression of the other nonsensorial somatic event. For example, the colonic disorder just mentioned produces the experience of pain. The pain is not a disorder but rather signals the possibility of disorder. A physician may palpate the abdomen and ask for reports of any painful or sensitive spots. From such symbolic expressions, that is, "symptoms," healers in all societies diagnose mental and physical disease. In many societies dream symbolism is interpreted as symptomatic of psychological disorder (e.g., Wallace 1959 on the Iroquois). Experience (in whatever phase of consciousness it arises) is considered as symptomatic of changes or problems existing outside the range of consciousness. This mechanism can perhaps account for the validity of Kleinman's (1980) distinction between "disease" (we would say operational disease) and "illness" (cognized disease). Because it is a neurognostic structure of consciousness, homeomorphogenesis leads to such cross-cultural regularities as diagnosis and symbolic healing.

Conversely, a sensorial system may produce a nonsensorial effect upon some other somatic system. For example, one can elicit a stress response from various bodily systems by merely evoking an image of a dangerous or painful experience. One may imagine cutting one's finger and evoke reflexes and endocrine activities appropriate to actually cutting a finger. Many societies use symbolic means in healing under the presumption that in some manner the symbols penetrate to the disorder and effect a cure (see Dow 1986; Moerman 1979; Young 1982). In fact, some interesting experiments are now being carried out by American physicians in the use of symbolic visualization techniques to treat cancer and other diseases. Symptoms, then, may be sensorial representations of somatic events and as symbols "invite" intentionality and multiple cognitive/affective associations which, for the patient, unite to form part of their "explanatory model" of disease (Kleinman 1980).

The usual state of affairs is, of course, a continuous feedback interaction between sensorial neural and nonsensorial neural and somatic systems. Causality is usually systemic and thus operates in both directions; but indicating which system initiates the interaction is central, for it affects the role played by the symbolic process in consciousness. It is thus fair to ask whether the symbol is an expression of unconscious processes in the being, or whether the symbol is the penetrator to unconscious processes. This bidirectional communication among discrete systems is crucial to the maintenance of whatever degree of fragmentation or integration of systems is characteristic of any particular consciousness. And as such, it is an important consideration in understanding how semiosis occurs in development.

METAPHOR

There is yet another symbolic process of keen interest to anthropology, the metaphor. *Metaphor* is the process by which imagery attained in one domain of experience is used to order, or provide meaning for, events in another domain of experience. For example, if we are involved in solving a difficult problem, we might say "the going got rough," or that we are "between a rock and a hard place." Experience in traversing or coping with the physical world is used to provide meaning for a mental quandary via imposition of imagery. The imagery draws with it significant cognitive and, perhaps, even effective and metabolic associations that enrich (whether appropriately or inappropriately) the associations available to conscious network at the moment.

As many theorists have noted (see Levi-Strauss 1964, 1966, 1978; Cassirer 1957; Boulding 1956; Fernandez 1986), the use of metaphor in the constitution of meaning is ubiquitous to the human species and is to be found in all cultures—in fact, is one of the basic structural "building blocks" of culture. Metaphor is a cognitive process by which a pattern is abstracted from memory of experience in one domain and applied to, or associated with, experience in another domain, which is being constituted within consciousness. The transference of cognitions is via imagery. One image (from memory) is superimposed on another image (currently present), and associations entrained to the memory image become entrained to the current image. If we say, "he is a worm," we drag cognitive/imaginal associations appropriate to the image of worm (say, a slimy and squirmy creature that is afraid of light and crawls in the dark under rocks) into cognition pertaining to "him." Piaget (1952) considers this type of cognition to be primitive and terms its operator *transductive logic*, a form of thought characteristic of the highly symbolic, preoperational thought of young children.

Metaphor is mediated by largely cortico-cortical homeomorphogenic entrainments, whose associative processes remain unconscious to the mind using metaphor. The association of "him" with "worm" may involve nothing more elaborate than a simple recognition of similarity and attribution of affects, say, revulsion, and no awareness of the analytical inappropriateness of the equation. Only a superimposition of the two images occurs and all else follows automatically. The combination of images may produce a kind of cross-phase transference if the imagery and other associations attributed in one phase of consciousness were encountered in, and are appropriate to, another phase of consciousness. If a person encountered during waking consciousness becomes equated with the imagery of a radiant being previously experienced during the dream phase, a cross-phase metaphorical association has been made. This kind of symbolism is very common to cultures with myth-laden cosmology and to cultures whose experiences attained in polyphasic consciousness are integrated via a single hermeneutical framework.

SYMBOLIC PENETRATION TECHNIQUES

All religious systems in the world use symbols to penetrate to and activate intentionalities that are either neurognostically present in all human brains (i.e., archetypes) or that have been developed through programs of enculturation. By manipulating symbols shamans are able to heal, evoke alternative phases of consciousness, stimulate inquiry and exploration, engender metaphorical-metonymic understanding, and transform ego identity. We have already shown how symbols and their intentionalities interact and have discussed how intentionalities may develop and how they may be penetrated and expressed by symbols. We now wish to examine how symbols are explicitly organized by societies to bring about specific intentional ends, including the evocation, development, and integration of gender-as-symbol for polar attributes of consciousness.

TECHNIQUES OF SYMBOLIC PENETRATION

Symbolic penetration takes on the mantle of technique through embedding symbols in ritual.[3] Symbolic penetration techniques are, in other words, ritualized practices of evocation, or the dramatic performance of metaphor (Fernandez 1986). We are using the term *technique*, not in the narrow mechanistic sense common to our culture, but in a broader Ellulian sense to mean "any complex of standardized means for attaining a predetermined result" (1964:vi). In a very real sense we are being penetrated all the time. Any nearby object, sound, texture, chemical, and so on, may be a symbolic stimulus penetrating to intentionality; for instance, music (Rouget 1985), imagery (Noll 1985), hallucinogens (deRios 1984), disease (Dow 1986), figures of speech (Fernandez 1986). Our concern now, however, is with the purposeful manipulation of symbols to attain some desired effect. We are especially interested in the use of penetration techniques in order to evoke significant warps of consciousness—an evocation that is a universal theme of transpersonal religious practices cross-culturally. Such techniques are to be found in the long training programs of apprentice shamans, as well as in Masonic initiation, Hindu and Buddhist tantric tradition, Sufism, and Kabbalistic mystical tradition.

Ritual is a complex of standardized activity that may operate to *amplify* a symbolic penetration technique. The symbolic information may be demarcated as sacred as opposed to profane and is thus raised in status to a level that attracts and holds the attention of the participant, thereby intensifying the penetration and maximizing the intentional field evoked. Again, the intentional impact of a cross in a Mass may be more intense than a cross used as personal ornament.

Ritual may also operate to prepare the consciousness of participants for optimal penetration. For example, a ritual may incorporate various drivers, which retune autonomic functioning to a balance appropriate to the introduction of (perhaps previously secret) symbolism, thus pairing the symbolic material with a discrete affective state. A ritual might pair both drumming and dancing (auditory and somaesthetic drivers) with the wearing of a mask and other regalia. The mask is designed not only to symbolize identification of the shaman with the consciousness and power of a supernatural entity, but also to incubate the direct experience of being that entity, and accruing the power obtainable by participation in the alternative reality of that entity (see Young-Laughlin and Laughlin 1988).

PENETRATION TO PALEONEUROGNOSTIC MODELS

We suspect that many religious practices found cross-culturally use symbolic penetration techniques in order to relevate, transform, and integrate previously latent or suppressed neural networks (see chap. 5). As we have said, symbols can penetrate to networks latent in their functioning or operating outside the bounds of awareness. Penetration to these networks may result in extraordinary experiences—experiences unaccessible to normal waking consciousness. Such techniques thus have two main properties of interest to us: (1) They may bypass inhibitions normally operating to suppress the activity of models; and (2) They may transform, elaborate, and even integrate with conscious network previously suppressed models.

Of particular interest is the potential for using symbolic penetration techniques for relevating and integrating neoneurognostic and paleo-neurognostic models (see page 72). Symbols of the right pattern penetrating with sufficient intensity may activate models in a broad field of intentionality. The field of intentionality may include phylogenetically older limbic and brain stem models, and by activation they may become transformed and, to an extent, more completely incorporated into a conscious network composed of phylogenetically more recent models. An eruption of this previously unconscious material may result in profound alteration in personality, autonomic balance, understanding, and behavior.

A member of our biogenetic structural group, Mark Webber (1980; Webber, Stephens, and Laughlin 1983), has used this theory to generate a compelling explanation of the course and effects of the Makah wolf ritual, as reported by Ernst (1952). A secret society among the Makah called Klukwalle offers an initiation *(Qua-ech')* each winter. During this ceremony new members are inducted into the society. During the four days of activity, initiates undergo fasting and other alterations of their daily routine.[4] Members act out wolflike traits. They later don wolf masks, speak and sing about wolves, and in general direct the attention of all to "wolfness." By the third night (the wolf is a nocturnal animal!) initiates are gashing themselves with knives to leave initiatory scars. They walk through the village imitating the behavior of the wolf. The climax of the whole affair is reached when initiates "dash about, as they experience the Wolf frenzy . . . putting the fire out and giving the wolf cry." Ernest describes the climax in this way:

> The singing is often lost in the noise of Klukwalle rattles and Wolf calls. The initiates at a certain point come out and circle about round the fire, "showing what they are" (i.e., that they are neophytes) until the fire is put out by those who go "He-guat 'luck," as the Wolf frenzy is called. During the He-guat'luck a certain ordained type of Wolf mask is worn . . . by the initiate; this is accompanied by a very vigorous mimetic dance in which the protagonist, his face duly painted and dagger or knife in either hand, is held by two men with ropes until his frenzy subsides. Although the third evening is the appointed time for the He-guat'luck, beginnings of it might appear as early as the second night. (1952:20)

The Makah ritual presents a pattern of activities not uncommon in the anthropological literature. Here we have the paired association of symbols in a standardized series of activities with such operators as ordeals, fasting, and sonic (whistles), somaesthetic (dancing), and photic (flickering firelight) drivers. Although some participants may be merely acting out the "frenzy," undoubtedly many enter a profound alternate phase of consciousness during which they experience directly the essence of "wolfness." We may interpret this experience as mediated by the older core limbic and brain stem networks which, when triggered to total eruption, relevate the fundamental, "bestial" functions of these systems into full awareness.

There is ample evidence supporting the view that the paleomammalian and reptilian complexes in humans are preadaptively wired for "archaic" neuroendocrine responses (Morgenson and Calaresu 1975; Gellhorn 1968; Malmo 1975). The "frenzy" of the Wolf cult initiate might well involve such responses as change in rate of respiration, heart rate, corticosteroid secretion, adrenalin secretion, endorphin and enkephalin secretion, muscle tonus, and facial expression; these along with other factors may be conditioned by the circumstances of the ritual into a "wolflike" package of responses with their experiential concommitants. Indeed, this phenomenon seems to be common cross-culturally where various ANS drivers are used to evoke various types of "frenzy" episodes in ritual (Winkelman 1986; see also Sargant 1974 for a semipopular account). The initiate experiences a gestalt of specific neurophysiological responses that become associated with the "wolf-frenzy" and the core SYMBOL, the wolf, particularly as depicted in masks. This experience and the resulting alterations in cognition constitute the conation of the ritual.

There exists the potential for a more complete integration of these archaic structures within the confines of conscious network. That is, the individual may now have more conscious access to these structures as they are more likely to be entrainable to conscious network. For those members of the Wolf cult who actually do experience the frenzy, cognitive, experiental, and physiological models become transformed by association with paleoneurognostic models and are reintegrated as intentionality around (penetrable by) a core SYMBOL. Presumably, by manipulating this core SYMBOL, the secret society is able to penetrate and access this new intentionality for its collective purposes.

PENETRATION AND BUDDHIST MEDITATIONS

As another example of penetration, we wish to describe and analyze a more elaborate system of symbolic penetration techniques. One of the authors (CDL) has worked for some years within the tradition of Tibetan Tantric Buddhism, and much of what we have to say here derives either from his own experiences or from those of his associates and informants.

Tibetan Buddhist adepts practice a form of contemplation originating in early Hindu tantrism that may be called for our purposes *arising yoga.* An adept is initiated into a particular practice of arising yoga by undertaking an empowerment ceremony, or *wang* (Tib. *dBang),* given by a *lama,* or teacher. The empowerment ceremony is rich with visual, auditory, olfactory, and somaesthetic symbolism, and is designed to introduce the initiate to a series of symbols and practices that are to be repeated frequently by the initiate later in his private meditation. The central task in the meditation is the construction of an image in the mind's eye, which becomes the object of concentration (see Noll 1985 for the cross-cultural literature on "mental imagery cultivation"). The object of the work, at least in its early stages, is the constituting of the image at will—hence the term "arising."

The actual practice of the meditation with its central visualization involves a ritual procedure of at least nine steps (see Laughlin, Mc-Manus, and Webber 1984):

1. *Purification.* The adept carries out initial practices in order to quiet the stream of thoughts and fantasies, to calm his body, to perceive his body as hollow, and his sensorium as an empty vessel.

2. *Constituting the Image.* The adept constructs an image of a deity within his empty sensorium. The construction of the total, often complex image is accomplished step by step and is a process of concatenating a number of constituent SYMBOLS such as bells, skulls, flowers, body parts, jewels, knives, and heads of different colors. The construction occurs in a series of discrete additions. The Tibetan text from which the adept is guided may read, ". . . arm, gold bracelet, head, jewelled crown, . . ." and the adept is to add each part to his internal image as it is named.

3. *Stabilizing the Image.* The adept meditates on the form of the completed image or on those portions of the image he is able to hold in his mind's eye. The meditation upon the image lasts for a varying period of time.[5]

4. *Identification with the Image.* At first the deity is imagined as outside the adept's body. Once the form is stabilized, however, the adept imagines the deity entering his own body and becoming one with him.

5. *Inner Meditation.* The adept may be given more advanced practices in which he imagines the internal energy flow within the body of the deity, which he has become (see chapter 11 on psychic energy). These inner meditations are also upon SYMBOLS constructed within the sensorium, but are imagined as existing within one's own (equals the deity's) body.

6. *Mantra Meditation.* Depending upon the practice, the adept may repeat an appropriate incantation (Skt. *mantra*) during all of steps 3 through 5 and during step 8 below. For example, if the deity being visualized is Chenrezig, then one appropriate incantation would be the famous *om mani padme hum* mantra.

7. *Dissolving the Image.* The adept dissolves the image, which is to say, his (the deity's) own form, part by part until all that is left of the image is a tiny spot of light. Then, the tiny spot is made to vanish and the adept meditates for a period of time on the place where the spot vanished.

8. *Reemergence of the Image.* The adept meditates upon the essential emptiness of phenomena for as long as he is able or until the image of the deity spontaneously reappears in the sensorium.

9. *Final Dissolution of the Image.* The image is finally dissolved back into the essential emptiness of the sensorium and the practice is completed with appropriate formulae.

This listing is a simplified breakdown of the essential steps in arising yoga practice. Readers interested in more complete examples of Tibetan *sadhana* techniques are urged to consult Beyer (1973), Willis (1972), or Blofeld (1974).

One feature that makes the various Buddhist contemplative traditions immensely interesting is that they explicitly recognize the stages of the penetration process and the stages of cognitive development they portend. What follows is a manageable, refined classification, which we have modified from a number of ancient Buddhist sources,[6] in order to make the scheme more useful for cross-cultural analysis. Although it will be presented here in the context of the Tibetan system, the stage model will prove particularly useful for understanding practices in societies where specialized meditation techniques are not practiced, and where a coherent indigenous ethnopsychological model of penetration cannot be found (see Noll 1985). We will outline the stages of penetration and then provide illustrative examples.

1. *Outer SYMBOL.* The first stage of penetration is concentration upon the outer SYMBOL. An object, or set of objects, is given to the adept for the purpose of concentration. The object may be literally any symbol presented via any one or more of the senses. In the Tibetan practice, the SYMBOLS used are most commonly visual and auditory and are introduced to the adept during the empowerment ceremony. Examples of appropriate outer SYMBOLS in the Tibetan tradition include a portrait of a deity, the sound of bell, and an incantation *(mantra).* From the earliest period of Buddhist tradition, monks were encouraged to concentrate upon objects they made that represented space, light, the different colors, and the elements (fire, air, earth, and water; see Buddhaghosa

1976: vol. I on *kasina* practice). Examples of outer SYMBOLS encountered in other religious traditions around the planet are such things as a wooden cross, the Prayer of the Heart and the Sacred Heart in Christian meditative tradition, masks worn by shamans in cultures throughout the world, a candle or firelight, a Navajo sand painting, an animal, crystalline spheres and other forms, skrying bowls, smoke, water, dance, drama, drumming, and many other objects. Any one of the sense modes may act as an entry gate to penetration into the cognized environment. The outer SYMBOL will tend to fall within the range of appropriate environmental and cultural patterning; for example, a mask of an animal indigenous to the environment (killer whale among Kwakiutl, tiger among natives of India).

2. *Inner SYMBOL.* The inner SYMBOL is created by holding an eidetic image internally without reinforcement from an external stimulus. Once the adept is able to constitute the requisite image in his mind's eye, the outer SYMBOL (painting, object, sound, etc.) is no longer required, and the practice begins thereafter with the inner SYMBOL. We presume from evidence presented earlier that the inner SYMBOL is mediated primarily by cortical models. There may, of course, be midbrain limbic or lower networks entrained to conscious network while concentration upon the inner SYMBOL proceeds, and these may well influence the form of the image. In any event, the inner SYMBOL does not remain static after internalization. Parts of a complex image may be missing, proportions among forms may change, and phenomena in other sensory modalities may arise due to cross-model transfer; for example, one may see patterns of colored lights while listening to a symphony, one may smell a visualization, touch an image, hear a deity speak. And the inner SYMBOL may "come alive" in the sensorium and begin to move and transform in conative ways not willed by the adept.

3. *Universal Symbol.* When an inner SYMBOL is stabilized as an eidetic image, and concentration upon it is intense and undistracted, the stage is set for the arising of one or more universal symbols. These are sensorial phenomena that arise unbidden from unconscious networks, and are the result of a radical reentrainment of networks producing a warp in consciousness. The inner SYMBOL is transformed or eliminated, and in its place occurs a sensory experience intuitively, but nonrationally related to the inner SYMBOL. In time, memories of encounters with universal symbolic material become the major intentionalities associated with the outer/inner SYMBOL. Such memories include phenomena, as well as affects and intuitive insights that have arisen as a consequence of contemplation of the inner SYMBOL. It is crucial to the scientific appreciation of the penetration process to understand that the universal symbols are rarely discussed with the adept prior to their arising. No

anticipatory set is established. The teacher assigns the work and knows from the adept's reports of his experiences and insights how far along the adept is in his practice.

4. *Absorption in the Universal Symbol*. If concentration is hyperintentional with the universal symbol as object, then the adept may experience absorption in the universal symbol. Absorption is the experience of total unity with the object of attention so that awareness is no longer dualistic. That is, there is no awareness of a distinction or phenomenological distance between ego and symbol; there is only the awareness of symbol. The concentration is complete so that all other phenomena are excluded from awareness. Absorption is a common experience in everyday life. Everyone has become "absorbed" in a good book, a movie, or in making love. But in this case, because the absorption is in a universal symbol, the experience is far more numinous. Absorption is commonly associated with ecstatic bliss and a profound sense of tranquillity. We interpret this experience as mediated by another radical reentrainment of conscious network so that the deep, often paleoneurognostic models mediating the universal symbol are entrained to consciousness. Intellection is absent during the period of absorption, and yet profound intuitive insights may arise as a consequence of the experience.

5. *Void Consciousness*. Absorption into the universal symbol *may*, under the right conditions, lead to Void Consciousness, the ultimate experience of many of the world's religions and one that may be interpreted in various cultures as unification with God, the attainment of "pure consciousness," union with the All, or any number of other labels. We will have more to say about Void Consciousness in a later chapter (also see Nishitani 1982).

ANOTHER EXAMPLE: THE WATER MANDALA

The use of mandalas (Skt. meaning "mind-device" or "mind door") as objects of contemplation may be found in virtually all contemplative traditions (see Jung 1968b; Tuci 1961; Arguellas and Arguellas 1972). Before returning once again to the more complex Tibetan system, we will give a simple example of a symbolic penetration technique from the early Buddhist *kasina* practices (Buddhaghosa 1976). We will select one of the meditations upon the elements, the *water kasina*. In this and all of the other *kasina* practices, the first step is to construct a *kasina;* that is, an outer SYMBOL. In the case of the water *kasina* the object of meditation is a neutral grey clay bowl filled with clear water which is positioned 2½ spans (one span equals the distance from the elbow to the tip of the middle finger) in front of the adept's body and at approximately a 45-degree angle below eye level. The adept then sits in a relaxed, yet alert posture and gazes at the water in the bowl for short intervals. The adept may repeat an incantation such as the word *apo* (water).

Between intervals of gazing at the *kasina* the adept attempts to hold eidetically the image of the water in his mind's eye. The object of the initial practice is to recall the image of water without requiring the *kasina*. When the recall is accomplished, the role of the outer SYMBOL is finished. The eidetic image—the inner SYMBOL—is the principal object of concentration throughout. The mandala of water is duplicated within the sensorium in the absence of the outer stimulus, with or without the eyes closed. In order to emphasize the independence of the inner from the outer SYMBOL, the traditional practice required the adept to leave the place of the water *kasina* and move to another spot for concentration upon the inner water SYMBOL.

Sustained and intense concentration upon the inner water SYMBOL will lead to several experiences that are not logically entailed or suggested by any of the adept's practices but are nonetheless predictable. Universal symbols are commonly reported by mediators as spontaneously arising in the sensorium (CDL's and Mark Webber's own experience, as well as the ancient meditation text: see Buddhaghosa 1976). For instance, one may perceive "streams" of movement running through the water, or "bubbles" emerging from the surface, or "steam" or "mist" rising from the surface. We place these phenomena in quotes because these are interpretations imposed upon the phenomena from our own, Western perspective. Different labels may be used by different individuals in different cultures. These symbols are considered in Buddhist practice to be forerunners for the eventual realization of the classic water mandala experience. They are indicators as well and signify to the teacher the adept's stage of development in meditation. The total realization of the water mandala may be accompanied by images of a crystalline network. These may appear in space in front of the adept or in the body, and tend to be paired with the maturing of intuitive knowledge pertaining to the essence of the water element. This knowledge consists of the connectedness, cohesiveness, concretion, or confluence of things, as symbolized by "network."

These are all universal symbols, for they are associated with discrete, alternative phases of consciousness in which the phenomenal aspects are devoid of personal or cultural conditioning. They are, as Jung was so fond of saying, archetypal. We should note that the universal symbols may arise even during the outer SYMBOL stage. This event should not be surprising, for the networks mediating the perception of the outer SYMBOL are neurological, and, hence, inner. Perfecting the inner SYMBOL is actually, in part, the transformation of the percept into an autoreverberative model, independent of evocation from the world. But penetration to the model's mediating the universal symbols may well occur before perfection of the inner SYMBOL is complete.

Absorption (dhyana, jhana) into the universal symbol may occur when the mind develops a very fine balance between deep tranquillity and concentrated alertness. As we have described, no separation between the symbol and the perceiver is experienced. For the duration of the experience, the entirety of consciousness becomes "network-connectivity," consciousness is "locked" to the universal symbol to the exclusion of all else. There is the experience of total union with this universal quality of consciousness. Just as the Makah initiate becomes fully transformed into "wolfness," so too does the Buddhist adept working on the water element become totally transformed into the quality of "concrescence."

SOME IMPLICATIONS

Several points may be made now relative to penetration. Statements collected from mature contemplatives suggest that any form whatever may be chosen as an outer SYMBOL, and with transformation through internalization and concentration, universal symbols will arise. We hypothesize that the outer/inner SYMBOL is the experience of the externally conditioned and developed model (i.e., the percept), while the universal symbols that arise as a consequence of concentration upon the outer/inner SYMBOL are the homeomorphogenic representations of the relatively unconditioned, undeveloped neurognosis from which the conditioned model develops. In other words, the universal symbol is mediated by the primitive, relatively undeveloped initial organization of models as they existed prior to external conditioning. Every conditioned model retains to some extent its predeveloped form.

We also hypothesize that traditional penetration techniques are not based upon a random selection of objects as outer SYMBOLS. Rather, as the term "technique" implies, forms are chosen with a purpose in mind. Knowledge of which SYMBOLS to assign is grounded upon generations of practice with SYMBOLS that have proved particularly efficacious in evoking experiences that significantly confirm the point of view or teaching that gives rise to the technique. The Makah ritual is designed to evoke an experience that confirms for each secret society member the great power associated with the wolf. In Buddhist tradition, SYMBOLS have been chosen (indeed, some are older than Buddhism itself) that, as it were, sidestep the ego and provide profound evidence of aspects and knowledge about the being and the world extrinsic to the adept's ego. Transpersonal experiences of this sort thus have the potential of accelerating and broadening the scope of personal growth.

The nonlogical, but predictable relationship between the outer/inner

SYMBOL and the universal symbols associated with it is methodologically and theoretically crucial. This relationship suggests that invariant principles exist in the relationship between conscious percipience and unconscious processes in the nervous system. The invariance indicated here is simply another incidence of cross-cultural invariance in the structure of alternative phases of consciousness. Eliade (1964) has amply demonstrated the structural commonalities in shamanic experiences cross-culturally. Such experiences involve trips to the sky or to the underworld, bright lights, and ecstasy, all of which, by the way, may arise during the course of meditation. In a similar vein, deRios (1984), Kluver (1966), and Siegel (1977) demonstrate structural invariance of perception in the reports of subjects under the influence of psychotropic drugs such as mescal, marihuana, and psilocybin. With Siegel (1977:139), we hypothesize that all such structural invariance is due largely to the effects of drugs or techniques upon neural structures that either directly mediate sensorial experiences or indirectly mediate them through homeomorphogenic entrainment. This hypothesis follows logically, of course, from the principle of experiential-physiological correspondence (see page 92).

Finally, it should be emphasized again that the arising of the universal symbol often occurs paired with an affect of intense ecstasy or bliss. The experience vivifies the adept—an effect that may be felt for as long as many hours. There is thus a numinous quality to the universal symbol. It is unexpected, it is often novel and dramatic, and it is frequently paired with both intuitive insight and ecstatic bliss. These factors combine to produce a particularly memorable experience, which is often given a sacred interpretation. The memory of the universal symbol(s) and its attendant knowledge and affects become the intentionality of the outer SYMBOL. Over time and with diligent practice, many such experiences may occur. The "meaning" of the outer SYMBOL is thereby experienced as dynamic, unfolding, and deepening. Moreover, the more intentionality accrues via direct, transpersonal experience, the more the "meaning" becomes experienced as ineffable. The "meaning" becomes vaster and deeper than any textual rendition could possibly describe.

YET ANOTHER EXAMPLE: GENDER IN TIBETAN ARISING YOGA

Returning now to our more complex example of penetration technique, there are several possible versions of Tibetan cosmology (Paul 1982:43ff; Stein 1972). Most versions depict the origin of the cosmos by reference to an absolute, undifferentiated realm that somehow becomes differentiated into the primordial paternal (associated with light or brilliance) and the primordial maternal (associated with darkness and torment; Paul 1982:51; Getty 1962:197). Other versions associate the Great Mother of Infinite Space with the absolute realm at the beginning of cosmogony (ibid.:52).

By way of a series of bifurcations, the world is created as an essential polarity with masculine light on the right hand and feminine dark on the left hand (ibid.:499). This splitting of the world in cosmogony into masculine and feminine is very common among the world's cultures (Neumann 1963; Eliade 1959:139). The associations between bright masculine and dark feminine, and right and left hand, respectively, was noted early in this century by the French sociologist Robert Hertz (1909).

Not surprisingly, the feminine aspect is further associated with the womb, which in turn is associated with hell and with death and rebirth (ibid.:255). The womb is transformed in myth into a sack or cave in which the hero (masculine) hides while awaiting birth (ibid.:261, 289). Those associations become the grounds for suppression of females, who are linked with demons and passion and are thus dangerous to masculine unity (ibid.:272). It should be noted that legendary teachers like Milarepa are often depicted as having spent years dwelling in caves and contemplating in cave mouths (Evans-Wentz 1969), a type of solitary meditation allowed only the most seasoned contemplatives. The cave mouth *qua* vulva is seen as the only route to rebirth, also a common motif among the world's mythologies (see Campbell 1949:297ff).

GENDER IN TIBETAN CONTEMPLATION

Because the Buddhism practiced in Tibet is an amalgamation of early *Bon-po* cosmology and Northern Indian Buddhist doctrine, the latter a blend of still older Buddhist teachings and Hindu *tantra*, Tibetan iconography is rich in gender-related symbolism. The word *tantra* is difficult to translate but is most commonly associated with the Sanskrit roots for "thread," "rope," and "loom." In the ancient Vedantic texts, the cosmos is seen as a lotus flower upon which occurs an eternal play between *Shiva* (male) and *Shakti* (female). Emphasis in tantrism is, as Walker (1982:9) points out, upon the feminine principle, which is associated with activities such as cooking, spinning, plaiting, and weaving. The feminine principle is the unfolding of the *prana* energies that constitute the world, energies that in their becoming reveal the inherent fabric of the world—she is the "undying body of illusion," as *samsara* (or the world of appearances) is often described.

A more accurate connotative and esoteric meaning of *tantra* refers to the process by which all the disparate aspects of consciousness become integrated through the disciplined practice of awareness. In this respect, there is a tacit recognition of a fundamental disparity or fragmentation between those aspects coded as masculine and those coded as feminine.

ༀ། །གདོད་མའི་མགོན་བོ་དོན་མི་འགྱུར། །དཀྱིལ་འབོ་ར་ན་རྒྱི་འབྱུང་གནས་མཆོ།།
མ་ཉིན་རབ་ཡེ་ཤེས་རྒྱ་མཚོ་བ་སྟེས། །ཁྱབ་བདག་ཨང་ཕྱམ་ལ་ཕྱག་འཚལ། །

FIGURE 21. A Tibetan *yab-yum* figure. The peaceful deity is Samantabhadra in sexual union with his consort Samantabhadri. Reprinted from K. Dowman, "The Nyingma Icons," *Kailash* (Kathmandu, Nepal) 2 (4): 331.

Meditation techniques are carried out among tantric adepts to bring about the "reweaving" of the masculine and feminine strands of consciousness into the integrated, undifferentiated totality whence consciousness originally derives.

The more advanced forms of Tibetan symbolic penetration techniques commonly work with male and female figures (*yidam*) linked in sexual union (e.g., figure 21). An adept is initiated into the mysteries of this work in the manner discussed on page 199, and the visualization practice proceeds along the lines indicated in the ideal *sadhana* practice. The deity used as outer SYMBOL may be male (called the *yab*; e.g., Samantabhadra in figure 21) or female (the *yum*; e.g., Samantabhadri).

In the more advanced *tantras* both the male and the female forms will be imagined, both separately and in sexual union (as in figure 21). The initiate may visualize first one figure and then the other, and then bring them together into union with the initiate, identifying first with ("becoming") the male and then the female and then both simultaneously. Exchange of energy (or communication) between the two forms may be, in some cases, accentuated by imagining a stream of tiny bubbles *(bindus)* moving with the breath from heart to heart via the nostrils (or genitals, or some other symbolic device).

It is significant that initiates into tantric practice receive instruction through both participation in ritual drama (the *wang*) and the reading of text (the *lung*). One is tempted to suggest that the Tibetan teaching techniques are directed at both right-lobe imaging and left-lobe conceptualizing faculties. There is, in any case, a balance in initiation between the semiological and the conceptual modes of presentation. The adept maintains this balance in his individual practice by working with both a text *(sadhana)* and where possible a full-color painting *(tanka)* of the deity(ies).[7] The paintings were once meticulously painted by adepts as an aid to internalizing the image of the deity—much as the ancient Southern Buddhists made their own *kasina*. Western psychology has frequently failed to appreciate the equal importance of imagery relative to language in learning, a misunderstanding that seems to be now in the process of rectification (see Arnheim 1969; Horowitz 1978; Randhawa 1978; Shepard and Cooper 1982; Rubinstein et al. 1984: chap. 8). We suggest that the balance of textual material and imagery in these practices has specific functions within a unified state of consciousness.

GENDER AND UNIVERSAL SYMBOLS

Given what we have said about penetration techniques thus far, it is not surprising that intense contemplation by a male or female adept upon male and female deities in sexual union may lead to experiences and insights about the masculine and feminine principles operating and interpenetrating in consciousness. It is not surprising that experiences associated with the feminine tend to relate to the unfolding of psychic energy, raw sensation, and intuitive knowledge; and those associated with the masculine tend to relate to conceptual knowledge about invariant patterns in the unfolding world of appearances (we have developed an explanation of this cross-cultural invariance elsewhere; see Laughlin 1984). More specifically, the adept comes to experience directly a dialogue between conscious conceptual knowledge (referred to variously in Sanskrit-Pali as *nana, vinnana,* or *panna;* in Tibetan, *rnam.par.shes.pa)* and the continually unfolding and developing organization of experience which, when revealed to awareness, becomes intuitive wisdom (in

Sanskirt, *prajna;* in Tibetan, *shes.rab)*[8]—in other words, between *logos* and *physis* respectively in the ancient pre-Socratic Greek tradition. The emphasis here, as in all forms of Buddhist insight work, is on the gradual process of merging these two orders or forms of knowledge into a dynamic and harmonious unity of awareness.

Experiences occurring in the course of contemplation are often ineffable. In part this ineffability stems from the problem of transposition (moving information from the rich domain of experience into the relatively poor medium of language) and in part from the subtlety of the experiences. However, generally speaking, we have found that experiences associated with the male aspect *(yab)* are involved mostly with qualities like nonattachment, recollection, intense concentration, and understanding, whereas experiences associated with the female aspect *(yum)* involve the release and flow of energy passing in a lawful order through consciousness. One must be cautious here because the more advanced the contemplation, the less gross and more subtle become the possible distinctions between *yab* and *yum* experiences. Rather, the two become increasingly integrated until experience itself begins to resemble the *yab-yum* in union—with emphasis upon *union.*

A clue to the nature of *yum*-related experiences is to be found in her customary body posture (see figure 21), which is one of blissful, mindful abandon, with head thrown back, arms and legs spread wide, and back arched. It is the position of ecstasy and orgasm, of letting go.[9] She represents the quintessence of flow. By contrast, the position of the *yab* is one of grounded and intense concentration upon the *yum.*[10] In these meditations the attachment to phenomena may become exceedingly tenuous, and the concentration so intense and detached, that previously repressed energy and activity are released with greater and greater force until the whole of consciousness appears to the adept to be filled by something like a roaring river of fire. Even so the *yab* consciousness remains unmoved. This is more clearly symbolized in other, more fierce forms where the *yab* and *yum* are dancing in flames while in sexual union (see figure 22).

Generally speaking, the masculine principle here is associated with the more passive aspects of consciousness and the feminine with the more active. But *active* connotes willful ordering of cognition and action—as in active compassion—while *passive* refers to the dynamic *order-as-given*, not stasis. Concentrated attention and awareness on the uninhibited flow of experience are the two essential qualities of consciousness defining the *yab* and *yum* respectively. The total integration of these two qualities are depicted by the *yab-yum* much as in the more famous *yin-yang* symbol. In fact, the former can spontaneously transform itself into the latter during contemplation.[11]

FIGURE 22. The fierce *yab-yum*. The deity is Yamantaka in sexual union with his consort while dancing in flames. Reprinted from K. Dowman, "The Nyingma Icons," *Kailash* (Kathmandu, Nepal) 2 (4): 390.

Once again, it is methodologically crucial to remember that the *yab* and *yum* are never defined by the *lama* in relation to these experiences prior to meditation work. Universal symbols are rarely referred to in instructing the initiate. Rather, after the initiation, the initiate goes off on his or her own to practice the meditation. The various cognitive associations arise spontaneously as universal symbols during the course of contemplation.

There is evidence that people often reexperience their womb-lives and births under hypnotic regression (Chamberlain 1980, 1983), during primal therapy (Janov 1972), and under the influence of psychoactive drugs (Grof 1979). However, it not generally recognized that experiences of womb and birth scenes spontaneously arise during meditation, particularly in an intense retreat situation. One of the authors (CDL) recalls meditating on the breath (*anapanasati*) while sitting in a straight-back chair when a tunnel image appeared. At the end of the tunnel was a light that grew brighter and more intense (accompanied by an increasing flow of blissful energy in his body). Overwhelmed by the visual and somaesthetic experience, he lost all awareness of his normal surroundings. When the climax of the experience had passed, he found himself lying on the floor exhausted, in fetal position with arms and legs twitching, and not knowing how he had gotten there. Meditation on the breath is well known among experienced meditators to be associated with hypermnesia, the capacity to remember in extraordinary detail, a phenomenon that also arises in the course of hypnotherapy (Chamberlain 1983:29).

YAB-YUM AND HOMEOMORPHOGENESIS

What we are suggesting here is that symbolic penetration techniques using gender as a symbolic attribute, as evinced by such practices as Tibetan *yab-yum* arising yogas, operate as top-down homeomorphogenic devices. That is, by symbolically enacting the arising of, identification with, and joining of the male and female principles in the sensorium, the greater intentional fields of the male and female principles are evoked, relevated, and (potentially) integrated. By manipulating male and female symbols in the theater of mind and into symbolic union, the *logos* and *physis* are evoked, simultaneously entrained to conscious network, and caused to interact under the canopy of awareness. The degree to which the two poles will integrate in the process depends on the extent of conditioned disparity between the poles, as well as the extent of neurotic reactivity of the male to the female principles (and vice versa). Also important will be the sophistication of awareness in the adept vis-à-vis these factors; that is, the extent to which the adept comprehends the play once it has been staged.

8 THE THEATER OF MIND

> Since the human resides in the brain, we cannot be satisfied with our
> explanations of human thinking until we can specify the neural substrates
> for the elementary information processes of the human symbol system.
> —Herbert A. Simon (1980)

ANTHROPOLOGY HAS SHOWN an enduring interest in the dramatic quality
of certain ritual social processes (see Firth 1973:194; Goffman 1967:30;
Turner 1974:23ff; Grimes 1982; Fernandez 1986; Schechner 1985). The
terms *drama, dramatization, dramatism,* have typically been used metaphorically to express the "bigger-than-life" texture of social action
involving role play, conflict, and transformation within the fabric of
social life. Anthropologists (e.g., Boas as noted in Goldman 1975:101–
102) have often been puzzled by the actual significance of the theatrical
quality of shamanic performances—performances which frequently use
illusionist tactics such as hidden strings and pebbles in the mouth,
crude demonic regalia, speaking tubes in the middle of fireplaces, highly
stylized gestures, and the like. Moreover, given the positivist, materialist bias of the discipline through most of its history, anthropological
theory has been embarrassingly incapable of accounting for the relationship between dramatic social activity and the psychology of participants
in and observers of that activity (see Turner 1982:12; Schechner 1985).

Some of the confusion dissolves when ritual drama is seen as a cross-
culturally common and effective method for inducing and controlling
phases of consciousness (see Hufford 1982 on this point). Much ritual
drama involves the expression of a society's cosmology via enactment
of elements and relations making up the cosmology (Eliade 1963:19).
Participation in the drama may induce alternate phases of consciousness
(dreaming, as well as so-called ecstatic states, trances, visions, etc.) in
which experiences arise that are interpreted so that they verify the
cosmology. We have already examined several principles and mechanisms by which ritual drama may achieve remarkable influence over
experience. These steps include control of cognitive complexity, orientation response, and autonomic tuning. Another means to attain this
control is by incorporating symbols as penetrating agents: symbols
(usually SYMBOLS) that can penetrate to the deepest levels of neurocognitive organization and produce changes in their entrainment. In chapter 7 we provided examples of ritualized symbolic penetration in the

ritual of empowerment in Tibetan Buddhist meditation tradition and in the Makah wolf ritual. Ritual manipulation of symbols is also central to the Catholic Mass and virtually every other Christian ritual routinely performed in our society.

Participation in full-blown ritual dramas, as in the medieval mystery plays, or in any of the examples noted above, is an encounter at whatever level of realization with esoteric mysteries; with a developmental sequence of experiences that gradually unfolds, matures, and becomes more global in significance. Irving Goldman writes that when considering participation in the Kwakiutl Winter Ceremony

> one arrives at an idea of hidden things, in the sense that the ceremonies deal with secret matters that are always hidden and can be experienced, therefore, only in a simulated form. The masks, the whistles, the ornaments, the dramatizations of mythical events simulate a hidden reality, a reality that does not literally exist on this side of the Cosmos, belonging only, as the Kwakiutl always say, "on the other side." The idea of simulating hidden things is one of profound religious sophistication, a recognition of the ineffable. (1975:102)

In our opinion, what is "hidden" and "ineffable" are direct transpersonal experiences of the shaman-adept for whom the mysteries are, strictly speaking, no longer hidden.

In many circumstances cross-culturally, ritual drama may be conceived as *theater of mind*. The target of ritual is the sensorium of the participant and audience member. The sensorium is the stage upon which an intentional play through ritual manipulation of symbols is produced in the world of experience. This play may in turn be a dress rehearsal for the "opening night performance," which is direct transpersonal experience attained in an alternative phase of consciousness.

For this reason, we want to explore the wider context of symbol and ritual in this chapter. We will consider ritual as theater of mind and then examine the role of theater of mind in the grand context of cosmology.

VICTOR TURNER AND RITUAL AS THEATER

No other anthropological theorist has come as close as Victor Turner to comprehending both the neurocognitive foundations of human symbolic activity (Turner 1983), and the essential function of ritual in producing and controlling experience (Turner 1982). Symbolism and ritual were always at the forefront of Turner's work. He saw the major portion of human life being carried out in a relatively static social field (*societas*) in which role-related performance predominates (Turner 1969). By contrast, the realm of ritual is one of fluid transformation in which the participant experiences an unencumbered consciousness, which is neither one thing nor another. The participant exists for a period of time in a "liminal," or transitional, state between social identities that is often accompanied by a sense of unity *(communitas)* with other participants, the group, or even with humanity (Turner 1974, 1982). "Liminal" ritual is thus antistructural in the sense that emphasis is upon experiential flow, dynamic transformation, and reorganization, rather than upon static role structure. It produces dissolution of, rather than dependence upon, normative behavior and expected form, and thus stands as a portal between the sacred and the profane. The major operator in ritual, according to Turner, is symbolism. All ritual is organized around a core symbol or set of symbols that imparts coherence to all activities composing the ritual (Turner 1969), a coherence that forms its most expansive intentionality in a culture's cosmology.[1]

THE CYCLE OF MEANING

There exists, then, a potential harmony or isomorphism among an individual's experience (or a group's collective experiences), their activity in the world, and their (at least metaphorical) understanding of the cosmos. Experience, activity, and knowledge are part of a single process so that (1) all three unfold from early pre- and perinatal life in mutual interpenetration; (2) they are operating in the neurocognitive development of every human being in every society; (3) they emerge in unison via recognizable stages reflected in activities beginning with spontaneous play, through social play, and cosmological ritual with full comprehension; but (4) they may also be influenced by cultural and other environmental factors to produce fragmentation and disharmony among each other.

The process of integration of knowledge and experience would seem to be very delicate because, we believe, social construction of knowledge and the experience of each individual are involved in a reciprocal feedback system whose properties may be changed in such a way that the link between knowledge and experience is broken. This delicate process is one that Paul Ricoeur (Reagan and Stewart 1978) calls the "hermeneutic circle," but one which we choose to call the *cycle of meaning*. This cycle of negative and positive feedback exists between cosmology, SYMBOLIC expression of cosmology, the world of experience, and interpretation of experience within the frame of reference provided by the cosmology.

COSMOLOGY

A *cosmology* is a culturally conditioned, cognized view of reality as a systemic, multicameral, dynamic, and organic whole. A cosmology is an account of all the significant elements and relationships that go to make up the universe, as well as their cosmogonic origins, and occasionally their eschatological demise. A cosmology defines the position of an individual, the group, or all of humanity within the universe by treating the individual as a microcosm within the greater macrocosm. In cosmological consciousness

> the world stands displayed in such a manner that, in contemplating it, religious man discovers the many modalities of the sacred, and hence of being. Above all, the world exists, it is there, and it has a structure; it is not a chaos but cosmos, hence it presents itself as creation, as work of gods. This divine work always preserves its quality of transparency, that is, it spontaneously reveals the many aspects of the sacred. The sky directly, "naturally," reveals the infinite distance, the transcendence of the deity. The earth too is transparent; it presents itself as universal mother and nurse. The cosmic rhythms manifest order, harmony, permanence, fecundity. The cosmos as a whole is an organism at once *real, living,* and *sacred;* it simultaneously reveals the modalities of being and of sacrality. Ontophany and hieropheny meet. (Eliade 1959:116–117)

The *cosmos,* as the term implies, is a great system, a totality consisting of well-demarcated realms, the realization of which is often expressed by a central metaphor, or *cosmogram* (George MacDonald, pers. com.). The universe is "like a beehive," or "like a mandala," for example. It is made up of all the elements of ordinary and extraordinary experience. It is populated by celestial bodies, rocks, rivers, winds, directions, rain, lightning, demons, animals, gods, people, enemies, and the like, and all are causally interrelated so that a change in one element affects the whole arrangement of the universe. (It is, by the way, this systemic and inherently lawful interactivity among elements that games and their rule structures may reflect when they are played in a greater cosmological frame.) For example, the Bushmen hunters of the Kalahari Desert in Southern Africa traditionally offered up prayers that a slaughtered animal be replaced by a similar form in order to maintain the balance of the cosmos, which they had disturbed. A cosmology will typically offer explanations for the origin of the universe (i.e., a *cosmogonous* cosmology) including its constituent elements and relationships. It may also, but not inevitably, account for the end of the cosmos as well (i.e., an *eschatological* cosmology). A cosmology tends to define the universe of known realities within both space and time (Eliade 1954).

What we are defining here is a set of universal structures of the cognized environment commonly found among preindustrial, traditional peoples. Cosmologies do not exist "out there" somewhere but are cognized worlds, which inform and are informed by the world of experience as it unfolds in each individual's sensorium. Cosmologies have their proper ontologies in the developing nervous systems of group members. They are points of view about experience. And they may be expressed in various symbolic ways, particularly through a culture's *mythopoea*; that is, through the SYMBOLISM embodied in game, myth, ritual, drama, art, tale, and so on (Count 1960). Note that we are distinguishing the internalized view of the world from its symbolic manifestation, the cosmological intentionality from its mythopoeic expression. Ignoring the distinction leads to a confusion about what is being examined, whether it is the individual understanding of the world, or a public textual rendition as a sort of collective understanding. The distinction is important relative to the interaction between cosmology and experience.

Cosmology is initially transmitted as culture through publicly available mythopoeic expressions. SYMBOLIC expression via games, tale-telling, and the like leads to semiosis in the young or in older initiates, whose brains readily model both the SYMBOLIC material and its intentionality as publicly expressed. SYMBOLS presented through mythopoeic means become objects of semiotropic response, and the models penetrated by those SYMBOLS gradually accrue multiple association and broader semantic fields via metaphoric application in direct experience. SYMBOLISM may be so pervasive in traditional society that one lives out one's life in a virtual "forest of symbols," to use Victor Turner's (1967) apt aphorism.

Cosmologies are typically *somatocentric* in orientation (George MacDonald, pers. com.). From a Jungian perspective, Erich Neumann notes that:

> Early man, who, without being aware of it, occupies a position in the center of the world, whence he relates everything to himself and himself to everything, fills the world around him with images of his unconscious. In so doing, he projects himself into three regions on the inner surface of the world-vessel that encompasses him. These three regions, in which the images of his own unconscious become visible as images of the world, are the heavens above him, the earth on which he lives along with all living things, and the realm that he experiences as the dark space "under" him, the underworld, the inside of the earth. . . . [W]hile the first relation consists in the body-vessel symbol in its cosmic projection upon the world as a world-body-vessel, the second, which is no less important, is expressed in the correlation of certain cosmic bodies, directions, constellations, gods, demons, with the zones and organs of the body. *This correlation is so universal for primitive man that the world-body correspondence may be looked upon as a law of the primitive world view.* (1963:41; *emphasis ours*)

George MacDonald notes that the somatocentricity of cosmological views are often symbolized in the significance of relationships among skeletal bones among a number of cultures in Siberia and North America:

> Skeletal parts are individually important, as an expression of *pars pro toto* or in anatomical order as an expression of the ordered relationships of the universe in ultimate terms. Throughout the coast much emphasis is placed on the spinal column as the prime structure of the animal, or human being, since it is the axis of the being. Its segmented structure is the ultimate cognitive form of all axes. (MacDonald n.d.)

The somatocentricity of cosmic views appears to be a universal principle upon which cosmologies are organized and may be explained only by reference to the characteristic relationship between cosmology and individual experience. Before exploring this relationship any further, we offer a few brief examples of cosmologies as publicly described in Symbolic cosmograms and other renditions in order to lay a common ground for understanding the cycle of meaning as it operates in traditional societies.

THE TUKANO

The Tukano Indians live in the rain forests of the Amazon (Reichel-Dolmatoff 1971). For them the universe is a closed system of energy, which must be tapped properly to make possible the return of the energy to its proper form. Energy for the Tukano seems to be synonymous with "vibration" in the sense encountered in Eastern mysticism (see chapter 11). Energy flows in circuits and becomes manifest in forms, thus exhibiting the female and male principles, respectively. As with most cosmologies, the Tukano divide the universe into three domains (figure 23), the upper (celestial), the intermediate (earth), and the lower (paradise). In their cosmogram, the Milky Way predominates in the upper realm, representing, among other things, the principles of fertility and contagion, the birth and death of forms. The blue of the upper realm is intermediate between the yellow of the sun and the red of the earth. Smoke is seen to unite earth and sky. The sun of perception is but a replica of the creator who dwells in paradise. Paradise is associated with the physiology of sex, with fertility and penetration. Different colors of light are interpreted as differing intensity of penetration by the sun. Paradise itself is associated with the color green.

> There can be no doubt the [Tukano] have observed the phenomenon of solar energy by its effects on living beings. The observation of organisms that glow in the shade; the reaction of a sick person who, after months of lying in a dark [house], goes out for the first time; the feeling of relief under the rays of the sun after long periods of rain or of low clouds; all of this has taught the native that, behind and above a concept of mere

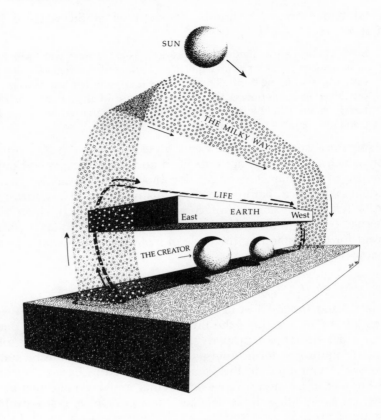

FIGURE 23. Cosmogram of the Tukano cosmos. The everyday world of earthly perception lies between the overworld and the underworld. Life, like the course of the sun, is a movement between worlds. Drawing by Donna Gordon, after Reichel-Dolmatoff 1971).

fertility imagined in sexual terms, there is an immeasurable vital energy emanating from the sun. Here then is the divinity in this energy, and its interpretation as a seminal force is only a rationalization of a phenomenon that is outside the native's knowledge. The chains and clusters of metaphors, images, and symbols are a mechanism to handle these manifestations. (Reichel-Domatoff 1971:48n)

The flow of energy is continuous, emanating from the creator in the lower realm, flowing in a grand arch from east to west across the celestial plane, fertilizing the earth below, and returning once again to paradise. The cosmos is thus an organism with divinity associated with skeleton (also with bone, uterus, penis, and, in the form of lightning, with ejaculation), earth associated with blood, the celestial realm with insemination. The metaphorical association of cosmic events with erotic events is quite marked. The cosmos "is hyperbiological in that it derives from the model of sexual physiology an endless number of associations, images, and symbols that withdraws farther and farther from physical facts until it constitutes a dynamic philosophy of equilibrium" (ibid.:55).

A Tukano may experience many numinous visions of cosmic relations during "profound concentration" (ibid.:43) or under the influence of hallucinogenic drugs. In fact, the deity is thought to be in a perpetual state of trance. It is in alternate phases of consciousness that humans may pass from one domain of reality to another, and interpretation of those experiences are expressed in terms of cosmological relationships. It is interesting that hallucinogens are stored in vessels that represent the cosmos and are ingested only under ritual circumstances.

THE DOGON

For the Dogon, who live in Burkina Faso in West Africa, the cosmos (see figure 24) was created by God along the cosmogramical lines of a basket granary.

> He took a woven basket with a circular opening and a square base in which to carry the earth and puddled clay required for the construction of a world-system, of which he was to be one of the counsellors. This basket served as a model for a basket-work structure of considerable size which he built upside down, as it were, with the opening, twenty cubits in diameter, on the ground; the square base, with sides eight cubits long, formed a flat roof, and the height was ten cubits. The framework he covered with puddled clay made of the earth from heaven, and in the thickness of the clay, starting from the centre of each side of the square, he made stairways of ten steps each facing towards one of the cardinal points. At the sixth step of the north staircase he put a door giving access to the interior in which were eight chambers arranged on two floors. . . . [T]he symbolic significance of this structure was as follows:
>
> The circular base represented the sun.
> The square roof represented the sky.
> A circle in the centre of the roof represented the moon.
>
> The tread of each step being female and the rise of each step male, the four stairways of ten steps together prefigured the eight-tens of families, offspring of the eight ancestors.
>
> Each stairway held one kind of creature, and was associated with a constellation as follows:
>
> The north stairway, associated with the Pleiades, was for men and fishes.

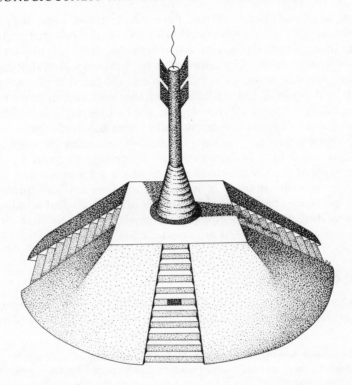

FIGURE 24. Cosmogram of the Dogon cosmos. The world of symbols is like an upside-down granary basket with an arrow stuck in the "roof" and a string from the arrow to heaven. The four sides of the basket are the cardinal directions. There is a door on one of the steps into compartments representing the structure of fertility. Drawing by Donna Gordon, after Griaule 1965.

The south stairway, associated with Orion's Belt, was for domestic animals.

The east stairway, associated with Venus, was for birds.

The west stairway, associated with the so-called "Long-tailed Star," was for wild animals, vegetables, and insects. (Griaule 1965:31–32)

All living things have their proper place on the steps of the cosmic structure including humanity, which stands, along with the fishes, on the northern stairway. Inside the granary are two stories, each divided into four compartments. "Each of these compartments contained one of the eight seeds given by God to the eight ancestors in the following order: little millet, white millet, dark millet, female millet, beans, sorrel, rice, and *Digitaria*. With each of these seeds were all the varieties of the same species" (ibid.:38). The compartments are also associated with organs of the human body: stomach, gizzard, heart, small liver, spleen, intestines, great liver, gall bladder (ibid.:39). Jars in the middle symbolize the womb and fetus. The inner partitions are associated with the skeleton. Four poles ending at the corners of the roof are arms and legs.

> Thus the granary [is] like a woman, lying on her back [representing the sun] with her arms and legs raised and supporting the roof (representing the sky). The two legs [are] on the north side, and the door at the sixth step [marks] the sexual parts. . . . [T]he granary and all it contained was therefore a picture of the world-system of the new order, and the way in which this system worked was represented by the functioning of the internal organs. These organs absorbed symbolic nourishment which passed along the usual channels of the digestion and the circulation of the blood. From compartments 1 and 2 (stomach and gizzard) the symbolical food passed into compartment 6 (the intestines) and from there into all the others in the form of blood and lastly breath, ending in the liver and the gall bladder. The breath is a vapour, a form of water, which maintains and is indeed the principle of life. (Ibid.:39)

On the roof of the granary lies a circle, representing the moon, into which God shot an arrow. He wound a thread around the arrow and, attaching it to another arrow, shot arrow and thread into "the vault of the sky to give it purchase" (ibid.:41). This celestial symbolism, combined with other ingredients to be found in Dogon mythical lore, account for the union of earth and sky, and for the continuous round of creation and destruction in the world. The male and female principles are represented at every level of construction, as is the principle of articulation of the human body. Even the most mundane objects such as sandals and spittle are given meaning via interlocking relations within the world-system. And when these relationships must be adjusted for the benefit of humans, sacrifice is made to redistribute the life-force thus appropriated (ibid.:130–37).

> The elements of Dogon cosmology may be enacted in masked dance: And the team of dancers, the society of masks, are a picture of the whole world, for all men, all activities, all crafts, all ages, all foreigners, all animals, can be represented in masks or woven into hoods. The masked dancers are the world; and, when they dance in a public place, they are dancing the progress of the world and the world-order. . . . [T]hus the whole complex of dancers, orchestras, and the place where they dance constitutes a picture of the smithy beating out the rhythm of the movement of the universe. (Ibid.:189)

The anthrolpologist who did the remarkable work among the Dogon was unfortunately not transpersonal in his orientation, therefore we

FIGURE 25. Cosmogram of the Beaver Indian cosmos. Divided into the cardinal directions and the three worlds. Drawing by Donna Gordon.

have little information about the experiences of Dogon dancers and dreamers as a consequence of enacting their cosmology.

THE BEAVER

The Beaver Indians live along the Peace River in northwestern British Columbia. They, too, conceive of a universe divisible into three realms: the earth, an upper sky world, and a subterranean underworld (Ridington and Ridington 1970). The cosmos (see figure 25) was created by the god *Yagesati* who drew

> a cross upon the primeval waters. It is this cross that fixed the middle earth and determines its qualities. Horizontally the cross defines the cardinal points or quarters of the earth: East, South, West, and North. Vertically its center is to become the link between the upper and underworlds. (ibid.:51)

The four directions are associated with various positive and negative qualities, as well as with interaction between the male and female principles operating in the world. The four quarters also metaphorically depict the stages of development of the child prior to embarking upon the vision quest. It is during the vision quest that a person moves to the center of the cross and engages the upper world (at the zenith) and the lower world (at the nadir) by taking his stance at the intersection of all axes:

Initiation comes through the experience of dreaming, and in his dream he sees himself going through his vision quest but in the perspective of knowledge of its cosmic significance. In these dreams he experiences, for the first time, the meaning of what happened to him as a child in terms of a shamanic cosmic structure. He has entered the center of the mandala and seen that the child, who was and is himself, became a god, an animal, a mythical supernatural being. The dreams reveal that his life in the bush was actually an entry into the dimension of mythic time and cosmic space. His communication with animals on this world took him into the internal world in which the myths of creation still exist and the giant animals that are the "boss" of the species are still alive. Spatially the inner dimension of meaning is symbolized by the upper and lower worlds inhabited, respectively, by the giant forms of game animals and birds, and the other, underworld animals. In anthropological terms, these dreamings constitute his totemic initiation and his entry into a shamanic cosmology. The myths in which giant animals had powers over humans exist not in the distant past, but in the experience of every Beaver Indian. The upper and underworlds to which they are sent by the culture hero, the first man to acquire power, are not geographical places but states of being that may be experienced. (Ibid.:58)

As with many native American societies, the experiences attained during the vision quest determine the nature and quality of personal power in relation to the cosmos. The Beaver receive their "song," "vibration," or power from significant animal symbols in their environment, symbols whose numinous meanings have been cognized by the initiate in accord with the culture's mythopoea. Direct transpersonal involvement in cosmic affairs may remain at the level of animal "song" and identification with the "boss" of the power species, or it may continue to unfold through the shamanic experiences of death, rebirth, and encounter with the creator. The latter experience occurs to few individuals, who use their shamanic powers for the benefit of all (ibid.:60).

BUDDHIST COSMOLOGY

The cosmos is represented in some Buddhist traditions by a mandala, or cosmic circle. At the center of the circle lies the axis, Mount Sumeru, around which the universe revolves and transforms. Upon the slopes of this primeval peak are various planes of reality in which forms continuously flow into and out of existence as the momentary concrescences of the five elemental principles: fire, air, earth, water, and space. The mandalic circle symbolizes the integrity of the cosmos in perpetual opposition to the forces of chaos and impurity roiling about in creation (Tucci 1961:23ff).

The peak of Sumeru is conceived as supporting the sky with its roots well buried in the primal stuff of creation. The great mountain is seen as a kind of *axis mundi* integrating the three realms of existence: subterranean, earthly, and celestial (ibid.:25). The form of cosmic mandalas will vary greatly according to place and ritual usage, and may be extremely complex, or may take the simple form of a circle enclosing the five basic colors: white (water), blue (space), yellow (earth), red (fire), and green (air). They may depict perfect mythological cities (so-called pure lands), deific retinues, and other ideal states of being.

An especially dramatic three-dimensional form of the mandala is the *stupa* (Tib., *chorten*) in figure 26. The *stupa* is an ancient symbol, dating from before the time of Sakyamuni Buddha, and like the mandala it has taken many forms through the centuries as metaphysical views have changed. The basic form of the Tibetan *stupa* is fairly representative: a white pot-shaped cupola (representing water) rests upon a yellow cube (earth) and is topped by a red cone (fire), which is topped by a hemisphere covered by a green umbrella or cup (air). The umbrella is then capped by a white moon crescent, a red sun disk above, and crowning the entire structure, a flame (space, void, "ether," or essence of mind; Govinda 1976, Blofeld 1974).

Buddhist cosmograms refer simultaneously to elements and relationships, and the development of these within the body. "Verily, I tell you," proclaimed the Buddha, "the world is within this six-feet high body!" (Govinda 1976:84). Mandalas and *stupas* are conceived as symbolizing energy relationships within the system of *chakras* and *nadis* discussed in chapter 11.

> The cakras [*sic*], as radiating centers of psychic force, gave new impetus to the interpretation of the human body as a cosmic manifestation. Not only was the spinal column compared to Mount Meru, the axis of the universe, and therefore called "meru-danda," but the whole psychophysical organism was explained in terms of solar and lunar forces, which, through five channels—the so-called nadis—moved up and down between the seven cakras which in their turn represented the elementary qualities of which the universe is built and of which the material elements are only the visible reflexes. (Govinda 1976:87)

The three sources of psychic energy running up the medial axis of the body have cosmological significance. Two lateral *nadis* wrap themselves snakewise round the central channel. The *nadi* originating on the left is white and associated with lunar creative energy, while the *nadi* on the right is red and associated with solar energy, feeding awareness and intellection. These and all other forces in the body must be harmoniously balanced for healthy personal development. The function of certain meditative practices, or yogas, assures the activation, balance, and growth of those forces.

FIGURE 26. A Buddhist cosmogram. A modern rendition of
some of the essential symbolic features of the ancient *stupa*.
Drawing by Donna Gordon.

CONSCIOUSNESS AND COSMOLOGY

Having briefly summarized some of the salient features of several
cosmologies, we are better placed to note some of the structural commonalities found in cosmologies cross-culturally. First, we have indicated that cosmologies tend to be somatocentric. Further, the key to
understanding the macrocosm is to be found in the realization of the
nature of the microcosm. "As above, so below," say Western mystics.

"The world is within this six-feet high body," says the Buddha. However stated, the significance is the same. Somehow we may at least metaphorically understand the rest of the universe by understanding our own being. The Kabbalistic Tree of Life (Knight 1965), the Buddhist Tree of Knowledge (Govinda 1973), and other such cosmograms actually refer, in part, to relationships obtaining within the body, the microcosm; by metaphorical extension from knowledge of these relationships, we may come to know the nature of the entire cosmos.

Again, we are referring to the *cognized* environment, and not the operational environment apart from perception of it. The "world" of traditional cosmology is the world constructed by the nervous system and portrayed in the sensorium. And, as we have seen, the nature of the cognized cosmos arising "in this six-feet high body" depends upon, among other things, the phase of consciousness within which it forms its concrescence.

As noted earlier, many peoples around the planet conceive of their existence as being lived-out in a world of *multiple realities* (Schutz 1945). There are typically three domains of reality, each consisting of one or more discrete realities, which may be related vertically: upper world, normal world, lower world. Experiential access to these domains and constituent realities is generally via discrete phases of consciousness, either available to all or to those who specialize in attaining the requisite phase of consciousness. For example, some traditional Native American groups conceive of what we would call "normal waking consciousness" as that unfortunate phase during which the soul and body are glued together. In alternative phases, like dreaming, the soul is freed from the body so that it can fly and commune with other souls and spirits.

What we Western theorists have failed to appreciate is the intimate relationship between attainment of experiences in alternative phases of consciousness and the multiple realities depicted in traditional cosmologies. As we have argued (see chap. 5), the reason for this oversight is that we tend toward monophasia and thus to give credence to events arising only in "normal waking consciousness" while discrediting, ignoring, or repressing experiences occurring in other phases of consciousness. Strenuous effort is required of a Western scientist to realize that his concrete view of reality is merely a construct, a set of entrainments, a system of creodes, and thus an impediment placed in the way of comprehending a unitary cosmos in which his cognized environment is only one of many alternative views. The failure to understand the cognized locus of multiple realities has led many an anthropologist astray when attempting to analyze native cosmology:

> Surely we do not still believe that savages imagine nonexistent worlds because of their poor understanding of physical reality. The real meaning

of the supernatural must be symbolic and the shamanic flight an inner journey into a realm of experience for which the symbols stand. The three worlds of a shamanic cosmology are not geographical places but internal states of being represented by a geometric analogy. The shaman does not really fly up or down, but inside to the meaning of things. (Ridington and Ridington 1970:51)

The drive to experience the inner realm of being appears to be universal and is reflected in the myriad ways the majority of human cultures find to incubate alternative phases of consciousness (Bourguignon 1973, 1976). A major significance of such transpersonal experiences in most cultures is that it offers incontrovertible, directly empirical evidence that (1) there is more to one's being than the empirical ego, and (2) there is more to reality than is experienceable in the "normal" phases of consciousness.

CYCLE OF MEANING

Cosmology is thus the cognized environment of an individual as it pertains to ultimate and global questions about being and the relationship between being and universe. In traditional societies, the cosmologies of individual members have more in common with each other than they have differences. But caution must be exercised in portraying "the" cosmology of a group, as we have just done, for variance in the individual understanding of, interest in, and participation within any particular culture's cosmological foundation may well be significant, as we shall see in the next two chapters.

For our present purposes, we may distinguish three general levels of knowledge about the cosmos among group members.[2] The first level of knowledge is *belief*, which is the introductory, catechismic level where knowledge is restricted to the symbolic expression of cosmos committed to memory. One "believes" in the experiences reported by others. Young monks in the Buddhist tradition spend thousands of hours memorizing and chanting textual material. The young of many cultures learn the mythic lore from elders around the evening's cooking fire. Ritual dramas and "mystery plays" may be observed and recalled. The outsider (e.g., an ethnographer) entering an alien cosmology must at least "suspend disbelief" in order to enter further the system of knowledge. At the level of belief, most of what is known about the cosmos is gleaned vicariously from others, not through direct experience. Yet this is the level at which most ethnography and anthropological theory relevant to the relationships among experience, action, and cosmology produces its literature (e.g., Perinbanayagam 1982 on the role of astrology in Jaffna society).

The second level of knowledge is *understanding*, the stage at which one's learning begins to "make sense" in light of direct experience. The cosmos appears to be a total system of knowledge, rather than bits and pieces of memorized material. The young monk may now relate experiences in daily life to what he has learned from the texts, and vice versa. The young Beaver Indian may enrich what he has learned about wolf or swan in myth with direct experiences of wolf and swan. Symbolic material and direct experience become increasingly and metaphorically intentional and gradually approximate a totality of knowledge about the world.

The third level of entry into cosmological knowledge is that of *realization*—the stage of *full* participation in the cosmos as modeled. Experience of cosmological relationships is now more direct than vicarious. The cosmos has become *real*. The monk, now a serious contemplative, is having experiences in extraordinary phases of consciousness that were previously only read or talked about. The Beaver Indian seeks his vision and is participating more fully in the cosmos in both waking and dream consciousness. The Tukano is ingesting drugs and experiencing the alternative realities previously known only by hearsay.

The impetus of all viable cosmological traditions is to guide members from belief, through understanding, to some degree of realization via experiences that verify the "reality" of the cosomology (see figure 27). The tendency will be to complete the cycle of meaning as a negative feedback loop. Entry into the cosmology will be considered incomplete if knowledge remains merely at the levels of belief and understanding, no matter how well the textual material has been learned. Vicarious experience must be transformed into direct experience, and the SYMBOLS must come to penetrate to their primeval intentionalities. Only then does mythopoeic doctrine become fully "religious" in the literal Latin sense of *religare*, "to rebind."

The steps that one takes on the path of realization are never left to chance. Rather, a society's mythopoea incorporates ritual practices, which operate, as Turner has so elegantly demonstrated, as liminal transformers, and these become essential to full participation in native life. Members of societies such as the Beaver, Tukano, and Dogon are prepared over many years for the realization of their cosmologies. Realization involves direct, transpersonal experiences, which are incubated in ritual, using many principles discussed earlier (see chapter 5). The experiences are predictable, and their metaphorical interpretations preestablished. Upon reflection such experiences "make sense" in the context of the cosmological views that originally impelled the experiences.

And so the cycle of meaning completes itself: cosmology gives rise to mythopoeic expression in myth, art, story, drama, and the like, and to

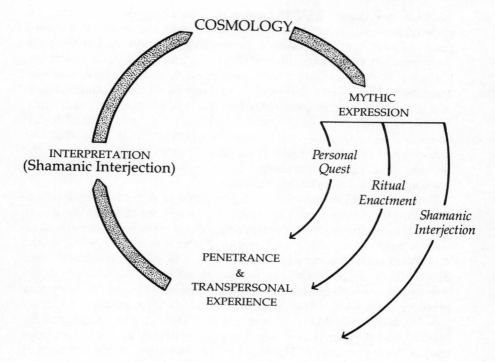

FIGURE 27. The cycle of meaning. A cosmology is symbolically expressed via myth, ritual, and shamanic activity, leading to transpersonal experiences that are in turn interpreted in such a way as to verify and vivify the cosmology. Drawing by Donna Gordon.

ritual performances that are made meaningful in the context of the total SYMBOLIC field. The practices result in symbolic penetration to the models mediating phases of consciousness, which evoke a warp in consciousness. Profound reentrainment of conscious network results in extraordinary experiences that produce an equally profound state of awe, curiosity, and vulnerability in the initiate. The experiences, or more accurately, the memory of the experiences, are then interpreted in terms of the mythopoea and are thus conceived by the initiate and by all those group members around him as verifying and vivifying the cosmology.

Cosmology and the cycle of meaning are never static. There is always positive feedback into the system due to environmental and cultural change, as well as transgenerationally divergent experience relative to the cycle (see Powers 1977 on change in Oglala cosmology). In fact, the cycle of meaning is quite vulnerable to change: the negative feedback round of SYMBOLIC expression, experiential realization, and mythopoeic interpretation may be completely broken at any point in development. If the break occurs, then it will likely cease to guide, vivify, and give meaning to life. What is left of the cycle may be relatively static artifacts of a previously dynamic interplay between knowledge and experience. All that may remain is the SYMBOLIC detritus in the form of rigid dogma or lifeless text, its penetrative influence upon spiritual life completely relinquished. Bereft of realization, the mythopoeia is no longer the enactment of a living cosmology, but merely the vestigial portrayal of ideology—a kind of Tylorian "survival."

If transpersonal experience is not incubated from a cosmology and its attendant expressions, and interpreted to verify the cosmic view giving rise to the experience, then (presuming it does arise) it will not articulate with a total view of life and world. No matter how profound and numinous such experiences may be, they will not be "religious" (see Bowker 1973: chap. 7), for they will not result in self-knowledge conducive to a totally integrated view of self and world. Ironically, they may promote even greater cognitive fragmentation than existed previously (see Wallace 1959). Many people in our society smoke marihuana for "kicks" and the experiences produced are generally coded (when positive) as "entertainment." The Rastafarians, however, imbibe the drug as a sacrament, which leads to experience imbued with sacred meaning within the context of their worldview.

We repeat, the cycle of meaning may be disrupted at any point. Rituals may be forbidden, shamans may die, a different worldview may replace the cosmology and its mythopoea. The mythic cycle may not be told, the annual initiations may not be held. Children may be sent off to modern schools and hospitals and away from the evening cooking fires and healing ceremonies. So vulnerable is the cycle of meaning, in fact, that it may be rendered developmentally inert in a single generation. Such cataclysms have not been infrequent in the wake of rapid sociocultural change, especially of the sort that seems to follow inevitably "modernization."

However, rather than being completely disrupted, a cycle of meaning may be *revitalized* (Wallace 1966, 1969). Change, too, may be accomplished at any point in the cycle. Fresh visionary experience, perhaps attained in the course of serious "spirit" illness or in spiritual retreat, may result in a new interpretation that transforms the cosmology and its SYMBOLIC expression and becomes the essence of many so-called revitalization movements from which new religious cults emerge (Wallace 1956). On the other hand, a new worldview or a modification of the old worldview may be promulgated by teachers or missionaries. The fresh material becomes wonderfully blended with the traditional so that it still leads to transpersonal experiences, but transforms the interpretive import of these experiences within the frameworks of the new cosmology. This transformative process will be especially fluid in cases where textual material is not written.

THE SHAMAN

The shamanic principle (see page 149) is usually an integral part of the cycle of meaning, whether there exists a special shamanic social role recognized in a society. Shamanism assumes significance in the cycle whenever the initiate perceives someone as having more experience than he in either controlling the ritual practices, relaying textual material, or offering an interpretation of the initiate's experiences. Anyone who is recognized by an initiate as a model of spiritual development, growth, or wisdom is in a shamanic position relative to the initiate. Of course it is cross-culturally common for certain individuals to be recognized socially and labeled as specialists in traveling within the extraordinary domains of the cosmos for the benefit of the group (so-called "flying shamans") and for the healing of patients ("healing shamans"). A shaman is normally perceived as having superior power, skill, or insight and is thus someone to attend and even emulate (*shamanic projection,* see page 150). As noted in figure 27, the points of interjection in the cycle of meaning where the shaman exercises his greatest effect are in controlling the ritual setting of initiation (for example, the sacred ground and activities at the Sun Dance) and the interpretation of transpersonal experiences when they arise (for one who has experienced Buffalo during the Sun Dance; see Jorgensen 1972).

The main operator in shamanic projection is what psychologists call *transference,* which is merely a special case of projection. In a real sense, the initiate assigns control over his neurocognitive and other physiological processes to another individual. He projects the locus of control to a significant other. The project can be limited or total. One is perhaps out of touch with the holistic operator in oneself but recognizes that facility personified in another. The other seems (or one is taught to see the other as) brighter, morally superior, more complex, happier, more interesting, more fulfilled, wiser, or calmer than oneself. He seems to have access to the Truth of Things and is able to speak from that realization. One perhaps experiences oneself as being "in a better place" when one is around the other. One may feel less confused about experiences or about life when one is being guided by the other. These are some of the aspects of the shamanic principle in action. Examples of this relationship abound in our society (see John-Steiner 1985). Physicians, chiropractors, dentists, and psychotherapists, all practice by virtue of shamanic projection. Priests, rabbis, and ministers, as well as some school teachers and counselors, depend upon this process. What is perhaps not obvious is that the principle can operate in rock concerts, where musicians assume a role similar to that of shaman. And, of course, the principle is at work in the myriad religious cults, like the Moonies, the Divine Light Mission, and the Scientologists, that have sprung up over the last generation or so in North America and have centered upon charismatic teachers.

Under the guidance of a shaman, an initiate may attain direct transpersonal experiences that vivify the multiple realities depicted in his culture's mythopoea. Flat, two-dimensional images become living entities. Realms of experience previously encountered only in story and drama are entered and explored, producing memories that profoundly enrich the intentionality of the culture's lore and core symbolism. And if the initiate continues this dialogue long enough, he, too, may become a recognized shaman. In virtually all undiluted shamanic traditions, the shaman *is* a shaman precisely because he has been empowered by treading the road others wish to follow, a course conceived by all as being arduous and dangerous, but tending toward greater personal health, power, and unity with the creative force behind all phenomena. As the Ridingtons note:

> Every Beaver Indian has, through his vision quest, entered into the inner dimension of mythical meaning, but only the shaman has followed this path to its beginning and end. Ordinary men must know that to take the lives of animals is to give them another form of life . . . but it is the shaman alone who knows through his own experience, the meaning of human life and death. His sharing of this knowledge is the basis of Beaver ceremonial life, a form of ritual that unites the life cycles of animals with those of men. Thus, the totemic experience that is entered into in the vision quest is completed in the death and return of the shaman. The mythic time and cosmic space that every adult Beaver knows is but the beginning of the road to heaven that has been explored by the shaman in whose footsteps he hopes to follow. (Ridington and Ridington 1970:60–61)

The shamanic principle is ubiquitous to religious, healing, and transpersonal activities throughout the world simply because those activities are ubiquitous to neurocognitive and physiological development. It is well to remind ourselves continually that we are symbols to each other. In one sense the shaman is "out there," a real person who has attained some degree of personal insight and growth. But essentially, the shaman is "in here," a percept which penetrates to those neurocognitive intentionalities associated with Turner's communitas: exploration of self and multiple worlds, transformation, and social flow. There is a cliché out of the East that runs something like, "When the student is ready, the teacher will appear." One interpretation of this doctrine is that when the models mediating shamanic intentionality are sufficiently mature, "shaman" will be projected upon another person who is then recognized as shaman. The shamanic other may or may not be recognized as such by the society. He may have exhibited dramatic power through extraordinary visions, or may have quietly accrued wisdom over the course of life. He may have inherited the position of shaman from a parent, or have spontaneously developed skills recognized by others as useful (see e.g., Sharon 1978). The details of case history will vary, but the process of projection remains the same: the recognition of the potential perfection of oneself in another.

COSMOLOGY AND SCIENCE

In the intimate relationship between consciousness and cosmology lies the crux of the inadequacy of modern science to provide meaning for most of us in our daily lives. Science simply does not produce a functional cosmology for most people in our society. The essential problem is that science produces a view of the world, a cognized environment, that is intentionally disconnected from the direct, everyday experience of people while profoundly affecting people's lives. When most scientists leave the rarified atmosphere of their laboratories and libraries, they face difficulties similar to our own. It is difficult to orient our life experiences in relation to notions like "black holes," "quarks," "ids," and "polypeptides." These ideas do not perform well as metaphors and simply do not inform our moment-by-moment sensorial experience. They do not help us to find purpose or meaning in what we do, nor do they satisfactorily account for why our desires are thwarted, why our goals seem unattainable, or why we suffer in the midst of apparent plenty. They do not help us to come to grips with why we and our loved ones must die. Yet, these are commonplace questions that arise from the experiences of people everywhere and are the central stuff of functioning cosmologies (see Tillich 1963; Capra 1978).

Whitehead (1964: chap. 2, 1978) spoke directly to this issue when he charged science with committing a "bifurcation" of nature. His language is, as always, difficult to comprehend in casual discourse, but he is worth quoting at length, for he saw clearly the problem of integrating the fragmentary conceptual by-products of science ("public prehensions") with experience ("concrete facts") to form a viable cosmology:

> The theory of prehensions is founded upon the doctrine that there are no concrete facts which are merely public, or merely private. *The distinction*

between publicity and privacy is a distinction of reason, and is not a distinction between mutually exclusive concrete facts. The sole concrete facts, in terms of which actualities can be analysed, are prehensions; and every prehension has its public side and its private side. Its public side is constituted by the complex datum prehended; and its private side is constituted by the subjective form through which a private quality is imposed on the public datum. The separations of perceptual fact from emotional fact; and of causal fact from emotional fact, and perceptual fact; and of perceptual fact, emotional fact, and casual fact, from purposive fact; *have constituted a complex of bifurcations, fatal to a satisfactory cosmology.* The facts of nature are the actualities; and the facts into which the actualities are divisible are their prehensions, with their public origins, their private forms, and their private aims. But the actualities are moments of passage into a novel stage of publicity; and the coordination of prehensions expresses the publicity of the world, so far as it can be considered in abstraction from private genesis. Prehensions have public careers, but they are born privately. (1978:290, *emphasis ours*)

The world is bifurcated into the cognized environment of science and the unfolding world of experience produced within the sensoria of people, thus propagating a disharmony between *logos* and *physis*. Little effort is expended by science to integrate the two worlds for the individuals it affects. Yet, science is and has been for several hundred years the main agent in disrupting traditional cosmologies, both in our own society, and to one extent or another in every society with which we interact. Indeed, positivistic science arose as a conscious strategy for excluding "metaphysics" from modern systems of knowledge.

Please understand, we are not leveling a blanket condemnation of science or proclaiming the existence of a scientific conspiracy against traditional cosmologies. Rather, we are concerned with accounting for the structures of experience, and the exploration of these indicates tendencies toward both integration and fragmentation of consciousness in different individuals, in different societies, and in the same society at different points in history. Some social institutions may facilitate integration, others may foster fragmentation. We are saying that the institution in our society called science generally fosters fragmentation, and at times even seems to impede the development of alternative institutions more conducive to cognitive integration. With the exception of certain scientific professions that may consciously act to thwart the activities of alternative professions (e.g., the legal and propagandistic efforts of the medical profession to eradicate or limit the activities of alternative health professions), most of this disintegrating effect is due solely to the preeminant position of science, scientists, and scientific views in the consciousness of people in our culture. Science, for many, is the ultimate font of truth. Science produces a significant fraction of school curriculum from the earliest grades through university, and pervades our awareness via television, magazines, and popular books. Yet, for most people science ironically does not offer a viable interpretation of life experiences in the way that a true cosmology does. Science, highly analytical and technological, produces the conditions conducive to alienation from productive activity in the marketplace through automation, conducive to pollution of the environment through production of noxious chemical wastes, and conducive to dread about the possibility (for many the probability) of thermonuclear annihilation. But science does not tell us how to cope with the personal consequences of these vast, seemingly impersonal forces.

Of course, we have not said that science *cannot* produce cosmology, only that it tends not to do so. But scientists are human beings with brains, and science is the product of institutionalized human neurocognitive activity (see Rubinstein et al. 1984). It should not surprise us, therefore, to find scientific formulations that exhibit many structural characteristics of traditional cosmologies. Cosmological elements are evident in many of the views of modern physics, especially those that have been generated in the wake of quantum mechanics. Quantum physicists have publicized a range of theoretical perspectives that are partial or quasi-cosmologies (see e.g., Bohm 1980; Prigogine 1980; Pagels 1982). Some writers have even pointed to the similarities between quantum physical theories and more traditional cosmologies (see e.g., Capra 1975).

There is no better example than the cosmological physics of John Archibald Wheeler (1982, 1983). Championing the position of Niels Bohr over that of Albert Einstein, Wheeler has gone far in returning the human observer to a previously mechanistic and positivistic physical universe:

> In today's words Bohr's point—and the central point of quantum theory—can be put into a single, simple sentence. *"No elementary phenomenon is a phenomenon until it is a registered (observed) phenomenon."* It is wrong to speak of the "route" of a photon in the experiment of the beam splitter. It is wrong to attribute a tangibility to the photon in all its travel from the point of entry to its last instant of flight. A phenomenon is not yet a phenomenon until it has been brought to a close by an irreversible act of amplification such as the blackening of a grain of silver bromide emulsion or the triggering of a photodetector. In broader terms, we find that nature at the quantum level is not a machine that goes its inexorable way. Instead what answer we get depends on the question we put, the experiment we arrange, the registration we choose. *We are inescapably involved in bringing about that which appears to be happening.* (Wheeler 1983:1984–85; *emphasis ours*)

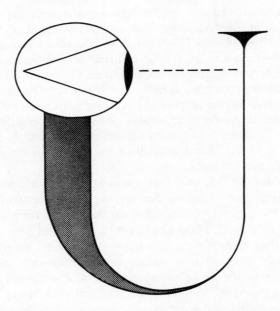

FIGURE 28. A modern cosmogram by John Archibald Wheeler, the particle physicist. The universe (U) begins on the upper right with the big bang and turns in on itself in self-awareness. Reproduced, by permission, from *Foundations of Physics*, Plenum Publishing Corp.

Although we obviously agree with this position—that phenomena are sensorial events—this view in physics demonstrates many elements we have been discussing: quantum reality according to one theory or another is seen as (1) *cosmogonic,* or having a dramatic beginning (e.g., the "big bang"); as (2) *eschatological,* or having an end (e.g., "the end of time," and "total entropy"); as (3) *interdependent* and noncasual in interaction between events (e.g., Bohm's "implicate order"); as (4) *teleological,* or purposive (e.g., Carter's "anthropic principle"; see Carr and Rees 1979); and as (5) *experiential* for full realization of phenomena (e.g., Wheeler's 1983 "observer-participancy"). Furthermore, Wheeler has even given us a cosmogram reflecting the interdependence of observation and cosmological phenomena (figure 28).

However, the resemblance between quantum physical cosmologies and traditional cosmological systems exists largely at a superficial textual level. Quantum mechanics is not, in fact, involved in a cycle of meaning in the sense described here. There are several reasons for this divergence. First, the elements and relationships modeled in quantum physics are not directly experiential. Talking bears and flying spirits can be "seen," whereas photons, electrons, and black holes cannot be experienced. Indeed, David Bohm (1980: chap. 1) chides his colleagues in physics for no longer looking at the world. What physicists actually "see" are measurements, numbers on counters, and not sensorial events that bring their cognized environment alive. Second, the phenomena being modeled in quantum physics lie within a very restricted *décalage* (see page 247). The domain of experience being modeled is a fraction of the range of experiences of any particular physicist, and is virtually nonexistent for nonphysicists. Third, the cycle of meaning is absent or incomplete outside the domain of experience addressed by cosmological physics. Fourth, the initiation process by which an individual engages direct experiences that verify cosmological physics is exceptionally arduous and progressively specialized. It does not produce an integrated consciousness and an accrual of power and control over everyday life comparable with the goals of shamanic traditions.

To what extent cosmological physics may inform the spiritual life of physicists will naturally vary from individual to individual. Our suspicion is, however, that for most scientists the restrictive scope of laboratory experiments addressed by cosmological theories will tend to exacerbate, rather than amalgamate, fragmentary consciousness. Science is for a very few what it can be for an Einstein or a Bohr, a quest for "a completely harmonious account of existence" (Wheeler 1982:1). But the reader must not mistake our intent here. We are not trying to expose science as a useless or hopeless pursuit; nor do we assert that physicists should drop what they are doing and run off to an ashram. Rather, we are modeling what we believe to be the fundamental structure of experience and how one and the same structures may operate to produce holistic and fragmentary consciousness alike. Modern physics is manifesting a trend away from the extreme fragmentation of earlier positivist science. It has far to go before its formulations can approximate the cycle of meaning requisite for optimal growth of consciousness without the argumentation of methods and cosmological views from outside the current boundaries of science.

PART THREE

CONSCIOUSNESS AND THE LIMITS OF EXPERIENCE

9 EMPIRICAL EGO, CONSCIOUSNESS, AND CONTEXT

Dark, dark my light, and darker my desire.
My soul, like some heat-maddened summer fly,
Keeps buzzing at the sill. Which I is I?
A fallen man, I climb out of my fear.
The mind enters itself, and God the mind,
And one is one, free in the tearing wind.
                          —Theodore Roethke, "In a Dark Time"

THE SENSORIUM IS FILLED with content which we see, hear, feel, intuit, and think about. Its structure imparts form and meaning to that content. We know only the content constructed within the sensorium. We *know* by applying the structures that organize that content; it is the organizing that *is* knowing. The outer operational environment and its own structuring impacts upon the structuring process of the organism, triggering reentrainments (or morphogenesis) whose forms we experience as the sensorium.

We have seen that we live in a world of symbols generated by our own being, namely, our own structuring process. The cognized environment is shaped and constrained by

1. its own previous history of development
2. its genetic history and phenotypic expression
3. its level of structural attainment
4. the structure and activity of the surrounding milieu

The contents of the sensorium, which we then experience, are symbolic equivalents of structural properties of ourselves under impact from the surrounding world.

We are a semiclosed system in a state of continuous dynamic transformation. We are transforming ourselves within particular constraints defined by our nature as biological beings, existing in continually adapting relationships to our world. We are part of a *field* including that world, an integral subsystem within it, yet distinct from it due to the properties defined by the boundaries of our being, which distinguish us from that milieu. Much of what lies within us is inseparable from reality owing to our structuring process, which is in continuous exchange with the world of which we are a part. We differentiate ourselves from the milieu by the distinct properties of our internal organization.

Any part of the milieu that enters within the boundaries of our organism is transformed into elements of our structuring process, and what we put into the world tends to change and modify it as well. Every event or property of the operational environment that we can perceive is

1. conditioned by the state and complexity of our own organization at that moment in time
2. manifested within our being as a transformation or equivalent of that event or property in the form of the percept

In human beings, the momentary state of manifestation has evolved over millenia for the species in general, and through the span of a lifetime for each of us within the constraints imposed by the species' evolution. Human experience is an extension of biological "experience," emerging first as awareness, then as self-awareness. Yet the root principles of self-organization and adaptation obtain at the level of the immaterial and intangible as well as at the level of the material and tangible. The difference here is in the greater complexity of organization and adaptation and in the milieu to which the being must adapt.

As biology approaches the immaterial from the material, the range of milieus requiring adaptive reorganization also expands. With each advance of increasingly complex internal organization, an increasingly complex and immaterial world is created anew, fostering both a deeper penetration into the material and an adaptive pressure we might characterize as requiring *comprehension*. The complex being we call human needs to learn behaviors that insure his biological survival; he requires "understanding" not only of his world of survival, but eventually of the immaterial world of thought that is the creation of the increasing complexity and subtlety of his own process of cognition. A self-conscious being who is unable to comprehend his mental milieu tends toward disintegration just as the biological being, unable to comprehend or adapt behaviorally to the physical world, will similarly tend toward disintegration. The history of mankind is the history of this evolution of structure, simultaneously biological and behavioral on the one hand, cognitive and emotional on the other. *They are two aspects of the same process.*

A human being constructs itself over a period of years as the species *Homo sapiens* constructs itself over a period of eons. No human being is ever complete, ever finally constructed, for each learns anew every day. The species as well is never complete but is in the process of constructing itself over an evolutionary frame of increasing rapidity, hurtling along a yet unknown trajectory. What we experience on the stage of the Theater of Mind, what we are calling the sensorium, is the momentary state of

the self-structuring individual embedded within the evolutionary species' trajectory, existing within an operational environment of which it
is an integral part and which it is also continuing to create and evolve.
Such is the spatiotemporal predicament of humanity.

The history of all humanity lives within each man and woman as does
the totality of his or her own history. The future of each person lives as
well within him or her, as does the future of all mankind. Man now sits
at the edge of The Great Divide, approaching, as a species, the level of
"autonomous man." Some among us have reached that point; the vast
majority of us move at various paces toward that point. A few among
us have passed through that point and their movements represent the
future trajectory of our species. At each moment a wide spectrum of
evolutionary organizations are present not only within the species, but
in each individual as well. Each person is a community of cells and
organizations of differing levels of development and structure, part
dispositionally determined, part situationally and functionally determined.

Each person is bounded by an adaptive surface with which he or she
greets and adapts to the operational environment. That surface is an
uneven topography of complexity of structures whose organization is
oscillating moment to moment. The adaptive surface is creating and
forming itself according to the demands of the situation and the constraints of its previous internal organization. Its optimal, most evolved
levels of complexity or adaptive capability define its limits and the range
of milieu within which it exists. But its momentary state may fall well
within those limits and its world will similarly shrink and expand
accordingly.

The adaptive surface constitutes the outer boundary of the being as a
whole, defining its range of operation while at the same time defining
its world. Paradoxically, that which seems relatively constant—the
world—is in actuality contingent upon the limits of the organism, a
cognized environment existing within it. Yet this is literally the case: the
being creates an "immaterial" dimension of the self-created world; it
creates a "world" with which others interact in a conceptual realm; it
creates a world to which others react in a material realm. Each world is
as real as is the other, each is *the* world; it is one world, an evolving
world.

THE EXPERIENCING EMPIRICAL EGO

It is our empirical ego that experiences, and the nature of our ego
usually controls the nature of our experience. This is a general statement

referring to the average person and to experience as we generally think of it. There are exceptions. But first it is advisable to begin in an area of familiarity.

To say our empirical ego experiences is to imply that there *is* an entity we call the ego which experiences *something*. To experience something is, in some sense, to know it, to apprehend it. This apprehension may be sensorial, emotional, cognitive, or as we generally use the term, all three. To these three we might also add the function of intuition, which usually refers to the implicit meaning of something. To experience something implies awareness, for many things happen within us or without, of which we are not fully aware, and we therefore do not experience these events. Our ego then is the part of us that apprehends entities or events outside of itself. When this apprehension is within the bounds of awareness, we call it our experience. This is our starting point in considering the nature of the ego.

What then is this ego that accounts for our experience? What is this experience? We will look at the potential structural properties of ego and experience. As suggested in the introduction to this chapter, we see structure as process. This is emphasized repeatedly to avoid the pitfalls of nominalization, which will skew our understanding of the phenomenon.

Structure as process is an activity with formal properties. It is biological in its roots and form, neurophysiological in its location, and conceptual and seemingly immaterial in its scope. Its internal manifestation is in the neurophysiology of the being; its external manifestation ranges from physical movement and reaction to the products of thought and imagination. It is in the latter realm, thought, image, and feelings, that the structuring process fully emerges as ego.

We'll begin at the borders of the "normally developed ego" and work our way both inward and outward in space, forward and backward in time. The border of the ego, the boundary of the maximally extended field of its operation, we will call its *primary adaptive surface*. The surface referred to here is the point of demarcation beyond which we find the outer operational environment. Below that surface we find the organization that adapts, the being. Within this boundary is the ego. It exists as an ongoing structural activity at the most complex point of a long process of development. It rests upon, and is to some degree interpenetrated by, similarly organized processes within the being and to some extent includes them. It is through the ego structure that primary contact with the world outside the being is made, and that point of contact is the adaptive surface.

The adaptive surface of the empirical ego is in a constant state of exchange with the environment that surrounds it. The currency of exchange can range, for any given structure, from the material to the immaterial. In some sense the currency can be seen as informational vis-à-vis the structure itself. The Swiss epistemologist Piaget used the term *aliment*, a nutriment appropriate to the level of systematic organization considered. For example, a wide variety of chemical compounds in the form of "food" is appropriate aliment for a biological system. Concepts and ideas are aliment for a conceptual system. The medium of exchange is *system specific* and provides information to that system; that is, through exchange the system absorbs materials or patterns that alter the state or mode of functioning of the system itself.

Our egos trade in the more abstract range of the media of exchange. They trade in information in the classic sense and feed on symbols and symbolic arrays. The human ego is a complex organization, biological in nature, symbolic in content, and adaptive in function. The border of the adaptive surface is the most abstract and complex level of organization of the organism within which it resides. The ego's contact with the world inside and outside itself is thoroughly symbolic. It is through this symbolic field and its constant internal organizing activity that both the survival and experience of the person is engineered.

Experience is symbolic because the system that generates experience processes only symbolic material. Lest this seem a radical statement, one may reflect on the notion that everything entering, encountered by, or registered by the sensory apparatus of the person, including the most minuscule and elementary sensations (dots!), is *transformed* immediately upon contact with the sensory apparatus and goes through manifold transformations as it ascends through the neurological structures. Those data now coded in form at each step are generally compounded with information internally generated at the most critical junctures, finally arriving in cortical areas where it is experienced. A description by Mountcastle is worth citing here:

> Each of us lives within the universe—the prison—of his own brain. Projecting from it are millions of fragile sensory nerve fibers in groups uniquely adapted to sample the energic states of the world about us; heat, light, force, and chemical compositions. This is all we know of it directly: all else is logical inference.
>
> Sensory stimuli reaching us are transduced at peripheral nerve endings, and neural replicas of them dispatched brainward, to the great grey mantle of the cerebral cortex. We use them to form dynamic and continually up-dated neural maps of the external world, and of our place and orientation, and of events within it. At the level of sensation, your images and my images are virtually the same, and readily identified one to another by verbal description, or common reaction. . . .
>
> Beyond that, each image is conjoined with genetic and stored experiential information that makes each of us uniquely private. From that complex

integral each of us constructs at a higher level of perceptual experience his own, very personal, view from within. (Mountcastle, quoted in Popper and Eccles 1977)

The ego, which is the person's primary adapting structure, experiences and adapts to symbolic elements within its own structure. Those symbolic elements are further abstracted; that is, symbolized by the transformative activity of the ego process itself. In order to be assimilated by the organization that is the empirical ego such material is finally transformed homeomorphogenically into aliment appropriate to the ego's structure. Remember here that aliment is system specific. The ego can assimilate and therefore experience only material (information) roughly compatible with its own organization or within its own range of modification. To a large extent, then, what the ego experiences is itself, its own organizing, symbolizing activities.

THE SYSTEMIC NATURE OF THE EMPIRICAL EGO

The empirical ego itself, as we normally conceive of it, is not easy to articulate. In Western intellectual tradition it has most often been assigned "the executive function": the control center for experience and behavior, and the seat of reason and rational interaction with the world. The outstanding feature of ego functioning is indeed its rationality.

Other attributes historically associated with a functioning ego are will, intentionality, purposefulness, and unity of experience. As we have noted previously, those attributes, while appropriate to a discussion of the organized process called ego, should be regarded carefully. Although definitions of the first appearance of an ego include these terms, in each person ego attributes (1) undergo a developmental course, generally increasing in their applicability throughout the life span; and (2) generally vacillate in complexity and pattern of entrainment within any one being at different points in time and in different situations. We therefore can speak of less or more developed egos, and better or poorer functioning egos, and still remain within the domain of the empirical ego.

It is therefore appropriate to talk of a process that fluctuates within a range of relatively optimal functioning. The organizational properties of such a system both developmentally and situationally determine its actual form and function. In addition it is a compound structure, constituting itself moment-to-moment from an enormous number of reentraining networks. We consider the ego (after Piaget 1975 and Mandler 1984) as the inclusive structure due to its rational and logico-mathematical properties, and its subsystems as networks. The distinction between ego and network is most visible at a network's molecular levels, organizing percepts and elementary coordinations of sensorimotor activity. The boundaries become more blurred when subsystems of the ego begin to have representational capacities.

The range of an adult's ego functioning is generally considered *concrete operational* and occasionally *formal operational* in Piaget's terms. Other theorists (e.g., Freud, Lovinger) set various criteria and focus on different aspects of ego functioning. We are primarily concerned here with the structural aspects as the principal determining factors. From our point of view Piagetian and similar formulations are the most relevant.

Roughly, the operational structures of thought (concrete and formal) are developed structures, which internally regulate themselves and direct a wide range of behavior. They are relatively abstract and propositional and have the property of reversibility; that is, they can test and rehearse mentally, without behavioral expression. Concrete operational thought is primarily applied to objects; formal operational thought has the capacity to reflect upon thought itself.

Ego structures are characterized by their relative endurance over time and their consistency in directing the being's interaction with the world. Their degree of developmental complexity limits their range of activity and the environment with which they interpenetrate. In other words, they are characterized by the degree of uniformity and creodization of their intentionality and the scope of their purposefulness. Formally operational systems are more complexly integrated internally, are less content and context dependent, and avail themselves of a wider range of cognized environments. Concrete operational structures stand in a relationship similar to developmentally prior structures (for a more extensive discussion see McManus 1979; Piaget 1971, 1977).

These ego structures constitute the primary adaptive surface of conscious network mentioned earlier. The work of Piaget and others suggests that ego structures are more consistent and pervasive than in fact they are. Piagetian experiments, for example, are almost exclusively concerned with children and their perceptions of the physical world. Others such as Kohlberg have ventured into areas of social and moral development. The general picture of the ego produced from those researches is one of pervasive and consistent structurization, of organizations relatively free from fluctuation in response pattern and applicable across domains. We see the issue somewhat differently when looking at the full range of adult ego experience and behavior.

DECALAGES

First, there is the question of unevenness of development termed *décalage* by Piaget. That is, development progresses at an uneven pace in the various networks and ego structures relative to the domain of experience. Within the context of Piagetian research, for instance, the concept of mass appearing during the emergence of concrete operational thought appears before the concept of volume is constructed. A structure is considered to be complete when the formal properties of that level of organization are applied uniformly to encounters with the operational environment. And indeed, this would seem to be the case in Piagetian research of the physical environment. However, things become less clear when we look at investigations of the social, moral, and conceptual environment. In Kohlberg's (1969, 1981) research, for example, we continue to find some mixture of response patterns and less indication of unity of structure.

It seems more likely that the adaptive surface of the ego, if we imagine the ego metaphorically as a sphere, would have an uneven surface more like the moon than a ping-pong ball. We would expect to find *décalages*, variable levels of structural complexity, in areas where (1) the individual is less experienced than in other areas; (2) the object of encounter is more flexible and indeterminate than others (for example, compare the unpredictability of human interaction with that of day-to-day physical objects); and (3) the emotional salience of the encounter is marked as "in threat" or "in love." In those areas we would expect to see inconsistencies in the organization of the overall system, entrainments that are developmentally more primitive than the dominant system characteristic of the overall ego. Yet they are included within the dominant system, comprise a portion of its adaptive surface, and may be influenced by the organization of the inclusive system. The ego's adaptive surface in a professional physicist dealing with thermodynamics may appear quite different and formally operational from that of a "green-haired freak, tripped-out on acid and trying to sell someone a bag of boa constrictors." We would, however, expect to see at least a tendency toward consistency in any one ego combined with a resistance from systemically included, yet less developed, networks.

FLUCTUATION

In addition to *décalages* in the adaptive surface, another issue generally not considered in studies of the empirical ego's formal properties is the oscillating nature of that surface in terms of its *momentary* entrainment. While *décalages* are developmental lags or indentations in the surface, *oscillations* are moment-by-moment, situational fluctuations in organizational complexity, which we have hypothesized in earlier works (McManus 1979). We see the ego structure and its primary adaptive surface as having a developmental limit in complexity that fluctuates, decrementing to previous modes of functioning contingent upon events occurring in the operational environment. Lack of stimulation, division of attention, intrinsic oscillation between hypo- and hyperintentionality, and stress variously defined, reduce complexity and range in ego functioning. In such cases, the ego structure is shrunk, in a sense, restricted and rigidified in its functioning. Encounters at the adaptive surface are perceived and subsequently dealt with more primitively, characteristic of earlier modes of development.

In summary, we consider ego functioning to be relatively average when there is

1. a range in the functional domain reflecting the cognitive complexity organizing and mediating it
2. an uneven topography of entrainments generating differences in functioning at the ego's adaptive surface
3. a continuous oscillation in the structural complexity underlying and defining the adaptive surface

The ego, thus conceived, is an active fluctuating process, internally self-regulated and organized. It contains within it numerous networks, models, and subsystems of varying degrees of complexity, entrainable in a wide variety of ways but subsumed under the functional constraints of the dominant, most advanced level of structure. This overall form is the principal defining structural feature of a particular ego's nature.

Ego as Self-Conservation

The empirical ego is thus an open system of transformational activity in a state of relative equilibrium and creodization. This equilibrium is never completely attained, nor is this system ever completely adapted, owing to transcendental perturbations of the inner and outer operational environment that require continual *re*-equilibration and *re*-adaptation. The ego, ever-striving toward equilibrium, continuously organizing and reorganizing itself, is resistant to change; its first priority is self-conservation. Once the empirical ego has emerged and taken root in the being, it struggles endlessly to preserve its identity and extend its domain.

By the latter we mean a lateral extension of the same level of structured complexity. From this perspective, growth or learning would seem to consist largely of internal differentiation within the system.

Assimilation

Self-maintenance is effected by the mechanism of assimilation, whereby the ego structure admits elements from outside into itself. As stated above, this is done indirectly and symbolically. The ego is a symbolic system, which is intentional, conceptual, and representational.

In lower, less developed systems physical entities are included within the response cycle of the relevant structures. At the ego level, however, representational entities are assimilated into the system. These entities as well as the more elementary physical ones must be recognized by the ego in order to be assimilated. A primitive ego structure developed only to the level of complexity appropriate to process concrete concepts, for example, will not recognize and assimilate abstract concepts (Turiel 1966).

This process of assimilation seems to have a sequence in which the range of recognition is considerably broader than that of the actual assimilation process. That is, the existence of a concept or representation may be recognized within the sensorium yet not be assimilable by the ego structure. A concept, or even a physical object, may be recognized, yet not be sufficiently isomorphic with the current properties of the ego structure that it can be taken in. Here a variety of outcomes is possible: (1) the object or idea is noticed or oriented to, but not internally processed (see Rubinstein et al. 1984 for a discussion of this phenomenon in scientific thought); (2) the object is denied or repressed (i.e., read out of the universe); (3) the structure differentiates itself to accommodate the recognized intrusion; (4) the system distorts the pattern sufficiently within the symbolic process that it can assimilate the distortion.

ACCOMMODATION

Accommodation is the bipolar compliment of assimilation, existing as a subfunction of the assimilation process (Piaget 1971). The overall function is the fundamental bipolarity that underlies the internal organization of the ego. Within that bipolar function, the accommodation pole controls change in the structure. As the organism encounters a noumenon, the sensorium will construct representations of the homeomorphogenic impact of that event. The nature of that symbolic representation will depend upon (1) the currently operative level of structural complexity of conscious networks, usually limited by that level ontogenetically and immediately preceding the operative ego level; and (2) the empirical constraints of the event itself (i.e., its pattern of penetration).

Should the event penetrating into ego via the sensorium be too far outside the structural range or have already been habituated to, it will be assimilated lower in the information-processing hierarchy and perhaps never reach awareness. If it should be closer to that range but outside the range of direct assimilation, or beyond the reaction norm of the accommodation mechanisms, it will be denied or left floating effervescently in the sensorium. However, if the event falls within the accommodative range of the structure, the system will differentiate internally and it, as well as subsequent noumena like it, will be assimilated. We suspect at this point in the process that repeated encounters with a noumenon has a cumulative effect. Although the impact of the initial encounter may not be sufficient to reverberate high enough to enter the sensorium, repeated encounters would produce a reverberative wavefront sufficient to manifest and model the noumenon at higher levels. This would be similar to Libet's findings for conscious awareness of cutaneous stimulation (Libet cited in Popper and Eccles 1977). It is well to remember once again that this process is one of successive intentional reorganizations as adjoining and related structures are penetrated by homeomorphogenesis. This multiple sequence of symbolic transformations constitutes what we earlier (McManus 1979) referred to as a sensory transformation, which is constrained in its range by the ego structure.

OVERASSIMILATION

The principle alternative to accommodation is a form of assimilation. In this case the structure does not differentiate through accommodation. Rather, it accommodates the noumenon to itself symbolically through what we call overassimilation; that is, essentially a distortion of the internal symbolizing of the noumenon dominated by the assimilatory pole. The noumenon is symbolized internally, not by the parameters generated by the noumenon, but by the process of assimilation into the ego structure. As the ego structure operates on the representation, it reduces the representation to its own parameters, rendering it compatible with the ego's structural properties, and assimilates it. This process has been demonstrated by Turiel (1966) in studies using Kohlberg's moral development scale.

Overassimilation is a systemic description of the mechanism of projection, wherein systemic properties dominate the interaction to the detriment of the transcendental nature of the noumenon and the properties are thus phenomenologically attributed to the object. Since the principal synchronic function of the ego structure, as with any similar structure, is its own conservation, overassimilation, and therefore projection, is an extremely common outcome. It would be fair to say that (1) overassimilation (projection) is a fundamental tendency of the empirical ego; and (2) overassimilation predominates relative to accommodation far more often than not. If the system criteria are biased toward self-preservation over learning and change, overassimilation would be the more probable resolution of any encounter with the transcendental that is not directly assimilable. In addition, both activities may function simultaneously— some accommodation to the noumenon occurs along with a compensatory overassimilation, varying in their predominance but probabilistically favoring assimilation—the essentially dominant functional pole.

Accommodation may be seen over time as a sequence of such actions, each dominated by the tendency to assimilate, yet progressively adjusting the structure through sequential accommodation to replications of that category of noumenon. The sequential adjusting through this combined process is what analytical psychology calls withdrawing projections. Although a thorough withdrawal of ego projections from the phenomenal world entails a more complex process (which includes a developmental transformation), this adjustment is essential to the differentiation required for transformation (we will discuss this issue later).

The interacting EMC polarity of assimilation and accommodation is the mechanism by which the ego structure stabilizes itself. Stability is maintained both by self-confirmation as executed through assimilation and by accommodation, the latter essentially a response to negation, which supplies flexibility of response and increased capacity through its differentiating function. Together, constituting a bipolar cycle of assimilating activity, these functions maintain the ego process in a state of relative equilibrium, regulating its exchanges with its operational environment through the symbolic medium of the sensorium. The sensorium as part of the overall system of internal transformations is a creature of those systems, feeding both itself and the ego structure. On the one hand, there is considerable input from the frontal cortex to lower, sensory junctures in the system, on the other hand, the ego structurally acts as an upper bound, or limit, interpenetrating the sensorium. The sensorium will reflect both the attitude that the ego takes toward it (Husserl's "natural attitude") and the operations the ego enacts upon it.

THE SELF-CONSTRUCTING EGO

It is evident, therefore, that the empirical ego is an immensely complex transformational system and the most abstract in the normally developed human being. It is a self-constructing, self-regulating system of neurophysiological entrainments emerging in a series of stages in the ontogeny of the individual. Through constant interaction with the operational environment, as constituted within its cognized environment, each stage of development replaces and subsumes its previous organizations within itself. It is the apex of human evolution and individual development and its most distinguishing features are reason and imagination. Yet, it remains a creature of symbolic activity, constructing, organizing, and living in an internally informed, symbolic world.

We hypothesize that the thinking, symbolizing ego emerges on the basis of a single developmental sequence. That sequence is transformational and incorporates the other basic transformation discussed earlier in the volume. In its simplest form it can be modeled as a sequence of separation, differentiation, and integration, the very process that produces cellular reproduction. Here, however, it is occurring in patterns of physiological entrainment and electrochemical activity within neural networks and experienced homeomorphogenically in the sensorium as symbolic form.

THE SENSORIMOTOR EGO

When first emerging into the world the human infant is equipped with a wide variety of internal coordinations mediated by neurognostic networks and other somatic structures. Among the most well known are the sucking and grasping responses. The sensory systems as well as the motor systems display a tremendous degree of organization. Through interaction with the environment these systems quickly become intercoordinated into more inclusive patterns of perception and action; that is, the various networks reciprocally assimilate one another. An ever-increasing field of coordinated action is the result. Such reciprocal assimilations occur through intentional entrainment of two or more networks to the same object. Two types of equilibration are occurring simultaneously, one between the two systems involved, and another between those systems and the outer operational environment. As these systems assimilate reciprocally, a third form of superordinate equilibrium is engendered between the two systems and the functions governing them in their coordination (Piaget 1977). During the first year and one-half of life a remarkable range of internal coordinations takes place, forming an overall system that eventually constitutes the adaptive surface ego of the child.

THE PREOPERATIONAL EGO

Perhaps the major accomplishment of this period is establishing within the system a constancy in the perceived environment. A constantly changing, appearing, and disappearing cognized environment begins to have some phenomenological permanence, due in part to accelerated maturation of prefrontal intentional processes. Where once things seemed to disappear from the world as attention wandered, now they remain to be *re*-attended. Some stability has been imposed upon the sensorium. The capacity to symbolize is developing and the world begins to take a more complex shape.

With object constancy, imitation and its eventual internalization as symbol, and increased reciprocal assimilation of substructures, language begins to appear and the ego rises from its background. For the next five or six years, the story of the ego is its emergence through increasing symbolic activity. Separation has occurred from the sensory ground and the ego has dug deeper roots in the biological system. Initial goals are formulated, extended behavior sequences develop and become more flexible, a symbolic cognized environment has become more extensive and with it glimmerings of a unitary intentionality. Where earlier each model and substructure had its own microintentionality and goal-directed behavior was brief and unstable, now the child increasingly displays a superordinate intentionality. This ability is possible through the maintenance of internal symbols defining goals and guiding behavior.

As the nascent ego separates itself from its sensorimotor functions, a simultaneous separation from the world is taking place. As the biological structure extends into the symbolic, it releases itself from its embeddedness in the world, becomes increasingly separate from that world and experiences, and recognizes that separateness. This separation is accomplished through action. Initially that action is sensory and motor, and eventually it becomes extended to and included in the symbolic and the intentionality. Each action upon the environment produces information and assists in symbolic representation of that toward which it is directed. Increasingly that action becomes itself symbolic, and a larger adaptive surface emerges to encounter a correspondingly enlarged world. It is this overall pattern of separation and internal differentiation that progressively constructs an ego. Cassirer put it nicely:

> All true action is *formative* in a twofold sense: the I does not simply impress its own form, a form given to it from the outset, upon objects; on the contrary, it acquires this form only in the totality of actions which it exerts upon objects and which it receives back from them. Accordingly, the limits of the inner world can only be determined, its ideal formation can only become visible, if the sphere of being is circumscribed in action. The larger the circle becomes which the self fills with its activity, the more clearly the character of objective reality and also the significance and function of the I are manifested. (Cassirer 1955:200)

> . . . for the unity of personality can be intuited only through its opposite, through the manner in which it manifests and asserts itself in a concrete multiplicity of forms of action. (1955:206)

Through differentiation the human ego emerges from an evanescent world with which it is mutually interpenetrated to construct its own greater cognized environment as it constructs itself. This world, however, is fairly static internally. A symbolic world is created that does but doesn't undo. A child can perform an action internally, but cannot undo it. He reasons transductively where part tends to stand for whole, where member and class tend to collapse upon themselves. It is still an immediate world ruled by affect. The conceptual operations of identity and reversibility have not completely taken root. It is experientially an animistic world where the moon may move as the child walks; where projections of feelings and intentions into the outside world occur easily; where sympathy occurs, but not yet empathy. The cognized environment of the nascent empirical ego is still stimulus bound, impulsive, and ego-centered. Although more separate now from the world than earlier, the young ego is not highly differentiated from that world. As physical action was necessary to separate self and world at an earlier stage, symbolic action is now necessary. But this action is also insufficient to reduce further a high degree of interpenetration between self and world. Yet, even here a new integration is formed. As the internal system reciprocally assimilates and equilibrates internally, a new level of integration is achieved with the outside world: a symbolic integration of meanings not previously registered in the sensorium, not existing in the world.

Within the internal structure, differentiation of subsystems remains in an intermediate state. The overlapping relationships among internal networks, evidenced by transductive logic, the confusion of part and whole, member and class, produce lateral associations, all-or-nothing responses, and emotional lability. Overall intentionality of the ego is limited and momentary as subsystems triggered in tandem owing to insufficient differentiation draw the attention and activity of the being first in one direction, then another. Attention is limited and highly dependent upon external stimulation or internal emotion. We have the beginning of an ego but not yet a completely formed ego. For that stage, a conceptual universe must construct itself; another act of separation is needed if these lower boundaries of ego are to be transcended.

THE OPERATIONAL EGO

Somewhere around the age of seven, another miraculous recreation of the world takes place. The world begins to explode into a universe of ideas about things. Higher rational order enters the cognized environment. Number, volume, mass, time—all begin to take root and relate. Newton has arrived upon the scene. As the child separates himself from a world of static imagery, these emerging systemic properties project themselves into the world arising in the sensorium. Further separating the ego from a phenomenal world defined sensorially and emotionally, he creates a more abstract world, and the ego now establishes new relationships with that world.

Intentionality continues to internalize more of the being and the world, extending itself in space and time. A world of action takes place increasingly within the being, and the range of action is extended, ever more capable of ordering its world rather than simply being ordered by it. The adaptive surface extends outward with another layer of growth, which is more mobile, more flexible, and more conceptual. And all that went before is reorganized in this development and subsumed within the newly created level of being. This is the realm of practical man where the world loses some of its magic to gain a modicum of practical order.

The ego becomes complete when it becomes *operational*. By operational we mean, as does Piaget, the application of mental forms of logical action upon objects in the sensorium—operations such as classification and seriation. This development brings thought into the cognized environment and thereby expands that world substantially: it becomes more mobile. While new operations can be performed in a conceptual realm and carried out in a physical realm, they can also be reversed internally, ordered in various ways, perhaps classified differently—all before being executed. Emotional responses can be differentiated and graded because of the emergence of classificatory schemes where specific members of a class of phenomena are more easily seen and therefore reacted to as such, rather than eliciting responses appropriate to the overall class. Transductive reasoning is transcended and similarity is no longer coded as identity. Several objects can be classified, here by one criterion, there by another, rather than being dominated by one rule. Conservation of physical properties becomes facile as two aspects of an object or process can be held in mind by the newly emerging operational system. Something can be longer and thinner rather than one or the other. Simultaneous comparison by multiple criteria becomes possible, and with it a more complex world and a more complex way of being-in-the-world.

With the advent of operational logic, the ego becomes an element in a nexus of other egos forming a new layer encompassing the world, a layer of biological processes extending themselves. Forming this layer the being forms the world encompassed within itself and forms itself in the process. The individual ego stands more separate from its surround than ever before, yet integrates itself within that surround at an entirely new level of action and being. Thought, still intimately tied to the physical objects of action and remaining interpenetrated by those ties, is at the same time more differentiated internally and more separate. The integrative relationship with the extended world is maintained by new equilibrating activity, conceptual in nature, showing a finer balance between the functional poles of assimilation and accommodation. The focus of this equilibration effort is the preoperational level now being transcended, and that system becomes reorganized as a field and becomes nested within the operational domain. Now experiencing itself more fully as a being in time, the ego seeks to extend its range of control over the world, regulating itself more precisely in the process.

The overall process of equilibration starts from a center anchored in the perceived constancy of the phenomenal object, and at each level the reorganization forms itself around that initial operation of constancy. At each level the reorganization of the ego begins again, redefining the object anew at each reformulation. Starting at this center the process works itself outward in ever-increasing radiations, first with physical objects, then the social sphere, and beyond. The objects of operational application are defined by greater freedom, more flexibility, and less predictability of response. *Décalages* manifest themselves, generally reflecting the difficulty of those properties. As a general rule, operational understanding of reality coalesces in physical reality before the social and eventually the ethical realities. Laterally extended, the process tends to recapitulate the developmental course, moving from the sensate and predictable, to the conceptual and fluid, through the intermediate zone of the purely representational.

The lateral extensions of the process are the surface transformations discussed earlier. Each is an organization of expanded reality based upon encounters reflecting the increasing complexity of the growing nervous system's information-processing structure. These transformations are synchronic and seek internal equilibrium as well as adaptive equilibrium with the perceived world outside as homeomorphogenically generated within the sensorium. More and more of the newly construed world is taken into the ego through its own self-constructing action, becoming at once a world more separate from self and a world constituted for and by self. Interactions between ego and world are controlled, constrained, and regulated by these internal autoregulations. Transformational activity composed of exchanges between self and world are defined by the surface manifestation of the underlying structure. The nature of these exchanges, sensory transformations, exhibit the dual quality of adapting to the world while in the act of constituting it. We see the world as we define it and structure it; we adapt to those definitions and cybernetically redefine the cognized environment in this overall cyclical action.

Of course, the process of equilibrium never achieves the hoped-for balance. As each transformational cycle is executed, coordinated, and reciprocally assimilated to others, it redefines the world toward which its efforts are directed. As this process proceeds, new questions are opened up, adaptations required, and problems posed. The cycle itself engenders uncertainty in its quest for certainty, imbalance in its search for balance. Laterally expressed it leads to internal differentiation of the structure and its networks in the form of accommodatory activity. This internal differentiation presses for additional modes of regulation, of systemic integration. The continual search for equilibrium reveals itself as one of *dynamic equilibration,* containing its own internal pressure, and containing the mechanisms of self-transcendence. The pressure toward more stable and adequate equilibrium engenders a systemic self-reflection producing developmental transformations in the process. Equilibration is thus the equilibrium process cast in a temporal and progressive dimension.

Developmental transformations occur when bipolar conflict is generated by the efforts of the adaptive surface confronted by a disadaption. Simultaneous penetration effects, entering the sensorium, present two opposing aspects or perceptions of an event. Initially, the system will recognize this conflict sequentially, emphasizing one aspect, then the other. Then, more rapid alternation between one facet and another initiates an attempt at synthesis. Should one or the other pole predominate, transformations remain at the surface level, either in the form of overassimilation, accommodation generating internal differentiation, or some combination favoring one or the other. A radical surface transformation may maintain structural integrity by flipping bipolarly in content—for example, the ardent capitalist turns socialist, the libertine joins the Moral Majority. The complexity of the ego and its adaptive surface remains the same; only the values attached to the polar position change. On a large scale, culture reflects a surface structure of all possible structurizations at a given level of complexity. Something quite different, however, occurs if properties of the event, or the degree of internal differentiation of the operating structures, occur simultaneously. It is at this point that the system may transcend its own organization.

The tripartite division of the transformation sequence can be further differentiated to reveal its internal mechanisms. At the center of the process we find stages of alternation in perception and perhaps also in behavioral expression. Alternation and the subsequent decision between alternatives is the fulcrum of transcendence. Should more than one perspective be attended, and the two supporting neural networks simultaneously activated in the sensorium, the possibility of reciprocal assimilation arises. Repetition of this event or the surpassing of a threshold of intensity will promote a fusion, the networks operating simultaneously within conscious network. A pattern of reverberation is thereby established, reinforced by repetitive exercise, deepening a creode, and creating a new and expanded organization entrainable to conscious network. A chain reaction over time and the superiority of adaptation generated by the new structure may initiate a generalization of the reciprocal assimilations, eventually generating a more complex regulatory structure from the original internal interactions. A new boundary forms, created by this activity, which encloses and includes the earlier mode. When this process occurs at the adaptive surface, a new level of ego is created, perhaps a further separation and a new level of ego-world integration attained.

THE FORMAL OPERATIONAL EGO

The supreme mode of organization is now propositional. Thought itself becomes the object of adaptive activity organized into a new system by a new level of thinking. At this level of abstract thought, separation from the world is considered complete and ego-world inter-action transpires in a realm more of its own creation. Biology has extended itself out of the material; the realm of practical man is sub-sumed within the world of philosophical man (Radin 1927). A Teilhar-dian noosphere encompasses more fully both the operational and the cognized environments. The universe turns in upon itself and recog-nizes itself. Thought, in addition to displaying the functions of identity and reversibility and a preoccupation with the material, formalizes itself further with the operations of negation and reciprocity. A fully autoreg-ulated structurization appears, and the ego to some extent breaks its bonds to the material. The ego disengages from the content it is structuring and becomes a fully operational, generally applicable mode of being-in-the-world, yet not quite a being-of-the-world. From most contemporary, scientific points of view, this is the apex of human evolution and individual development of the ego.

A formally operational ego is an intentional ego *par excellence*. Its capacity for self-regulation, its de-centering vis-à-vis the cognized envi-ronment composes a system of exquisite stability and far-ranging adapt-ability. A formally operational, fully rational, and self-reflective being is more a master in its own house. It constructs a world of ideas, which interact among themselves and downward through the neurocognitive hierarchy and perhaps manifest physically in the world. It operates in a world no longer fixed but fluid, relative, and relational. As it organizes more complexly within itself, it penetrates more deeply into the struc-tures of the operational environment.

THE EGO IN RETROGRESSION AND TRANSCENDENCE

We've described the ego as a system, as its own expanding universe, continually separating, differentiating, reintegrating, and displaying two constant functions: its own self-organization and adaptation to the operational environment. It arises out of the operational environment, biology expressing itself in formation. The functional poles of assimilation and accommodation constitute the basic mechanisms of a progressive equilibration extending itself into the universe (Piaget 1971a). With each developmental transformation the ego surpasses itself, and in the act of transcendence, creates a new world with its growth. Yet within the ego are nested all the previous structures developed and coordinated along its trajectory, and these remain as parts of the encompassing whole. They are organizations of living cells incorporated into more developed organizations of living cells.

The adaptive surface, interfacing with the world, is a membranelike boundary self-generated by its own reciprocal assimilations and by those structures enveloped within it. This boundary varies in its permeability depending on its overall assimilation-accommodation balance. Within optimal ranges of coordination, this balance provides both maximally effective adaptation and optimal openness to its surround. A predominance of assimilation closes the boundary, while an excess of accommodation increases the homeomorphogenic effect of the environment. The former increases projection, rigidifies the system, yet emphasizes its own conservation. The latter tends to destabilize the internal organization, often stressing the system and initiating compensatory action from the other pole. Here the destabilization of excessive accommodation can provoke a competition of sorts resulting in overassimilation, which increasingly distorts the perceptions of the external operational environment and initiates increasing maladaptive behaviors. The sensorium correspondingly reflects this activity and becomes conceptually and imaginatively chaotic, even threatening. The self-regulation of the ego is jeopardized and the being is at risk.

THE DEVELOPED EGO

In this section we want to focus on the inner composition of the developed ego, whose structure ranges from concrete to formal operational organization. Relatively little is known experimentally about formal operations compared with the three preceding levels of structurization for several reasons: (1) the vast majority of work addressing the problem has been carried out with children as subjects; (2) formal operational thought is not achieved by everyone in this or any other culture; (3) some cultures may produce none, or relatively few such individuals; and (4) it is unknown how this structure extends across content areas beyond that of the physical universe. We suspect that fully formal operational individuals, manifesting no *décalages* and highly developed in all areas, are undoubtedly rare (Laughlin and Richardson 1986). Lacking extensive epidemological data, we would expect the general population to evidence a wide variety of developmental levels with *décalages* in many areas. The structural topology of any population would have an uneven surface composed of individuals varying considerably in developmental level and individuals displaying a range of variation at any moment in time.

If we peer underneath the primary adaptive surface as we did in chapter 2 and examine the supporting structural activity, we see essentially a map of the ontogenesis of the individual's higher neurocognitive processes. Neural networks are nested within neural networks, reciprocally assimilating with some networks, less or not at all with others. Within these networks lie nested more molecular models, all regulated by the organizing process producing the adaptive surface of the ego. Heretofore, the adaptive surface has been described principally by its adaptive exchanges with the operational environment. It is the agent of equilibration with the world. It can be seen from the inside, however, reflecting an adaptive surface toward the elements of its own organization. An equilibrium must also be effected in this direction in order to maintain the integrity and regulation of the internal structure.

RELEGATION AND A WELL-PLACED CINEMAGRAPHIC METAPHOR

Experience is the conjunction of the intentional and cognitive structures and the organized perceptual content of consciousness. Both the cognitive structures and the perceptual content lie within fields of transformational activity produced by the nervous system. These fields extend beyond and beneath both the cognitive structures that organize, define, and act upon the cognized environment and the neurognostic homeomorphogenic penetrations from the operational environment, which constitute the phenomenal world as essentially presented. Both structural activity and sensorial content have been relegated to lower-level systems, and out of conscious access. In a sense, our experience is much like a well-edited film—a great deal has been left on the cutting-room floor. We are left to experience the cleaned-up narrative where the story-line tends to hold together in a coherent whole. Still, there are parts of scenes, even entire scenes that potentially could be edited back in but are either nonessential or destructive to the current plot.

Outside of our current experience lie actors and scenes, which are potentially usable and available. These are the relegated structures of earlier development, contents previously experienced but forgotten or repressed, material vaguely and peripherally processed, latent material waiting in the wings. These can be relevated into consciousness and enacted in the sensorium with varying degrees of ease. Still further offstage lurk additional plots, alternative scripts, and actors yet unknown. These are not relegated elements because they have never been on the stage of the sensorium; they have never played a role in consciousness. Here, relatively inaccessible to relevation, roam figures that rehearse alternative scenes out of sight of the ego, alternative phenotypic expressions of the genotypic master plots from which the current scenario enacted by the ego was hatched. Yet, the ego of contemporary man, basking in the spotlight of the leading role, spins a reality blissfully unaware that the world is only a play and he is only one of many possible actors vying for the leading role.

The ego sings and dances his way through life, however, with a nagging doubt, stronger in some than in others, that all is not well in the scripting department, that there are other characters on the stage occasionally hogging the light meant only for him. Beneath the production staged in the sensorium and experienced as ego lie neural structures with intentionalities all their own. Some of these are occasionally recruited to fill out the cast or to enter the adaptive surface to enact roles not quite right for the ego. Most often the ego, with the stereotypical vanity of the leading player, takes credit for the applause, denies the boos are meant for him, at best gives a grudging nod to the supporting player and nudges him—or especially *her*—gently off the stage (the opposite being the case for females). All this time the ego does not know, or at least would not admit, that both he and they stem from parents and an ancestral lineage that are organizations of living cells within the being, and are always standing in the wings, pulling many of the strings that keep this show on the road.

The ego has an infuriating and flagrantly limiting tendency to deny its relatives, friends, and parents. Framing, creodically constraining, and giving life to habitual patterns of entrainment are the basic networks and neurognostic foundations from which the ego has sprung. True, it would often seem that the ego is the brightest light in the family, but he is definitely not the only one. Deep in the background of experience are an unknown number of genotypic, archetypal progenitors for, not only the ego, but the other phenotypic expressions in the form of neuropsychological complexes. The neurognostic archetypes constitute the basic neurological ground plans out of which later structures develop, the ego being the most developed of these due to its greater contact with the world. However, sibling structures do develop, mostly kept out of consciousness or cast out as unacceptable to the ego's vain desires. Substructures that qualify for the status of neurotic complexes are those that are partially but incompletely entrained to the ego and conscious networks. They are occasionally recruited into an overlapping neural network when environmental penetration elicits them or when the ego's attention flags or is distracted. Under these conditions they may pop out from the wings and do their act. There are intermediate states as well where the environmental press or internal perturbations activate them and they sway the ego, distort ego responses in their direction, and alter his character just out of range of the spotlight of consciousness. Some are frequently entrained to ego, others frequently less so; some easily seen, others seen only with the greatest difficulty and considerable coaxing.

RELEVATION AND THE EGO

From the ego's point of view, looking at its own supportive field and developmental context is like looking down into a massively spiraling vortex of dancing shapes, receding further into haze and eventual murky darkness. Ego has forgotten whence he has come, oblivious to ancestors he has never known. The structural array we have just discussed descends through a roiling sea of reciprocally assimilating substructures, each with its own quasi-intentionality, increasingly diffuse yet interpenetrating. One finds as one penetrates these depths carefully and systematically—whether through insight meditation, or, as one author (McManus 1979) has done, along a Jungian-alchemical path— that these structures spring to life, relevate themselves into consciousness, become entrained to conscious network, and appropriate a sensorial life of their own. They tend to objectify themselves on the stage of the sensorium, taking symbolic shape as persons, figures, and personae. They may surprise and startle the ego, reveal themselves one by one, and react to the ego's attention. Often they bring others with them, creatures with similar affiliations. They tend to be uncovered in reverse order to their initial occurrence in the developmental ascent of the ego. They are substructures left behind, relegated to the chorus with developmental transformations or potential paths not taken in the formation of this particular ego.

In pursuit of the greater being, one generally descends through a field of incessant chatter lying slightly lower in the structural field, relating complex to complex in a concrete fashion, each less evolved than the ego, each less separate from its mates. Still further down, images predominate, more nonhuman forms materialize and relate to each other and ego in a transductive, figurative fashion. Both extreme fragmentation and intensive interpenetration are more frequent at this level. Still deeper layers throw up figures more imaginary or geometric, more primitive and less articulately formed. With each deeper descent the figures filling the sensorium are more compelling, more energetic, more numinous, more encompassing. Deep at the base of the structural field lie the archetypes, the fundamental neurognostic organizations, out of which our ego and our thought patterns have evolved.

In Western culture as have been conditioned not to make this arduous descent. Indeed, the spectacular advance of the Western ego and its accomplishments in the world may be largely due to this caveat. By ignoring, repressing, and suppressing the depths of its own being, the Western ego has at once molded the earth to its will, has streaked past many peoples in politicoeconomic and technological development, and has deluded itself about its own primacy, its own separateness, and its own essential nature. It has extended itself expansively, devoured the world voraciously, and taken that world into itself. It has penetrated the world technologically to its finest constituent particles while forgetting it is of that world and interpenetrated by that world. It has constructed an adaptive surface turned almost exclusively toward phases of consciousness and attendant experiences it conceives as the outside world, only vaguely aware of the activities of the operational environment inside; that is, the *being*.

The sensorium produces an edited movie with a preference for action dramas written for the ego. It hears the grumblings within, the noise of the cast in unbidden images, perplexing fantasies, and endless, (to the ego) meaningless internal chatter. Much of this activity forces itself upon the stage of the sensorium, often arising accompanied by feelings, emotions, and moods. But these transformations are acceptable and therefore assimilable to the ego. And they are, compared to the ego and its exalted reason, diffuse, unarticulated, and often troublesome. The door to the dressing rooms has been effectively sealed, with only the occasional interloper slipping through. An iron gate, it seems, has been erected across the land of images and myth, roughly at the preoperational level of development. The passage of material through the gate is difficult, strained, and usually disguised, and as symptom or feeling it will only distract the gatekeeper. Only under the shade of slumber, when the house lights are dimmed, do the players gain access to the stage. Not realizing that it is but a module in a vast field of living neural organization, the ego's adaptive surface remains a semicircle equipped to deal with the outside world, but walled off in consciousness (but not in effect) from its outside world.

When the ego stops devouring the aliment of the world that confirms, reinforces, and equilibrates its existing level of structurization; when it refrains from finer and finer accommodations to differentiate itself further, the ego finds that all is not as it has seemed. This conclusion may be voluntary, as in therapy or meditation, or it may be thrust upon one in reaction to stress. In either case, the world as previously known to the ego is shaken and perhaps shattered; the ego must confront a new world little known. Depending upon the strength of the ego, and the guidance and techniques available to it, the result will vary between development and collapse. In any event the result will follow the same transformational outcomes previously described for the encounters between the outwardly turned ego and the operational environment. They will be

1. an encounter, destabilization, recovery, overassimilation, and no change
2. assimilation-accommodation vacillation to the extreme, overassimilation to the extreme, and potential collapse of the ego structure
3. instability with overassimilation maintaining the structure but effecting a surface transformation (as in some political or religious conversions)
4. a balance of assimilation and accommodation, a new integration, and the beginning of a course of developmental transformation

Resolution may (1) leave the status quo intact; (2) move the ego out of adaptive equilibrium with the environment and even destroy the ego altogether; (3) inflate the ego and realign it adaptively to the environment in a new stance; or (4) align the ego with its own affiliative structures to establish an entirely new construal of, and relation to, the operational environment. The first and third are actions at the surface, structurally the same but differing because the first holds its original position; the third flips to its opposite or complement. Numbers two and four take place diachronically, altering the nature of the structuring process itself. The second damages or destroys the empirical ego, intentionality regressing it to diffuse, conflicting, and scattered arrays. The fourth increases overall viability by recruiting and entraining structures outside the ego into a larger, reciprocally assimilating structure, inclusive of more of the being than the ego. Here the ego advances to the status of a major player in an ensemble, aware of the other players on the stage, now capable of greater combined vision, and acting in a more profound play.

If regression occurs, the ego tumbles backward down the backstage stairs, grasping at doorknobs and bannisters as it goes. In actuality this is better described as a retrogression in which the structures strain, twist, and often come apart (disentrain). Yet, sectors of functional entrainment remain; some structures continue intact. With good fortune, should a "cure" be affected, the ego system will find a relative equilibrium and identify with the bannister that held, whether bolstered by therapy, teaching, or faith. The demons will be repressed, denied, or assimilated to a "normal" frame, and ego will go on in the world much as before. Later eruptions will be controlled through drugs, therapy, or will, and the backstage doors will be sealed once more.

In transcendence a very different course is charted and a very different set of results attained. As stated previously, the result is growth; a displacement of ego from center stage and a clear vision of both self and world. With this change comes a more separate and integrated being, a being more at one with its world. Over time and with success awareness dawns of how much "out there" is really "in here," still projected unknowingly on the world-out-there. Through time as the figures we have described are encountered, accommodated to, and assimilated with, awareness of the extent of the overall being expands consciousness by virtue of this integration. The figures will dissolve to reveal the structurization process itself that composes and supports not only the ego but its related structures and, beyond, the construction of the world itself. Potentially, the field of being may reveal itself and the illusion of a separate subject in an objective world is replaced, not by merely a unitary view of the world, but by a unitary being-in-the-world.

10 Dreaming, the Shaman's Journey, and Polyphasic Awareness

> Now, Kitty, let's consider who it was that dreamed it all. This is a serious question, my dear, and you should *not* go on licking your paw like that—as if Dinah hadn't washed you this morning! You see, Kitty it *must* have been either me or the Red King. He was part of my dream, of course—but then I was part of his dream, too!
> —Lewis Carroll, *Through the Looking-Glass*

RETURNING TO OUR EARLIER DISCUSSION of phases of consciousness, we wish now to apply the theoretical views we have constructed to an explanation of various alternative phases of consciousness encountered both by anthropologists cross-culturally, and by individuals in their own pursuit of self-knowledge. In particular we are interested in the relationships between symbolism and cross-phase transference of information into alternative phases of consciousness, and the role of the ego in that process. We are also interested in experiences that arise as a consequence of cross-phasing, as well as the neurobiological concomitants of the process. We will begin our application by examining the most obvious and common set of alternative phases of consciousness—dreaming. We will first look at dreaming in relation to the empirical ego and then in the context of the shamanic experience. Then we will consider the neurobiology and anthropology of dreaming. This inquiry will set the stage for our later exploration of mature contemplation.

DREAMING

For most people in Western culture dreams constitute a lower bound of consciousness. The brain is active, processing quantities of symbolic material; yet ego consciousness, at least as described in the previous chapter, seems to be out of the picture. Formal principles of organization that define the adult ego are notably absent. Linear logic and rational continuity is suspended, and the images and scenes in the dream revert to a transductive mode where elements are linked through partial similarity of configuration or meaning. There is a great deal of similarity between the organization of a dream, Piagetian notions of preoperational thought (Piaget 1975; Piaget and Inhelder 1969), and Cassirer's (1955) descriptions of mythical thinking. Dreams appear to be the mind at play when the ego is on holiday.

During dreams we find access to the activity and content of the operational infrastructure upon which ego consciousness rests. This activity, a process of constant structurization produced by organizations of living cells, never pauses. When dreams emerge, the activity of the supporting structures, as well as structures disentrained from ego through repression, mediate the dream and thus reveal themselves. Active as well are systems never having entered consciousness, and behind all this activity are the fundamental neurognostic organizations often referred to in Jungian terms as *archetypes*.[1] In dreams we have a chance to see the activity of our internal structurization normally out of range of the constraints of ego consciousness. Thoughts, too, being residues and elements of ego consciousness, all mingle in the field of play. It is through the world of dreams that ego may get the idea that there is more than "he" or "she" in there and that encounters with these images begin to clear a path to transcending empirical ego consciousness.

In monophasic Western culture the dream has been denied a place in consciousness (see Tedlock 1987). Indeed dreams are to be ignored, repressed, and overcome. Until the advent of psychoanalysis, little use was seen in studying dreams. Even Freud, while recognizing their utility in therapy, saw the material as reflections of the culturally aberrant. Only Jung saw them as a vehicle of transcendence. But civilization seems to organize itself as does the mind. While technologically advanced cultures pushed the dream world more and more into the background and worshipped at the altar of reason, in outlying areas less "developed" and preliterate peasants and traditional peoples maintained their affinity for the dream world. In myths and fairy tales, legends and stories, contact with and concern for dreams and dream imagery and their import continues. As the ego emerges into reason and forgets the other aspects of the overall structuring process, so civilization arose leaving similar material to its own periphery, denying and denigrating it just as the ego does its challenging complexes. In both cases, however, pressure from the periphery continues to penetrate. In both cases the holistic imperative to unitary intentionality is influenced and thwarted by the neglected aspects of the being. Nevertheless, for ego and Western civilization the world of myth and dream continues to penetrate, erupt, and draw the attention of consciousness toward it. The ego and its civilized context are rooted in myth and unknowingly follow its design while rationalizing that they intended this route for very conscious reasons. And when things go terribly wrong, both egos and nations project the intentionality they will not or cannot own as parts of their being onto something outside of themselves—another being or another nation.

Many cultures nurture a concept of a golden era when all was well with the world. Egos, too, secretly nourish a fantasy, often projected into the future, of a Garden of Eden to come. At different times and in different places, contact with this garden was broken and to one degree or another access to it was lost or forfeited. Polyphasic cultures leave certain doors and windows open to those other worlds (MacDonald et al. 1989); monophasic cultures attempt to cement the entire wall. Yet, everywhere there is nostalgia for the place left behind or yet to come, and everywhere there have been men and women who still knew the way back or the way ahead. Of course, at all times and in all cultures there exist people who bridge the gap erected by ego and culture and maintain the link to the rest of being and the world. There have always been individuals, and sometimes whole groups, who know there is more to consciousness than is socially condoned, no matter how or where defined.

The dream world is the unconscious territory adjoining normal consciousness. It is experientially the closest point of contact to the nonego. Explorers of a wider consciousness have always known the world of dreams in one way or another. Often it is their first contact with transpersonal modes of consciousness. The dream world is, naturally, to one degree or another, accessible to everyone. For most of us it is simply smatterings of phenomena we call "a dream" and exclude from our definition of consciousness and ourselves. For some individuals in our culture and for everyone in some polyphasic societies, dreams are an extension of, or part of, their normal conception of consciousness. Still others encounter this material unintentionally as dreams thrust themselves into waking life, and complexes threaten the stability of their world. These latter folks experience the dream world as a living nightmare, one from which escape is desperately desired. Some are shattered by the experiences; their ego structures crumbling, they are pulled into the abyss of madness. Yet there are others who survive and even thrive on such encounters and out of them forge a wider understanding of being and consciousness. These are the egos which transcend themselves, and it is to the pioneers of this work that we now turn our attention.

SHAMANS AND THE DREAM WORLD

Our thesis is congruent with one proposed by Wilber (1983), that the early explorers of this realm of expanding consciousness were the

270 CONSCIOUSNESS AND THE LIMITS OF EXPERIENCE

shamans. Shamans have appeared the world over within traditional cultures (Eliade 1964; Roe 1982). These cultures by our developmental criteria would lay closest to the boundary that we Westerners construct between image and concept. If these cultures have formally operational members, they are extremely rare (Dasen 1972). In those cultures living close to the immediate contingencies of survival and largely lacking in what we term *formal education*, the adaptive pressure for such development is often not there (see e.g., Laughlin and Brady 1978). Development for these people often assumes a different course and the shaman is the principal exemplar of this path. His or her world is made of ritual, symbol, and myth generating a phenomenological cosmos with depths below and heights above the world of normal consciousness. This nonprofane world is approached first through a phenomenological descent and then a magical flight (see Eliade 1964; Grim 1983).

THE DESCENT AND EXPERIENTIAL DISMEMBERMENT

One way or another, the incipient shaman enters his own being, advancing into the lower realms of the land where dreams are made. He most likely doesn't know, as more advanced adepts surely do, that this land lies within himself. Yet he enters it nonetheless and makes the first discoveries of the world beyond the ego. This realm is also cast upon the neurotic and the psychotic, but there is a difference here: a difference in their personal character, in interpretation, and eventually a difference in their method and relation to the cultural worldview and the social order.

Like the neurotic or psychotic, many shamans are cast into this world involuntarily. Frequently a history of hypersensitivity, instability, or disease accompanies the shaman during his growth. Often a severe emotional crisis eventually occurs and the incipient shaman is introduced to the world of wonders and terrors. But again there is a difference. For the neurotic it is a lifelong battle, for the psychotic a shattered world. For the shaman, however, it is the commencement of an initiation leading to the construction of a greater world. Although some shamans are appointed or gain their role through social descent and take this journey by intention and technique, a great many find their role thrust upon them by transformations spontaneously occurring within themselves. Unlike the modern neurotic or psychotic, they live in times and in cultures that have an understanding of and a container for such experiences. These people are thoroughly socialized in and surrounded by a cosmology that describes and explains the world of wonders and terrors—a cycle of meaning. These cultures have methods as well, discovered and transmitted by previous explorers, that assist in the extension and control of these journeys. In such cases the shaman is a person of strong character who suffers an initiatory sickness and transcends himself in the curing of himself (Grim 1983:172ff). This sickness, cure, and transcendence sets him apart, the conventional connection with the world left behind, and a new world opening before him.

Often, the shaman first encounters the depths through a vision or a lucid dream. Not ordinary dreams or mundane fantasies, they are archetypal dreams in the Jungian sense, intense and compelling. Often prophetic, they carry an announcement from the other side. Such events may be singular or repetitive, but in either case constitute a phase of internal fragmentation or dismemberment. Experientially, the cognized environment is being torn apart internally. Symbolically, it is a rendering by animals, or spirits, or a cutting to pieces by figurative or shadowy entities. In all cases it is a very painful first step. Its medieval European counterpart occurs as described in the first phase of the alchemical process called the *Nigredo* or *blackening,* a time of painful despair and doubt. In Jungian individuation it is the analytic phase, the examining and taking apart. In Christian mysticism it is the Dark Night of the Soul of St. John of the Cross. In these cases it is the dismembering of the current ego and the commencement of developmental transformational activity.[2]

In normal development as discussed in the previous chapter, the transition from one level of development to another takes a period of years, extending and consolidating itself over time. It, too, is based on doubt and contradiction and their synthesis, occurring in incremental steps and in the bright light of day. But the suddenness and intensity of the shamanic ordeal distinguish it and give it its force. The sudden reversal of apparent trajectory from the centrifugal to the centripetal, extraversion to introversion, staggers the being. But the process is a de-structurization essential to transformation either into progression or regression. Its suddenness and change of direction intensify its shattering effect; it is the pressure of development accelerating itself. The de-structuring homeomorphogenically experienced as dismemberment is the internal structure literally coming apart under powerful and impelling intrusion from unassimilated neural structures. If they do not shatter the ego, those structures eventually may reciprocally assimilate with ego into a greater structure producing a wider vision.

The trip through this territory is very different from the original, extraverted, and gradual development. For one thing, there is a functioning ego. To some extent even the psychotic's ego, which has been largely shattered, faintly remains. It is the ego awareness that engenders the fear in these experiences. In the shaman it is the relative integrity of the ego that makes this retrogression a step in an ultimately progressive transformation. This notion is extremely difficult to articulate or to diagram without mistakenly conveying that his journey is either a conceptual reduction or a purely pathological experience. It is neither. Shamanic cultures metaphorically use the terms descent and ascent as does medieval alchemy. They are symbolic expressions of what is, over time, an expansive, developmental transformation of consciousness.

The shaman's ability develops in stages of experience, usually supported by instruction and embedded in a cosmology. Over time the sequence of experiences informs a growth. It all becomes of a piece. But in its initial stages leading up to spiritual crisis and the initial revelations, "downward" is an apt metaphor for the attendant introversion and the experience of dismemberment. It is apt as well from an external point of view because during the early stages the individual is too dislocated to conduct optimal adaptive behaviors toward the world; nor does his divided consciousness permit him to function at peak cognitive capacity. This introversion and fragmentation of consciousness (leading to a dimming of intentionality) is the initiatory sickness often characterizing shamanism cross-culturally.

This separation phase demarcates transformational junctures. As Eliade (1964) correctly points out, the shaman undergoes spontaneously, then formally, the sequence characterized as rites of passage (van Gennep, 1960). The separation is internally driven by the introversion and restructuring that disassociates the shaman from mundane ego consciousness. This phase also separates him externally from his fellows, often acted out by the incipient shaman in a retreat to the wilderness, solitude, and letting go into possession states. Such separation is often ritually and institutionally prescribed as part of the shaman's training. Nevertheless, the separation starts the transformational sequence, breaking the shaman from comfortable awareness of the known world, and preparing him for entry into another and unknown world.

The second phase, differentiation, has two aspects as well. Experientially, the shaman differentiates his new world and dawning consciousness with each encounter, whether spontaneously or ritually provoked. As with any new development, continued experience forces accommodation to and assimilation of the material encountered. Formal instruction and guided experiences with their interpretation at the hands of experienced shamans constitute the second aspect of the differentiation phase. Over time those experiences facilitate a growing familiarity with the expanding world and control over the experiences themselves. Increasingly they are entered and left behind at will. Internally, a new developmental process coalesces and equilibrates. Externally, the shaman adapts to his newly created world and adapts anew to the old world, which it now includes and subsumes. Integration takes place progressively and the world is seen anew. Reciprocal assimilations develop internally between ego and other structures fulfilling the overall intentionality of the being. This process is represented as the relationships between the shaman and his spirits, phenomenological symbols of internal functional relationships held together within an expanded and regulated structure.

With both guidance and experience the shaman gains mastery over his new realm of experience. He becomes expert at cross-phasing warps and transcending levels of his own internal structures (Grim 1983:138). What was earlier experienced as dismemberment and madness now becomes an exploration. As Neumann (1954:411) remarks about the process of individuation: "The ego ceases to be overwhelmed as consciousness becomes more capable of assimilating and understanding the individual symbols. The world grows clearer, orientation more possible and consciousness enlarged."

THE ASCENT: MAGICAL FLIGHT

A universal attribute of the shaman is his magical flight. The shaman is commonly conceived to fly, free from the body, to worlds unseen (Eliade 1964; Halifax 1979). In states of ecstasy the shaman leaves this world, as well as his own body, and enters a world of spirit forms. Within this greater world enacted within the shaman's sensorium, he learns to benefit the mundane world to which he will return.

Flight is not only a characteristic of the shaman's vision, it is also an appropriate metaphor for his experience as he encounters the greater, sacred imaginal world associated with states of trance and ecstasy. The sensorial input from the external world is progressively shut out through the internal mechanism of habituation (see McManus 1979). Consciousness is turned inward and the sensorium fills with homeomorphogenically symbolic transformations of internal neurological processes. Images appear, experienced in the sensorium as real in the same way the external world is experienced as real. Free of his body and separate from the world, the shaman flies into the symbolic world of his own interior, usually via some sort of portal, door, or tunnel (MacDonald et al. 1989). Here he is greeted by the symbolic enactments of the structures common to mankind and given shape, form, and meaning by his culture's cosmology.

Experientially, the shaman meets many figures on the other side, both human and animal in form. A common experience, especially for the male shaman, is a female form, a psychopomp who initiates and guides him from the start. She is the connection between the sacred and profane worlds with instructions concerning the former and messages for the latter. This figure is also encountered in the experiences of modern Jungian individuation in the form of the *anima*, the contrasexual structures linking the conscious empirical ego to the nonconscious.

Other structures express themselves in the form of animals whom the shaman must come to know or master (see e.g., Webber, Stephens, and Laughlin 1983). As these figures differentiate themselves through experience and reciprocally assimilate themselves to some extent to consciousness, the internal world stabilizes and takes overall form, generally congruent with the shaman's culturally framed cosmology. Some of those figures accompany the shaman for life as tutelary spirits and helpers, upon whom the shaman calls during his periodic flights. These figures, in turn, will have affinities and relationships with other figures, internal structures reciprocally assimilating and interpenetrating in various ways. In knowing these beings, the shaman comes to know his internal structural pattern and its effect in phenomenologically creating the profane world as it is experienced. In this manner the shaman brings knowledge back into the profane world and applies it as healer, sage, and oracle (Halifax 1979, 1982). To the extent that the shaman has great power, that he penetrates deeply into the basic roots of the structurization process, he will bring valid information back into the world of the ego.

We really do not know, owing to meager relevant ethnographic data and direct phenomenological accounts, the total range of experiences encountered by the many shamans over historical and prehistorical time. Considering an evolutionary change in the development of consciousness and the more primitive cultural surround of earlier epochs, we think it is likely that the majority of shamans experienced encounters with this internally generated symbolic field as a world-out-there, rather than a world within. Some, however, may have come to understand, as do adepts in more highly developed phenomenological traditions, that they were exploring the interior of their own selves. For the more primitive shaman, expansion of consciousness may well have stopped at the awareness of a greater world of multiple realities inhabited by figures encountered while in dream or other alternative phases of consciousness. The mature contemplative becomes aware of the emphemeral and illusory nature of this world and its figures through sustained discipline and inquiry; most shamans may know only of that world's existence and, on the basis of that limited knowledge, may function as psychopomps and interpreters of one world for the other. But as we say, the data are insufficient to resolve this question.

The nature of the shaman's experience seems to have both universal and culturally specific attributes. Universality of experience across cultures is seen in phenomena such as the experiences of portaling, flight, magical heat, dismemberment, ecstatic trance, and encountering spirits in both human and nonhuman form. This universality would be attributable in the present model to the consistent organization and entrainments of neurognostic structures existent within the human nervous system. As one experientially converges toward the vortex of the internal structuring process, individual and cultural variations vanish to reveal a profound, common structure. This structure embedded neurognostically in the human brain is experienced by shamans everywhere in their realization of the interrelatedness of all things, of energy flow, and of the existence of a nonprofane world outside the bounds of conditioned normal perceptions. Closer to the surface and the boundary defining normal experience, we find experiential variation across cultures and cosmologies. Determined by the surface structures, these individually and culturally conditioned variations are generated by the deep neurognostic structural underpinnings of human cognition.

From central initial neural networks emerge split-off formations of a general order, which produce generic internal functional relationships and which reflect average, abstract modes of adapting to the operational environment. Consciousness experiences these generic structures as affectively laden archetypal entities relevated to the sensorium and interpreted as real. The homeomorphogenic symbolization of what is essentially structure and process is a function of the confluence of the structuring activity of the ego and the extravagant production of a cognized environment by the sensorium. Consciousness constitutes these encounters in a phenomenal way that can be digested, assimilated, and comprehended. As they emerge closer to normal consciousness, they further differentiate into complexes more articulated and molecular. These complexes are experienced in more familiar forms as animals and humanlike figures, reflecting the developmental level of structure encountered. Near the surface we find the greatest cultural variation, the cultural definitions having greater formative influence in determining the experience of structuring activity. And as we made clear in chapter 7, culturally generated cosmologies determine the interpretive nature of the experiences at all levels. Even with experiences of the deeper levels, Christians interpret aspects as manifestations of Christ, Plains Indians as Wakan Tanka, alchemists as the philosopher's stone.

Culturally formulated surface structures have their effect at two levels. First, the determining effect of surface structures on experience is greatest at levels of structurization most closely resembling the ego structure. This effect lessens as deeper processes are experienced. As the central structures are approached, the experience becomes more universal and less personal. Second, the interpretation of the experience defined by the cosmological frame characteristic of a given people is the *post hoc* activity of reason as it attempts to assimilate and comprehend what has transpired. The two domains of influence are mutually reinforcing and integral parts of the cycle of meaning, partially molding the experience of one world and reciprocally assimilating it with another.

STRUCTURE OF THE SHAMAN'S JOURNEY

Thus the world of the shaman consists of the application of myth, symbol, and ritual to the generative ground of dreams and visions. Myth provides the context, which frames both the experience and its interpretation. Symbols provide the ideographic mode of access, portals through which the shaman enters his world as well as giving form to the experiences encountered within. Ritual is the means by which the shaman plots his flight, separating him socially from the external world and phenomenologically empowering his flight into the internal domain. "Descent" is metaphorically descriptive of the shaman's early encounters and his experience of unknown territory, while "ascent" is descriptive of the entry into a new world now known through direct experience. "What for the rest of the community remains a cosmological ideogram for the shaman becomes a mystical itinerary" (Eliade 1964:265).

RITUAL

Ritual is the driving force behind the shaman's flight, the engine of ecstasy. It is the shaman's stock-in-trade. It is on the wings of ecstasy that the shaman flies to worlds unseen by most, and ritual is its source. Often interwoven with symbols, augmented by drugs, and possessing various forms, ritual is the behavioral component inducing the shamanic trance. Ritual behavior is patterned, repetitive, and structured to produce generally inter- or intraorganismic coordination (see d'Aquili et al. 1979, chaps. 4 and 5).

In the case of the shaman a notable characteristic of ritual is its autonomic driving function (see chapter 5). Driving may be accomplished by stimulating either the sympathetic or the parasympathetic system (see chapter 11) to various extremes, producing atypical modes of functioning. One such effect, sensory stimulation induced visually, auditorily, or behaviorally through repetitive movement such as dance, is to habituate the sensory systems to input from the outside world (see McManus in d'Aquili et al. 1979). When presented or enacted in multiple modalities, the impact from the outside world reduces to a single wavefront, effectively eliminating competing external stimulation from the sensorium. This wave may entrain a field of neural networks into synchronization and elicit penetration from internal systems, which then predominate on the stage of the sensorium. The principal effect of ritual behavior individually, and ritualized sensory input contextually, may be to block the activity of the dominant cerebral hemisphere and reduce the normal adaptive surface of ego to nonlinear, image- and affect-ridden thought processes. That model suggests that a decrement in dominant lobe functioning invites a shift in predominance toward the atemporal, image-based functioning of the nondominant hemisphere (d'Aquili 1983).

In essence, ritual techniques neutralize in various ways the functioning of the analytic, conceptual mode, bringing to the fore developmentally earlier functioning somewhat characteristic of preoperational thought. This mode associates aspects of experience transductively; that is, it makes lateral associations among the elements of thought and perception based upon similarity, overlapping class membership, or emotional affinity. This mode is more participatory and less decentered than is conceptual thought and consists of images embedded in fields of affect rather than concepts embedded in fields of logical relationships.

Because ritual behavior drives and tunes the autonomic nervous system into specific patterns, its effect on cognitive organization should be predictable, based upon the inverted U-curve hypothesis stated in the preceding chapter. In terms of this model, either over- or understimulation of the neurocognitive system may drive its functioning below normal. Understimulation may occur either by lack of stimulation as in extreme isolation, or certain meditative states, or by repetitive stimulation such as saying mantras, chanting, or drumming. Overstimulation can be accomplished in numerous ways combining multiple sensory modes, including ordeals and stresses of various sorts, and is particularly relevant to the shaman's brand of ecstasy. The emergence of image-based, atemporal functioning and the temporary integrative state forged by structural synchronization tend to eliminate internal conflict and produce euphoria and release.

In meditative states (discussed in chapter 11) the ego is more likely to be detached and stable, whereas in trance states, particularly those induced by overstimulation, the ego is immersed and overwhelmed. A state of *participation mystique*[3] in Levy-Bruhl's sense is generated in which the ego participates in the events of the sensorium, driven there, and eventually returned through ritual action. Driven deeply enough, the shaman will enter into such worlds, not simply observe them. Ego position in some cases may be entirely displaced. In others some self-consciousness may be retained. A continuum of experiences between single visions and total immersion into an entire phantasmal world exists for the shaman. In any event, such experiences are generally interpreted as both numinous and real.

SYMBOL

While ritual is the engine of shamanic ecstasy, intention-inviting symbol is its pilot. Shamanic rituals are replete with symbols, from the shaman's costume to the masks and implements used. Symbols and ritual behavior are essentially inseparable from the shaman's repertoire, constantly intermingling and mutually supporting each other. Yet, while the repetitive action of ritual serves to turn off the conceptual mind, symbols act to stimulate nonanalytical modes of knowing. Symbols embedded within ritual penetrate homeomorphogenically to entrain networks to conscious network and relevate them to prominence within the sensorium. They may do this in two ways: (1) as a portal or entry into an internal symbolic world; and (2) as containers giving form and meaning as they evince that symbolic world.

Symbols may operate as a door or passageway through which consciousness may pass to an alternate world (see McDonald et al. 1989). Supported by ritual-driving techniques, intense concentration upon a particular symbol can center the mind on a redundant visual pattern in a hyperintentional way that eventually fills the whole of consciousness. The practitioner may identify with or pass through this state, penetrating to a chain of associations perceptually linked to the portal. Noniconic portals such as mirrors, crystals, or blank slates may produce the same effect, the principal differences being the degree of constraint that the form of the portal imposes upon the experience. A highly detailed iconic symbol suggests a more definite experience than does a mirror, which allows greater freedom of projection of the shaman's internal state. Iconic symbols, therefore, may be more useful in contacting a particular spirit, familiar, or experience; noniconic portals would be more useful for generic explorations. In either case, additional constraint will be imposed by other symbolic material in the ritual context.

A variety of interrelated symbols in the ritual context may reflect and define relationships expected to exist in the shaman's mythical world. Transductive association, expected to be prevalent within this world, reasons from part to whole, indeed assimilates one to the other. In the ritual context masks, statues, aspects of an animal or spirit, hair, pairs of horns, and the like, grouped together, may help to define the elements and interrelationships existing on the "other side." Experience with this symbolic material, as well as with the continual accrual of memories of journeys beyond, helps the shaman to differentiate that world, understand it as a whole (Grim 1983), and incorporate it into a total cosmology.

Knowing the "other world" involves the organization of a symbolic field, as does the knowing of the external operational environment. It requires an act of construction, actually re-construction, in which external symbols and their relationships are used to execute an internal transformation within a field of potential neural entrainments. That is, the process of initiation may be assisted or accelerated through the manipulation of external symbols. This manipulation would have homeomorphogenic effects on the internal structure, essentially entraining it to the external pattern, but according to its own internal logic.

Repetitive use and exercise of a variety of symbols on the outer plane would tend to elicit and differentiate structures to which they penetrate upon the internal plane. Repeated collaborative use of certain symbolic combinations would both elicit and reciprocally assimilate the corresponding structures within the neurocognitive system. New patterns of entrainment, repetitively coelicited over time, would tend to effect a restructuring of the internal system itself, forging a new integration. The neurophysiological mechanisms for establishing such new entrainments are known and are discussed in chapter 2.

This gradual reconstruction of structures mediating perception and thought are generally taking place instinctively below the conceptual or operational levels of thought. A rearrangement of substructures is being effected in this manner, progressively entraining them through individual and sequential exposure (differentiation) and combined elicitation (varying levels of integration), forging a new substrate in the neurocognitive system. It is taking place at levels of internal entrainment, which are more fluid and less constrained by the rules of logic characteristic of the operational levels of thought. As children at this level, our thinking was iconic (Piaget 1975). As an adult accessing this level by neutralizing later-developing analytic thought, the shaman again reenters this world and reforms it away from the limitations normally imposed by later modes of thinking. The shaman accesses and reshapes a world of almost pure experience. The reformed structures will in turn exert pressure upon these later systems. That is, differentiation and reintegration of the developmentally earlier substructures will homeomorphogenically penetrate upward and outward, generating adaptive activity by the entire conceptual apparatus. The movement is commonly from pure experience, through feeling and intuition, to reason—bringing all four functions into a more mature harmony.

Techniques such as those discussed, ancient as they are to shamanic traditions, are increasingly coming into vogue in modern psychotherapy. They are integral to hypnotic interventions, especially those based on the work of Milton Erikson (Erikson, Rossi, and Rossi 1979; Bandler and Grinder 1975). Gestalt therapy has used techniques based upon such methods for many years, and cognitive therapy is turning to them as well. As in these modern techniques, which are essentially attempting to discover, monitor, and reconcile discrepant internal models often ascribed to the different cerebral hemispheres, the shamanic cultures seek a similar reconciliation. Yet, these cultures place a higher premium on, and assign a greater veridicality to, those experiences we now attribute to internal cortical and subcortical entrainments. Their world is much closer to the boundary of experiences emerging from that mode of functioning, one that has become a virtual gulf in modern Western culture. Therefore, they cross that boundary more easily, maintain the techniques to do so more faithfully, and integrate the differences with greater facility.

MYTH

Finally, the mode of conceptual integration available to and used by shamans and shamanic cultures is myth, which forms the bridge between the iconic and the verbal or rational. Myth includes elements of both. Within the mythic world, imagery and feeling are cast into a narrative. Story line and causality become more linear and thus more satisfying to the newly analytic mind. Myth mediates between the sacred and the profane, between the transpersonal and the personal. Although myth explains and applies to the realm of the practical, it comes from the realm of the sacred. Existing in manifest form within the world of the "real," myth is the container for, and integration of, the land of the "unreal." Although the notion of what is or is not real may vary substantially in shamanic cultures relative to ours, the degree of accessibility to mythic experience engenders the need for the shaman. It is myth that instructs, stabilizes, and integrates the shaman's experiences and provides the context and meaning without which he might sink into psychosis. It is myth that identifies, indeed often forms, the experiences through symbolic penetration. And it is myth that tells the shaman what he's seen and how it fits into a coherent whole.

Myth acts as the field of external constraints molding the ego from the outside as the shamanic experience remolds him from the inside. The surface structure defining the ego's particular expression of consciousness is a joint function of the level of ego development and the mythical context within which it grows. In the shaman's case, however, myth can have a role in transcending the ego. To the extent that myth reflects the dreams and visions of previous shamans who have surpassed the empirical ego, it can assist and guide them to further transcendence. As a map of the relationships of internally integrated structures, it can help forget that integration within the shaman. If myth leads not only to awareness of a world outside boundaries of ego knowledge, but also to a world transcending the ego; and if the structures ritually activated are reciprocally assimilated to that ego, then a structure greater than that ego is gradually integrated into a wider consciousness. The ego of the shaman then exists as a subsystem, albeit an important one, within an unfolding neurocognitive structure with increasingly unified intentionality and one flying free of the constraints of mundane time and personal viewpoint.

The shamans actually attaining a highly developed state may have been proportionally very few. Many more took partial steps, entering to various degrees the worlds beneath and beyond the ego. We have only sketchy records of a few of their arduous journeys, some glimpsing little on their way, others glimpsing considerably more. Often bound by their facility in encountering the nonordinary, many were undoubtedly chained to a world of mystery and fantastic visions. These remained mired in their ego condition, often what we might term a *protoego* state. Yet they were the ones who kept the fire, maintained the knowledge and techniques that other adepts later built upon. They were the first explorers of the human mind who forged the trail, which will become the future of self-reflection for those who follow them.

THE FUNCTION OF DREAMING

Having examined the relationship between the empirical ego and dream experience, and having expanded our view to include how shamans used their dreams and visions, we will discuss more fully the function of dreaming within the context of psychology and anthropology. In that way we can appreciate the importance of alternative phases of consciousness for the development of all beings, regardless of their self-awareness.

Because every normal human being on earth sleeps and dreams, and every warm-blooded animal sleeps, and very likely dreams (Jouvet 1975:516), sleeping and dreaming are obvious universals (Laughlin and d'Aquili 1974:164) with which every human can potentially identify. Everyone has experienced the need for sleep, the association between sleep and dreaming, and perhaps the effects of sleep disturbances. What is therefore remarkable is that the actual function of sleep, and especially dreaming, remains largely a mystery to science. Naturally, there are many competing theories about the function of sleep and dreaming (see C. S. Hall and Nordby 1972; J. A. Hall 1983; O'Nell 1976 for reviews). Many of these theories are purely psychological and refer little to the psychophysiology of sleep, whereas others consider the psychophysiology of sleep and ignore the experiential aspect of dreaming. By now the reader recognizes the typical dualism involved, and, as usual, we wish to develop all aspects of the question so that we may speak from a single perspective regarding the biology, behavior, and experience of the phenomenon.

After presenting an abbreviated form of our theory of sleep and dreaming, we will elaborate on the views entailed in the theory, which have not been fleshed out in previous chapters. In brief, *sleep* refers to a set of neurocognitive and somatic entrainments, whose function is to facilitate the interpenetration of networks and organs, and the intraorganismic adaptation of these relative to each other and to the requirements of the total organism. *Dreaming* refers to a set of phases of consciousness in which experiences arising in the sensorium of the organism homeomorphogenically portray the activities of sleep entrainments. The homeomorphogenic sensorial events may be the expression of activities in the greater organism, or they may initiate those activities, depending upon several factors. The central query we pursue is how active are the structures of awareness and attention in the entrainments mediating sensorial events.

INNER AND OUTER ADAPTATION

The hallmark of sleep in humans and all other higher animals is diminished arousal and tonic inhibition of the skeletal muscle systems. It is as though the body "shuts down" its activities in order to rest and perhaps conserve energy for important events ahead. Although it is true that sleep involves the "shutting down" of certain neurocognitive and other somatic systems, it is not true that all systems have become quiescent. Far from it. In fact, as our own dream experiences reveal, much activity may go on during sleep.

Paradoxically, the sleeping organism appears inactive, but from the inside looking out, so to speak, the activity may be quite intense. In this seeming paradox lies the clue to the essential function of sleep and dreaming, for it exhibits the bipolarity of the adaptive processes inherent in all animals with big brains: the necessity of constituent organs and networks to "pull together" in adaptation to outer reality, and to adapt to each other within the inner reality of the organism.

The cycle of reentrainment of neural systems mediating phases of consciousness would seem to recur in a daily round; that is, according to a circadian rhythm (Broughton 1975). The cycle of phases alternates between those especially entrained to process information about the outer operational environment and those entrained to process information about the inner being. In Western culture we call the former set of phases being "awake" and the latter set being "asleep." As we saw in chapter 5, many phases may be nested within the grand phase "awake"—subphases like "reading," "drunk," and "eating." We recognize these phases by their attributes, their recurrent qualities that alert our self-awareness to our current phase. But in Western culture, apart from scientific investigations of sleep and dreaming, we tend not to be aware of embedded "asleep" phases while they are happening, and only reflexively in the waking phase if we happen to remember a dream. There are individual exceptions to this indifference in Western culture, of course, as in the minority of people who have "lucid dreams." But we will speak more of this later.

THE PSYCHOPHYSIOLOGY OF SLEEP AND DREAMS

The alternation between outer and inner orientation of the nervous system and the rest of the body seems to be controlled by warps primarily originating in the reticular activating nuclei in the brain stem. There is evidence that the onset and progression of deep slow-wave sleep is brought on by the activity of serotonergic neurons located in the so-called anterior raphe system (portions of the dorsal raphe nucleus and centralis superior; Jouvet 1975:505). Onset of sleep is associated with an increase in the threshold of arousal owing to external stimuli (like noises or movement) and a deepening generalized tonic inhibition (or paralysis) of the skeletal musculature. The process appears to turn off gradually systems that are primarily concerned with external events, preparatory to periods of intense inner-oriented activity. The gradual, cautious retreat from active involvement with the outer operational environment Jouvet (1975:506) calls the "fail-safe" mechanism of sleep onset.

Deep slow-wave sleep paves the way for what has been variously called paradoxical sleep, or rapid eye movement (REM) sleep. It is called paradoxical because, although the body is heavily relaxed and quiescent, the general tonic inhibition spares the oculomotor systems and the eyes move in a manner suggesting scanning. These "rapid eye movements" are the outward signal of intense inner neurocognitive activity. As Jouvet puts it, this REM sleep is characterized by "intense endogenous phasic and synchronous activity of most cerebral neurons, including pyramidal and extraparamidal motorneurons" (1975:507).

Such global activity requires both a "pacemaker" and the massive tonic inhibition already established during slow-wave sleep. The "pacemaker," or endogenous generator of cerebral rhythms during REM, is provided by networks in the pons, which are in turn entrained to tissues in the lateral geniculate areas and higher cortical areas—this being the so-called PGO system (Jouvet 1975:507). The tonic inhibition is delivered by the caudal portion of the locus coeruleus in tandem with the vestibular nuclei in the spinal cord (Jouvet 1975:511), to insure that no gross body movements are made as a consequence of the intense cerebral activity of REM sleep.

Interestingly, human beings do not begin to show electroencephalo-graphic evidence of a clear awake-sleep differentiation until somewhere after the thirty-second week of gestation (Niedermeyer 1982:109). Prior to this the child would seem to be in and out of wakefulness and sleep with little detectable differentiation between the two. Some differentiation within sleep begins to occur between REM and non-REM stages. Between the thirty-sixth and thirty-eighth week, sleep features appear similar to those of full-term newborns (ibid:110). It is important to note that a major proportion of sleep in the newborn is of the active, REM-type sleep, which may constitute from 50 to 64 percent of the baby's time asleep. Newborns will enter stage REM almost immediately after falling asleep and will develop recognizable slow-wave sleep patterns gradually over the first month of life (ibid:114). By the third to the fifth month after birth, the proportion of REM sleep has dropped to 40 percent and between the twelfth and twenty-fourth months to 30 per-cent of total sleep time. The relative predominance of active, REM-type sleep in the very young is a pattern found throughout the animal kingdom:

> In mammals, and probably also in birds, the amount of [REM] seems to be very closely related to the degree of development of the central nervous system. . . . Thus a newborn rat with a brain almost totally immature at birth has a very high proportion of [REM] during the first week after birth and [REM] reaches adult levels . . . only when the maturational process is almost completed. On the other hand, a newborn guinea pig, whose central nervous system is almost totally mature at birth shows a very low proportion of [REM], similar to that of the adult. . . . However, recordings taken in utero . . . have indicated a very significant level of [REM]: the amount of [REM] of a guinea pig 20 days before birth is the same as that of a newborn rat (for an identical level of development of the brain).
>
> (Jouvet 1975:516–17)

Jouvet notes that the amount of REM seems to be a good index of the stage of brain development in mammals and that it plays a major role in the development of the brain "when genetic factors are more important than epigenetic events" (ibid.:517).

DREAMING AS HOMEOMORPHOGENIC PLAY

Activity of sensorial structures during dreaming should be conceived as operating according to most of the same principles as during waking phases. What has changed is that the nervous system withdraws its concern for events external to the being and becomes oriented upon growth and reorganization of internal relationships. Sensorial events will ordinarily reflect this alteration of orientation. In order to understand the relationships between sensorial events and global neurological events during sleep, we must turn again to our concept of homeomorphogenic entrainment (see page 192).

We would argue that dreams are phases of consciousness during which *any reality desired by the being, or by any neurocognitive structure within the being, may arise in the sensorium.* During dream phases all sorts of events may occur, many of which may depict relationships, properties, and causal interactions considered irrational by the waking ego. The key element in determining the phenomenal nature of experiences during sleep is suggested by the term *desire*. It is therefore crucial that we examine what we mean by that term and its implications relative to our model of dreaming. It will also prove useful in the next chapter when we consider the structure of contemplation.

DESIRE

We began this volume by taking the position that the nervous system may be understood as a community of cells, and that the billions of cells composing the nervous system become organized through development in a hierarchical structure of networks. These networks may become involved in patterns of entrainment mediating control, perceptual, associative, affective, and many other functions in the body, including the mediation of phenomenal experience, the empirical ego, and consciousness. We later said that patterns of entrainment become conditioned to recur so that phases of consciousness are recognizable by their characteristic attributes.

Emphasizing that the networks mediating phases of consciousness are composed of living, goal-seeking cells, and thus living, goal-seeking networks, we may speak in general of the *desire* of any network as its inclination to "do its thing"—that is, to operate in a fashion that optimizes the positive (depolarizing) activity of its constituent cells. Desire, therefore, is relative to the network of reference. The desire of conscious network at any particular moment, which is a function of the interplay between the desires of the networks entrained to it, may be unitary and yet may conflict with the desires of alternative networks not entrained to it. Furthermore, the desire of conscious network may be relatively fragmented owing to the conflicting desires of its entrained networks. Of course, in the absence of a strongly integrated conscious network, the run of sensorial events may reflect a teaming, discontinuous play of symbolic motifs and themes reflective more of the scattered desires of momentarily active networks than any unitive experience resulting from control exercised through intense attention and unitive awareness. This view of the competitive activity of networks within a being obviously relates to the issues of dual consciousness, multiple personality, and other forms of fragmented consciousness discussed in chapter 5.

HOMEOMORPHOGENIC PLAY

The phases of consciousness we call "dreaming," then, are ones during which homeomorphogenic plays depict the interactions occurring in the global neurophysiological field. In other words, dream phenomena are symbolic expressions of neurological activities occurring largely outside the sensorium. For most people in any culture, and perhaps all people in some cultures, the entrainment of sensorial and nonsensorial activities is initiated outside the bounds of conscious network. Conscious network and entrained sensorial networks are relatively responsive recipients of penetrations from the global neurological field. The sensorium is penetrated by nonsensorial networks, and the field of activity among the sensorial networks mediating the field of dots constituting the "dream" is a partially isomorphic depiction of the more global neurocognitive activities occurring *at that moment*.

Penetration need not be in one direction, of course, but we are speaking here in relative terms. During lucid dream phases and under conditions of *hyper*intentional awareness in the dream phases during advanced dream yoga (or comparable disciplines), the direction of predominance of causality may be reversed. Conscious manipulation of dream symbolism and experience may penetrate to nonsensorial structures and homeomorphogenically entrain them to the events occurring in the sensorium at that moment. We will have more to say on this reversal of causality later.

ADAPTATION AGAIN

It is significant that phases of consciousness exhibit a cycle of recurrence alternating in orientation from concern with adaptation to events in the outer operational environment to concern with adaptation of competing networks within the inner operational environment (the being). Several observations may be made about this alternation. First, phases of consciousness at either pole tend to exhibit both active and passive phases. Within the waking phase there occur phases of consciousness that are relatively excited ("jogging," "eating," "making love," etc.) and those that are relatively relaxed ("resting," "reading a novel," "sunbathing," etc.). Likewise, there are active and passive phases within dream phases. So called non-REM or slow-wave sleep tends to be metabolically relaxed, while REM or fast-wave sleep and associated dreaming is usually active. We have introduced the neurophysiological structures mediating excitation and relaxation in chapter 5, and will further elaborate on those structures in the next chapter.

Second, the warp(s) mediating the transition from outer orientation (waking phase) to inner orientation (sleep phase) is designed to function optimally under relaxed autonomic tuning. The normal transition from waking to sleep involves a phase of relaxed "drowsiness" followed perhaps by presleep rituals like changing clothes, "reading a good book," having a hot drink, lying down in an appropriate spot and accustomed body posture, and other more subtle activities ("counting sheep," praying, etc.) during which the consciousness is preparing and is being prepared for sleep (Shearer et al. 1979). Laboratory work with animals and clinical work with humans suggests that the organism resists sleep and concomitant dream phases in the presence of perceptible danger or stress in the world. Even in slow-wave sleep, normally preparatory to active REM sleep, noises or other stimuli may block the onset of REM (Jouvet 1975). As sleep, tonic inhibition of somatic systems, and withdrawal from concern with the world deepen, a higher threshold exists that may reverse the reentrainment leading to sleep and arouse the organism (ibid.:506).

Third, there is a significant similarity between this "fail-safe" (Jouvet 1975) aspect of sleep and the conditions requisite for waking play. We consider it more than a coincidence that immature animals in the wild will not play in the absence of a perceived secure environment (e.g., among young lion cubs when their parents are not around, or among many organisms when they are hungry). Play is a waking phase in which somatic systems are "freed-up" from the immediate demands of outer adaptation in the interests of optimizing development of neurocognitive and somatic structures, which will be used in future adaptations (Laughlin and McManus 1982). An intrinsically driven activity, it is nonetheless outer-oriented. Solitary and social play facilitate growth of systems that are used primarily in outer adaptation. We are suggesting that dreaming is another form of play in which neurocognitive systems (to the exclusion of other somatic systems) optimize their development and integration "freed-up" from the demands of activity in the outer operational environment.

Fourth, keeping in mind, as always, that the brain is a community of living, goal-seeking cells organized into myriad networks and entrainments of networks, we can see that dreaming is the sensorial concomitant of play among cells and networks over the entire brain. Dreaming is "free time," a recess from class in the "school of hard knocks" of waking adaptation. During sleep individual networks are relatively free to act and to interact with each other. It seems likely that the imperative to act during sleep will be strongest among those networks *least* free to act during waking phases. In other words, those networks heavily inhibited by other networks that are preeminently involved in adaptation to the world may become free from inhibition during sleep and become active with a vengeance. But we must be cautious here, for we are saying neither that (1) all inhibition is released during sleep, nor that (2) all activity of neurocognitive systems during sleep is expressed in the sensorium. The reader will recall that much of what any network does is inhibit competing networks. What we are suggesting here is that during sleep there tends to be a freer play among competing networks than is the case during waking adaptation. And the function performed by this relatively free play among networks does not normally require expression in the sensorium. But the sensorium is composed of cells and networks too! They are active during sleep and are entrained to, and are driven by, some of the nonsensorial networks active in the free play of the moment. This sensorial activity is the "dream." Whether there is involvement of intentionality, awareness, or memory structures in the process of dreaming is another matter altogether.

MYTHOLOGICAL TIME

For reasons that perhaps lie in the more subtle interplay of views developed in this book, we are in partial agreement with James Hillman's (1979) assessment of our culture's rather distorted treatment of dream interpretation. His criticisms of Freudian and Jungian methods is based upon their insistence that an adequate account of the meaning of dreams must be couched in the language and logic of the waking ego. As Hillman notes:

> We may compare three approaches to dream persons. The first, let us call it Freudian, takes them back to the actuality of the day by means of association or by means of the objective level of interpretation. Other people are essential for understanding dream persons. The second, which we may call Jungian, takes them back to the subject as an expression of a person's complexes. My personality is essential for understanding dream person's complexes. The third, archetypal method, takes them back to the underworld of psychic images. They become mythic beings, not mainly by amplifying their mythic parallels but by seeing through to the imaginative persons within the personal masks. Only the persons of the dream are essential for understanding the persons in the dream. (1979:63–64)

The classic Freudian view of the function of dreaming is that in dreams we encounter the repressed wishes of the unconscious—the bestial, antisocial feelings and desires that we keep hidden from ourselves and others during our waking life (Hall and Nordby 1972). The Jungian view, which is more complex, considers dreams a compensatory mechanism for the distortions of the true self caused by the waking ego. Dreams may be compensatory in the sense of providing a more comprehensive picture of the psyche's dynamics as a whole, or in the sense of engaging the ego's intimate and active participation in psychic growth (Hall 1983:23–24). In either case, Hillman would hold that these perspectives conceive of the function of dreaming only in reference to the waking ego, either meaningful material hidden from ego, or messages directed at ego to some integrative or transcendent purpose.

Hillman's criticisms of modern psychodynamic theories of dream function and interpretation mirror the broader criticisms of Paul Ricoeur (1962; see also Rasmussen 1971; Price-Williams 1987) directed at traditional methods of textual analysis in philosophy and anthropology. Western interpretive bias is in favor of *demythologization;* that is, meaning must be recovered from symbolic materials, and recovery requires the transposition of highly symbolic dream (or mythological) material into the rational logic of natural language before the material may be said to "make sense." And making sense is, of course, with reference to waking ego. Ricoeur's point, and Hillman's as we read him, is that mythological texts and dreams are meaningful in themselves and do not require imposition of rational and linguistic overlays, or "exegetical methods," in order to retrieve meaning. The meaning inherent in myth and dream are apprehended directly in the lived experience of them. It is interesting, in this respect, that Hillman regards dream phases as entry into a mythological "underworld." For Ricoeur, the retrieval of meaning from mythological material requires the direct experience of the reality symbolized in the myth, and only after the material has fully come alive in consciousness may "philosophical" reflection proceed upon the dialectic between text and experience. Like Hillman, Ricoeur is highly critical of exegetical, demythologizing methods of myth interpretation such as those used by semiotic structuralists like Levi-Strauss and Propp.

EGOCENTRIC VERSUS POLYPHASIC AWARENESS

Somewhere on the continuum between monophasic awareness on the one hand, and fully polyphasic awareness on the other hand, is an awareness that remains egocentric but also minimally polyphasic (see e.g., Hillman 1987). That is, conscious network is not entirely constrained to a set of entrainments operating only within the waking phase, as is the case with monophasic awareness. There exists some cross-phase transference of symbolic material—some "leakage" from alternative networks into conscious network's awareness. Consciousness remains fragmented to some extent, but conscious network does have access to memories of experiences (entrainments) occurring in alternative phases of consciousness during which conscious network is far less alert, aware, collected, and concentrated (i.e., is *hypo*intentional).

The preceding state of affairs elicits egocentric and demythologizing interpretive strategies. The orientation is toward waking ego—that is, the self-view operating within conscious network among the set of waking entrainments—as the preeminent arbiter of meaning of all experiences arising in whatever phase of consciousness. Events in the cognized environment must make sense to waking ego if they are to make sense at all.

Fully polyphasic awareness is subtly different from egocentric awareness of transpersonal material. Polyphasic awareness describes a consciousness that is operating within the same intentional range of attention, concentration, and awareness in every phase of consciousness, whether waking, or dreaming, or trance (see e.g., Price-Williams 1987 on the "waking dream"). The intentionalities of all networks that become entrained to it are "meaningful" to conscious network within the frame of reference provided by whatever pattern of entrainment prevails at the moment. In other words, to the fully polyphasic consciousness, experience is meaningful as it is occurring, regardless of the phase of consciousness during which it arises. Polyphasic consciousness does not require interpretation of events occurring within one phase of consciousness to be rendered in another phase of consciousness in order to be meaningful. Yet, because cross-phasing is fluid, each phase of consciousness may interpret events in other phases according to its own context, intentionalities, and logic of events.

The difference between egocentric and polyphasic awareness is somewhat analogous to the difference between two metaphorical elementary schools. At the egocentric school the teacher (i.e., the cortical intentional structures) supervises the activities of the children in the classroom but not in the schoolyard during free play. The teacher's concern is primarily with events occurring in the classroom, and there is minimal interest in what is happening during recess. He is aware only of schoolyard events as they are recounted to him by pupils when they return to class. Perhaps he hears rumors of conflicts or of children playing in the yard that never show up in the class. The meaning of events in the yard perhaps attain real significance only when conflicts and other problems arising during recess somehow leak into the classroom.

At the polyphasic school, however, the teacher supervises and participates in the activities of both the classroom and the schoolyard. His awareness of free-time events is direct and meaningful, without requiring reports from pupils in the classroom, and vice versa. The presence and participation of the teacher during free-time events changes those events and their meaning, just as the presence or absence of the teacher in the classroom changes the nature of classroom events. Classroom and schoolyard events are fully meaningful to the teacher as they are occurring, and he has access to the memories of those events in alternative circumstances.

Without belaboring the metaphor, polyphasic consciousness is potentially fully informed about all phases of consciousness in each phase of consciousness, just as the polyphasic teacher is potentially fully informed of both classroom and schoolyard events whether in the classroom or the schoolyard. Egocentric consciousness (as well as fully monophasic consciousness) is informed about alternative phases only insofar as memory of events arising in those phases cross-phases to normal waking consciousness and is considered meaningful, just as the egocentric teacher is informed of schoolyard events only via (childlike) hearsay.

From our view of dreaming as homeomorphogenic play, the schoolyard analogy is not that farfetched. The free play among neural networks, so important to their growth and reorganization, is much like a schoolyard full of children. The presence of an aware, fully participating adult teacher among the children will obviously alter the activity, and perhaps result in greater cohesion and purpose to the total field of activity, without stultifying the free-play aspect of the activity. The logic changes, as it must, in order for the play to be free. Too much "leakage" from the classroom could have the effect of stifling play and could result in problems not only in the yard, but later in the classroom. That is, intense "leakage" of waking-phase material and logic into the dream phases may result in psychological problems. The play must occur, yet the presence of an integrated, concentrated awareness among the field of playing networks alters the organization of sensorial events, and as a consequence the field of play among networks.

TYPES OF DREAM CULTURES

We noted in chapter 5 that societies may be distinguished according to how monophasic or polyphasic they are in facilitating cross-phase transference among alternative phases of consciousness. We wish to return to this issue and expand that notion to include the variety of ways societies treat dreaming: the incidence of dreaming, the significance of dreaming, the interpretation of dreams, and the degree to which dreams become integrated into a polyphasic consciousness.

THE MONKEY AND THE MOON

There is a story told in the East about a monkey who often sat on a favorite branch in a tree where he could watch both the moon in the sky and the moon in a pool of water. But one day he became so entranced with this lovely view that he lost his balance and fell into the water. It was then that he suddenly realized the relationship between beauty and suffering. The monkey thereafter spent the rest of his life trying to get the moon out of the water. This story illustrates an essential point that we made in chapter 1 and must reemphasize here: a clear distinction must be maintained between direct sensory experience and the possible interpretations of that experience (see Stace 1960). But once the distinction is made, we must also add that the sensory and interpretive aspects of experience exist in a state of mutual interaction. Our monkey sat, perhaps for years, enjoying his view of the two moons, unaware that the one in the pool is a reflection of the one in the sky. Suddenly, he has an awakening, an "aha!"—he falls in the pool and learns to associate the beauty of the vista with suffering. A new interpretation of the old experience is made. It changes his life radically, and he spends the rest of his life trying to free the pool-moon.

What gives this story a tinge of silliness is that we know what the monkey does not. The moon in the pool is only a reflection of the real moon in the mirrorlike surface of the water. We would know better than to try to get the reflection out of the pool. We would know that all we would have to do is move to another branch to see only the real moon. This seems like common sense to us. And yet, we lose sight of the fact that other interpretations are possible. Perhaps there are interpretations more advanced than our commonsense view, as our view is more advanced than that of the monkey's.

The monkey is concerned with both moons. He positions himself so that he has an excellent view of both. We, on the other hand, would perhaps ignore the pool-moon as "unreal," and thus of no practical value. But perhaps another consciousness might continue to position itself to see both moons, but interpret both as unreal, both as reflections of a real moon existing in a supramundane realm of Platonic forms. This consciousness might know that it can come to understand the real moon by careful study of both of its imperfect reflections. Still other interpretations are possible, but the reader will no doubt have gotten the point by now. Every normal, healthy individual on the planet dreams. And, as far as we know, the sensoria of all dreamers functions in much the same way. Yet, how we value dreaming relative to our ego view, and how we interpret sensorial events during the dream phase, varies widely from culture to culture.

FOUR TYPES OF DREAM CULTURE

From the theory of cross-phase transference (see page 150), it is obvious that one may position individuals, regardless of their cultural background, on a continuum indicating the degree of cross-phasing, integration of phases, and maturity of contemplation of which they are capable. At one end of the continuum would reside extremely monophasic individuals and at the other end totally polyphasic individuals who perhaps have realized Void Consciousness.

Likewise, it is possible to align societies on such a continuum indicating to what extent they either (1) evidence knowledge of polyphasic consciousness and Void Consciousness in their cultural materials (symbolism, texts, ritual practices, selection of leaders and shamans, etc.), or (2) encourage individuals via an institutionalized cycle of meaning to explore polyphasic phenomenology, transpersonal experience, and perhaps Void Consciousness. The first alternative allows distinction between societies without reference to evidence of individual group members' actually attaining degrees of realization. The second alternative recognizes that regardless of a society's place on the continuum, individual members will also range on a continuum of realization.

To make matters easy, we will treat the continuum as a series of four ideal types defined primarily upon the second method of distinguishing societies. The reader is well advised to remember that these types are unreal and that we are talking about four locations on the continuum. The four types are described below.

1. *Monophasic Societies.* Monophasic societies tend to institutionally value experiences occurring only in normal waking phases of consciousness. That is, these are societies whose cultures give credence to phases of consciousness adapting only to the outer operational environment. Exploration of dream and other alternative phases is typically proscribed, disparaged, or simply not facilitated. Institutional measures may be taken to limit creodically the range of neurocognitive entrainments composing conscious network to those having only "practical" application to the world. Exploration of alternative phases may be restricted to treatment of pathology. Individuals found to engage in exploration of alternative phases, with or without the use of drugs, may be perceived by others as deviant, "crazy," antisocial, and perhaps, "criminal" and dangerous ("sorcerer," "evil," etc.). This type of culture is associated with a materialist society, one that tends toward a worldview depicting reality as full of concrete, physical, soulless objects to be exploited for economic ends. Individual group members may themselves be perceived as objects of exploitation by others. A monophasic society is the epitome of Sorokin's (1941) sensate society. Institutional means may be negatively in place to sanction and control the incidence of spontaneous, or willful exploration of, alternative phases of consciousness.

2. *Minimally Polyphasic Societies.* These are societies that seem primarily oriented toward waking phases of consciousness, but that also give minimal credence to the exploration of dreaming and other phases. Exploration of alternative phases is encouraged within ritualized contexts, and great emphasis is placed upon interpretation of dreams and other experiences in terms comprehensible to the waking ego. A polyphasic cycle of meaning will provide a cosmology, and perhaps professional dream interpreters that offer interpretations of dream experiences strictly in accordance with the dominant ideology. No significant facility is encouraged for mastery of anything like active dream exploration of "higher" phases of consciousness. There is no recognition or legitimation of shamans adept at traveling to alternative realities or adept as guides for realization of "higher" phases. Shamans are recognized strictly for practical purposes relative to waking consciousness—for healing, dream interpretation, astrological and other forms of divination, and so forth. Every effort is made to transpose transpersonal experiences to waking-ego terms. Demythologization of transpersonal reports is the norm.

3. *Maximally Polyphasic Societies.* The cosmology of this type of society codes reality in much the way described in chapter 8. Reality is conceived as existing in multiple levels that may be experienced and verified in different phases of consciousness. All, or a portion of the population, are guided into confirmatory experiences via symbolic text, ritual action, or instruction, often under the aegis of a shaman or master adept. Extreme measures may be used to evoke such experiences, including formal meditation techniques, psychotropic drugs, ordeals, fasting, and so on. Transpersonal experiences are encouraged, actively sought, and highly valued. The dream world or trance world may well be valued more highly than "mundane" waking reality. There are commonly a few individuals recognized as especially adept at entering alternative realities (alternative phases) and manipulating the "power" derived through such experiences for the benefit or detriment of others. This type of culture tends not to be materialistic and to epitomize Sorokin's ideational pole. No great emphasis is placed upon demythologization in the interpretation of experiences, although interpretations will still tend to be couched in cosmological terms.

4. *Polyphasic Void Societies.* These are societies that are maximally polyphasic and code in their cosmology an ultimate, transcendental Void Consciousness. Institutions in these societies encourage exploration of dream and other alternative phases, not as ends in themselves, but as means to the realization of a phase of consciousness beyond any phenomenal reality. Individuals who are recognized as having attained

Void Consciousness accrue high social status as the greatest healers, guides, leaders, sages, and teachers—those who are wise relative to ultimate truth. This type of culture is the most difficult to operationalize, for it would be quite easy for an ethnographer to work for years in such a society without having twigged to the significance of Void Consciousness, presuming there were adepts there who had attained that level of realization. Furthermore, as symbols (which are after all phenomena!) are used to describe metaphorically an experience that is essentially beyond phenomenology, there might be no easy way of distinguishing between a mythopoea derived from a merely polyphasic society from one originating in a Void Consciousness society. In any event, one may expect only a handful of living Void Consciousness adepts, if any, in a Void Consciousness society. More frequently, the situation will be one in which Void Consciousness is inferred from the data on an otherwise maximally polyphasic society, without any living informants having attained that level of realization.

11 MATURE CONTEMPLATION

> Do you remember how that life yearned out of its childhood for the "great"? I see that it is now going on beyond the great to long for the greater. For this reason it will not cease to be difficult, but for this reason too it will not cease to grow.
>
> —Rainer Maria Rilke, *Letters to a Young Poet*

> Neither common sense nor science can proceed without departing from the strict consideration of what is actual in experience.
>
> —Alfred North Whitehead, *The Organization of Thought*

WE HAVE DEVELOPED a theory of the structures of consciousness, showing how the nervous system as a community of cells organizes and reorganizes itself to mediate the flow of experience and alternative phases of consciousness into which strips of experiences congregate.[1] Furthermore, we have demonstrated how symbols operate to participate in their own meaning and in communication both between conscious and unconscious parts of the nervous system, and between the organism and the world. In the last chapter we applied this theory to a better understanding of dreaming and shamanism. It is our task in the present chapter to examine the biopsychological principles operating in higher phases of consciousness, and in particular, those attained as a consequence of various mystical practices.

The key to understanding the structures mediating higher phases of consciousness is to be found in the relationships of higher cortical processing and lower metabolic, autonomic, and endocrine activity. We will be centering our discussion primarily on those relationships producing phases of consciousness interpreted in various cultural traditions as *contemplation*, the systematic exploration of consciousness by means of trained introspection. In order to model those relationships, however, we must avoid the pitfalls of mind-body dualism, this time in the guise of different languages for speaking about phases of consciousness on the one hand, and the "somatic correlates" of those phases on the other. We will avoid dualism in this case by the simple expedient of introducing Gellhorn's unaccountably neglected theory of ergotropic-trophotropic processing. But before we do so, we will return to the discussion of the sensorium and the fields of dots for an operational definition of psychic energy, and we will review the literature on the psychophysiology of meditation. We will then be in a better position to account for some of the structural invariants that seem to occur in the development of higher phases of consciousness.

PSYCHIC ENERGY

Mystical traditions from many cultures describe extraordinary experiences that involve a sense of movement of energy within the body. These experiences are typically profound, are the consequence of entering an alternative phase of consciousness, and are coded as both numinous and sacred. We wish to operationalize the concept of psychic energy so that cross-cultural comparison of such experiences is possible. We will describe the basic structure of psychic energy experiences, with examples. We will then look at the scientific literature on meditation and suggest a tentative neurocognitive model to account for the structural invariants in those experiences. There are, however, two basic issues relative to the language and scope of description that need clarification before we move directly to that objective.

THE LANGUAGE OF DESCRIPTION

The Indian Vedantic and tantric traditions provide perhaps the most colorful, thorough, and sophisticated description of psychic energy phenomena available in literature. The temptation is great, therefore, to use the Sanskrit terminology elevated to the status of scientific concept for cross-cultural comparison. After all, it is a time-honored tradition in anthropology to borrow native terms for phenomena where English terms are not available (e.g., *shaman, mana, taboo,* etc.).

However tempting this course may at first appear, it would be as fatuous, as it would be logically fallacious, to borrow a set of terms without including some of the culturally specific Vedantic theory, which gives the terms their common meaning. It is one thing to borrow the odd term from a native tradition, and quite another to lift an entire system of terminology, especially one enjoying the popularity of Hindu philosophy. Furthermore, we could end up in the ludicrous position of making sense of, say, Christian mystical experience using Hindu insights and interpretations, whereas it may well turn out that Christian experiences are conditioned by distinctly Christian interpretations. In any case, we would have failed to meet our original goal, namely, to construct a framework for cross-cultural comparison and scientific theory construction. Professor R. S. Perinbanayagam, in his book *The Karmic Theater,* has noted the same problem with using Hindu terminology to account scientifically for Indian social institutions:

> The somewhat romantic claim that Indian civilization should be investigated with its own epistemological categories—the so-called monism of

Indian thoughtways—seems to me rather self-defeating. It may lead to a properly Vedantic sociology but hardly a scientific or comparative one. Indeed, such a method will produce only data, demanding further probing and comparative evaluation and analysis. (1982:10)

Every attempt will be made, therefore, to develop a set of descriptive terms consonant with the views already developed in this book. Furthermore, in keeping with the stated aims of biogenetic structuralism (see chapter 1) the terminology we elect to use here will allow both an empirical description of direct transpersonal experiences and an account of those experiences based upon sociocultural and biopsychological findings.

EMPIRICAL VERSUS THEORETICAL CONCEPTS

Concepts of psychic energy are rife in the theories of Western philosophy, physical science, and psychology. But the scope of concern in this study is with empirical, rather than with theoretical notions. We are interested in abstracting the invariant qualities of a range of experiences and giving them cross-culturally useful labels. To be sure, theories may be built upon those terms, and we will use them here to further a biogenetic structural theory of consciousness. But we wish to make clear at the outset that the invariant qualities being labeled are intended as *empirical generalizations grounded in direct experience* (like "respiration," "red," "straight," etc.), and not as theoretical entities (like "id," "wave function," "photon," etc.). As empirical generalizations they are open to both experimental replication within an appropriate transpersonal frame and theoretical explanation within a scientific frame.

PSYCHIC ENERGY

The word *energy* derives from the Greek word *energeia*, which means "activity," the concatenation of the two roots *en*, "in," plus *ergon*, "work" or "action." And, of course, the word *psychic* comes from the Greek *psyche*, which means soul or mind, and which also carries the connotations of life principle or "breath." Thus the term *psychic energy* connotes the activity of, or within, consciousness, mind, or soul. Operationalizing the term within the present framework, we may say that *psychic energy refers to the experience of the activity of dots within the sensorium*. The direct perception of psychic energy is the perception of the movement, unfoldment, transformation, or flow of dots and patterns of dots in consciousness, whether the existence of dots *per se* is recognized by the perceiver.

It is presumed in this definition that the activity of a field of dots is a pan-human universal. It is universal because the physiological structure of the sensoria of all humans is the same. As a pan-human universal, the activity of fields of dots composing the experiential component of the cognized environment will produce a recognizable pattern of invariance in the reports of introspection cross-culturally. As we noted in chapter 1, this presumption amounts to a strong, biologically grounded form of W. T. Stace's (1960:29) *principle of causal indifference*. This requires that methods of cross-cultural comparison must also be sensitive to the invariance embedded in the seemingly variant, culture specific, traditional modes of symbolic expression. In short, there is the immediate perception of sensorial events, and there is the interpretation of them vis à vis traditional symbolism and cosmological understanding (Stace 1960:31).

PSYCHIC ENERGY AND HIGHER PHASES OF CONSCIOUSNESS

Although psychic energy as defined here is apparent to disciplined introspection at any time, we are interested primarily in certain regularities in the experiences of psychic energy while practitioners are in extraordinary phases of consciousness. By the phrase *higher* phases of consciousness, we imply a developmental (or maturational) aspect to the neural entrainments mediating certain experiences and knowledge (see Maslow 1968, 1971; Wilber 1980; Boucouvalas 1980). Phases of consciousness, even extraordinary ones, are produced by discrete patterns of entrainment of neural networks and are thus open to diachronic, developmental processes, as well as synchronic structural ones. We are less interested in extraordinary experiences that may occur as a consequence of a chance and novel entrainment, and are more interested in the experience and knowledge that arises as a consequence of *advanced development* of patterns of entrainment. This advanced development is rare in human cultures and inevitably requires the conscious participation of the individual in his or her own development—what C. G. Jung might have considered advanced individuation.

The following are, we believe, some cross-cultural invariant features of the higher experience of psychic energy.

FLOW

The experience of greater flow of energy in the body/sensorium is an inevitable consequence of sustained and intense concentration on a physical activity such as racing, dancing, swimming, and the like, or on some object of contemplation.

> Flow is the holistic sensation present when we act with total involvement, a state in which action follows action according to an internal logic, with

no apparent need for conscious intervention on our part. Flow is experienced in play and sport, in artistic performance and religious ritual. There is no dualism in flow. . . . Flow is made possible by a centering of attention on a limited stimulus field, by means of bracketing, framing, and often a set of rules. There is a loss of ego, the self becomes irrelevant. Flow is an inner state so enjoyable that people sometimes forsake a comfortable life for its sake. (Turner 1979:154)

Flow (see Csikskentmihalyi 1975) is an experience that may be associated with the unfettered release of all bodily and mental tension. Total flow experience is the experiential polarity of total, "up-tight" distress. Depending upon how blocked the energy resources are under stress conditions, flow may or may not involve the experience of a marked release or upsurge of energy, which may be interpreted at the time as "floating," "bliss," "rapture," "ecstasy," or "exhilaration." Full flow will be characterized by the cessation of internal verbal chatter and fantasy. Consciousness is notably clear of worry, defensiveness, and ego-centeredness. Entering flow is commonly reported to be like "breaking through" to another plane of consciousness, as "attaining one's second wind," and as if the "bottom had fallen out from under" the normal limits of consciousness. During the experience of uninhibited flow, there is a sense of access to an endless source of energy, and the awareness of bodily movement as smooth, effortless, and blissful (Csikskentmihalyi 1975).

CENTEREDNESS

A more refined, and presumably more advanced, form of flow involves the movement of energy toward (or into) or away from (or out of) the central axis of the body.[2] The centering of bodily energy in a vertical axis may be experienced directly as bodily (i.e., proprioceptive) sensations and symbolically in visual imagery. One of the authors (CDL) had a relevant experience while participating in Maulavi (Sufi dancing) in which the activity was to spin around to music while visualizing a central crystal-form axis running up the center of his body and colorful streams of energy flowing out of his palms. There came a point in the dance when concentration intensified and consciousness shifted—the energy centering in that axis and the entire world of phenomena appeared to be spinning around the center of consciousness, which was the axis. This experience was associated with intense and blissful energy stirring in the axis. A moment later the absorption was broken by thoughts about the experience, and the author immediately fell down.

Individuals having a central axis experience may see in a vision the movement of energy in a central tube or shaft, the trunk of a tree, a waterfall, or the like. The symbolic variations are endless, and undoubtedly are related to the *axis mundi* motif in cosmological myth (Eliade 1964).

CIRCULATION

Centered psychic energy is often experienced as circulating around the body axis, and often concentrated at one or more points along the axis. The classic example of circulating, concentrated energy is the *chakra*, a Hindu term that literally means "wheel" (Kakar 1982:201; see also discussion below). Again, a discrete center of psychic energy may be experienced somaesthetically as a concentration of heat, bliss, or movement at a particular locus, and symbolically as a scintillating bubble or sphere; a rotating wheel, ball of fire, "space station," lotus or other flower; rings around a planetlike sphere; or some other image. References to "circulation of light" within the body and the cosmos to be found in an ancient Chinese meditation text, *The Secret of the Golden Flower* (Wilhelm 1962), provide one example of such experiences.

Circulation of energy may be experienced as moving centrifugally away from the center, or centripetally toward the center (Woodroffe 1974:7). The center may feel like a spot of intensely hot and blissful energy radiating outward from the body and into the world. One may perceive a radiant "sun," "moon," or other astrological body emitting rays of light outward into the world. On the other hand, one may feel energy moving inward, concentrating upon a particular spot in the body. One may see the image of an inwardly spiraling vortex of light, perhaps condensing at a particular spot.

ASCENDING AND DESCENDING

It is not uncommon for a report of centeredness to emphasize the ascending or descending direction of energy flow. Energy may be experienced as originating from below (the nadir) and moving up the body axis, originating above (the zenith) and moving down the axis, or both. Once again, the experience may be a somaesthetical flow of energy from above or below, producing bliss or ecstasy in the body. One may feel like a virtual conduit or hollow shell through which all imaginable energy is flowing from someplace unseen to someplace unseen. The experience may also have a visual component such as radiant light from a source above or below (see Eliade 1965; Bucke 1961 for various descriptions), a waterfall down the central visual field, a shaft of light, a tube of flowing particles, movement of a mist or cloud of energy, or vertical movement of consciousness. Movement of energy up and down the central axis is frequently associated with emotional outbursts and the spontaneous release of tension, the latter called "dearmoring" by Reichian psychologist Alexander Lowen (1976).

Of notable significance seems to be the interaction of polarized energy sources, especially those associated with above and below, left and right. The highest phases of consciousness and the most profound illumination or insight are frequently associated with the linking of these polarities by axes of energy flow. In some cases, establishing a free flow of energy between an energy center above (e.g., in or above the head) and one below (e.g., the belly, genital-anal area, or somewhere below the spine) is requisite for a phase of consciousness during which profound and numinous experiences are attained. This phase, commonly described in terms of a "clarification," or an "expansion," of consciousness, is one in which superior power, illumination, and transcendent insight and vision are attainable. It is in this phase of consciousness, often described in the ethnographic literature as "trance," "ecstasy," or "altered state," that a shaman may experience a journey into the ethereal or chthonian realms of cosmological reality. The journey to one or another of these cosmic realms is a common motif both in mythopoeic texts and dramas and in dream reports.

DREAMBODY

The flow of psychic energy in the body, revealed in various phases of consciousness as somaesthetic sensations and symbolically as visual forms, may be interpreted in some cultures as a *dreambody* (after Mindell 1982). The dreambody (i.e., "soul," "subtle body," "energy body," etc.) is the conceived or imagined "real" body of perceived energy flow within the sensorium. The perception of energy flow within the body is, of course, dependent upon the phase of consciousness being attended. Viewing the body as a concrete, physical "thing" or entity is typical of the phases of consciousness most concerned with adaptation to the external environment. But this perception, like all perceptions, is a construct combining somaesthetic, visual, and tactile inputs with conceptual and imaginal components to form a basic *body image*. Views of the body in other phases (e.g., dream, lucid dream, meditation, hallucinatory drug experience, etc.) tend to drop the dominant body image and to be more evanescent in substance and plastic in form. The dreambody is perhaps capable of extraordinary deeds, able to metamorphose or vanish at will, and free to travel to other worlds.

EXAMPLES OF HIGHER PSYCHIC ENERGY EXPERIENCES

There are numerous examples of higher psychic energy experiences in the literature (see e.g., Bucke 1961). It might be useful to describe three of the more dramatic reports available:

BUSHMEN !KIA AND N/UM

A clear example of higher psychic energy experiences from the ethnographic literature, and one that incorporates some of the structural motifs just noted, is that found among the Kalahari Bushmen. Richard Katz (1976, 1982) describes for the Bushmen a "transcendental experience" called *!Kia*, an extraordinary state of consciousness during which

> a !Kung experiences himself as existing beyond his ordinary level of existence. !Kia itself is a very intense physical and emotional state. The body is straining against fatigue and struggling with convulsion-like tremors and heavy breathing. The emotions are aroused to an extraordinary level, whether they be fear or exhilaration or fervor. Also, a !Kung practices extraordinary activities during !Kia. He performs cures, handles and walks on fire, claims x-ray vision, and at times says he sees over great distances. He does not even attempt such activities in his ordinary state. (Katz 1976:287)

The *!Kia* mindstate is attained through the mastery of *n/um*, an "energy" which, the Bushmen say, dwells in the pit of the stomach. Individuals are known to master this energy, which may be evoked by repetitious dancing.

> As the master of n/um continues his energetic dance, becoming warm and sweating profusely, the n/um heats up and becomes a vapor. It then rises up the spine, to a point approximately at the base of the skull, at which time !Kia results. (Katz 1976:286)

According to one of Katz's informant adepts:

> You dance, dance, dance, dance. The n/um lifts you in your belly and lifts you in your back, and then you start to shiver. N/um makes you tremble; it's hot. Your eyes are open but you don't look around; you hold your eyes still and look straight ahead. But when you get into !Kia, you're looking around because you see everything, because you see what's troubling everybody. . . . Rapid shallow breathing, that's what draws n/um . . . then n/um enters every part of your body, right to the tip of your feet and even your hair. . . . in your backbone you feel a pointed something, and it works its way up. Then the base of your spine is tingling, tingling, tingling, tingling, tingling, tingling, tingling . . . and then it makes your thoughts nothing in your head. (Katz 1976:286–87)

The motifs apparent in these descriptions are strikingly similar to those found in other cultures. An energy source from below is tapped by some spiritual exercise (in this case dancing and intense concentration). Energy, whose movement is associated with heat, emotion, release of tension, and bliss, rises up a central axis to a center above, and a higher phase of consciousness, *!Kia*, is attained. Thoughts are transcended and extraordinary powers are experienced.

HINDU KUNDALINI

A similar phenomenon has been described for ages among Indian Hindu yogis who recognize the existence of a primal, infinite source of psychic energy called *kundalini*, which is considered to be the font of all religious states of consciousness:

> Thus the rousing of the Kundalini is the one and only way to the attaining of divine wisdom, super-conscious perception, realization of the Spirit. The rousing may come in various ways: through love for God, through the mercy of perfected sages, or through the power of the analytical will of the philosopher. Wherever there has been any manifestation of what is ordinarily called supernatural power or wisdom, there a little current of the Kundalini must have found its way into the Sushumna [central axis]. (Vivekananda 1956:58)

The goal of yogic practice is to open the central channel, which runs up the center of the body just in front of the spine, of the psychic energy body to the *kundalini* energy. "When the current begins to rise through the Sushumna, we go beyond the senses, and our minds become supersensuous, superconscious, we go beyond even the intellect, where reason cannot reach" (ibid.:63). There exist several major energy centers ranging along the central axis, but the most important are the *kundalini* centers at the base of the spine, at the heart, and the crown of the head. "All the energy has to be taken up from its seat in the *Muladhara* [basal center] and brought to the *Sahasrara* [head center]" (ibid.). To this end yogis practice a number of techniques involving rhythmic breathing and physical exercise to loosen and direct the *kundalini* energies.

It should be emphasized that the tantric view of the structure of the energy body is based, not upon metaphysical speculation or theological revelation, but upon direct, empirical observation of psychic energy events in the body during yogic practice. The symptoms of *kundalini* activity are complex and varied. For example, Dhyananyogi Madhusudandas has described many symptoms related to the activity of the *kundalini*:

> . . . creeping sensations in the spinal cord, tingling sensations all over the body, heaviness in the head or sometimes giddiness; automatic and involuntary laughing or crying; hearing unusual noises, seeing visions of deities or saints. Dream scenes of all kinds may appear from the heavenly to demonic. Physically the abdomen wall may become flat and be drawn towards the spine; there may be diarrhea or constipation, the anus contracts and may be drawn up, the chin may press down against the neck. (Mookerjee 1982:71)

Not everyone will experience the same symptoms, but from a constellation of many of those symptoms one may know that their *kundalini* is active. Pandit Gopi Krishna experienced a particularly dramatic and spontaneous eruption of *kundalini* energy:

> One morning . . . I sat cross-legged in a small room. . . . I was meditating with my face towards the window on the east through which the first grey streaks of the slowly brightening dawn fell into the room. Long practice has accustomed me to sit in the same posture for hours at a time without the least discomfort, and I sat breathing slowly and rhythmically, my attention drawn towards the crown of my head, contemplating an imaginary lotus in full bloom, radiating light. . . . The intensity of concentration interrupted my breathing; gradually it slowed down to such an extent that at times it was barely perceptible. My whole being was so engrossed in the contemplation of the lotus that for several minutes at a time I lost touch with my body and surroundings. During such intervals I used to feel as if I were poised in mid-air, without any feeling of a body around me. . . . During one such spell of intense concentration I suddenly felt a strange sensation below the base of my spine, at the place touching the seat. . . .
>
> . . . suddenly, with a roar like that of a waterfall, I felt a stream of liquid light entering my brain through the spinal cord. . . . the illumination grew brighter and brighter, the roaring louder, I experienced a rocking sensation and then felt myself slipping out of my body, entirely enveloped in a halo of light. . . . I felt the point of consciousness that was myself growing wider, surrounded by waves of light. It grew wider and wider, spreading outward while the body, normally the immediate object of its perception, appeared to have receded into the distance until I became entirely unconscious of it. I was now all consciousness, without any outline, without any idea of a corporeal appendage, without any feeling or sensation coming from the senses, immersed in a sea of light simultaneously conscious and aware of every point, spread out, as it were, in all directions without any barrier or material obstruction. I was no longer myself, or to be more accurate, no longer as I knew myself to be, a small point of awareness confined in a body, but instead was a vast circle of consciousness in which the body was but a point, bathed in light and in a state of exaltation and happiness impossible to describe. (Krishna 1971:11–13)

Pandit Krishna had many painful symptoms arise during the weeks and months following this extraordinary experience. For example, the "heat grew every moment causing such unbearable pain that I writhed and twisted from side to side. . . . But the heat increased and soon it seemed as if innumerable red hot pins were coursing through my body, scorching and blistering the organs and tissues" (Krishna 1971:13). Itzhak Bentov in working with *kundalini* experiences of Western meditators described similar symptoms reported by his subjects. He termed the collection of symptoms the "sensory motor cortex syndrome":

> . . . a transient paresthesia of the toes or ankle, with numbness and tingling. Occasionally, there is diminished sensitivity to touch or pain, or

even partial paralysis of the foot or leg. The process most frequently begins on the left side and ascends in a sequential manner from foot, leg, hip, to involve completely the left side of the body, including face. Once the hip is involved, it is not uncommon to experience an intermittent throbbing of rhythmic rumbling-like sensation in the lower lumbar and sacral spine. This is followed by an ascending sensation which rises along the spine to the cervical and occipital regions of the head. (Bentov 1977:34)

The list of weird and exotic symptoms associated with the awakening of *kundalini* is almost endless. Completing this process may take as little as three days, as in the case of Sri Ramakrishna, or months as in Pandit Gopi Krishna's case, or even years.

CHRISTIAN SACRED HEART

Reports of higher psychic energy experiences come to us from several sources within the Christian mystical traditions. There is no better source for our purposes than that of the Sacred Heart tradition that began in the twelfth century (see Laughlin, Chetelat, and Sekar 1985). A number of saints reported significant visions pertaining to the Sacred Heart of Jesus; predominant among them was Margaret Mary Alacoque (1647–90). She had four profound visions over the course of her life, experiences which directly resulted in full development of the symbol of the Sacred Heart, and in the consecration of the Sacred Heart devotion as a rite within Roman Catholicism.

Margaret Mary described her first vision in her autobiography. Tickell, writing in the nineteenth century, quotes from her work in describing that experience:

> The following, as it seems to me, is the way in which the thing occurred. Jesus said to me, "My Divine Heart is so full of love for men, and for you in particular, that being unable to contain within Itself the flames of Its burning charity, It must needs spread them abroad by your means, and manifest Itself to them to enrich them with the treasures It contains. I discover to you the price of these treasures; they contain graces of sanctification and salvation necessary to draw them from the abyss of perdition. I have chosen you, in spite of your unworthiness and ignorance, for the accomplishment of this great design, in order that it may better appear that all is done by Me."
>
> After these words, our Lord asked her [Margaret Mary] for her heart. She begged of Him to take it. This He did, and placed it in His own Adorable Heart, where He showed it to her *as a little atom which was being consumed in this burning flame in form of a heart*. He restored it to the place from whence He had taken it, saying to her "See, My well-beloved, I give you a precious pledge of My love. I have enclosed within your side a little spark of the vivid flames of that love to serve you for a heart, and to consume you to the last moment of your life. Its ardour will never be

extinguished, and you will be unable to find any relief from it, except some slight relief by bleeding. And even this remedy will bring you more humiliation and suffering than relief. . . . You have taken, hitherto, only the name of My slave, I give you from this time that of the beloved Disciple of My Sacred Heart." (Tickell 1869:128–29; *emphasis ours*)

After this vision Margaret Mary suffered from searing pains in the chosen side on the first Friday of every month. She received her second vision the following year:

One day . . . on the Feast of St. John the Evangelist 1674, after having received from my Divine Savior a favour almost similar to that bestowed upon the beloved Disciple on the evening of the Last Supper, the Divine Heart was represented to me *as on a throne of fire and flames, shedding rays on every side brighter than the sun and transparent as crystal*. The Wound which He received upon the Cross appeared there visibly; a crown of thorns encircled the Divine Heart and It was surmounted by a Cross . . . He gave me to understand afterwards that it was the great desire He had to be perfectly loved by men that had made Him form the design of disclosing to them His Heart, and of giving them . . . this last effort of His love by proposing to them an object and a means so calculated to engage them to love Him. (Ibid.: 141–42; *emphasis ours*)

The third vision appeared the same year. Jesus presented himself to Margaret Mary "all resplendent with glory, his five wounds shining like so many suns" (Stierli 1957:117), and ordered her to carry out a number of ritual acts. In her last vision, Christ requested the liturgical celebration of the mystery of the Sacred Heart. The period following the last vision was filled with pain, physical illness, and humiliation at the hands of other sisters in the Order.

These examples illustrate the profound alterations that may occur to both consciousness and physiology as a consequence of intensively practicing one or another spiritual discipline. It would therefore seem reasonable to review the scientific literature on the psychophysiology of meditation in order to glean whatever clues we may find to the structural principles upon which these experiences are based.

THE PSYCHOPHYSIOLOGY OF MEDITATION

Great interest in meditation has developed in Western science over the past generation. One would expect a concomitant rise in interest among scientists as well (see Murphy and Donovan 1983). And indeed, there has been a flurry of research on the topic, but the scientific literature on the physiology of meditation is, unfortunately, incomplete at best, and downright impertinent at worst. The apparent lack of experience in meditation of many researchers and the unavailability of a technology appropriate to complete inquiry about meditation result in inadequate information (Shapiro 1983). Research is frequently impertinent when it fails to address the naturalistic circumstances of meditation within traditional cultural contexts. The literature is spotty, for example, when it fails, as it usually does, to distinguish clearly between the great variety of practices available cross-culturally, often generalizing from a single tradition (usually Transcendental Meditation, or TM) to all meditation traditions. For example, research often fails to note that many meditation traditions intentionally set the stage for extraordinary transpersonal experiences—conditions and experiences that almost never occur under laboratory conditions and are thus almost impossible to replicate within the unrealistic strictures imposed by current scientific paradigms. It is also impertinent when it refuses to consider lengthy retreat work often presupposed by paths of advanced spiritual development.

GLOBAL RELAXATION VERSUS MULTIPROCESS MODEL

However, many of the more extreme shortcomings of scientific research on the physiological and psychological effects of meditation are being corrected, albeit slowly, and there is some information available relevant to our topic. By "meditation" we refer to any number of techniques for the formal practice of concentration and awareness. Several useful reviews of the literature have been published over the past decade and a half (Pagano and Warrenburg 1983; Schuman 1980; Davidson 1976; Woolfolk 1975; Shapiro 1980; Holmes 1984). One problem in dispute is whether meditation produces a "unique hypometabolic state" in practitioners as claimed by Wallace and colleagues (1971). That is, does the practice of meditation—usually "passive" types of meditation like TM—produce a distinct pattern of somatic relaxation not also produced by simple relaxation or an alternative relaxation technique such as progressive relaxation? Some of the more elaborate claims along this line have proved to be unfounded, or at least have failed to be replicated (see Holmes 1984). Quoting Pagano and Warrenburg:

> We regret to report that our search for a unique or dramatic effect directly attributable to meditation thus far has not been successful. In this area many practitioners have made sweeping claims about the effectiveness of their techniques. Frequently, this is based on subjective experience, and often the claims are "shored up" on the basis of "research." All too often, this research turns out to be not very rigorous—really only of pilot nature. This has been especially true within the TM movement. Our experience has been that when good scientific methodology has been used, the claims made have been extravagant and premature. (1983:203)

Comparable relaxation effects have been demonstrated for other techniques (Steptoe 1978; Pagano and Warrenburg 1983). Some authorities have argued from these reports that individuals are capable of a base level of relaxation (a "floor effect"; Pagano and Warrenburg 1983:165) attainable through a variety of means: "passive" meditation, normal relaxation, progressive relaxation, biofeedback, autogenic training, and exercise. Some researchers have reasoned, therefore, that each of these techniques taps (drives) a singular, generalized "relaxation response" (Benson, Beary, and Carol 1974; Hoffman et al. 1981; Holmes 1984).

Other researchers continue to find distinct physiological differences when comparing meditators to controls along such dimensions as respiration (Wolkove et al. 1984), decreased oxygen consumption, and relative increase of cerebral blood flow (Jevning et al. 1978, 1982). Still other researchers have pointed to the distinctiveness of effects of different techniques used in different situations. They argue that decreased arousal is not a singular process, but rather a complex of processes that may be organized in different ways under different circumstances (Davidson 1976; Davidson and Schwartz 1976).

Personality factors may well have an influence on patterns of meditation. For example, Pagano and Warrenburg (1983:204) reported evidence suggesting predispositional factors may determine the success of a particular technique. They showed that subjects already measurably high in the capacity for absorbed attention tended to persist with meditation (see Davidson, Goleman, and Schwartz 1976). In other research, Schwartz, Davidson, and Goleman (1978), distinguishing between cognitive and somatic components of anxiety, compared the effects of physical exercise and meditation upon reports of anxiety. They found that meditators report less cognitive and more physical anxiety, whereas exercisers report less physical and more cognitive anxiety.

Several studies have indicated that the presence or absence of stressful conditions is corrolated with differential somatic reactions by practitioners of various relaxation techniques: whereas their responses under optimal conditions seem much the same (thus seeming to support the singular relaxation response model), their responses under various stressful conditions may diverge significantly (thus supporting a multiprocess model, see Pagano and Warrenburg 1983:165, Steptoe 1978; Lehrer 1978; Stroebel and Glueck 1978; Schwartz, Davidson, and Goleman 1978; Davidson and Schwartz 1976).

EXCITATION VERSUS RELAXATION

Most meditation research has been carried out upon "passive" meditation techniques such as TM and Zen. The trend in the literature is to demonstrate the calming effects of those techniques. In sharp contrast to those findings are those from research on various yogic techniques such as Ananda Marga (a form of Hindu tantric yoga; see Elson, Hauri, and Cunis 1977; Corby et al. 1978; Elson 1979), which show some *elevation* of excitation rather than simple relaxation (see Woolfolk 1975 for a review of the literature). Corby and colleagues (1978) found that the more advanced the meditator, the more actively alert he was during meditation as indicated by measures of skin conductance, frequency of GSR (galvanic skin response) responses, heart rate, and EEG sleep scoring. This finding contrasts with some research on "passive" meditation using EEG scoring measures that indicates that "passive" meditators, at least inexperienced ones, often spend some time asleep while meditating (Pagano and Warrenburg 1983:156). Corby's results are in keeping with other studies of active Indian yogic techniques (Das and Gastaut 1955; Wenger and Bagchi 1961; Anand, China, and Singh 1961; however, see Elson et al. 1977 for conflicting results). Their subjects reported experiences associated with "good to excellent" meditation sessions that are in keeping with somatic and sensorial arousal:

> "I experienced many feelings of energy rushes, as if energy were pouring into my body: more and more as my breathing deepened and slowed," ". . . chills, laughter, changing and varied emotions: early life flashes," ". . . total energy and absorption gradually coming down, concentration with an intense yearning to be one with the object of ideation," ". . . feelings of rushes of energy, pouring over my body," and ". . . becoming mantra, not doing it but being it. A great sense of merger and understanding of experience and its meaning." (Corby 1979:606)

It should also be noted that little scientific research exists to date on the psychophysiology of meditation systems that use visualization or imaging extensively, such as the Tibetan tantric (Chang 1963) and Japanese Shingon (Kiyota 1978) forms of Buddhism. There exists some evidence that both the process and the content of imaging can influence activities of the autonomic nervous system (see di Giusto and Bond 1979, Qualls and Sheehan 1981 for reviews of the literature). We may reasonably expect that certain imagery may operate to increase and other imagery to decrease autonomic arousal.

ATTENTION, ABSORPTION, AND THETA ACTIVITY

Potentially the most important finding in meditation research is ironically one of the least understood. We refer to the observation of increased production of low- to high-amplitude, low-frequency theta activity recorded by EEG from meditators (Zen, TM, Ananda Marga) and practitioners of other relaxation techniques (autogenic training; see Schacter 1977, Woolfolk 1975, Pagano and Warrenburg 1983:171–172 for numerous citations). Elson and colleagues (1977) and Corby and colleagues (1978) found that yogic ("active") meditators produced more theta power than nonmeditators, and that more proficient meditators produce more theta than less proficient meditators. Kasematsu and Hirai (1966, see also Hirai 1974) found that Zen meditators showed continuous theta production, even when eyes were open, after the end of the meditation session. Interestingly, an analysis of resonance frequencies of a sample of mantras gave values of 6 to 7 Hz, which is within the theta range (reported in Stroebel and Glueck 1978:420).

Whereas most meditation researchers seem reluctant to attribute psychological correlates to theta activity, some evidence exists that sustained low-amplitude theta is correlated with sustained attention or vigilance (Pigeau 1985, Ishihara and Yoshii 1972, Schacter 1977). High-amplitude theta bursts may well be correlated with the brief, intense absorption (hyperintentional) states common to more proficient meditators. Heightened vigilance leading to absorption (see Tellegen and Atkinson 1974) would seem to be an individual "special trait" (Pagano and Warrenburg 1983:188), already functioning in persons likely to become long-term meditators (see Qualls and Sheehan 1981). Smith (1978) reported that subjects benefiting the most in terms of anxiety reduction from TM meditation tended to score highly on a section of a personality test that relates specifically to the capacity for absorption.

PEAK EXPERIENCES

Psychophysiological research pertaining to peak experiences in meditation is understandably rare. Corby and others were fortunate enough to record some measures during a period when a yogi experienced a brief near-absorption state:

> One expert meditator reported the experience of "having my breathing taken over by the *mantra*" during the meditation condition, and felt it might represent what she termed a "near-*Samadhi*" experience. The concurrent respiratory record . . . showed a pattern of respiratory acceleration with little change in respiratory amplitude followed by cessation of respiration for approximately 100 seconds. . . . A dramatic decrease in skin resistance of approximately 200 kohms preceded the respiratory acceleration.
>
> Visual inspection of the meditation EEG record of this subject disclosed large amounts of high amplitude (up to 100 μV) alpha range frequencies and also large amounts of theta range frequencies (up to 150 μV). Occasionally there were discrete bursts of theta range frequencies of amplitudes up to 300 μV. No particular EEG changes were associated with the "near-*Samadhi*" event. (1978:574)

This indication of significant autonomic arousal during peak or "ecstatic" experience is in keeping with previous research on yogic practice (Das and Gastaut 1955, Wenger and Bagchi 1961).

MEDITATION AND HEMISPHERIC ASYMMETRY

The early hypothesis proposed by Ornstein (1972) and others that meditation changes predominant processing from left to right lobe, and thus from linguistic-analytic to imaginal-gestalt modes of cognition, has proved to be unfounded (see Pagano and Warrenburg 1983:174ff). Indeed, the prevailing evidence seems to favor the view that "passive" meditation in general leads to a less asymmetrical, more balanced processing of information (Stroebel and Glueck 1978) and that different types of meditation, particularly "active" meditations accompanied, as they always are in traditional settings, by cosmological beliefs and mythopoeic symbolism, may result in different neurocognitive entrainments and thus different experiences (see Davidson 1976:372 on this point). This combining of cultural elements will involve variant entrainment of left- and right-lobe functions, depending upon the tradition in which the technique is embedded, and the proficiency and psychological makeup of the individual meditator.

One would not really expect a dramatic shift from left- to right-lobe processing for the meditation techniques usually researched in laboratories. As any mature contemplative knows, progress along the path of meditation involves the cessation of *both* conceptualizing and imagery. In fact, many techniques encourage disattention to, even active suppression of, both verbal chatter and fantasy. In Zen, for example, the mind is trained to watch without attachment the arising and passing away of whatever enters consciousness (Suzuki 1970). However, in traditions using visualization practices in which concentration is upon an eidetic image, we would expect to find some evidence for a predominance of right- over left-lobe processing, at least in the early stages of meditation.

Relative to cerebral dominance and yoga practice, research by Werntz and colleagues (1982) has shown that the nasal cycle (that is, the shift in nasal dominance during breathing) is directly correlated with activity in the cerebral hemispheres as measured by cortical EEG. As the relations between hemisphere and autonomic system are ipsilateral (same side), rather than contralateral (crossed over), they reason that greater cerebral efficiency is facilitated by greater sympathetic (excitatory) arousal on the ipsilateral side (increasing air flow) and greater parasympathetic (vegitative) arousal on the contralateral side (decreasing air flow). There is evidence that relative dominance of cerebral activity changes cyclically during the day (Broughton 1975), and nasal dominance would seem to correlate to some extent with this cycling. It is interesting to note that yogic traditions recognize the significance of the nasal cycle for balancing the flow of psychic energy in consciousness. For example, Tibetan tantric practice specifically suggests waiting to do certain meditations until the breath is flowing equally through both nostrils (Chang 1963:63). Yogis will in fact use simple breathing techniques to assure an equal flow. We may suggest that the optimal condition for carrying out some "active" meditations exists when both hemispheres are balanced in their activity.

It should be evident from our very brief survey of the psychophysiology of meditation that the picture is far more complex than some early reports led one to believe. The question is, does there exist a model of neurocognitive activity sufficiently complex to account for the many and varied phenomena being reported in the recent literature?

TUNING THE ERGOTROPIC AND TROPHOTROPIC SYSTEMS

Following the pioneering work of W. R. Hess (1925, 1957), E. Gellhorn and his associates (Gellhorn 1967; Gellhorn and Loofbourrow 1963; Gellhorn and Kiely 1972) developed a model of the hierarchical integration of somatic, autonomic, and higher neural systems, which in part accounts for the complex intercausality between activities at every level of processing (see also Lex 1979, Davidson 1976). The somatic system that controls the distribution and utilization of metabolic energy in the body is conceived as being composed of two complementary (sometimes antagonistic) systems. One system is called the *ergotropic system* and the other the *trophotropic system* (Gellhorn 1967; Gellhorn and Loofbourrow 1963).

THE ERGOTROPIC SYSTEM

The ergotropic system subserves our so-called fight-or-flight responses; that is, the physiological components of our adaptation strategies to desirable or noxious stimuli in the world. Anatomically, the ergotropic system incorporates the functions of the sympathetic nervous system (one-half of the autonomic nervous system discussed in chapter 5), certain of the endocrine glands, portions of the reticular activating system in the brain stem, the posterior hypothalamus, and portions of the limbic system, and the frontal cortex. The principal function of the ergotropic system is the control of short-range, moment-by-moment adaptation to events in the world. It is activated when the possibility of responding to stimuli arises and is constructed to shunt the body's metabolic energy away from long-range developmental activities, and to initiate and carry out action directed either at acquiring or avoiding stimuli of interest to the organism.

Under generalized ergotropic arousal, many organic responses may be experienced, including shivering, constriction of the surface veins and capillaries (paling of the skin), dilated pupils, increased heart rate and blood pressure, increased muscle tension, decreased salivation ("dry-mouthed"), constriction of the throat, increased rate of respiration, erection of body hair ("hair standing on end"), and desynchronization of cortical EEG patterns (indicating discordant or disharmonic cortical functioning). These responses, all subserving adaptation in one way or another, are commonly associated in experience with positive or negative emotion. Objects or events associated with responses will typically be perceived as desirable or undesirable, attractive or repulsive, friendly or hostile, beautiful or ugly. The ergotropic system prepares the organism to obtain objects (like food, water, or a mate) required for the continued survival of the organism or species, and to avoid objects (like poisons, enemies, and predators) dangerous to survival. A fundamental problem in nature is how to eat without being eaten. The ergotropic system in humans is the product of millions of years of selection for responses that solve that problem. It is the ergotropic system that mediates stress relative to events in the world (Selye 1956).

THE TROPHOTROPIC SYSTEM

The trophotropic system is far less dramatic in its activities but is nonetheless the system responsible for regulating all the vegetative functions, such as reconstruction and growth of cells, digestion, relaxation, sleep, and so on. Anatomically, the trophotropic system incorporates the functions of the parasympathetic system (the other half of the autonomic nervous system discussed in chapter 5), various endocrine glands, portions of the reticular activating system, the anterior hypothalamus, and portions of the limbic system and frontal cortex. The trophotropic system controls the somatic functions responsible for the long-term well-being, growth, and longevity of the organism. This system operates to maintain the optimal internal balance of bodily functions for continued health and development, both of the body and consequently of the mind.

Under the influence of the trophotropic system, a variety of physical and mental responses may be experienced, like warmth and "blushing" at the surface of the body due to release of sympathetic constriction of veins and capillaries, constriction of the pupil of the eye, decreased heart rate and blood pressure, relaxation of tension in the muscles, increased salivation, relaxation of the throat, slowing and deepening of respiration, erection of the penis and clitoris, and synchronization of cortical EEG patterns (indicating harmonized higher cortical functions). Relaxation (reduced arousal) and its concomitants are commonly associated either with disinterest in events in the environment, or with dispassionate concentration upon some object (Jacobson 1938; Benson et al. 1974). Judgments about the desirability or undesirability of the object are suspended. The relaxed person is typically experiencing a comfortable, warm, womblike indifference to the environment. The fundamental function of relaxation is perhaps less obvious than that of ergotropic arousal, but is nonetheless crucial to the survival of the organism. It is mainly during relaxation, and particularly during undisturbed sleep, that the body processes nutrients and uses these to repair and grow. In other words, when the body is not finding food and avoiding becoming food (ergotropic reactivity), it is reconstructing and developing itself (trophotropic reactivity).

COMPLEMENTARITY

The ergotropic and trophotropic systems have often been described as "antagonistic" to each other—the increased activity of the one tends to produce a decreased activity in the other. Each system is physically designed to inhibit the functioning of the other under most circumstances. If a person gets excited about something (angry, anxious, afraid, strongly desirous, etc.) the ergotropic system not only produces the requisite physiological, emotional, and behavioral responses, it also suppresses (via reciprocal inhibition pathways) the trophotropic system, which was previously subserving digestion and other conservative metabolic activities. Likewise, when a person relaxes (say, after a heavy meal), the trophotropic system actively suppresses the activity of the ergotropic system. A summary of the reciprocal functions of the two systems may be studied in table 1.

TABLE 1

A Summary of Some Functions of the Trophotropic
and Ergotropic Systems

Trophotropic System	*Ergotropic System*
Storage of vital resources	Expenditure of vital resources
Digestion and distribution of nutriments	Digestion stopped
Bronchi leading to lungs constricted and coated with mucus	Bronchi opened
Heart rate and blood pressure reduced	Heart rate and blood pressure increased
Collection of waste by-products	Endocrine system releases chemicals that increase efficiency of muscles
Constricts pupils	Dilates pupils
None	Erection of body hair
Synchronized EEG	Desynchronized EEG
Erection of penis	Ejaculation
Increased salivation	Decreased salivation
Respiration slower and deeper	Respiration faster and shallower

The relationship between the two systems would be better described as complementary, rather than antagonistic, for each serves the short- and long-range well-being of the organism. It is really a matter of balance of functions, the trophotropic system maintaining the homeo- static balance necessary for health and growth while the ergotropic system facilitates the moment-to-moment adaptation of the organism to its environment. As such, they are not anatomical mirror images of each other. The "wiring" of the ergotropic system is designed to arouse the entire body for potential response to threat. Under normal conditions, when the ergotropic system is activated, the entire body/mind becomes aroused. By comparison, the trophotropic system is "wired" for the fine tuning of organs in relation to each other as the demands of internal maintenance shift and change. Its resources can be activated for one organ or body part, or it can turn on globally as during sleep when the entire skeletal musculature is "turned off."

The point to emphasize is that whereas the trophotropic system is designed for continuous activity, the ergotropic system is designed for occasional activity. We are "wired" for short, infrequent bursts of adaptive activity interspersed with relatively long durations of rest, recuperation, and growth. Prolonged ergotropic reactivity may cause depletion of vital resources stored by the trophotropic system in various organs, and may cause fatigue, shock, body damage, and in extreme cases, death (Selye 1956; Antonovsky 1979).

TUNING

The particular balance of ergotropic and trophotropic activities under particular environmental circumstances is susceptible to conditioning (Thomas 1968; Hofer 1974; L. E. Roberts in Schwartz and Shapiro 1978), and there is evidence that their characteristic balance under stress is established as early as pre- and perinatal life (Grof 1976; Richmond and Lustman 1955; Wenger 1941; Thomas 1968; Chamberlain 1983; Verny 1982). The learned (conditioned) ergotropic-trophotropic balance rela- tive to any stimulus is called *tuning* (Gellhorn 1967:110ff). When we say that someone "gets up-tight around authority figures," we are referring to a discrete ergotropic-trophotropic tuning relative to people perceived to be in authority. Or when we say that someone "calmed-out when he got a back-rub," we are referring to a different discrete tuning relative to being stroked.

As we have noted in chapter 5, a change in the characteristic ergo- tropic-trophotropic balance relative to a stimulus is called *retuning* (Gell- horn 1967; see also Miller 1969). Events like football games, rock con- certs, and combat patrols, that previously elicited excitement (ergotropic reactivity), may after retuning be met with a relaxed response (trophotropic reactivity). Some theorists have argued that ritual control of ergotropic-trophotropic balance is fundamental to virtually all primitive healing techniques and to the evocation of alternative phases of consciousness (Gellhorn and Kiely 1972; Kiely 1974; Lex 1979).

There are several ways that ergotropic-trophotropic retuning may be accomplished:

1. *Rational Mediation.* Under certain circumstances the rational faculties mediated by the cerebral components of the two systems may intercede to modify tuning. A particular emotional response may come to be recognized as inappropriate to a situation, and this knowledge may result in some retuning. This response is common to many forms of group therapy.
2. *Heightened Awareness.* Increased attention to one's own psychodynamics may result in perceiving and intuiting the cognition producing an ergotropic response. The relevating of the operation into consciousness may be sufficient to produce a retuning. An example would be the cognitive therapy of A. T. Beck (1967) in which techniques are used to uncover the operations mediating affective disorders.
3. *Abreaction.* By "reliving" a traumatic event in our past, the characteristic tuning of ergotropic-trophotropic functions may be altered. This is particularly useful in cases where autonomic and limbic responses are linked to images operating unconsciously to ego.
4. *Drivers.* As noted earlier, lower autonomic systems may be tuned and retuned directly by penetration from external stimuli without necessary intervention of higher ergotropic-trophotropic centers (Gellhorn and Loofbourrow 1963, Lex 1979). These stimuli are called *drivers* and may take the form of repetitive stimulation such as drumming, flickering light, chanting, or sexual intercourse. Drivers may be used in ritual circumstances to generate simultaneous discharge of both systems (e.g., orgasm), which sets the stage for a radical retuning of the systems relative to particular stimuli (Lex 1979). Such drivers are an example of symbolic penetration at the level of the autonomic nervous system.

The first three methods of retuning—rational mediation, heightened awareness, and abreaction—tend to be evoked, so to speak, from the top down ("top-down retuning"). The fourth method, the use of drivers, may work from the bottom up ("bottom-up retuning"). That is, the first three tend to require retuning of higher cortical systems before lower limbic and autonomic-endocrine systems follow suit, but the last method operates directly upon lower autonomic-endocrine-somatic systems first, followed by higher-center retuning. Rational mediation is notoriously ineffective when the system has been tuned in association with image-centered trauma. Such associations (entrainments) are typically established during pre- and perinatal life, or early childhood, when virtually all learning involves autonomic-somatic and imaginal systems, rather than higher cortical processing (Piaget and Inhelder 1969).

The Physiology of Psychic Energy

We have distinguished many structural invariants in the experience of psychic energy in higher phases of consciousness. We have examined theoretical concepts by which we may speak of the relationships among neural and other somatic systems and sensorial events. And, we have surveyed the literature on the psychophysiology of meditation, particularly relevant to metabolic processes and consciousness. We have determined that the best perspective from which to formulate a tentative theory of psychic energy is via the ergotropic-trophotropic model of metabolic energy distribution. We now wish to link these elements to suggest an account of psychic energy experiences in higher phases of consciousness. We realize that not only sensorial events but also their structural invariance must be explained.

We have defined psychic energy as the experience of activity of fields of dots within the sensorium. All that we are, or ever can be, phenomenally aware of is composed therefore of psychic energy, which includes our awareness of metabolic events occurring in our body. We know that we need nutriment when we feel hungry, that we are injured when we feel pain, that we are relaxed when we feel calm, and aroused when we feel excited. Some people have unfortunate neurophysiological disorders that prevent them from feeling pain when they have been injured. And many of us walk around not knowing that we are hypertense, unaware mainly because we are "disconnected" from our bodies. But when the systems of the body are operating in an ideal state of uninhibited or unobstructed interpenetration, we may say that a process of homeomorphogenic interpenetration exists between the sensorium and its activities and the greater organism and its activities. This is tantamount to a microcosm-macrocosm relationship—one of partial isomorphism—in which events in the body are represented by (expressive mode), or produced by (integrative mode), patterns in the flurries of dots within the sensorium. The cognitive system is designed to detect invariance in the patterns formed within the field of dots and to construe a cognized environment from the totality of such patterns.

Thus, patterns of sensorial psychic energy may be in some instances the consequence of metabolic events in the body, and in other instances may be the cause of metabolic events in the body. One feels pain when a finger is cut, but one can also produce somatic responses characteristic of injury by vividly imagining a cut finger. The causality between sensorial and nonsensorial somatic events is interactional.

Furthermore, the sensorium, like the rest of the nervous system, participates in ergotropic-trophotropic balance. That is, the sensorium registers somatic events energized by the bicameral ergotropic-trophotropic system, and is thus a part of their organization. Simply put, an excited somatic system produces an excited consciousness, and vice versa. A calm consciousness is mediated by a calm body. There is no such thing as a calm mind in an excited body. When tuning is in favor of trophotropic activity, this activity includes a predominance of trophotropic activity within the sensorium. The same may be said for predominantly ergotropic tuning. An ergotropically tuned sensorium may be a welter of rapid, even confused thoughts, sensations, and images, whereas a trophotropically tuned sensorium may be fairly clear, even blank.

HIGHER PSYCHIC ENERGY EXPERIENCES

Homeomorphogenic relationships between sensorial and nonsensorial ergotropic-trophotropic events continue to operate in higher phases of consciousness and experiences of psychic energy. From the model presented above, we may hypothesize four categories of ergotropic-trophotropic events and their sensorial concomitants, which may occur during extraordinary phases of consciousness:

1. *Hypertrophotropic Tuning.* Trophotropic activity is tuned exceptionally high resulting in an extraordinary state of relaxation. This activity happens of course in normal sleep but may paradoxically occur during meditative phases accompanied by keen alertness and vigilance. In extreme form, hypertrophotropic tuning may be experienced as a sense of oceanic tranquillity and peace in which no thoughts or fantasies intrude upon consciousness and no bodily sensations are felt. The meditator feels as though he were floating on a waveless sea. In Buddhist psychology this state might be termed *access concentration (upacara samadhi).*

2. *Hyperergotropic Tuning.* Ergotropic activity is tuned exceptionally high, resulting in an extraordinary stage of unblocked arousal and excitation. This stage may occur under various circumstances where output of motor activity is continuous and rhyth-

mical, as in dancing, long-distance running, swimming, or rock climbing; or where continuous processing of information becomes so voluminous that interjection of thought and ego-centered decision making would prove disadvantageous, as in motor car racing, or piloting a jet fighter. This state will also be associated with keen alertness and concentration in the absence of superfluous thought and fantasy. The practitioner feels as if he were channeling vast quantities of energy effortlessly through his consciousness. This is the quintessential flow experience noted earlier.

3. *Hypertrophotropic Tuning with Ergotropic Eruption.* As noted by Gellhorn and Kiely (1972), under certain circumstances both systems may discharge simultaneously. In this case, the meditator is in a state of oceanic bliss, and perhaps by intensifying his concentration upon the object of meditation, he experiences absorption into the object *(appana samadhi* in Buddhist psychology), an experience inevitably accompanied by the sense of a tremendous release of energy. The meditator may experience one or another of the "active" blisses, energy rushes, and other movements and sensations in the body.

4. *Hyperergotropic Tuning with Trophotropic Eruption.* Simultaneous discharge of both systems may be attained via the opposite route. The practitioner may experience a trophotropic discharge in the midst of hyperergotropic tuning as a consequence of enhanced concentration and of trophotropic drivers such as rhythmic stimuli like mantra. The practitioner may experience an orgasmic, rapturous, or ecstatic rush arising from a generalized sense of flow. This experience may occur as a result of practices like Sufi dancing and marathon running.

DRIVING AND PEAK EXPERIENCES

Both the ergotropic and the trophotropic systems may be driven directly, either from the top down or from the bottom up. The dancing of the Bushman adept that evokes the arising of *n/um* is an example of hyperergotropic activity driven by rhythmic motor activity, erupting, under proper conditions, in a trophotropic experience in which the *!Kia* mind state arises. The dancing, a bottom-up driver, is also operating initially upon the lowest level of ergotropic-trophotropic organization. Another common bottom-up driver is fasting, a practice often preceding or accompanying other more active ritual procedures (e.g., North American Indian vision quests). Fasting is known, not only to reduce caloric and other nutriments available to cells, but also to decrease the amount of important hormones in the blood, as well as their receptor-cell

sensitivity, thus providing a probable mechanism of energy conservation at the cellular level (Schussler and Orlando 1978). Fasting may thus
be interpreted as a bottom-up driver of trophotropic activity, due to its
tranquilizing effect upon the body.

The two systems may be driven as well from the top down. This event
is frequently accomplished by concentration upon imagery, which we
have already noted may produce an increase or a decrease in somatic
arousal, depending upon the content. Prolonged and intense meditation
("devotion") upon a lotus above the head, or upon a Sacred Heart in
the chest, may first result first in ever more enhanced concentration
leading to hypertrophotropic activity and, under the proper conditions,
to an ergotropic discharge—perhaps a minor release at one of the
sympathetic plexes, or a complete discharge throughout the system
experienced as Pandit Krishna's *"kundalini* awakening" or St. Margaret
Mary's sustained "rapture."

THE PRINCIPLE OF HOMEOMORPHOGENIC RECRUITMENT

Psychic energy is usually felt as bodily sensations, or "seen" as
visions of energy flows as just described. Occasionally there may be
auditory or other sensory modal components to the experience. The
point to emphasize is that the sensorial components of the experience
bear a homeomorphogenic, causal relationship to the ergotropic-trophotropic transformations associated with them. If they are expressions of
those transformations, sensorial events are brought into synchronous
entrainment with the ergotropic-trophotropic events. If they are initia-
tors of those transformations, then sensorial events bring the greater
ergotropic-trophotropic events into entrainment.

Whether top-down or bottom-up drivers are operating, the key element is usually concentration upon a single process or object leading
eventually to harmonious, homeomorphogenic entrainment of operating systems at all levels of the hierarchy. We may thus define a *principle
of homeomorphogenic recruitment:* sustained concentration of attention
upon an object or process, if carried out with sufficient intensity, will
tend to recruit and eventually entrain most, if not all, somatic systems
at every level of hierarchy within the body. Bentov (1977) has hypothesized that certain meditative procedures lead ultimately to the synchronization of all standing waves of the body to the rhythm of the dominant, aortic standing wave. This explanation could be considered a
special case of our principle.

Whether the experience of psychic energy flow is the result of explicitly applied drivers, or due to the spontaneous retuning of the systems
as an unintended consequence of inadvertent drivers, the "higher up"
the ergotropic-trophotropic systems the effect reaches, the more diver-

gence may be experienced: the range of possible entrainments is most limited at the lower end of the hierarchy (i.e., in autonomic, endocrine, and other somatic systems), whereas it is less limited in the midrange structures (i.e., midbrain and limbic systems), and least limited at the higher end (i.e., in cortical structures). In other words, we would expect the imagery and intuitive insights associated with psychic energy experiences to vary substantially more from individual to individual, and from culture to culture, than we would somatic and affective components. Much of the apparent diversity in psychic energy experiences cross-culturally derives primarily from different codes used *after the fact* to describe the more symbolic and interpretive aspects of the experience—precisely those aspects that are most easily recalled and described in natural language and art.

STRUCTURAL INVARIANTS
AND ERGOTROPIC-TROPHOTROPIC TUNING

And yet, as we have seen, despite different cultural and symbolic traditions, a recognizable structural invariance recurs in the reports of higher psychic energy experiences. We suggest that the sensations of flow common to these experiences derive from the breakdown of body-image entrainment in favor of direct entrainment with proprioceptive fields (i.e., sense receptors that deliver information from muscles, tendons, arteries, etc.) in the body. This breakdown amounts to interpenetration of proprioceptive neural networks and the neurocognitive systems mediating consciousness. The distinct sense of centering, as well as ascending and descending psychic energy, likely derives from proprioceptive sensing of autonomic and endocrinal functions, which are most active in the center of the body. The obvious origins of such activity are the two sympathetic trunks (part of the ergotropic system), which lie on either side of the spine, and the great vagus nerve of the parasympathetic system (part of the trophotropic system), which sweeps down from the base of the brain to emerge at the base of the spinal column to innervate the sexual and other organs. Sensations of circulation and heat at discrete centers of the body, such as the heart region, may be accounted for as proprioception from one of the sympathetic plexes (see Motoyama and Brown 1978).

Visual and other sensory components of "visions" may be accounted for, in part, as homeomorphogenic representations within the sensorium of these proprioceptive inputs. As the usual body image is replaced by the experience of flow, the visual system may become entrained to the process, thus providing the image of a radiant energy body, perhaps as glowing energy centers perceived as a radiant heart, or lotus, or sphere with Saturnian rings. The culturally conditioned expectation of the practitioner will determine the details of the vision and, in particular, the interpretation of symbolic material encountered.

In any event, the unbounded simultaneous discharge of the ergotropic and trophotropic systems seems to set the stage for an ultimate mystical experience, which again exhibits cross-cultural structural invariants (see Stace 1960; d'Aquili 1982). *!Kia,* visitations from Christ, the arising of *kundalini,* all are anticipated and accompanied by profound alterations in the flow and form of psychic energy. As we have shown, those alterations can be explained, in part, by reference to principles of organization operating in the human nervous system.

CLARITY OF CONSCIOUSNESS AND THE THEATER OF MIND

Retuning of the ergotropic-trophotropic balance not only may lead to profound experiences of energy flow within the body and the perception of energy flow events, it may also profoundly alter one's experience of self, world, and cosmos in a manner that has often formed the core of religion in society. The changes may be more or less permanent, as was surely the case for Gopi Krishna and St. Margaret Mary. The simultaneous discharges of both systems after years of meditational ("devotional") discipline have all the earmarks of a Thomian catastrophe (Thom 1975)—that is, a dramatic morphogenesis resulting from a period of less dramatic change. The period of actual structural transformation at every level of hierarchic organization took months, and very likely years in each case.

This issue is reminiscent of the age-old argument waged among some of the Chinese schools of Buddhism over whether enlightenment occurs in a sudden moment of blinding insight or whether it requires years of maturation. The answer might well be both, depending upon whether one is referring to a moment of overwhelming morphogenesis experienced as a dramatic shift in consciousness, or to the relatively longer period of maturation of the structures to an organization capable of producing that shift in consciousness.

TRUE CONTEMPLATION

In any event, we suggest that there may occur a structural reentrainment produced by a full-scale ergotropic-trophotropic retuning that we may call the phase of *true contemplation.* Just as with the dream phases, this phase of consciousness is one in which *any reality desired by the being may arise in the sensorium.* During a phase of true contemplation, an individual may experience insight, a divine vision, the cessation of all form and even more subtle phenomena, infinite power, and journeys to far-off lands and multiple realities. The key variable in determining the phenomenal nature of experiences during contemplation is the term *desire*.

DESIRE AND CONTEMPLATION

In the last chapter we developed the notion that phases of consciousness tend to arise cyclically to maximize adaptation to events in the outer operational environment during part of the cycle, and to optimize harmonious adaptation of competitive internal systems vis-à-vis each other during another part of the cycle. It is the task of conscious network to facilitate both of those functions, neither of which may predominant for a long time if the organism is to remain optimally functional. However, in the present context of higher phases of consciousness, those processes have been reintegrated into phases that transcend the rudimentary demands of the organism. The desire giving rise to activity among networks are transcendent—Maslow's (1971) higher "needs"— and result, via homeomorphogenic recruitment, in transcendent or transpersonal experiences arising in the sensorium. Generally speaking, a transcendent experience profoundly disconfirms one's point of view and results in activation of the EMC and growth.

The desires that elicit phenomena in the contemplative phase of consciousness will depend upon many factors, including the stage of development of the contemplative, the cosmology and mythopoeic systems influencing the contemplative through the cycle of meaning, the extent of integration or fragmentation of competing neural networks, and other somatic systems within the being as well as the environmental conditions surrounding the contemplative. The Sun Dance practitioner may have to participate in the ritual many years before a vision occurs. The Buddhist student may meditate for months or years before sufficient calm (trophotropic tuning) arises, enabling higher insights to mature (see e.g., Dubs 1987). The Christian devotee may spend years of purification before the grace of a vision is bestowed. We are referring here to desire elevated to the level of volition, aspiration, and purpose (in the psychological sense).

We are suggesting that a singular stage in neurocognitive development exists, the stage of contemplation, which is relatively rare to human experience because it requires a radical retuning of ergotropic-trophotropic balance. Further, there may arise a variety of so-called mystical experiences, whose phenomenal contents will depend on what is desired by competing networks in the being. This stage of development is in fact coded in some of the more sophisticated esoteric traditions: *upacara samadhi* in Theravadin Buddhism, *mahamudra* in Vajrayana Buddhism, *tiferet*, or Beauty, in Kabbalah, and perhaps Bushman *!Kia*.

It is a stage characterized by the cessation—at least for the moment—of lower-order distractions such as discursive thought and imaginal fantasy, bodily aches and pains, and mundane worries, and also by the distinctive clarity of perception, and intense, effortless concentration upon whatever object of contemplation spontaneously arises, or is assigned, or is chosen.

THEATER OF MIND

Contemplation is the stage of fruition of the theater of mind. When the practitioner has reached this stage, the multiple realities coded in cosmology and enacted in mythopoeic drama may "come alive" in direct experience. Those networks whose functions are the intentionalities of mythopoeic symbolism are free to express themselves in sensorial events via homeomorphogenic recruitment. But unlike the homeomorphogenic interplay during normal dreaming, the interplay of sensorial events during contemplation is accompanied by, and therefore transformed by, intense concentration and keen awareness. The sensory components of the experiences arising during contemplation are typically lucid, and memory of the events is exceptionally numinous and detailed.

Generally speaking, the phenomenal experiences that may emerge during contemplation may be either ethereal or cthonic, depending upon the degree of integration (thus harmony) or fragmentation (thus competition) in the organization of networks entrained to conscious network. Ethereal experiences might include journeys to the overworld, the realm of deities or radiant beings, or more subtle absorption into radiant light. Cthonic experiences may include journeys to the underworld, the realms of demons or hellish states, the encounter with primordial darkness. All such experiences, we would emphasize, originate and pass away within the sensorium, and are composed of forms within the field of sensorial dots.

Insight tends to arise fluidly during true contemplation, and in direct correlation to the nature and intensity of curiosity—curiosity being but another form of desire, in this case desire for knowledge. Insight may arise through the medium of symbolic imagery in vision or in direct apprehension of knowledge relative to some stimulus event. In paths of insight such as Buddhist *satipatthana* or kabbalistic tarot meditations, the round of curiosity and insight leapfrog until some ultimate experience arises. In the absence of desire, either for symbolic expression on the part of neural networks, or for insight, the sensorium tends to remain blank to everything save, perhaps, sensations of bliss. In some Buddhist schools this experience has been termed "frozen ice" *samadhi*, and is considered a hindrance due to the lack of curiosity about the nature of phenomena and mind.

No matter how advanced the practice, or mature the contemplative, experiences arising during contemplation are then the object of *post hoc* interpretation (see Reichel-Dolmatoff in Furst 1972; Stace 1960)—Ricoeur's "philosophical reflection"—which tend to be framed within the cosmological views that initially led to the attainment of the experiences. Thus the contemplative participates, at whatever level of attainment, in the cycle of meaning in which his cultural being is lodged. It is this interpretive phase, which usually sets in after the contemplative phase has passed, that facilitates through ratiocination the integration of knowledge gleaned in contemplation with the wider self and cosmological views of the practitioner, and perhaps his fellows.

PORTALING AND INVARIANCE IN CONTEMPLATION

To note the range of variation of detail in experiences during contemplation, either among individuals or cross-culturally, is not the same as saying that no invariant structural features exist among these experiences. Indeed, structural invariance is apparent in all "mythical" experiences once reports are shorn of their idiosyncratic, ideological, and cultural overlays (see Stace 1960; Ring 1974, 1976; Wilber 1980). We have already examined many components of psychic energy in these experiences. There are other universal structural motifs we might discuss as well.

A very common theme in ritual and visionary reports is the passage from one realm of reality to another through a symbolic limen, or portal (see Turner 1974, 1979, 1982). This process is experienced typically as the passage through a door, mirror, hole, or tunnel to emerge, like Alice stepping through the looking-glass, in an alternative reality. We have termed this experience *portaling,* and the symbols and instruments used ritually to evoke the experience, *portal symbols* (see MacDonald et al. 1989). Many objects may be used as portal symbols in ritual, including mirrors, gems and crystals, skrying bowls and pools, cave mouths, and doorways.

We consider portal symbols, and practices accompanying them, to be thoroughly archetypal, and as such we may expect them (1) to be universal, or nearly so, in the mythopoea of cultures valuing experience of multiple realities; (2) to be utilized cross-culturally in a similar manner within the context of ritual practice; and (3) to evoke under proper conditions similar experiences cross-culturally. In particular, we hypothesize that portal symbols will penetrate to the neurocognitive structures controlling the entrainment of phases of consciousness, and will produce often profound reentrainment of those systems. In other words, portal symbols produce warps in consciousness by penetrating to mechanisms that are internal to the nervous system and that control the transformation of consciousness.

Metaphorically speaking, portal symbols are precisely like doors between rooms, or perhaps keys to the doors between rooms. If we conceive of the rooms as relatively durable phases of consciousness, then the doors are warps. Much of the symbolism in multiple-reality cosmologies pertains to elements and relationships within discrete rooms, but additional symbolism pertains to the relationships between rooms, and to ways of moving between rooms. We are suggesting that transformational symbols have predictable forms cross-culturally because of their efficacy in penetrating to the mechanisms that produce reentrainment of neurocognitive systems mediating the play of experience unfolding in the sensorium.

Furthermore, by directing a practitioner's attention to the warp between phases of consciousness, portal symbols result in opening up the warp to awareness and thereby to cognitive restructuring as a phase. The practitioner thus becomes aware of the process of transformation from one reality to another by focusing awareness upon the portal between realities.

The universal and archetypal potency of portal symbols points the way toward another effective transpersonal methodology for experimentation with and study of such symbols. Very simply, one may meditate upon portal symbols in a disciplined way (i.e., generate a willful semiotropism) and explore the experiences that arise from concentration. Those experiences may then be treated as data concerning the "meaning" or intentionality of the portal symbols (i.e., semiosis). However, the experiences arising for the anthropologist are not necessarily the same as for the native practitioner. The anthropologist and the native usually carry divergent cultural baggage into the experience. Cognized phases of consciousness will differ from culture to culture, and from individual to individual within a single culture—the furnishings in the various rooms of consciousness will perhaps differ from house to house. However, if the portal symbols are indeed archetypal, then a fundamental similarity of experience should occur, if only structurally—all houses of consciousness will have rooms, however furnished.

The anthropologist must be mindful of the warnings that come with the various meditative traditions: the initiate shaman must learn to find his or her way back to "normal" reality. Various safety measures are built in to techniques of portaling. In terms of the present theory we may interpret this common admonition to mean that one must learn to reentrain the phase of consciousness from which one began the exploration. This is usually automatic owing to the lifelong conditioning of "normal" phases of consciousness. But certain measures are generally taken to avert the fear that may easily arise from meditative practices.

AN EXAMPLE: THE TIBETAN MANDALA OFFERING

One of the preliminary meditations (ngon-dro) carried out by practitioners of Tibetan tantric Buddhism is termed dkyil-'khor, or mandala offering (Beyer 1973:437ff). The root dkyil refers to the middle or center, and the root 'khor to a wheel or circle. There are variations on the practice, but they all involve constructing a mandalic form with rice on a round metallic surface and then wiping the surface clean. The practitioner concentrates intensely on the operation of constructing and disassembling the mandala and repeating a mantra, or chant (gzuns, snags: Govinda 1973:92), which speaks of the construction of the mystical cosmos surrounding the mythical Mount Sumeru. The beginning practitioner is expected to repeat this operation at least a hundred thousand times during the process of foundation work. An additional hundred thousand repetitions may be required of a practitioner (usually a monk) who has entered the traditional three-year retreat. The mandala offering is found in abbreviated form as an element in most ceremonies performed in temples. The mirror-rice mandala may be represented using a ritual hand gesture, or mudra (phyag-rgya).

The base upon which the rice mandala is constructed is a circular bowl made of silver or copper, often with symbolic engraving and, occasionally, gold inlay around the rim. It is called sa-gzhi in Tibetan, the root sa meaning earth or ground and the root gzhi meaning foundation. The bowl is used upside down and has a flat, matte-finished surface upon which the rice mandala is constructed.

One of the authors (CDL) undertook the mandala-offering practice during his study of Tibetan arising yoga (see Laughlin, McManus, and Webber 1984). He completed his hundred thousand repetitions during two retreats, a one-month retreat in Canada in 1979, and a two-month retreat in Scotland in 1982. During the first of these retreats he completed approximately eighty-five thousand repetitions while combining the mandala-offering work with meditation on the breath (Skt. anapana-sati). He worked on the mandala-offering meditation during five one-hour sessions a day. The mirror used was the glass taken from a standard five-inch shaving mirror, which was glued to the bottom of a tea saucer. The saucer provided a handle by which to hold the mirror in the left hand while the mandalic form was constructed with the right hand. Five pounds of long-grained rice was used, died yellow using ordinary food coloring, and lying in a plastic bowl in the lap. A handful of rice was taken up, the mandala completed, the mirror and rice offered up to the guru, and then the mirror swept clean with the right hand, the rice falling back into the plastic bowl, all the while repeating the appropriate mantra.

A journal was kept describing meditation experiences and dreams throughout the retreat. Several experiences and insights arose during the course of that retreat illustrating the experiences that may be evoked by portaling devices. For one thing, most experiences obviously evoked by or related to the mirror work occurred during sleep. CDL, who is a lucid dreamer, had mandalic lucid dreams virtually every night, once the retreat was well under way. A common feature of these episodes was the appearance of a circular, opaque disk upon which a variety of symbolic forms arose. These episodes usually occurred as lucid phases immediately after a more ordinary dream. According to his dream diary, on one occasion

> the disk was back, consisting of two concentric circles, the inner more opaque than the outer, and there developed for several moments a rapidly transforming series of abstract characters flowing from a central vertical diagonal toward the periphery in a horizontal flow. Not all characters were symmetrical. . . . I was staring through this mandala at scenes beyond . . . [scenes being common hypnopompic imagery].

On another occasion, there arose

> a brief mandala episode during which a field of bright yellow flowers sprang out of a circular mirror and emitted great energy and, as it were, spit a blob of black something out of its center which then paused a moment and then melted into black drops and fell away. This occurred, as usual, several times.

Relevant motifs often arose in the normal dream state as well:

> I am in the ocean in a very sunny clime, flying a round, yellow-orange kite which pulls me out into the ocean and up to some interesting rock formations that seem to be made of piles of rice. I have gotten deeper in the water, but just as I am about to go under, I note that the rock formations begin to take on an ominous quality with eye sockets, etc. I lock my concentration into a "real" dark profile of a male driving the car I'm in. I can't seem to make out the face clearly. Then I am aware of the lights increasing in intensity from above (I am fully aware at this point and am entering lucid phase) and concentrate on the lights and that brings on a full-blown mandala experience.

By "full-blown mandala" experience is meant an intense light-show during which the entire visual screen is filled with brilliant lights usually appearing to emerge at the center in waves that radiate outward to the periphery in a continuous flow. As constantly shifting and changing patterns, sometimes incorporating human and other forms, sometimes remaining amorphous, the experience is associated with intense bliss and ecstasy and an extremely keen awareness and deep concentration. When these lucid dream experiences first arose many years prior to the mirror exercises just described, they would last only a few minutes. During this retreat CDL was able to sustain the experiences up to thirty minutes at a time by maintaining intense concentration on the center of the everchanging mandala.

Associations were frequently made in dream state between mirror, opaque disk, and bodies of clear water. All seemed to be equivalent metaphors for the reflexive quality of mind. This association is hardly surprising. In Buddhist tradition the most commonly mentioned symbols signifying the illusory nature of phenomena arising in the mind are motifs such as the reflected image in a mirror, the moon reflected in a pool of water, and a continuously moving stream.

Lucid mandala phases commonly involved a three-dimensional effect of traveling through tunnels into radiant light or into space. Sometimes in dream and in meditative vision, a tunnel would become a "space door" or portal into vast interstellar spaces and radiant spheroid forms, or spacious landscapes. These portals would usually constitute a limen signifying the point of transformation between one state of consciousness and another. Over time, the range of states became increasingly varied and differed ever more subtly one from another. Sometimes there was fear of passing through the portal, sometimes the awareness would pass through and shoot down a passage or tunnel at great speed into brighter and brighter light, or into expansive, crystal-clear awareness of empty space. The mind grew to understand that it could either resist passage because of fear or let go into whatever experience lay ahead. The consciousness often seemed to be polarized relative to the mirror, a part that wished to "pass over" and a part that wished to remain behind, and depending on which part was stronger at the moment, the experience would follow it.

The mirror and yellow ricelike energy particles became core symbols in dream and meditation vision thereafter. CDL recalls an occasion two years or so after the retreat when he was visiting the monastery of one of his teachers in Nepal. It was late at night and frightening apparitions were appearing before him in a lucid dream phase. In despair, he called out mentally to his teacher for help, and the image of his teacher appeared in a vision sitting on a throne and concentrating upon a gilt-edged mirror hanging on the wall. The vision zoomed in on a close-up of the mirror. A ray of yellow light composed of distinct particles beamed down onto the mirror and was reflected away. Laughlin became simultaneously aware that all of the apparitions that had been so frightening were merely transient piles of rice grains on the mirror of mind—in other words, insubstantial. The sense of despair lifted and, although apparitions continued to arise, the knowledge of their illusory nature was never forgotten.

Mirror surface motifs seem to be of two types: reflective mirror surfaces that we in the West commonly associate with the concept "mirror," and opaque surfaces that resemble the matte surfaces of Tibetan, Chinese, and shamanic ritual "mirrors." It is interesting that of the two types the opaque surface proved to be the most common in CDL's experiences, even though he used a reflective mirror, unlike the matte ones used by Tibetan yogis.

A split-image motif was very common in the mandala-offering work, and has proved a common feature of other types of mediation, both in CDL's personal experience and in the reports of other meditators he has interviewed. The lateral asymmetry may take a diverse form including, for example, the left side murky or dark and the right side clear or bright, a flow of energy streaming left and right from a central vertical seam or axis, and different human figures appearing on the left and right sides. In true mandalic form, the center of the visual field was often the locus of symbolic significance, with or without lateral asymmetry of form. Foveal symbolism included gemstones, spheres, tunnels, geometrical figures of various sorts, eyes, and nexes of crosses. It will be remembered that the classic definition of a mandala is a quartered circle with a center (Jung 1969).

Void Consciousness

There is a good deal of evidence that portaling symbolism and full-scale portaling experiences arise spontaneously, particularly under the influence of psychotropic drugs (Kluver 1966; Siegel 1977). Portaling is a common motif in shamanic art, and presumably in shamanic "journey" experiences, as recounted for cultures over much of the world (McDonald et al. 1989). We have emphasized portaling because some work has been done on the psychological concomitants of the phenomenon, and because this symbolic motif is directly associated with warp control discussed in an earlier chapter (see page 143). We have also emphasized the significance of gender symbolism in contemplative phases. At this time we could as easily discuss other universal features of higher phases of consciousness such as the experience of mystical light or illumination (Eliade 1965), or of totality (Chang 1971), for they are motifs equally amenable to a biogenetic structural approach.

However, we wish to end this chapter by noting that many mystical traditions report the occurrence of ultimate awareness (see Walsh and Vaughan 1980; Wilber 1980; Nishitani 1982). This experience has been labeled in many ways: God Consciousness, *kether*, Cosmic Consciousness, nirvana, *satori*. Kenneth Ring (1974:172; 1976:78) uses the term *Void* in his useful typology of transpersonal experience. D'Aquili (1982:366) has used the phrase "absolute unitary being" for the same level of consciousness, and reports some interesting psychiatric and philosophical aspects of related experiences.

The direct experience of Void Consciousness has been repeatedly affirmed by adepts from many cultures and many eras (see Goleman 1977). The experience is described as ineffable, either positive or neutral, and, therefore, best expressed using metaphor (d'Aquili 1982). Yet it is possible to articulate both the logical and empirical necessity of the experience (as David Bohm 1980 has implied; see also Wilber 1982:44ff), and the cognitive transformations that occur as a consequence of the experience (as Franklin Merrell-Wolff 1973a, 1973b has done; see also Burridge 1979: chap. 11). The resulting changes in cognition are most important from our point of view, for the cognitive transformations wrought by the attainment of Void Consciousness have major implications for the anthropological enterprise when viewed from a transpersonal perspective.

Merrell-Wolff has described very clearly the changes in his consciousness leading to, and subsequent to his attainment of, Void Consciousness. Of particular note is his characterization of the series of insights ("Recognitions") leading to the realization of Voidness and its effect upon his general philosophical outlook:

> Probably the most important permanent effect of the whole group of Recognitions is the grounding of knowledge, affection, and the sense of assurance on a base that is neither empirical nor intellectual. This base is supersensible, superaffective, and superconceptual, yet it is both conscious and substantial and of unlimited dynamic potentiality. I feel myself closer to universals than to the particulars given through experience, the latter occupying an essentially derivative position and being only of instrumental value, significant solely as implements for the arousing of self-consciousness. As a consequence, my ultimate philosophic outlook cannot be comprehended within the forms that assume time, the subject-object relationship, and experience as original and irreducible constants of consciousness or reality. At the same time, although I find the Self to be an element of consciousness of more fundamental importance than the foregoing three, yet in the end it, also, is reduced to a derivative position in a more ultimate Reality. So my outlook must deviate from those forms of Idealism that represent the Self as the final Reality. In certain fundamental respects, at least, the formulation must accord with the anatmic doctrine of Buddha, and therefore different in important respects from any extant western system. (1973a:76)

The experience of Void is, in part, one of recognition, of knowledge. From our perspective, Voidness is perceived only when the neural structures mediating the cognitive aspects of experience within the sensorium are sufficiently matured in their development that this advanced knowing may arise. The realization of the experience itself is sudden—a rapid "coming together" of knowledge and experience, and the instantaneous obliteration of all conceptual distinctions, including those maintaining any boundaries to consciousness. The experience of the Void is a phase preceded by a warp—what we will call the *transcendental warp*.

The "coming together" (entrainment) of neural structures at the transcendental warp seems to be a permanent stage in the development of the perceiver's neurocognitive system. It bears the plateau characteristics of other previous stages of cognitive development (à la Piaget), and its effects as a developmental transformation eventually permeate all cognition and experience.

Two of the effects most evident from Merrell-Wolff's description are the loss of ego-centeredness in experience and the loss of the view of the world as a concrete objective reality. Completely absent is any view of self as permanent, impermeable, seamless entity, or empirical ego. Gone as well is a cognition grounded in the belief that the phenomenal world is solid or fixed. Awareness is now grounded upon Voidness, which is to say upon the direct experience of a reality that is beyond transient phenomena, beyond feeling, and beyond concept. All phases of consciousness are experienced, in a sense, as equivalent, and there is no ego-identification with one phase rather than with other phases.

It is the dissolution of those views—that is, the reentrainment of the operating neural structures mediating the cognized environment—that *is* the transcendental warp. An effect of this transformation is to reorganize the conditioned entrainments mediating the experience of a permanent "me" as somehow distinct and removed from an objective world "out there." Because the shift in view affects experience of self and world simultaneously, the changes we are addressing do not result in simply a shift from a positivism to a subjectivism. Rather, there is a complete reorganization of operating neural structures so that neither a positivistic nor a subjectivistic paradigm accurately describes observation informed by the experience of the Void. Both positivism and subjectivism are oversimplistic and dualistic in relative to a *transcendental paradigm*. In a transcendental paradigm observation is carried out from an experience of totality in which "subject," "object," and "observation" are only labels for a partial view of what is really a single, completely integrated process—a process which is inseparable from the field of potentialities that is the Void.

12 CONCLUSION: NEURAL ORGANIZATION AS EPISTEMIC PROCESS

> We perform the epoche—we who are philosophizing in a new way—as a transformation of the attitude which precedes it not accidentally but essentially, namely, the attitude of natural human existence which, in its total historicity, in life and science, was never before interrupted. But it is necessary, now, to make really transparent the fact that we are not left with a meaningless, habitual abstention; rather, it is through this abstention that the gaze of the philosopher in truth first becomes fully free: above all, free of the strongest and most universal, and at the same time most hidden, internal bond, namely, of the pregivenness of the world.
> —Edmund Husserl, *Crisis*

EMBEDDED WITHIN OUR various discussions of brain, symbol, and experience is the thread of an argument leading toward a neuroepistemology. We want to conclude this volume by considering that argument and its implications for science, but first it would be useful to summarize the argument as it has unfolded in these pages.

THE ARGUMENT IN SUMMARY

Our task has been to understand the nature of consciousness and experience within their broadest possible context. This problem requires that we understand the structures of consciousness that produce the patterns of invariance in human experience cross-culturally. In order to understand the essential structures of experience it has been necessary to abandon all notions of dualism between consciousness and the nervous system for such notions preclude the grounding of those structures in the neurophysiology of the being.

The human being is a community of cells that is organized both to adapt to the world and to grow. The nervous system may also be conceived as a community of cells that has evolved first to regulate the being's internal metabolic activities and external motoric responses to the world, then to control those activities, and finally to constitute a cognized environment—an internally simulated world within which the more important of those activities may be staged as experience. Consciousness is produced by a field of neural entrainments that is constantly in flux but exhibits recurrent patterns of reentrainment, or creodes. Neural models and networks of models have an initial structure and a characteristic course of maturation that involves adaptation to the operational environment. Patterns of reentrainment occur phasically and are cognized as such. Phases of consciousness are punctuated by relatively rapid periods of reentrainment that exert the principal influence upon the overall structure of the phase. Neural models and networks that are not entrained to conscious network are nevertheless alive and have their own intentionalities. They may act in concert or competition with conscious network to produce a relatively harmonious or fragmented consciousness.

Consciousness is essentially intentional; that is, conscious network, being entrained in a dialectic field arising between frontal intentional processes and the sensorium, is always organized about some object (be that a thing, quality, feeling, idea, or process). Consciousness is also essentially a symbolic process by which a totality of cognitive associations comes together about the object as focus. Society has a vested interest in assuming control over much of the conditioned learning (semiosis) required to assure the proper associations are entrained to the object. Society not only controls much of the conditioning of neural entrainments, but is also able to control the cognized environments and behaviors of group members by manipulating objects as symbols. Noumena in the operational environment produce sensations in the sensoria of individuals that penetrate to a field of conditioned entrainments, which become operative within the overall organization, the conscious network. Penetration may also occur wholly within the being as activity in a somatic system external to conscious network produces a homeomorphogenic activity within a neural model entrained to conscious network. A good deal of the ritual drama encountered by anthropologists in the course of ethnographic fieldwork among non-Euramerican cultures would seem to be designed as penetration devices to stimulate enactment within the cognized environment as a kind of "theater of mind." Cosmological understanding is depicted in symbolic dramas that in turn lead to individual experiences, which are then interpreted within the framework of the cosmology that first produced the experience—thus completing a "cycle of meaning."

Human experience is most commonly constrained by the adaptive surface of the empirical ego. The ego is a system of recurrent patterns of adaptation mediated by creodic structures entrained to conscious network. Similarly, like other aspects of the being as a community of cells, the ego and its attendant networks undergo a neurognostically structured process of maturation involving a balancing act between the twin demands of assimilation of and accommodation to the press of the operational environment. Stabilization of an empirical ego is not, however, the ultimate stage in the maturation of the human nervous system. As the shamanic traditions of many of the world's cultures attest, there are means of expanding the scope of human experience that are considered fundamentally important to the well-being of the cosmological and social fabric, as well as to the health of the individual. Socially established means are prescribed for transcending the habitual bounds of ego consciousness, and for allowing the experience of multiple realities—realities which are here interpreted as alternative fields of neural activity entrainable to conscious network.

Transcendental phases of consciousness are attainable only by mature contemplatives who have, to some extent, become free of traditional constraints upon neural development, a freedom that unleashes relatively unfettered development of consciousness beyond that attained by most shamans. Viewed in this way, transcendence is a process of extraordinary neural development, which may require arduous dedication and lengthy maturation to produce a fundamental reorganization of the nervous system in just the same neurognostic way as does the construction of a stable ego. Whereas the ego is largely the product of adaptation and creodization, the course of producing mature contemplation results from the application of awareness to the very processes that produce the ego, the object, and the entire cognized environment. The ego is the maturation of adaptation, mature contemplation is the maturation of reflection. Both are mediated by the same neurobiological processes.

EPISTEMIC PROCESS

Epistemology, from our vantage point, is a genetic, evolutionary process, not merely a historical or normative discipline. Moreover, it is a process involving the evolution, development, and conditioning of the nervous system. As such our view of the epistemic process is in sympathy with, if not congruent with, Donald Campbell's (1974) "evolutionary epistemology," Jean Piaget's (1971a) "genetic epistemology," Hartwig Kuhlenbeck's (Kuhlenbeck and Gerlach 1982) "neurological epistemology," and Francisco Varela's (1979) "natural epistemology." Unlike the views of Campbell and Piaget, but in accord with those of Varela and Kuhlenbeck, our theory of the epistemic process is (as all such theories now can and should be) firmly grounded in the neurosciences. Thus by the term "epistemic process" we mean, in brief, a process incorporating all of the neurocognitive processes discussed earlier in this book. The epistemic process involves neurognosis, the empirical modification cycle, the prefrontosensorial polarity principle, relegation/relevation, the cognized environment, and so on.

According to our account, humans are social animals, and thus the human epistemic process may be considered as having three aspects: phylogenetic, ontogenetic, and sociogenic: The (1) phylogenetic aspect is represented in the process of encephalization. As Jerison (1985) has noted, the areas of the cortex that have allometrically expanded in hominid phylogenesis are precisely those that mediate the construction of a cognized environment and attendant knowledge. The (2) ontogenetic aspect is indicated by the invariant patterns of neuropsychological development of the individual during the life course. The (3) sociogenic aspect is seen in the influence and control exercised by societies in conditioning paradigmatic views of the operational environment in their members. It therefore follows that observation of the operational environment by any persons, be they scientist, shaman, or householder, is contingent upon the momentary concatenation of these three aspects. That means that any single observation, any momentary experience or perception, is generated by neural organizations that have been influenced by the evolution of the species, the development of the individual, and the forces of social conditioning.

As we have argued in chapter 1, the epistemic process that lies at the heart of science is always state-specific. Scientists are human beings, and as such they inherit brains and a process of neurocognitive ontogenesis that is developmentally prior to their social conditioning as scientists. An obvious implication from the most cursory exploration of findings in the neurosciences is that the observer is *never, under any circumstances perceiving the noumenon, or the object "out there," but is always operating upon the cognized object constituted within the sensorium of the observer*. Keeping this fact in mind can preclude the projection of erroneous notions of objectivity into the epistemic process—a system of projection that is at the heart of any positivist account of the process: "The naive materialist describes an introspective process while disclaiming or forgetting that it is introspective" (Kuhlenbeck 1982: vol. 2, p. 223). As Francisco Varela notes:

> If, on the other hand, we do keep in mind that all invariances and regularities are our construction, this awareness necessarily alters our idea of what is called "empirical investigation" and, indeed, our idea of science itself. We shall come to pay attention to the structure of our concepts and the origin of the categories, rather than assume that any structure and any categories have to be *there* as such. . . . [This view] shows that, in nature and culture alike, every unity that can be called a knower constructs

the world he knows and, in doing so, determines his way of knowing. (1979:276–278)

Given this relationship between the knower and the object known, at the present moment in our understanding we contend that the most comprehensive (but not the only) approach to the structures of experience is a blend of mature contemplation—or of mature phenomenology, if you will—and neuroscience. In a word, the brain, or consciousness, is the only object in the universe that we can come to know both from the inside out and from the outside in. That is, from our structural monist standpoint, the structures of experience may be known via both exteroceptive exploration of the body and interoceptive intuition of essences—a methodological advantage understood by many philosophers and scientists since, at least, the work of Schopenhauer. In order that this melding of perspectives take root in institutional science, the pervasive, paradigmatic views of the scientific endeavor must now change to accommodate it. Thus we will spend some time addressing the nature of this change of view.

THE FALLACIOUS DUALISM BETWEEN SCIENCE AND CONTEMPLATION

A major impediment to the merger of neuroscience and contemplation is the fundamental dualism inherent in the positivist account of science. According to the positivist account, contemplation, or "introspection," is productive of intuitive insight, wisdom, and metaphysics, but not of rational understanding, factual observation, and empirically testable theory requisite to the scientific enterprise (see e.g., Lyons 1986; Weissman 1987). This view sets contemplation apart from the practice of science and blocks any dialogue between the perspectives, a dialogue which may otherwise fructify both.

This dualistic conception of human knowledge was foisted upon science in the nineteenth and early twentieth centuries by theorists rightly wishing to wrest control of the creative exploration of the world from the grips of ideology. But this dualism has inadvertently produced an uncritical, illusory understanding of the scientific enterprise on the part of practitioners and an attendant projection by them of an erroneous view of contemplation. According to this attitude, science is fundamentally grounded in an objective world of empirical observations, which are the source of facts used to test the truth value of theories. In that positivist view, productive theories are verifiable and thus cannot become rigidified and false in the way ideology can become, for those theories are exoteric and always tested in the crucible of objective reality. Contemplation, according to positivism, is the opposite of science; it is essentially esoteric, spiritual, introspective, nonempirical, and mythological in expression. Positivism holds that contemplative truths are rarely, if ever, open to empirical verification, and contemplative laws and formulations are transmitted as received wisdom and socially imposed interpretations and do not change due to empirical disconfirmation.

The trouble with the positivist account is that neither science nor contemplation are really carried out in the way the account claims. As anyone knows who is familiar with the Kuhnian and post-Kuhnian developments in the history and philosophy of science, science as actually practiced is a social institution that generates its own cultural values, orientations, practices, and so on, that are transmitted between generations thus perpetuating its own statuses, social relationships, ritual activities, and other meaningful behaviors (Rubinstein, Laughlin, and McManus 1984). All scientific disciplines and explorations operate to assimilate observations to structures—theories—which are embedded in a context of paradigmatic expectations, professional initiations, and processes of legitimation, and the enculturative processes that canalize the cognitive development of practitioners.

As developments in modern quantum physics have underscored, any scientific exploration properly understood involves the concatenation of three sets of variables: the phenomenon to be observed, the technology and criteria for measurement, and the cognitive-perceptual organization of the observer. Of these three sets of variables, it is the latter that is *under the least conscious control* during experimental or naturalistic observation. This lack of awareness does not mean that the latter set is the least important. Rather, it means that scientists are conditioned to pay less attention to their own processes of observation than to the variables in the other two sets. Yet the enculturative process that produces the scientist is geared precisely toward producing the proper scientific "frame of mind" without which requisite observation is impossible. The variables operating within the observer are the structures of experience, and their activity is present in all scientific observations, whether the scientist is aware of them or not—and scientists generally are not aware of these processes. As W. H. Gantt put it, "On the same basis as we assess the science of the external universe, we have no adequate science for the internal universe" (1987:115).

CONTEMPLATION INCREASES SCIENTIFIC RIGOR

To enhance observer awareness of the processes of his or her own perception requires some form of phenomenology or contemplation. As Edmund Husserl (1970) no doubt would have agreed, rather than being an activity a pole apart from the scientific enterprise, contemplation *increases scientific rigor* by (in our own terms)

1. Relevating the processes of observation more fully into awareness, thus escaping recurrent errors unconsciously projected out of a naive scientific "natural attitude."
2. Providing mechanisms of control for the structures of experience that are operating during observations; mechanisms that can be built into the process of training new practitioners.
3. Integrating the entire process of observation under a single system of comprehension, which allows a range of control of the process including the most "exoteric" to the most "esoteric" aspects.
4. Allowing statements of contingency to be built into the theoretical frame (i.e., specification of state dependency of cognitive organization relative to perception, description, outcome, interpretation, and meaning within a greater interstate comprehension).

Contemplation and science can operate as complements for each other, thus serving both as contexts of validation and as sources of hypotheses for each other.

Phenomenological input into the act of scientific observation is not the task of New Age "flakes" (as some popular science renditions might have it), but is an activity carried out by experienced, trained, dedicated practitioners that are "scientific" in precisely the same sense that orthodox Western science is "scientific"; namely, training is directed at critical curiosity about the formations of consciousness, training is based upon an explicit system of empirical methodology (e.g., see penetration techniques described in chapter 7, and in MacDonald et al. 1989; Laughlin 1985a, 1985b; Laughlin, Chetelat, and Sekar 1985; Laughlin, McManus, and Webber 1985; Laughlin et al. 1986), knowledge is, ideally, experientially grounded, activity is professional and respectable, and the results of activities are "publicly" verifiable (see our discussion of "public event" in chapter 1). As Ken Wilber (1984) notes, phenomenological exploration of perception, in keeping with orthodox science, involves

1. *Injunction:* "If you want to know this, do this."
2. *Apprehension:* cognitive apprehension and illumination of "object domain" addressed by injunction.
3. *Communal confirmation:* results are checked with others who have adequately completed the injunctive and illuminative operations.

What is relevated into awareness and given professional legitimacy in this phenomenological account is the recognition of state-specificity of the injunction and illumination phases of observation, and the possibility of "public" confirmation in any object domain (or discipline) by others in the same enculturative process—all of which is implied in the Kuhnian view of the progress of science.

We cannot overemphasize the problem of state-specificity, for the simple reason that realization of state-specificity is exceptionally difficult for most people, including most scientists. "Normal," empirical ego-bound introspection is of necessity state specific—for all the reasons noted in chapter 9. What is observed is contingent upon, indeed *constituted* by, the internal structural organization of the observer/intro-spector, and as such is effected by the level of developmental structuri-zation processing the information at the moment (see the U-curve hypothesis in chapter 9).

As we have seen (chapter 10), one cross-culturally common resolution to the constraints imposed by the empirical ego upon the epistemic process has been the *shamanic principle*. The shaman learns to transcend empirical ego constraints by altering his ego state, allowing him to immerse himself and participate in a broader, more destructured phe-nomenal field. Yet, even this solution produces its own state-specificity that is subject to bias due to (1) ego-distortion during the descent stage of the journey, and (2) the ideological origins of interpretation imposed upon experience subsequent to the descent (see chapter 10).

The mature contemplative, on the other hand (see chapter 11), offers another solution to the problem of state-specificity; he is trained to maintain a *detached intentional field* (or watcher) that observes the process of reduction during transformations of state and thus maintain a *relative* objectivity about his own phenomenal processing. We emphasize *relative* objectivity, for here acts of contemplation correspond to acts of scientific enterprise: their training, technique, and paradigmatic institutions strive to achieve the same end, objectivity, but as we have seen, the pull of subjective bias is always present. The amalgamation of the two methods, science and contemplation, carry us as far as we can go toward the goal of objectivity by producing a complementary check upon the excesses of bias in each, while providing the most auspicious climate for optimal development of the epistemic process. As Aron Gurwitsch wrote: "By virtue of achievements in the course of mental development, the stream of experience is substantially transformed so as to exhibit features varying according to the stages of mental development" (1964:103).

HOW SCIENCE CAME TO MISUNDERSTAND
MATURE CONTEMPLATION

The received view (i.e., positivism) of the scientific enterprise led to an erroneous perspective vis-à-vis contemplation and its place in the epistemic process for the following reasons. First, early Western "scientific" attempts at introspection were primitive, unsophisticated, and *prima facie* wrong. Second, those attempts at introspection were undisciplined and lacked the rigor of a confirmed body of observation, a wealth of communal experience, and a system of control (see Lyons 1986). Third, those attempts lacked any knowledge or guidance from Eastern or other systems of relatively sophisticated introspection. And, fourth, those attempts could never transcend the enculturated "natural standpoint" of the scientists' understanding of mind, perception, ego, intentionality, and so on; as a consequence, their bias gave birth to fifty years of behaviorism. This abuse of introspection caused inevitable and erroneous comparisons to be drawn between a relatively successful, developed, sophisticated, and professionally institutionalized *science* and a relatively amorphous, unsophisticated, methodologically sloppy fringe activity that quickly became labeled as "occult" and "mysticism."

ESOTERIC VERSUS EXOTERIC

The terms most generally used for this comparison are *exoteric* and *esoteric*, the former meaning that methods, theories, and results are available to everyone, and the latter meaning that they are available only to the initiated. The positivist view is that science is wholly exoteric, and that mystical traditions commit the heinous sin of esotericism. The truth is that both scientific disciplines and mystical traditions are largely esoteric and will frequently react to the public or exoteric personae of each other. Historically one of the major impediments to an accurate understanding and evaluation of contemplative traditions by science has been either the lack of a written tradition within, or the unavailability of the written texts of, the more sophisticated phenomenological disciplines. Similarly, Husserl apparently never had an opportunity to consult texts from other, non-Western phenomenological traditions. But, of course, in modern times such texts abound and can easily be consulted.

Moreover, even here, when we look at how the profession of science is actually performed, we find that much of the initiation of practitioners is carried out within an essentially *oral tradition*, that is, the relationship between mentor and student. Kuhn's "exemplars" with correction of the student by the mentor, repetition in the practice of experimentation and method, review by the mentor's peers (faculty committees) are essentially oral procedures augmented by the written text. The pattern is much the same as one finds in the training, say, of a Tibetan Buddhist monk. The mentor (*lama*, guru, shaman) interacts with the student and sets initiative practices that are repeated over and over until the proper results are achieved. There is peer review of both master and student, and the process is essentially oral, even when, as with the Tibetan or Western Mystery traditions, there are written texts used in the training.

Thus science, which is essentially esoteric but conceives of itself (at least in the positivist view) as exoteric, compares itself with mysticism, which it considers wholly esoteric; but science's knowledge only of mysticism's public face allows science to invalidate all forms of phenomenology by means of a "straw man" argument. The truth is that science and mysticism—indeed any institutional manifestation of the epistemic process—are essentially esoteric in nature, but have public, exoteric aspects.

Perhaps we can make this clearer by schematizing all this in a fourfold table (table 2).

TABLE 2

	Popular View	*Actual Practice*
Science	1. Mass perception, stereotypy, imagined procedures, exoteric	2. Professional, trained perception, esoteric
Contemplation	3. Mass perception, stereotypy, romanticized, exoteric	4. Professional, trained perception, esoteric

We see that both science and contemplation have a public or mass aspect and an actual, professional aspect. Each may be viewed from its public aspect by the other, while each knows itself (to whatever extent) from its actual aspect. The error has been that science (as it knows itself from the vantage point of cell 2) evaluates contemplation by its public face, cell 3; and in so doing, concludes that science is superior, using supposedly "scientific" criteria—criteria summarized by Wilber as injunction, apprehension, and confirmation. Science has failed to conceive of and evaluate contemplation in its actual aspect, cell 4, in which the same "scientific" (i.e., epistemic) criteria would prove applicable.

The same epistemic evaluations may be applied to contemplation toward science, and to science toward contemplation, and most definitely are applied internally by each in the course of routine training and exploration. In fact, science is as vulnerable to charges of nonobjectivity, nonreplication, appeal to authority, tautological propositions, and ideological reverence as is mysticism, and perhaps more so owing to its ignorance of the structures of perception and experience. When science divorces observation from the observer and "assumes the extreme objectivity" that is embedded in the positivist paradigm, it sets the stage for a profound distortion of understanding, which returns to haunt all disciplines sooner or later. No contemplative tradition would make the error of that distortion because the unitary nature of the epistemic process is transparently and intuitively obvious to even fledgling contemplatives.

UNITING SCIENCE AND CONTEMPLATION

Bringing a mature contemplative component into science, as seems to be happening in certain of the disciplines today (e.g., Bohmian physics), can be beneficial. Far from diluting scientific discipline and a returning to nonempirical metaphysics, a melding of essentially similar training can only extend the scope of science, increase its rigor, bring the entire field of entrainments that mediates the epistemic process under more global relevation and control, and declare the observer, as well as the scope of inquiry and technology of measurement, *as a variable, rather than a relative constant.*

It is important to remember that the epistemic process always manifests a transcendental aspect. It is also a process inherent in the nature and activity of the nervous system and is thus an aspect of the operational environment that becomes a problem to understand via empirical exploration, not one to be defined away through normative imposition. *Epistemology* is the formalization of the epistemic process. Epistemologies in science and philosophy are generally rule systems organized at the logical level of Piagetian formal operations. When these formalizations are treated as theories of knowing useful in guiding initiates into the proper mind states conducive to empirical exploration, they are performing well as heuristic instruments. They do not impose a closure to the transcendental aspect of the epistemic process. But when such formalizations are elevated to the cultural status of "The Proper Method" (i.e., *the* scientific method, statistical methods, etc.), when they are projected onto a discipline and sanctioned, they force a closure to the epistemic process and doom the discipline's methods to scientific sterility. Most important, scientistic methods come to treat the epistemic process as nontranscendental, fully known, and thus as nonproblematic.

Moreover, because closed, normatively imposed epistemologies tend to be structured at a formal operational level of cognitive complexity, they fail to appreciate and take advantage of the possibility that the human nervous system may well be capable of structural organizations that developmentally transcend formal operations (incidentally, a possibility alluded to by Piaget in several places) and that such higher levels may be fundamental to optimal creativity in the epistemic process. This openness does not mean that the transcendental nature of the epistemic process stops operating upon the world. Rather, scientistic disciplines overemphasizing methodological strictures fail to recognize the transcendental ("intuitive," "creative," "artistic," "ingenious," etc.) aspects when they do occur, and will rationalize results in terms of formal epistemology rather than acknowledge the essentially mysterious complexion of the discovery process. The philosophy of science has recognized this error as mistaking the "context of justification" for the "context of discovery."

Understanding the productive role of epistemology both as theory leading to further exploration of the mysteries of consciousness, and as guide to initiation into the discipline, permits a developmental transformation of epistemology commensurate with the development of consciousness itself. Naturally it is impossible to predict accurately the effects that a universal recognition of the transcendental nature of the epistemic process would have upon science. But most likely such a transformation of view would at least

1. Produce a full recognition of, and an integration of rational processes with, *intuition*, which already has a strong, though largely tacit role in scientific discovery.
2. Tend to balance the developmental *decalages* that inhibit integration of asymmetrical processing of information in the brain; that is, integrate left- and right-lobe processing during theory construction.
3. Produce a science that would *transcend disciplinary boundaries* to a greater extent than is now the case. Interdisciplinary cooperation would become the norm rather than the exception.
4. Allow the use of broader-based skills and *more broadly trained personnel* as scientists than is currently the practice.
5. Facilitate *more global and flexible paradigms*, and more holistic, interdisciplinary theories than is the case under the current regime of specialization.
6. Make it far easier for practitioners to remain ever mindful of the distinction between the *cognized and operational aspects* of their inquiries and of themselves as observers, and that the interface between those aspects is the epistemic process—a process characterized by its own cognized and operational aspects.

The ultimate effect of a merger of the scientific and contemplative orientations is easier to anticipate and will no doubt generate a system of state-specific sciences that exhibit greater flexibility and interdisciplinary cooperation due to its grounding in a more sophisticated comprehension of the epistemic process. If the distinction continues to be made between science and contemplation within this merger, it will be used more to characterize two complementary orientations of the epistemic process and less as two alternative ways of knowing. When the epistemic process is oriented toward internal processes of the observer, it may be called "contemplation" or "phenomenology." When it is oriented outward by the observer toward the world, it may be called "science," or this or that discipline.

EVOLUTION OF THE EPISTEMIC PROCESS AND SCIENCE

A successful merger of science and contemplation would, we believe, initiate a transcendent stage in the evolution of the epistemic process, grounded in its own self-reflection and relevation. As Schrödinger (quoted in Gantt 1987:116) has put it, "One can say in a few words why our perceiving and thinking self is nowhere to be found within the world picture, because it itself is this world picture." This realization is fundamental to this volume and may, if generalized throughout the scientific disciplines as predicted by Husserl, produce a new kind science: a "science of tomorrow" that promises a new range of scope and rigor in which

1. All operations, methods, observations, experimental and naturalistic situations, and conclusions, as well as the determined status of the observer, are couched in state-specific terms. All variables are consciously conceived as determined by the epistemic status of the observer: one's phase of consciousness, theoretical approach, assumptions, expectations, paradigmatic allegiance, affective state, cognitive-perceptual limitations, point of view, phenomenological sophistication, and so forth.
2. The field of observation is conceived as a kind of phase hyperspace of contingency statements, something like Donald Campbell's (1963, Campbell and Fiske 1959) multitrait, multimethod matrix.
3. The polarized view of knowledge, which produces dichotomized concepts like esoteric-exoteric, will become ameliorated, if not entirely eliminated. This amelioration would inhibit the tendency of individuals to identify with one pole or the other as the "proper way of knowing," a tendency that can propel entire cultures to flip from what Sorokin (1941) called a *sensate* to an *ideational* pattern of epistemology. By relevating the bipolar tendency of the epistemic process—the tendency of the brain to know and adapt to the world and to reflect upon its own being—the activities of each pole remain entrainable to conscious network and neither is relegated to unconscious activity.

ANTHROPOLOGY-PLUS

We began this book by acknowledging that our approach was fundamentally anthropological, plus the addition of neurological, transper-

sonal, and phenomenological expansions. We hope that by now we
have made our case that

1. Embedding the question of consciousness in ethnology renders
   the scope of inquiry more global relative to culture and more
   evolutionary relative to our species as a whole.
2. Incorporating a transpersonal and a phenomenological perspective within ethnology provides the broadest range of human
   experience and the data base for recognizing many of the
   universal aspects of experience, which point to the existence of
   universal structures mediating experience.
3. Incorporation of the neurosciences into ethnology makes possible a more sophisticated, empirically grounded, ontogenetically and phylogenetically relevant theory of the structures of
   experience.

It is evident to students familiar with the history of anthropology that
current ethnological theory is virtually moribund. There has been no
major infusion of theory into ethnology since the discipline began to
waken to the implication of Levi-Straussian structuralism in the seven-
ties. Most of the current attraction to semiotic approaches is actually the
discovery of perspectives, like those of Victor Turner and Clifford
Geertz, that have existed for decades. There are those who are rummag-
ing through Marxist notions and interpretations, but even this probing
obviously reverts to a theoretical perspective generated long ago.

Our explanation for this quiescence of theoretical creativity was implied in earlier works (see Laughlin and d'Aquili 1974; Rubinstein,
Laughlin, and McManus 1984) and should be much more evident from
what we have said in the current volume. Any discipline that restricts
itself to the study of behavior and excludes the organization of the
biological organism that produces that behavior is clinging to one
window among other possible windows open to inquiry. Moreover,
exclusion of all but behavior (including symbolic behavior like speech
and writing) from the data base renders the discipline incapable of any
means other than deduction for formulating notions about the structures producing the behavior. Meanwhile, the burgeoning neurosciences produce almost daily information and insights of direct relevance
to the explanation of those behaviors, but these insights cannot be used
by anthropologists poorly trained in the neurosciences.

As we took great pains to point out from the beginning, the same
criticism applies to the very limited appreciation by ethnologists of the
transpersonal aspects of human experience. There is great truth to the
Eastern adage that one can teach only to the level of one's realization.
Ethnologists cannot comprehend the full range of human experience

until they have relinquished the culturally conditioned boundaries limiting their own experience and come to experience more of the vast range of possible cognized environments among humans on the planet.

The need of anthropology for its "plus-factors" is clear. More to the point, we see indications that anthropology is rapidly realizing its need for "plus-factors." And we suspect that it will not be long before a new breed of anthropologist will arrive on the scene as conversant with sulci, neocognitrons, and transmitter substances as they are with demes, mythemes, and patrilateral cross-cousin marriage. It may take longer for a cadre of transpersonal ethnographers to emerge from graduate schools and to enter the field to pursue the meaning of the Vision Quest, and still longer perhaps, for a cadre of mature contemplatives to inform the epistemic foundations of the discipline. However long it takes, these changes will come—and they will be welcome.

NOTES

CHAPTER 1: INTRODUCTION: BIOGENETIC STRUCTURALISM AND MATURE CONTEMPLATION

1. See McCall (1983) for an excellent critique of behaviorism from a phenomenological point of view.
2. We have elaborated the distinction between semiotic and evolutionary structuralism in d'Aquili, Laughlin, and McManus 1979:3ff.
3. We are particularly grateful for the discussions we have had with philosopher John R. Schumacher, who has, along with David Bohm, made us aware of the potential power of incorporating as much of quantum theory as possible into our formulations. We have made some attempt to address this inclusion in Laughlin 1986.
4. According to *Webster's Third New International Dictionary*, the word *epoche* means "suspension of judgment: (a) in ancient skepticism: the act of refraining from any conclusion for or against anything as the decisive step for the attainment of ataraxy [read tranquillity]; (b) the methodological attitude of phenomenology in which one refrains from judging whether anything exists or can exist as the first step in the phenomenological recognition, comprehension, and description of sense appearances: *transcendental reduction.*"

CHAPTER 2: THE NATURE OF NEUROGNOSIS

1. No one knows how many neurons comprise the human nervous system. There certainly are hundreds of millions of them. The commonly cited number of ten billion refers to the estimated number of neurons comprising each half of the cerebral cortex. The number has erroneously been quoted as referring to the number of cells in the entire brain (see Calvin 1983:xix on the issue).

CHAPTER 3: CONSCIOUSNESS AND THE COGNIZED ENVIRONMENT

1. The Tripitaka consists of the Sutra Pitaka, the discourses of the Buddha of various lengths; the Vinaya Pitaka, the rules of the order of monks; and the Abhidharma Pitaka, the high philosophical and psychological teachings of the Buddha. The Abhidharma is essentially a guide to the contemplative study of consciousness; see Narada Maha Thera (1975); Guenther (1976).

2. We have used the terms "cognized" and "operational environments" after Rappaport (1968; see d'Aquili et al. 1979:12ff; Rubinstein et al. 1984:21ff), but have substantially changed their meanings.
3. There is a school of thought in psychology called "attribution theory" that has a lot to say about this issue; see Jones et al. 1972.
4. Another school of thought in psychology called "cognitive dissonance theory" informs us here; see Festinger 1957.
5. For other examples of such illusions, see Gregory 1971; Luckiesh 1922.

CHAPTER 4: INTENTIONALITY AND THE SENSORIUM

1. See figure 1 in chapter 1.
2. This is an implication that may also be drawn from the so-called split-brain research (Sperry 1982).
3. We are particularly grateful for the feedback we received from John R. Schumacher, Radhika Sekar, and Lois and Gerard Chetelat while we were developing the notion of dots.
4. A generator potential is the action potential emitted by a sensory receptor cell at the periphery in response to stimulation within the discrete range of its receptivity.

CHAPTER 5: PHASES OF CONSCIOUSNESS

1. The law of homology states that similar biological structures will perform similar functions.
2. For much more extensive discussions of the evolution of cortical and subcortical areas of the brain, see Laughlin and d'Aquili 1974; and Jerison 1973.
3. These various functions are summarized in Kimura (1973); Goben et al. (1972); Shankweiler and Studdert-Kennedy (1967); and Levy; (1972).
4. See the film *Trance and Dance in Bali* made by Gregory Bateson and Margaret Mead.

CHAPTER 7: SYMBOLIC PENETRATION

1. Portions of this chapter have been adapted from previous writings, particularly from Webber and Laughlin 1979; Webber, Stephens, and Laughlin 1983; and Laughlin and Stephens 1980. The authors wish to thank Mark Webber and Christopher D. Stephens for their part in developing these ideas.
2. Homeomorphogenesis is a neologism, as we could find no currently used term in either systems theory or mathematics, much less in the neurosciences, for the kind of relation we wish to emphasize. The term combines

the concept *morphogenesis* from biological formulations (see Thom 1975; Sheldrake 1981; Waddington 1957) with the root *homeo* (as in the word *homeomorphic*, meaning of similar form or structure) to denote causally linked transformations of similar, but not exact, structures.

3. We are particularly grateful for the help of Mark Webber in formulating some of these ideas (Webber and Laughlin 1979; Webber, Stephens, and Laughlin 1983; Webber 1980).

4. Fasting is known to affect reception of hormones. Receptor binding for triiodothyronine is reduced and thus causes a decrement in thyroid activity. This mechanism conserves calories during the fast (see Schussler and Orlando 1978).

5. This task is the most difficult for the Westerner to learn. Because we are not taught to create and stabilize an internal image, we require considerable practice to master this technique. But most Tibetan adepts, who have practiced visualizing forms from an early age, learn the practice more easily.

6. One source is the Abhidharma, a Buddhist meditative and philosophical tradition (see Narada Maha Thera 1975), another is the Visuddhimagga, an ancient text in Buddhist meditation (Buddhaghosa 1976), and yet another is from the Tibetan Buddhist meditative tradition (see Beyer 1973).

7. In modern, postexile times, adepts have recourse to full-color photographs made from the more traditional paintings.

8. Our use of *prajna* and *vinnana* agrees more with Suzuki (1967:66) than with Turner (1974:47ff); *prajna* reflects the order-as-given in raw perception, and not the fundamentals of social organization, although the latter may be presented to consciousness in the former.

9. One of CDL's informants who has experienced full Void Consciousness (or "stream entry" in the Theravadin Buddhist lexicon) likened the experience to a "great cosmic shit—letting everything go!"

10. More accurately, his gaze is upon the Void from whence she arises and into which she passes away. Even more accurately, he represents the awareness of nonduality between the unfolding phenomenal world (*samsara*) and the Void (*nirvana*).

11. CDL's own experience during a lengthy retreat bears evidence of this. The *yab-yum* spontaneously refined themselves into a blue and red sphere respectively, and then each entered clouds of the contrasting color. The clouds then gradually interfolded into the classic *yin-yang* form with the contrasting bubbles at the appropriate spots. These imaginal transformations occurred over a period of time when the consciousness was increasingly centered and concentration increasingly intense and undistracted.

CHAPTER 8: THE THEATER OF MIND

1. Turner became aware of the formative relationship between the "liminal" aspect of ritual transformations in adult culture and the transformative functions of play in childhood cognitive development (Turner 1982:27). As a sidelight on the matter, Turner had just begun to appreciate the work of our

biogenetic structural group just prior to his death, and had gently chided us for having failed to address the issue of play (Turner 1983:233). It is a sad irony that he was unaware that our work on the evolution of play and games was being published even as he was giving his talk (Laughlin and McManus 1982). We now view that a developmental sequence exists in humans beginning with play, progressing to social play, then games, and finally to adultlike ritual, and that much of semiosis producing the core symbolism around which adult ritual is organized occurs within that developmental process.

2. We are very grateful to Dr. G. Ronald Murphy, S.J., for suggesting this approach to us.

CHAPTER 10: DREAMING, THE SHAMAN'S JOURNEY, AND POLYPHASIC AWARENESS

1. Archetypes as used here are a special case of our notion of neurognosis. They are neurognostically typical forms of perception and apprehension, and are structural or formal in nature. The archetypes, as Jung saw them, lie beneath and are separate from their representation in our experience. As neurognostic structures they are open to development, following the sequence of differentiation and integration discussed in the previous chapter. Beginning as species-specific response capabilities intrinsic to human neural organization, they form the ground plan of perceptions and feelings about the external world.

2. Any developmental transformation implies a liminal period of destructurization, of increased disorganization preparatory to the restructurization that defines a transformation. Often this is experienced as a time of tension, uncertainty, or stress, as any veteran of adolescence or midlife crisis knows only too well. In the current case, this experience is compressed, compacted, and intensified both structurally and experientially and as such contains great risk to emotional stability and adaptive capacity.

3. Participation mystique in this sense is an immersion in a field of one's own projections. The phenomenological field fills with internally generated images and relationships, which are experienced outside oneself as "real." These projections are symbolic representations of the neurognostic internal structural relationships and the emotional fields within which they are embedded. By way of note, Levy-Bruhl's principal mistake was not the validity of his principle, which he later recanted, but its range of definition. *All* people, to some degree, live in this state and project their own veil of Maya on others and the world outside. The earlier error was to assume reason as characteristic of modern man and participation mystique characteristic of traditional cultures. In fact, such a phenomenon is ubiquitous to man and varies in degree and area of application in different cultures and individual situations.

CHAPTER 11: MATURE CONTEMPLATION

1. Portions of this chapter were presented in Laughlin, Chetelat, and Sekar 1985. The authors wish to thank Lois Chetelat and Radhika Sekar for their immeasurable help in developing this perspective. We wish also to thank Dr. Arni Sekar, M.D., and Gerard Chetelat for aiding in the library research upon which this chapter is based.

2. It is interesting that the word *axis* derives from the Latin for *axle*, thus denoting a center around which something turns.

BIBLIOGRAPHY

Ackoff, R. L., and F. E. Emery. 1972. *On Purposeful Systems*. Chicago: Aldine-Atherton.

Adams, J. 1973. *The Gitksan Potlatch*. New York: Holt, Rinehart and Winston.

Adrian, E. D. 1951. "Olfactory Discrimination." *Année Psychologie* 50:107–113.

Adrianov, O. S. 1978. "Projection and Association Levels of Cortical Integration." In *Architectonics of the Cerebral Cortex*, eds. M. A. B. Brazier and H. Petsche. New York: Raven.

Almeder, R. F. 1980. *The Philosophy of Charles S. Peirce*. Totowa, N.J.: Rowman and Littlefield.

Altman, S. A. 1967. "The Structure of Primate Social Communication." In *Social Communication Among Primates*, ed. S. A. Altman. Chicago: University of Chicago Press.

Anand, B. K., et al. 1961. "Studies on Shri Ramanand Yogi During His Stay in an Air-Tight Box." *Indian Journal of Medical Research* 49:82–89.

Annett, M. 1970. "A Classification of Hand Preference by Association Analysis." *British Journal of Psychology* 61:303–321.

Antonovsky, A. 1979. *Health, Stress, and Coping*. San Francisco: Jossey-Bass.

Arbib, M. A. 1972. *The Metaphorical Brain: An Introduction to Cybernetics as Artificial Intelligence and Brain Theory*. New York: Wiley.

Arbib, M. A., D. Caplan, and J. C. Marshall. 1982. *Neural Models of Language Processes*. New York: Academic Press.

Archer, J. 1976. "Biological Explanations of Psychological Sex Differences." In *Exploring Sex Differences*, eds. B. Lloyd and J. Archer. San Francisco: Academic Press.

Ardener, E. 1971. "The New Anthropology and Its Critics." *Man* 6 (3): 449–467.

———. 1977. "Some Outstanding Problems in the Analysis of Events." In *Yearbook of Symbolic Anthropology*, ed. E. Schwimmer. London: Hurst.

Ardener, S. 1975. *Perceiving Women*. London: Malaby.

Arguelles, J. A. 1975. *The Transformative Vision*. Boston: Shambhala.

Arguelles, J. A. and M. Arguelles. 1972. *Mandala*. Boston: Shambhala.

Armstrong, E. 1983. "Relative Brain Size and Metabolism in Mammals." *Science* 220:1302–1304.

———. 1984. "Allometric Considerations of the Adult Mammalian Brain with Special Emphasis on Primates." In *Advances in Primatology*, ed. W. L. Jungers. New York: Plenum Press.

Armstrong, E., and D. Falk, eds. 1982. *Primate Brain Evolution*. New York: Plenum Press.

Arnheim, R. 1969. *Visual Thinking*. Berkeley, Calif.: University of California Press.

Assagioli, R. 1965. *Psychosynthesis*. New York: Penguin.

Aurobindo, Sri. 1960. *The Future Evolution of Man*. Bury St. Edmunds, Suffolk: East Midland Printing Co.

356 BIBLIOGRAPHY

Bainbridge, L. 1974. "Problems in the Assessment of Mental Load." *Le Travail Humain* 37:279–302.

———. 1978. "Forgotten Alternatives in Skill and Work-Load." *Ergonomics* 21:169–185.

Baldwin, J. D., and J. I. Baldwin. 1973. "The Role of Play in Social Organization: Comparative Observations on Squirrel Monkeys (Saimiri)." *Primates* 14:369–381.

Bandler, R., and J. Grinden. 1975. *Patterns of the Hypnotic Techniques of Milton Erikson, M.D.* Vol. 1. Cupertino, Calif.: Meta Publications.

Barlow, G. W. 1977. "Modal Action Patterns." In *How Animals Communicate*, ed. T. A. Sebeok. Bloomington, Ind.: Indiana University Press.

Barlow, H. B., and J. D. Mollon, eds. 1982. *The Senses*. Cambridge: Cambridge University Press.

Barnett, H. G. 1938. "The Nature of the Potlatch." *American Anthropologist* 40 (3): 349–358.

Barnouw, V. 1942. "Siberian Shamanism and Western Spiritualism." *Journal of the American Society for Psychical Research* 36:140–168.

———. 1946. "Paranormal Phenomena and Culture." *Journal of the American Society for Psychical Research* 40:2–21.

Basso, A., et al. 1973. "Neuropsychological Evidence for the Existence of Cerebral Area Critical to the Performance of Intelligence Tasks." *Brain* 96:715–728.

Basso, K. H., and H. A. Selby, eds. 1976. *Meaning in Anthropology*. Albuquerque, N.M.: University of New Mexico Press.

Bateson, G. 1955. "A Theory of Play and Fantasy." *Psychiatric Research Report* 2:39–51.

———. 1956. "The Message 'This Is Play'." In *Group Processes*, ed. J. B. Schaffner. New York: Macy Foundation.

Baumgardt, E. 1972. "Threshold Quantal Problems." *Handbook of Sensory Physiology* 7 (4): 29–55.

Beaglehole, E., and P. Beaglehole. 1938. *Ethnology of Pukapuka*. Honolulu: Bishop Museum Bulletin 150.

Beals, K. L., C. L. Smith, and S. M. Dodd. 1984. "Brain Size, Cranial Morphology, Climate, and Time Machines." *Current Anthropology* 25 (3): 301–330.

Beck, A. T. 1967. *Depression: Causes and Treatment*. Philadelphia: University of Pennsylvania Press.

Becker, E. 1973. *The Denial of Death*. New York: Free Press.

———. 1975. *The Escape from Evil*. New York: Free Press.

Bekoff, M. 1972. "The Development of Social Interaction, Play and Metacommunication in Mammals: An Ethological Perspective." *Quarterly Review of Biology* 47:412–433.

———. 1974. "Social Play in Mammals." *American Zoologist* 14:265–436.

Bekoff, M., and M. Fox. 1972. "Postnatal Neural Ontogeny." *Developmental Psychology* 5:323.

Bellugi, U., and E. S. Klima. 1976. "Two Faces of Sign: Iconic and Abstract." In *Origins and Evolution of Language and Speech*, eds. S. R. Harnad et al. 514–538. Annals of the New York Academy of Sciences 280.

Benson, H., J. R. Beary, and M. K. Carol. 1974. "The Relaxation Response." *Psychiatry* 37:37–46.

Benton, A., and M. W. Van Allen. 1968. "Impairment in Facial Recognition in Patients with Cerebral Disease." *Cortex* 4:344–358.

Bentov, I. 1977. *Stalking the Wild Pendulum*. New York: E.P. Dutton.

Bergson, H. 1907. *L'evolution Creatrice*. Paris.

Bergstrøm, R. 1969. "Electrical Parameters of the Brain During Ontogeny." In *Brain and Early Behavior*, ed. R. J. Robinson. New York: Academic Press.

Berkson, G., et al. 1963. "Situation and Stimulus Effects on Stereotyped Behaviors of Chimpanzees." *Journal of Comparative and Physiological Psychology* 56:786–792.

Berridge, M. J., and P. E. Rapp. 1979. "A Comparative Survey of the Function, Mechanism and Control of Cellular Oscillators." *Journal of Experimental Biology* 81:217–279.

Berry, H., and J. M. Roberts. 1972. "Infant Socialization and Games of Chance." *Ethnology* 11:296–308.

Bertallanffy, L. von. 1968. *General Systems Theory*. New York: George Braziller.

Beth, E., and J. Piaget. 1966. *Mathematical Epistemology and Psychology*. Dordrecht, Holland: D. Reidel.

Bevilacqua, L., et al. 1979. "Does the Hemisphere Stimulated Play a Specific Role in Delayed Recognition of Complex Abstract Patterns? A Tachistoscopic Study." *Neuropsychologia* 17:93–97.

Beyer, S. 1973. *The Cult of Tara*. Berkeley, Calif.: University of California Press.

Bharati, A. 1975. *The Tantric Tradition*. New York: Samuel Weiser.

Biesele, M. 1978. "Religion and Folklore." In *The Bushmen: San Hunters and Herders of Southern Africa*, ed. P. V. Tobias. Cape Town: Human and Rousseau.

Bischof, H. J. 1983. "Imprinting and Cortical Plasticity: A Comparative Review." *Neuroscience and Biobehavioral Reviews* 7:213–225.

Blakemore, C. 1974. "Developmental Factors in the Formation of Feature Extracting Neurons." In *Neurosciences Third Study Program*, eds. F. O. Schmitt and F. G. Worden. Cambridge: MIT Press.

Blofeld, J. 1974. *The Tantric Mysticism of Tibet*. New York: Causeway Books.

Blumenberg, B. 1983. "The Evolution of the Advanced Hominid Brain." *Current Anthropology* 24 (5): 589–623.

Bogen, J. E. 1961. "The Other Side of the Brain—II. The Appositional Mind." *Bulletin of the Los Angeles Neurological Societies* 34:162.

———. 1969. "The Other Side of the Brain—II. The Appositional Mind." *Bulletin of the Los Angeles Neurological Societies* 34:135–162.

———. 1977. "Some Educational Implications of the Hemispheric Specialization." In *The Human Brain*, ed. McWittrock. Englewood Cliffs, N.J.: Prentice-Hall.

Bogen, J. E., et al. 1972. "The Other Side of the Brain—IV. The A/P Ratio." *Bulletin of the Los Angeles Neurological Societies* 37 (2): 49–61.

Bohm, D. 1965. *The Special Theory of Relativity*. New York: W. A. Benjamin.

———. 1980. *Wholeness and the Implicate Order*. Boston: Routledge and Kegan Paul.

Borges, J. L. 1961. *Antologia Personal*. Buenos Aires: Sur.

Boucouvalas, M. 1980. "Transpersonal Psychology: A Working Outline of the Field." *Journal of Transpersonal Psychology* 12 (1): 37–46.

Boulding, K. 1956. *The Change: Knowledge in Life and Society*. Ann Arbor: University of Michigan Press.

Bourguignon, E. 1973. *Religion, Altered States of Consciousness, and Social Change*. Columbus, Ohio: Ohio State University Press.

———. 1976. *Possession*. San Francisco: Chandler and Sharp.

Bowker, J. 1973. *The Sense of God*. Oxford: Oxford University Press.

Brazelton, T. B., et al. 1977. "Neonatal Behavior Among Urban Zambians and Americans." In *Annual Progress in Child Psychiatry and Child Development*, ed. S. Chess and A. Thomas. New York: Brunner/Mazel Publishers.

Brazelton, T. B., and H. Als. 1979. "Four Early Stages in the Development of Mother-Infant Interaction." *The Psychosomatic Study of the Child* 34:349–369.

Breland, K., and M. Breland. 1971. "The Misbehavior of Organisms." *American Psychologist* 61:681–684.

Brentano, F. [1874] 1973. *Psychologie vom empirischen Standpunkte*, trans. A. Rancurello et al. New York: Humanities Press.

Brodal, A. 1975. "The 'Wiring Patterns' of the Brain." In *The Neurosciences: Paths to Discovery*, eds. F. G. Worden et al. Cambridge: MIT Press.

Brody, H. 1955. "Organization of the Cerebral Cortex." *Journal of Comparative Neurology* 102:517–557.

Broughton, R. 1975. "Biorhythmic Variations in Consciousness and Psychological Functions." *Canadian Psychological Review* 16 (4): 217–239.

Brown, D. P. 1977. "A Model for the Levels of Concentrative Meditation." *The International Journal of Clinical and Experimental Hypnosis* 25 (4): 236–273.

Brown, D. P., and Engler. 1980. "The Stages of Mindfulness Meditation: A Validation Study." *The Journal of Transpersonal Psychology* 12 (2): 143–192.

Brown, J. 1977. *Mind, Brain and Consciousness*. New York: Academic Press.

Brown, R. 1963. *Explanation in Social Science*. London: Routledge and Kegan Paul.

Browuer, B. 1934. "Projection of the Retina on the Cortex in Man." *Association for Research in Nervous and Mental Diseases* 13:529–534.

Browuer, B., and W. P. C. Zeeman. 1926. "The Projection of the Retina in the Primary Optic Neuron in Monkeys." *Brain* 49:1–35.

Bruner, J. 1972. "Origins of Problem Solving Strategies in Skill Acquisition." In *Logic and Art*, eds. R. Rudner and I. Scheffler. New York: Bobbs-Merrill.

———. 1974. "The Early Organization of Action." In *The Integration of a Child into a Social World*, ed. M. P. P. Richards. Cambridge: Cambridge University Press.

Bruner, J. S., J. Goodnow, and A. G. Austin. 1967. *A Study of Thinking*. New York: Science Edition.

Bruner, J. S., et al. 1966. *Studies in Cognitive Growth*. New York: Harcourt Brace.

———. 1976. *Play—Its Role in Development and Evolution*. New York: Penguin.

Bryant, P. E., P. Jones, V. Clanton, and G. M. Perkins. 1972. "Recognition of Shapes Across Modalities by Infants." *Nature* 240:303–304.

Buber, M. 1958. *I and Thou*. New York: Basic Books.

Buchtel, H. A. 1982. *The Conceptual Nervous System*. Oxford: Pergamon.

Buchtel, H. A., et al. 1978. "Hemispheric Differences in Discriminative Reaction Time to Facial Expressions." *Italian Journal of Psychology* 5:159–169.

Bucke, R. M. 1961. *Cosmic Consciousness*. Secaucus, N.J.: Citadel Press.

Buckley, R. M. 1968. *Modern Systems Research for the Behavioral Scientist*. Chicago: Aldine.

Buddhaghosa, B. 1976. *The Path of Purification (Visuddhimagga)*. Vols. 1 and 2. Boston: Shambhala.

Bunge, M. 1977. "Emergence and the Mind." *Neuroscience* 2:501–509.

Burns, D. D. 1980. *Feeling Good: The New Mood Therapy*. New York: New American Library.

Burridge, K. 1979. *Someone, No One: An Essay on Individuality*. Princeton, N.J.: Princeton University Press.

Butters, N., et al. 1970. "Role of the Right Parietal Lobe in the Mediation of Cross Modal Association and Reversible Operations in Space." *Cortex* 6:174–190.

Caianiello, E. R. 1968. *Neural Networks*. New York: Springer-Verlag.

Caillois, R. 1955. "The Structure and Classification of Games." *Diogenes* 12:62–75.

Cairns, D. 1976. *Conversations with Husserl and Fink*. The Hague: Martinus Nijhoff.

Caldwell, D. K., and M. C. Caldwell. 1972. *The World of the Bottlenosed Dolphin*. Philadelphia: J. B. Lippincott.

Calvin, W. H. 1983. *The Throwing Madonna: Essays on the Brain*. New York: McGraw-Hill.

Campbell, D. T. 1963. "Social Attitudes and Other Acquired Behavioral Dispositions." In *Psychology: A Study of a Science*, ed. S. Koch. New York: McGraw-Hill.

———. 1974. "Evolutionary Epistemology." In *The Philosophy of Karl Popper*, ed. P. A. Schilipp. Vol. 1. Peru, Ill.: Open Court.

Campbell, D. T., and D. W. Fiske. 1959. "Convergent and Discriminant Validation by the Multitrait-Multimethod Matrix." *Psychological Bulletin* 56:81–105.

Campbell, J. 1949. *The Hero with a Thousand Faces*. New York: World Publishing Co.

Campbell, K. 1984. *Body and Mind*. Notre Dame, Ind.: University of Notre Dame Press.

Campbell, R. L. 1977. "Emergent Cultural Systems: The Psychocultural Evolution of Man." *Phoenix: The Journal of Transpersonal Anthropology* 1 (1): 17–26.

Campbell, R. L., and P. S. Staniford. 1978. "Transpersonal Anthropology." *Phoenix: The Journal of Transpersonal Anthropology* 2 (1): 28–40.

Caplan, D., and J. C. Marshall. 1975. "Generative Grammar and Aphasic Disorders: A Theory of Language Representation in the Human Brain." *Foundations of Language* 12:583–596.

Capra, F. 1975. *The Tao of Physics*. New York: Fontana Books.

———. 1978. "The New Physics as a Model for a New Machine." *Journal of Social and Biological Structures* 1 (1): 71–77.

Carr, B. J., and M. J. Rees. 1979. "The Anthropic Principle and the Structure of the Physical World." *Nature* 278:605–612.

Carver, C. S., and M. F. Scheier, 1981. *Attention and Self-Regulation: A Control Theory Approach to Human Behavior*. New York: Springer-Verlag.

Case, P. F. 1975. *The Tarot: A Key to the Wisdom of the Ages*. Richmond, Va.: Macoy Publishing.

Cassel, Z. K., and L. W. Sander. 1975. "Neonatal Recognition Processes and Attachments: The Masking Experiment." Paper presented at the Society for Research in Child Development, Denver, Colo.

Cassirer, E. 1955. *The Philosophy of Symbolic Forms*. Vol. 2, *Mythical Thought*. New Haven, Conn.: Yale University Press.

———. 1957. *The Philosophy of Symbolic Forms*. Vol. 3, *The Phenomenology of Knowledge*. New Haven, Conn.: Yale University Press.

Chagnon, N. 1977. *Yanomamo: The Fierce People*. New York: Holt, Rinehart and Winston.

Chamberlain, D. B., 1980. "Reliability of Birth Memories: Evidence from Mother and Child Pairs in Hypnosis." Paper presented at 23rd annual meeting of American Society of Clinical Hypnosis, Minneapolis.

———. 1982. "Symposium Commentary on Lloyd de Mause's Origins of History." *Journal of Psychohistory* 10 (2): 222–229.

———. 1983. *Consciousness at Birth*. San Diego, Calif.: Chamberlain Communication.

Chang, G. C. C. 1963. *Teachings of Tibetan Yoga*. Secaucus, N.J.: Citadel Press.

———. 1971. *The Buddhist Teaching of Totality*. University Park, Penn.: Pennsylvania State University Press.

Changeux, J. P. 1983. "On the 'Singularity' of Nerve Cells and Its Ontogenesis." In *Molecular Interactions Underlying Higher Brain Functions*, ed. J. P. Changeux. *Progress in Brain Research* 58:465–478.

———. 1985. *Neuronal Man: The Biology of Mind*. Oxford: Oxford University Press.

Changeux, J. P., P. Courrege, and A. Danchin. 1973. "A Theory of the Epigenesis of Neural Networks by Selective Stabilization of Synapses." Proceedings of the National Academy of Sciences, USA 70:2974–2978.

Changeux, J. P., and A. Danchin. 1976. "Selective Stabilization of Developing Synapses as a Mechanism for the Specification of Neoronal Networks." *Nature* 264:705–712.

Chapple, E. D. 1970. *Culture and Biological Man*. New York: Holt, Rinehart and Winston.

Chapple, E. D., and C. Coon. 1942. *Principles of Anthropology*. New York: Holt, Rinehart and Winston.

Cheek, D. B. 1974. "Sequential Head and Shoulder Movements Appearing with Age Regression in Hypnosis to Birth." *American Journal of Clinical Hypnosis* 16 (4): 261–266.

Chevalier-Skolnikoff, S. 1973. "The Primate Play Face: A Possible Key to the Determinants and Evolution of Play." Paper presented at the annual meeting, American Anthropological Association, New Orleans.

———. 1975. "The Ontogeny of Primate Intellectual Development and its Implications for Communicative Potential." In *Origins and Evolution of Language and Speech*, eds. S. R. Harnad et al. Annals of the New York Academy of Sciences 280.

Chomsky, N. 1968. *Language and Mind*. New York: Harcourt Brace.

———. 1980. *Rules and Representations*. New York: Columbia University Press.

Churchland, P. S. 1986. *Neurophilosophy: Toward a Unified Science of the Mind-Body*. Cambridge: MIT Press.

Clark, W. E. LeG. 1957. "Inquiries into the Anatomical Basis of Olfactory Discrimination." *Proceedings of the Royal Society of London* 146b:229–319.

Cohen, L. B. 1979. "Our Developing Knowledge of Infant Perception and Cognition." *American Psychologist* 34 (10): 894–899.

Corby, J. C., et al. 1978. "Psychophysiological Correlates of the Practice of Tantric Yoga Meditation." *Archives of General Psychiatry* 35:571–577.

Coult, A. D. n.d. "LSD, Sex and Religion." Typescript.

Count, E. W. 1958. "The Biological Basis of Human Sociality." *American Anthropologist* 60:1049–1085.

———. 1960. "Myth as World View." In *Culture in History*, ed. S. Diamond. New York: Columbia University Press.

———. 1973. *Being and Becoming Human*. New York: Van Nostrand Reinhold.

———. 1974. "Homination: Organism and Process." *Bevolkerungsbiologie*. Stuttgart: Gustav Fischer Verlag.

———. 1976. "Languages of Organism." In *Origins and Evolution of Language and Speech*, eds. S. R. Harnad et al. 456–466. Annals of the New York Academy of Sciences 280.

Cove, J. J., and C. D. Laughlin. 1977. "Myth, Cognition and Adaptation." Paper presented at the meetings of the Canadian Ethnological Society, Halifax, N.S.

Cowan, W. M. 1979. "Selection and Control in Neurogenesis." In *Neurosciences: Fourth Study Program*, ed. F. O. Schmitt and F. G. Worden. Cambridge: MIT Press.

Cowey, A., and L. Weiskrantz. 1975. "Demonstration of Cross-Modal Matching in Rhesus Monkeys." *Neuropsychologia* 13:117–120.

Crabtree, A. 1985. *Multiple Man: Explorations in Possession and Multiple Personality*. Toronto: Collins.

Crail, T. 1983. *Apetalk and Whalespeak: The Quest for Interspecies Communication*. Chicago: Contemporary Books.

Crook, J. H. 1980. *The Evolution of Human Consciousness*. Oxford: Oxford University Press.

Csikskentmihalyi, M. 1975. *Beyond Boredom and Anxiety*. San Francisco: Jossey-Bass.

d'Aquili, E. G. 1972. *The Biopsychological Determinants of Culture*. Reading, Mass.: Addison-Wesley.

———. 1982. "Senses of Reality in Science and Religion: A Neuroepistemological Perspective." *Zygon* 17 (4): 361–384.

———. 1983. "The Myth-Ritual Complex: A Biogenetic Structural Analysis." *Zygon* 18 (3): 247–269.

d'Aquili, E. G., and C. D. Laughlin. 1974. "Myth, Language and the Brain: The Evolutionary Importance of Vicarious Experience." Conference on Linguistic Typology and Interdisciplinary Issues in Linguistics, State University of New York, Oswego, N.Y.

————. 1975. "The Biopsychological Determinants of Religious Ritual Behavior." *Zygon* 10 (1): 32–58.

d'Aquili, E. G., C. D. Laughlin, and J. McManus. 1979. *The Spectrum of Ritual.* New York: Columbia University Press.

Daren, M. 1953. *Divine Horsemen: The Living Gods of Haiti.* London: Thames and Hudson.

Darling, F. F. 1964. *A Herd of Red Deer.* Garden City, N.Y.: Doubleday.

Das, N. N., and H. Gastaut. 1955. "Variations de l'activité-electrique due cerveau, du coeur et des muscles squelletiques au cours de la méditation et de l'extase Yogique." *Electroencephalography and Clinical Neurophysiology* 6 (sup): 211–219.

Dasen, P. R. 1972. "Cross-Cultural Piagetian Research: A Summary." *Journal of Cross-Cultural Psychology* 3:23–39.

————. 1977a. "Are Cognitive Processes Universal? A Contribution to Cross-Cultural Piagetian Psychology." In *Studies in Cross-Cultural Psychology,* ed. N. Warren. New York: Academic Press.

————. 1977b. "Cross-Cultural Cognitive Development: The Cultural Aspects of Piaget's Theory." *Annals of the New York Academy of Sciences* 285:332–337.

Davenport, R. 1976. "Cross-Modal Perception in Apes." In *The Origins and Evolution of Language and Speech,* eds. S. Harnad et al. Annals of the New York Academy of Sciences 280.

David-Neel, A. 1932. *Magic and Mystery in Tibet.* New York: Dover.

Davidson, J. M. 1976. "The Physiology of Meditation and Mystical States of Consciousness." *Perspectives in Biology and Medicine* 19:345–379.

Davidson, J. M., and R. J. Davidson. 1980. *The Psychobiology of Consciousness.* New York: Plenum.

Davidson, R. J., D. J. Goleman, and G. E. Schwartz. 1976. "Attentional and Affective Concomitants of Meditation: A Cross-Sectional Study." *Journal of Abnormal Psychology* 85 (2): 235–238.

Davidson, R. J., and G. E. Schwartz. 1976. "The Psychobiology of Relaxation and Related States: A Multi-Process Theory." In *Behavior Modification and Control of Physiological Activity,* ed. D. Mostofsky. Englewood Cliffs, N.J.: Prentice-Hall.

De Beauvoir, S. 1972. *The Second Sex.* London: Penguin.

Deikman, A. J. 1966. "Deautomization and the Mystical Experience." *Psychiatry* 29 (4): 324–338.

De Mause, L. 1981. "Fetal Origins of History." *The Journal of Psychohistory* 9 (1): 1–89.

De Mille, R. 1980. *The Don Juan Papers: Further Castaneda Controversies.* Santa Barbara, Calif.: Ross-Erikson Publishers.

Denenberg, V. H., et al. 1978. "Infantile Stimulation Induces Brain Lateralization in Rats." *Science* 201:1150–1152.

de Rios, M. D. 1984. *Hallucinogens: Cross-Cultural Perspectives.* Albuquerque, N.M.: University of New Mexico Press.

Devereux, G. 1956. "Normal and Abnormal: The Key Problem of Psychiatric Anthropology." In *Some Uses of Anthropology,* eds. J. B. Casagrande and T. Gladwin. Washington: American Anthropologist Press.

DeVore, I. 1963. "Mother-Infant Relations in Free-Ranging Baboons." In *Maternal Behavior in Mammals*, ed. H. L. Reinhold. New York: Wiley.

Dewson, J. H. 1977. Some Behavior Effects of Removal of Superior Temporal Cortex in the Monkey." In the *Proceedings of the 6th Congress of the International Primatological Society*. New York: Academic Press.

Dharmasena, C. B. 1968. *Aids to the Abhidhamma Philosophy*. Kandy, Sri Lanka: Buddhist Publication Society.

Diamond, M. C., et al. 1964. "The Effects of an Enriched Environment on the Histology of the Rat Cerebral Cortex." *Journal of Comparative Neurology* 123:111–119.

Diamond, M. C., et al. 1966. "Increases in Cortical Depth and Glia Numbers in Rats Subjected to Enriched Environment." *Journal of Comparative Neurology* 128:117–126.

diGuisto, E. L., and N. W. Bond. 1979. "Imagery and the Autonomic System: Some Methodological Issues." *Perceptual and Motor Skills* 48:427–438.

Dimond, S. J., and J. G. Beaumont. 1974. *Hemisphere Function in the Human Brain*. New York: Wiley.

Dobbing, J., and J. L. Smart. 1974. "Vulnerability of the Developing Brain and Behavior." *British Medical Bulletin* 30 (2): 164–168.

Dobzhansky, T., et al. 1977. *Evolution*. San Francisco: Freeman.

Doty, R. W. 1975. "Consciousness From Matter." *Acta Neurobiol. Exp.* 35:791–804.

Douglas-Hamilton, I., and O. Douglas-Hamilton. 1975. *Among the Elephants*. New York: Viking.

Dow, J. 1986. "Universal Aspects of Symbolic Healing: A Theoretical Synthesis." *American Anthropologist* 88:56–69.

Dowman, K. 1975. "The Nyingma Icons: A Collection of Line Drawings." *Kailash* (Kathmandu, Nepal) 2 (4): 320–416.

Dreyfus, H. L. 1982. *Husserl, Intentionality and Cognitive Science*. Cambridge: MIT Press.

Dubs, G. 1987. "Psycho-Spiritual Development in Zen Buddhism: A Study of Resistance in Meditation." *Journal of Transpersonal Psychology* 19 (1): 19–86.

Durden-Smith, J., and D. Desimone. 1983. *Sex and the Brain*. New York: Arbor House.

Durham, W. H. 1982. "Toward a Co-evolutionary Theory of Human Biology and Culture." In *Biology and the Social Sciences*, ed. T. C. Wiegele. Boulder, Colo.: Westview Press.

Dykes, R. W., and A. Ruest. 1986. "What Makes a Map in Somatosensory Cortex?" In *Cerebral Cortex*, eds. E. G. Jones and A. Peters. Vol. 5. New York: Plenum.

Eccles, J. C. 1953. *The Neurophysiological Basis of Mind*. Oxford: Oxford University Press.

———. 1970. *Facing Reality*. New York: Springer-Verlag.

———. 1973. *The Understanding of the Brain*. New York: McGraw-Hill.

———. 1987. *Mind and Brain: The Many-Faceted Problems*. New York: Paragon House.

Edelman, G. M., and V. B. Mountcastle. 1978. *The Mindful Brain*. Cambridge: MIT Press.

Edgerton, R. B. 1974. "Cross-cultural Psychology and Psychological Anthropology: One Paradigm or Two?" *Reviews in Anthropology* 1 (1): 52–64.

Edwards, P. 1967. *The Encyclopedia of Philosophy*. London: Collier-MacMillan.

Eggan, D. 1955. "The Personal Use of Myth in Dreams." *Journal of American Folklore* 33:445–453.

Eggan, F. 1954. "Social Anthropology and the Method of Controlled Comparison." *American Anthropologist* 56:743–763.

Ehrenwald, J. 1978. *The ESP Experience*. New York: Basic Books.

Eibl-Eibesfeldt, I. 1970. *Ethology*. New York: Holt, Rinehart and Winston.

———. 1972. *Love and Hate: The Natural History of Behavior Patterns*. New York: Holt, Rinehart and Winston.

Eliade, M. 1954. *The Myth of the Eternal Return*. Princeton, N.J.: Princeton University Press.

———. 1957. *Myths, Dreams and Mysteries*. New York: Harper.

———. 1958. *Birth and Rebirth*. New York: Harper.

———. 1959. *The Sacred and the Profane: The Nature of Religion*. New York: Harper and Row.

———. 1963. *Myth and Reality*. New York: Harper and Row.

———. 1964. *Shamanism*. Princeton, N.J.: Princeton University Press.

———. 1965. *The Two and the One*. Chicago: University of Chicago Press.

———. 1967. *From Primitives to Zen*. New York: Harper and Row.

Elias, N., and E. Dunning. 1970. "The Quest for Excitement in Unexciting Societies." In *The Cross-Cultural Analysis of Sports and Games*, ed. G. Luschen. Champaign, Ill.: Stipes Publishing.

Ellingson, R. J. 1967. "Cortical Electrical Responses to Visual Stimulation in the Human Infant." In *Behavior in Infancy and Early Childhood*, eds. Y. Brackbill and G. G. Thompson. New York: Free Press.

Ellul, J. 1964. *The Technological Society*. New York: Random House.

Elson, J. C. 1979. "Ananda Marga Meditation." *Archives of General Psychiatry* 36:605–606.

Elson, J. C., P. Hauri, and D. Cunis. 1977. "Physiological Changes in Yoga Meditation." *Psychophysiology* 14 (1): 52–57.

Emery, F. E. 1969. *Systems Thinking*. Harmondsworth, Middlesex: Penguin.

Erikson, M., E. Rossi, and S. Rossi. 1979. *Hypnotic Realities*. New York: Halstad Press.

Ernst, A. H. 1952. *The Wolf Ritual of the Northwest Coast*. Eugene, Oreg.: University of Oregon Press.

Etkin, W. 1967. *Social Behavior from Fish to Man*. Chicago: University of Chicago Press.

Evans, E. F. 1974. "Neural Processes for the Detection of Acoustic Patterns and for Sound Location." In *The Neurosciences: Third Study Program*, eds. F. O. Schmitt and F. G. Worden. Cambridge: MIT Press.

Evans-Pritchard, E. E. 1965. *Theories of Primitive Religion*. Oxford: Clarendon Press.

Evans-Wentz, W. Y. 1958. *Tibetan Yoga and Secret Doctrines*. Oxford: Oxford University Press.

———. 1960. *The Tibetan Book of the Dead*. New York: Galaxy.

————. 1966. *The Fairy Faith in Celtic Countries.* New York: University Books.

————. 1969. *Tibet's Great Yogi Milarepa.* London: Oxford University Press.

Feldman, C. F., et al. 1974. *The Development of Adaptive Intelligence.* San Francisco: Jossey-Bass.

Fernandez, J. W. 1986. *Persuasions and Performances: The Play of Tropes in Culture.* Bloomington, Ind.: Indiana University Press.

Festinger, L. 1957. *A Theory of Cognitive Dissonance.* New York: Harper.

Feyerabend, P. K. 1962. "Explanation, Reduction, and Empiricism." In *Scientific Explanation, Space, and Time,* eds. H. Feigl and G. Maxwell. Minnesota Studies in the Philosophy of Science 3.

————. 1965. "Problems of Empiricism." In *Beyond the Edge of Certainty,* ed. R. G. Colodny. New York: Prentice-Hall.

Fichtelius, K. E., and S. Sjolander. 1972. *Smarter than Man? Intelligence in Whales, Dolphins, and Man.* New York: Random House.

Fillmore, C. J. 1976. "Frame Semantics and the Nature of Language." In *Origins and Evolution of Language and Speech,* eds. S. R. Harnad et al. 20–30. Annals of the New York Academy of Sciences 280.

Firth, R. 1967. *Tikopia Ritual and Belief.* Boston: Beacon Press.

————. 1973. *Symbols: Public and Private.* Ithaca, N.Y.: Cornell University Press.

Flavell, J. 1963. *The Developmental Psychology of Jean Piaget.* Princeton, N.J.: Van Nostrand.

Foster, M. 1974. "From the Earth to Beyond the Sky: An Ethnographic Approach to Four Longhouse Iroquois Speech Events." *Canadian Ethnology Service Paper* 20. Ottawa: National Museum of Man.

Foucault, M. 1970. *The Order of Things.* New York: Random House.

Foulkes, D. 1982. *Children's Dreams: Longitudinal Studies.* New York: Wiley.

Fox, M. W. 1973. "Social Dynamics of Three Captive Wolf Packs." *Behavior* 47:290–301.

————. 1974. *Concepts in Ethnology: Animal and Human Behavior.* Minneapolis: University of Minnesota Press.

————. 1975a. "Evolution of Social Behavior in Canids." In *The Wild Canids,* ed. M. W. Fox. New York: Van Nostrand Reinhold.

————. 1975b. *The Wild Canids.* New York: Van Nostrand Reinhold.

Fox, M. W., and A. Clark. 1971. "The Development and Temporal Sequencing of Agonistic Behavior in the Coyote (Canis latrans)." *Z. Tierpsychol.* 28:262–278.

Frampton, G. G., A. D. Milner, and G. Ettlinger. 1973. "Cross-Modal Transfer Between Vision and Touch of Go, No-Go Discrimination Learning in the Monkey." *Neuropsychologia* 11:231–233.

Franco, L., and R. W. Sperry. 1977. "Hemisphere Lateralization for Cognitive Processing of Geometry." *Neuropsychologia* 15:104–114.

Frederickson, F. S. 1960. "Sports and the Cultures of Man." In *Science and Medicine of Exercise and Sports,* ed. W. R. Johnson. New York: Harper and Row.

Freud, S. 1950. *Totem and Taboo.* New York: Norton.

Fried, I., et al. 1982. "Organization of Visuospatial Functions in Human Cortex: Evidence from Electrical Stimulation." *Brain* 105:349–371.

Friederici, A. G., and P. W. Schoenle. 1980. "Computational Dissociation of Two Vocabulary Types: Evidence from Aphasia." *Neuropsychologia* 12:11–20.

Fries, M. E. 1977. "Longitudinal Study: Prenatal Period to Parenthood." *Journal of the American Psychoanalytic Association* 25:115–140.

Fromm, E. 1962. *The Art of Loving*. London: George Allen and Unwin.

Furst, P. T. 1972. *Flesh of the Gods: The Ritual Use of Hallucinogens*. London: George Allen and Unwin.

Fuster, J. M. 1980. *The Prefrontal Cortex: Anatomy, Physiology, and Neuropsychology of the Frontal Lobe*. New York: Raven.

Gantt, W. H. 1987. "The Science of Behavior and the Internal Universe." In *Mind and Brain*, ed. J. Eccles. New York: Paragon House.

Gardner, H. 1983. *Frames of Mind*. New York: Basic Books.

Gazzaniga, M. S. 1970. *The Bisected Brain*. New York: Appleton-Century-Crofts.

———. 1985. *The Social Brain*. New York: Basic Books.

Geertz, C. 1963. *Agricultural Involution*. Berkeley: University of California Press.

———. 1973. *The Interpretation of Cultures*. New York: Basic Books.

———. 1983. *Local Knowledge*. New York: Basic Books.

Geldard, F. A. 1972. *The Human Senses*. 2nd ed. New York: Wiley.

Gellhorn, E. 1967. *Principles of Autonomic-Somatic Integration*. Minneapolis: University of Minnesota Press.

———, ed. 1968. *Biological Foundations of Emotion*. Glenview, Ill.: Scott, Foresman and Co.

Gellhorn, E., and W. F. Kiely. 1972. "Mystical States of Consciousness: Neurophysiological and Clinical Aspects." *Journal of Nervous and Mental Diseases* 154:399–405.

Gellhorn, E., and G. N. Loofbourrow. 1963. *Emotions and Emotional Disorders: A Neurophysiological Study*. New York: Harper and Row.

Gennep, A. L. van. [1909] 1960. *The Rite of Passage*. Chicago: University of Chicago Press.

Geschwind, N. 1965. "Disconnection Syndromes in Animals and Man." *Brain* 88:237–294, 585–644.

———. 1970. "The Organization of Language and the Brain." *Science* 170:940–944.

Geschwind, N., and A. M. Galaburda. 1984. *Cerebral Dominance*. Cambridge: Harvard University Press.

Getty, A. 1962. *The Gods of Northern Buddhism*. Rutland, Vt.: Charles Tuttle.

Ghuman, P. A. S. 1975. *The Cultural Context of Thinking*. Windsor, Berkshire: NFER-Nelson.

Gibson, E. J. 1969. *Principles of Perceptual Learning and Development*. New York: Appleton-Century-Crofts.

Gibson, J. 1979. *The Ecological Approach to Visual Perception*. Boston: Houghton Mifflin.

Globus, G., et al. 1976. *Consciousness and the Brain*. New York: Plenum.

Goffman, E. 1967. *Interaction Ritual*. Garden City, N.Y.: Doubleday.

Goldman, I. 1975. *The Mouth of Heaven*. New York: Wiley-Interscience.

Goldschmidt, W. 1966. *Comparative Functionalism*. Berkeley, Calif.: University of California Press.

Goleman, D. 1977. *Varieties of the Meditative Experience*. New York: E.P. Dutton.

Gorer, G. [1935] 1962. *Africa Dances*. New York: Norton.

Gough, K. 1961. "Nayar: Central Kerala." In *Matrilineal Kinship*, ed. D. M. Schneider and K. Gough. Berkeley, Calif.: University of California Press.

Gould, S. J. 1977. *Ontogeny and Phylogeny*. Cambridge: Harvard University Press.

Govinda, A. 1973. *Foundations of Tibetan Mysticism*. New York: Samuel Weiser.

———. 1974. *The Psychological Attitude of Early Buddhist Philosophy*. New York: Samuel Weiser.

———. 1976. *Psycho-Cosmic Symbolism of the Buddhist Stupa*. Emeryville, Calif.: Dharma Publishing.

Goy, R. W., and B. S. McEwen. 1979. *Sexual Differentiation of the Brain*. Cambridge: MIT Press.

Granit, R. 1977. *The Purposive Brain*. Cambridge: MIT Press.

Gray, J. A. 1982. *The Neuropsychology of Anxiety*. Oxford: Oxford University Press.

Greeley, A. M. 1975. *The Sociology of the Paranormal*. Beverley Hills, Calif.: Sage Publications.

Gregory, R. L. 1971. *The Intelligent Eye*. London: Weidenfeld and Nicolson.

Griaule, M. 1965. *Conversations with Ogotemmeli*. London: Oxford University Press.

Grim, J. A. 1983. *The Shaman: Patterns of Siberian and Ojibway Healing*. Norman, Okla.: University of Oklahoma Press.

Grimes, R. L. 1982. *Beginnings in Ritual Studies*. Washington: University Press of America.

Grindal, B. T. 1983. "Into the Heart of Sisala Experience: Witnessing Death Divination." *Journal of Anthropological Research* 39 (1): 60–80.

Grinder, J., and R. Bandler. 1976. *The Structure of Magic* 2. Palo Alto, Calif.: Science and Behavior Books.

Grinker, R. R. 1968. *The Borderline Syndrome*. New York: Basic Books.

Grof, S. 1972. "Varieties of Transpersonal Experiences: Observations from LSD Psychotherapy." *Journal of Transpersonal Psychology* 4:45–80.

———. 1973. "Theoretical and Empirical Basis of Transpersonal Psychology and Psychotherapy: Observations from LSD Research." *Journal of Transpersonal Psychology* 5:15–54.

———. 1976. *Realms of the Human Unconscious*. New York: Viking.

———. 1979. *LSD Psychotherapy*. Pomona, Calif.: Hunter House.

Grossman, M. 1980. "A Central Processor for Hierarchically-Structured Material: Evidence from Boca's Aphasia." *Neuropsychologia* 18:299–308.

Gruber, H. E., and J. J. Voneche. 1977. *The Essential Piaget*. New York: Basic Books.

Grunebaum, G. E. von, and R. Caillois. 1966. *The Dream and Human Societies*. Berkeley, Calif.: University of California Press.

Guenther, H. 1976. *Philosophy and Psychology in the Abhidharma*. Boston: Shambhala.

Guenther, H. V., and L. S. Kawamura. 1975. *Mind in Buddhist Philosophy*. Emeryville, Calif.: Dharma Publishing.

Gurwitsch, A. 1964. *The Field of Consciousness*. Pittsburgh, Penn.: Duquesne University Press.

Halifax, J. 1979. *Shamanic Voices*. New York: Dutton.
———. 1982. *Shaman: The Wounded Healer*. London: Thames and Hudson.
Hall, C. S. and V. J. Nordby. 1972. *The Individual and His Dreams*. New York: New American Library.
Hall, J. A. 1983. *Jungian Dream Interpretation*. Toronto: Inner City Books.
Hanson, N. R. 1958. *Patterns of Discovery*. Cambridge: Cambridge University Press.
Harlow, H. F. 1963. "Basic Social Capacity of Primates." In *Primate Social Behavior*, ed. C. H. Southwick. Princeton, N.J.: Van Nostrand.
———. 1969. "Age-mate of Peer Affectional Systems." *Advanced Studies of Behavior* 2:333–338.
Harlow, H. F., and M. K. Harlow. 1962. "Social Deprivation in Monkeys." *Scientific American* 207:137–146.
Harlow, H. F., et al. 1970. "Learning in Rhesus Monkeys After Varying Amounts of Prefrontal Lobe Destruction During Infancy and Adolescence." *Brain Research* 18:343–353.
———. 1971. "From Thought to Therapy: Lessons from a Primate Laboratory." *American Scientist* 59: 538–550.
Harlow, M. K., and H. F. Harlow. 1966. "Affection in Primates." *Discovery* 27:11–17.
Harman, G. H. 1971. "Three Levels of Meaning." In *Semantics*, ed. D. Steinberg and L. Jakobovits. Cambridge: Cambridge University Press.
Harner, M. J. 1973. *Hallucinogens and Shamanism*. Oxford: Oxford University Press.
———. 1980. *The Way of the Shaman*. New York: Bantam Books.
Harvey, O. J., et al. 1961. *Conceptual Systems and Personality Organization*. New York: Wiley.
Hatten, M. E., and J. C. Edmondson. 1988. "Mechanisms of Neuron-Glia Interactions in Vitro." In *From Message to Mind: Directions in Developmental Neurobiology*, eds. S. S. Easter, K. J. Barold, and B. M. Carlson. Sunderland, Mass.: Sinauer Association.
Haug, H. 1972. "Steriological Methods in the Analysis of Neuronal Parameters in the Central Nervous System." *Journal of Microscopy* 95 (1): 165–180.
Hawkes, T. 1977. *Structuralism and Semiotics*. Berkeley, Calif.: University of California Press.
Hayward, J. 1984. *Perceiving Ordinary Magic*. Boston: Shambhala.
Hebb, D. O. 1949. *The Organization of Behavior*. New York: Wiley.
———. 1968. "Concerning Imagery." *Psychological Review* 75 (6): 466–477.
Herrnstein, R. J. 1982. "Stimuli and the Texture of Experience." *Neuroscience and Biobehavioral Reviews* 6:105–117.
Hertz, R. [1909] 1960. *Death and the Right Hand*. Aberdeen, S. Dak.: Cohen and West.
Hess, W. R. 1925. *On the Relations between Psychic and Vegetative Functions*. Zurich: Schabe.
———. 1957. *Functional Organization of the Diencephalon*. New York: Grune and Stratton.
Hilgard, E. R. 1977. *Divided Consciousness: Multiple Controls in Human Thought and Action*. New York: Wiley.

Hilliard, R. D. 1973. Hemispheric Laterality Effects on a Facial Recognition Task in Normal Subjects." Cortex 9:246–258.

Hillman, D. J. 1987. "Dream Work and Field Work: Linking Cultural Anthropology and the Current Dream Work Movement." In *Variety of Dream Experience*, ed. M. Ullman and C. Limmer. New York: Continuum.

Hillman, J. 1979. *The Dream and the Underworld*. New York: Harper and Row.

Hinde, R. A. 1970. *Animal Behavior*. 2nd ed. New York: McGraw-Hill.

———. 1974. *Biological Bases of Human Social Behavior*. New York: McGraw-Hill.

———. 1982. *Ethology*. New York: Fontana Books.

Hirai, T. 1974. *Psychophysiology of Zen*. Tokyo: Igaku Shoin.

Hofer, M. A. 1974. "The Role of Early Experience in the Development of Autonomic Regulation." In *Limbic and Autonomic Nervous System Research*, ed. L. V. diCara. New York: Plenum.

Hoffman, J. W., et al. 1981. "Reduced Sympathetic Nervous System Responsivity Associated with the Relaxation Response." *Science* 215:190–192.

Holloway, R. L. 1968. "The Evolution of the Primate Brain: Some Aspects of Quantitative Relations." *Brain Research* 7 (2): 121–172.

———. 1972. "Australopithecine Endocasts, Brain Evolution in the Hominoidea, and a Model of Hominid Evolution." In *The Functional and Evolutionary Biology of Primates*, ed. R. Tuttle. Chicago: Aldine.

———. 1975. "The Role of Human Social Behavior in the Evolution of the Brain." 43rd James Arthur Lecture, 1973, American Museum of Natural History, New York.

Holloway, R. L., and M. C. de la Costa-Lareymondie. 1982. "Brain Endocast Asymmetry in Pongids and Hominids." *American Journal of Physical Anthropology* 58:101–110.

Holmes, D. S. 1984. "Meditation and Somatic Arousal Reduction." *American Psychologist* 39 (1): 1–10.

Horowitz, M. J. 1978. *Image Formation and Cognition*. 2nd ed. New York: Appleton-Century-Crofts.

Horton, R., and R. Finnegan 1973. *Modes of Thought: Essays on Thinking in Western and Non-Western Societies*. London: Faber and Faber.

Hubel, D. H., and T. N. Wiesel. 1962. "Receptive Fields, Binocular Interaction and Functional Architecture in the Cat's Visual Cortex." *Journal of Physiology* 160:106–154.

Hufford, D. J. 1982. *The Terror that Comes in the Night*. Philadelphia: University of Pennsylvania Press.

Huizinga, J. 1938. *Homo Ludens*. Boston: Beacon Press.

Husserl, E. 1931. *Ideas: General Introduction to Pure Phenomenology*. New York: The MacMillan Company.

———. 1964. *The Phenomenology of Internal Time-Consciousness*. Bloomington, Ind.: Indiana University Press.

———. 1967. *The Paris Lectures*, trans. with an introduction Peter Koestenbaum. The Hague: Martinus Nijhoff.

———. 1970. *The Crisis of European Sciences and Transcendental Phenomenology*. Evanston, Ill.: Northwestern University Press.

———. 1977. *Cartesian Meditations: An Introduction to Phenomenology*. The Hague: Martinus Nijhoff.

Hutchinson, G. E. 1957. "Concluding Remarks." *Quantitative Biology* 22:415–427.

———. 1965. "The Niche: An Abstractly Inhabited Hypervolume." In *The Ecological Theater and the Evolutionary Play*, ed. G. E. Hutchinson. New Haven, Conn.: Yale University Press.

Ihde, D. 1971. *Hermeneutic Phenomenology: The Philosophy of Paul Ricoeur*. Evanston, Ill.: Northwestern University Press.

———. 1983. *Existential Technics*. Albany, N.Y.: State University of New York Press.

———. 1986. *Consequences of Phenomenology*. Albany, N.Y.: State University of New York Press.

Inhelder, B., and J. Piaget. 1958. *The Growth of Logical Thinking from Childhood to Adolescence*. New York: Basic Books.

Inhelder, B., et al. 1974. *Learning and the Development of Cognition*. Cambridge: Harvard University Press.

Ishihara, T., and N. Yoshii. 1972. "Theta Rhythm in the Mid-Frontal Region During Mental Work." *Electroencephalography and Clinical Neurophysiology* 35:701.

Jacobs, L. 1976. "Serotonin: The Crucial Substance that Turns Dreams On and Off." *Psychology Today* (March): 70–71.

Jacobson, E. 1938. *Progressive Relaxation*. Chicago: University of Chicago Press.

Jacobson, M. 1978. *Developmental Neurobiology*. 2nd ed. New York: Plenum.

Jakobson, R. 1971. "Results of a Joint Conference of Anthropologists and Linguists." In *Selected Writings by Roman Jakobson*. Vol. 2. The Hague: Mouton.

James, E. O. 1962. *Prehistoric Religion*. New York: Barnes and Noble.

James, W. [1890] 1981. *The Principles of Psychology*. Cambridge: Harvard University Press.

———. [1902] 1963. *Varieties of Religious Experience*. New York: University Books.

Janov, A. 1972. *The Primal Revolution*. New York: Simon and Schuster.

Jantsch, E. 1981. "Unifying Principles of Evolution." In *The Evolutionary Vision*, ed. E. Jantsch. Boulder, Colo.: Westview Press.

Jantsch, E., and C. H. Waddington. 1976. *Evolution and Consciousness: Human Systems in Transition*. Reading, Mass.: Addison-Wesley.

Jay, P. 1965. "The Common Langur of North India." In *Primitive Behavior*, ed. I. DeVore. New York: Holt, Rinehart and Winston.

Jaynes, J. 1976. *The Origin of Consciousness in the Breakdown of the Bicameral Mind*. Boston: Houghton Mifflin.

Jerison, H. J. 1973. *Evolution of the Brain and Intelligence*. New York: Academic Press.

———. 1985. "On the Evolution of Mind." In *Brain and Mind*, ed. D. A. Oakley. New York: Methuen.

Jevning, R., A. F. Wilson, and J. P. O'Halloran. 1978. "Behavioral Increase of Cerebral Blood Flow." *Physiologist* 21:60.

———. 1982. "Muscle and Skin Blood Flow and Metabolism During States of Decreased Activation." *Physiology and Behavior* 29:343–348.

Jilek, W. G. 1982. *Indian Healing*. Surrey, B.C.: Hancock House.

John, E. R. 1967. *Mechanisms of Memory*. New York: Academic Press.

John, E. R., et al. 1967. "Effects of Visual Form on the Evoked Response." *Science* 155:1439–1442.

John-Steiner, V. 1985. *Notebooks of the Mind: Explorations of Thinking.* Albuquerque, N.M.: University of New Mexico Press.

Johnson-Laird, P. N. 1983. *Mental Model: Towards a Cognitive Science of Language, Inference, and Consciousness.* Cambridge: Harvard University Press.

Johnston, W. 1978. *The Inner Eye of Love.* London: Fount Paperbacks.

Jones, E. E., et al. 1972. *Attribution: Perceiving the Causes of Behavior.* Morristown, N.J.: General Learning Press.

Jones, E. G., and T. P. S. Powell. 1970. "An Anatomical Study of Converging Sensory Pathways within the Cerebral Cortex of the Monkey." *Brain* 93:793–820.

Jorgensen, J. G. 1972. *The Sun Dance Religion.* Chicago: University of Chicago Press.

Jouandet, M., and M. S. Gazzaniga. 1979. "The Frontal Lobes." In *Handbook of Behavioral Neurobiology,* ed. M. S. Gazzaniga. Vol. 2. New York: Plenum.

Jouvet, M. 1975. "The Function of Dreaming: A Neurophysiologist's Point of View." In *Handbook of Psychobiology,* ed. M. S. Gazzaniga and C. Blakemore. New York: Academic Press.

Jung, C. G. 1955. *Mysterium Coniunctionis.* London: Routledge and Kegan Paul.

———. 1966. "Principles of Practical Psychotherapy." In *The Practice of Psychotherapy.* Princeton, N.J.: Princeton University Press.

———. 1968a. *Analytical Psychology.* New York: Pantheon Books.

———. 1968b. *The Archetypes and the Collective Unconscious.* Princeton, N.J.: Princeton University Press.

———. 1969. *Mandala Symbolism.* Princeton, N.J.: Princeton University Press.

———. 1971. *Psychological Types.* Princeton, N.J.: Princeton University Press.

Jung, E. 1978. *Animus and Anima.* Zurich: Spring Publications.

Kachetkova, V. I. 1978. *Paleoneurology.* New York: Wiley.

Kakar, S. 1982. *Shamans, Mystics and Doctors: A Psychological Inquiry into India and Its Healing Traditions.* Boston: Beacon Press.

Kalidasa, Sri. 1977. *Raghuvamsa Mahakavya,* Canto 4, trans. T. K. Ramachandra Iyer. Kalpathi, India: R. S. Vadhyar and Sons.

Katz, R. 1976. "Education for Transcendence: !Kia-Healing with the Kalahari !Kung." In *Kalahari Hunter-Gatherers,* eds. R. B. Lee and I. DeVore. Cambridge: Harvard University Press.

———. 1982. *Boiling Energy: Community Healing Among the Kalahari Kung.* Cambridge: Harvard University Press.

Kaufmann, F. 1974. *Nietzsche.* Princeton, N.J.: Princeton University Press.

Kawai, M. 1965. "Newly Acquired Precultural Behavior of the Natural Troop of Japanese Monkeys on Koshima Islet." *Primates* 6:1–30.

Keil, F. C. 1981. "Constraints on Knowledge and Cognitive Development." *Psychological Review* 88 (3): 197.

Kessen, W., M. M. Heath, and P. Salapatek. 1970. "Human Infancy: A Bibliography and Guide." In *Carmichael's Manual of Child Psychology,* ed. P. Mussen. New York: Wiley.

Keyes, D. 1981. *The Minds of Billy Milligan.* New York: Bantam Books.

Kilborne, B. 1974. "Dream Symbols and Culture Patterns: The Dream and Its Interpretation in Morocco." Ph.D. diss., Université de Paris.

Kimura, D. 1973. "The Asymmetry of the Human Brain." *Scientific American* 228 (3): 70–78.

Kirk, V. 1983. *Neuropsychology of Language, Reading and Spelling.* New York: Academic Press.

Kiyota, M. 1978. *Shingon Buddhism.* Los Angeles: Buddhist Books International.

Kleinman, A. 1980. *Patients and Healers in the Context of Culture.* Berkeley, Calif.: University of California Press.

Klopf, A. H. 1982. *The Hedonistic Neuron: A Theory of Memory, Learning and Intelligence.* New York: Hemisphere Publishing Co.

Kluver, H. 1966. *Mescal and Mechanisms of Hallucinations.* Chicago: University of Chicago Press.

Knight, G. 1965. *A Practical Guide to Qabalistic Symbolism.* New York: Samuel Weiser.

Kockelmans, J. J. 1967. *Phenomenology: The Philosophy of Edmund Husserl and Its Interpretation.* Garden City, N.Y.: Doubleday.

Kohlberg, L. 1969. "Stage and Sequence: The Cognitive Developmental Approach to Socialization." In *Handbook of Socialization Theory and Research,* ed. D. Goslin. Chicago: Rand McNally.

———. 1981. *The Philosophy of Moral Development: Moral Stages and the Idea of Justice.* Vol. 1. New York: Harper and Row.

Kohlberg, L., and C. Gilligan. 1971. "The Adolescent as a Philosopher: The Discovery of the Self in a Postconventional World." *Daedalus* 100:1051–1086.

Köhler, W. 1927. *The Mentality of Apes.* 2nd ed. London: Routledge and Kegan Paul.

Krishna, G. 1971. *Kundalini: The Evolutionary Energy in Man.* Boston: Shambhala.

Kroeber, A. L. 1931. "The Culture-area and Age-area Concepts of Clark Wissler." In *Methods in Social Science,* ed. S. Rice. Chicago: University of Chicago Press.

Kuhlenbeck, H., and J. Gerlach. 1982. *The World of Philosophy.* Vol. 3, *The Human Brain and Its Universe.* New York: S. Karger.

Kuhn, T. S. 1970. "Logic of Discovery or Psychology of Research." In *Criticism and the Growth of Knowledge,* eds. I. Lakatos and A. Musgrave. Cambridge: Cambridge University Press.

———. 1974. "Second Thoughts on Paradigms." In *The Structure of Scientific Theories,* ed. F. Suppe. Urbana, Ill.: University of Illinois Press.

Kummer, H. 1968. *Social Organization of Hamadryas Baboons.* Basel, Switzerland: S. Karger.

Kurland, J. A., and S. J. Beckerman. 1985. "Optional Foraging and Hominid Evolution: Labor and Reciprocity." *American Anthropologist* 87:73–93.

LaBerge, S. P. 1981. "Lucid Dreaming: Directing Action as it Happens." *Psychology Today* 15 (1): 48–57.

LaBerge, S. P., et al. 1981. "Lucid Dreaming Verified by Volitional Communication During REM Sleep." *Perceptual and Motor Skills* 52:727–732.

Ladavas, E., et al. 1980. "Evidence for Sex Differences in Right-Hemisphere Dominance for Emotions." *Neuropsychologia* 18:361–366.

Laing, R. D. 1967. *The Politics of Experience*. Baltimore: Penguin Books.

————. 1982. *The Voice of Experience*. London: Allen Lane.

Landes, T., et al. 1979. "Opposite Cerebral Hemispheric Superiorities for Visual Associative Processing of Emotional Facial Expressions and Objects." *Nature* 178:739–740.

Lang, A. [1894] 1896. *Cock Lane and Common Sense*. New York: AMS Press.

————. 1897. *The Book of Dreams and Ghosts*. London.

————. 1898. *The Making of Religion*. New York: AMS Press.

Langstaff, E. deS. 1978. *Andrew Lang*. Boston: Twayne Publishers.

Langworthy, V. R. 1933. "Development of Behavior Patterns and Myelinization of the Nervous System in the Human Fetus and Infant." *Contributions to Embryology* 24:139. Washington: Carnegie Institute.

Larroche, J. C. 1966. "The Development of the Central Nervous System During Intrauterine Life." In *Human Development*, ed. F. Falkner. Philadelphia: W. B. Saunders.

Lashley, K. S. 1942. "The Problems of Cerebral Organization in Vision." In *Biological Symposia*, ed. H. Kluver. Vol. 7. Lancaster, Penn.: Jacques Cattell Press.

L'at, J. 1967. "Nutrition, Learning and Adaptive Capacity." In *The Chemical Senses and Nutrition*, eds. M. R. Kare and O. Maller. Baltimore: Johns Hopkins.

Laughlin, C. D. 1973. "Causality and Transformational Law: A False Dichotomy." Paper presented at the annual meeting of the American Anthropological Association, New Orleans.

————. 1974. "Maximization, Marriage and Residence Among the So." *American Ethnologist* 1:129–141.

————. 1983. "Relaxation, Retuning and Flow: Some Neuropsychological Aspects of Stress Management." *Royal Canadian Mounted Police Gazette* 45 (10): 35–39.

————. 1984. "Methodological Issues in Transpersonal Anthropology." Paper presented at meeting of the Canadian Ethnological Society, Montreal, Canada.

————. 1985a. "On the Spirit of the Gift." *Anthropologica* 27 (1–2): 137–159.

————. 1985b. "Womb = Woman = World: Gender and Transcendence in Tibetan Tantric Buddhism." *The Pre- and Perinatal Psychology Journal* Spring: 18–26.

————. 1986. "Dots, Quanta, and the Necessity for the Phenomenological Reduction." Typescript.

————. 1988. "Time, Intentionality and a Neurophenomenology of the Dot." Typescript.

Laughlin, C. D., and I. A. Brady. 1978. *Extinction and Survival in Human Populations*. New York: Columbia University Press.

Laughlin, C. D., L. Chetelat, and R. Sekar. 1985. "Psychic Energy: A Biopsychological Explanation of a Cross-Cultural Transpersonal Experience." Paper presented at the annual meeting of Northeastern Anthropological Association, Lake Placid, N.Y.

Laughlin, C. D., and E. G. d'Aquili. 1973. "Human Universals: The Cognitive Evidence for Neurognostic Models." Typescript.

———. 1974. *Biogenetic Structuralism*. New York: Columbia University Press.

Laughlin, C. D., and J. McManus. 1975. "The Nature of Neurognosis." Typescript.

———. 1979. "Mammalian Ritual." In *The Spectrum of Ritual*, eds. E. G. d'Aquili et al. New York: Columbia University Press.

———. 1982. "The Biopsychological Determinants of Play and Games." In *Social Approaches to Sport*, ed. R. M. Pankin. Rutherford, N.J.: Fairleigh Dickinson University Press.

Laughlin, C. D., J. McManus, R. A. Rubinstein, and J. Shearer. 1986. "The Ritual Control of Experience." *Studies in Symbolic Interaction* 7, Part A, ed. N. K. Dengin. Greenwich, Conn.: JAI Press.

Laughlin, C. D., J. McManus, and J. Shearer. 1984. "Dreams, Trance and Visions: What a Transpersonal Anthropology Might Look Like." *Phoenix: The Journal of Transpersonal Anthropology* 7 (1/2): 141–159.

Laughlin, C. D., J. McManus, and C. D. Stephens. 1981. "A Model of Brain and Symbol." *Semiotica* 33 (3/4): 211–236.

Laughlin, C. D., J. McManus, and M. Webber. 1985. "Neurognosis, Individuation, and Tibetan Arising Yoga Practice." *Phoenix: The Journal of Transpersonal Anthropology* 8 (1/2): 91–106.

Laughlin, C. D., and S. Richardson. 1986. "The Future of Human Consciousness." *Futures* (June): 401–419.

Laughlin, C. D., and C. D. Stephens. 1980. "Symbolism, Canalization, and P-Structure." In *Symbol as Sense*, ed. M. L. Foster and S. Brandais. New York: Academic Press.

Leach, E. R. 1964. *Political Systems of Highland Burma*. Boston: Beacon Press.

———. 1976. *Culture and Communication*. Cambridge: Cambridge University Press.

Lederer, W. 1968. *The Fear of Women*. New York: Harcourt Brace Jovanovich.

LeDoux, J. E., and W. Hirst. 1986. *Mind and Brain: Dialogues in Cognitive Neuroscience*. Cambridge: Cambridge University Press.

Lee, R. B., and I. DeVore. 1968. *Man the Hunter*. Chicago: Aldine.

Lee, S. 1980. "Association for Transpersonal Anthropology." *Phoenix: The Journal of Transpersonal Anthropology* 4 (1/2): 2–6.

Leehey, S. C., and A. Cahn. 1981. "Lateral Asymmetries in the Recognition of Words, Familiar Faces and Unfamiliar Faces." *Neuropsychologia* 17:619–635.

Lenneberg, E. H. 1967. *Biological Foundations of Language*. New York: Wiley.

Levi-Strauss, C. 1964. *Mythologiques: Le Cru et le Cuit*. Paris: Plon.

———. 1966. *The Savage Mind*. Chicago: University of Chicago Press.

———. 1967. *Structural Anthropology*. Garden City, N.Y.: Doubleday.

———. 1969. *The Elementary Structures of Kinship*. Boston: Beacon Press.

———. 1971. *L'Homme Nu*. Paris: Plon.

———. 1976. *Structural Anthropology*. Vol. 2. New York: Basic Books.

———. 1978. *Myth and Meaning*. London: Routledge and Kegan Paul.

Levine, S. 1974. "Differential Response to Early Experience as a Function of Sex Difference." In *Sex Differences in Behavior*, eds. R. C. Friedman et al. New York: Wiley.

Levy, J. 1972. "Lateral Specialization of the Human Brain: Behavioral Manifestations and Possible Evolutionary Basis." In *The Biology of Behavior*, ed. J. A. Kiger. Corvallis, Oreg.: Oregon State University Press.

Levy-Agresti, J., and R. W. Sperry. 1968. "Differential Perceptual Capacities in Major and Minor Hemispheres." *Proceedings of the National Academy of Science* 61:1151–1154.

Levy-Bruhl, L. [1923] 1966. *Primitive Mentality*. Boston: Beacon Press.

Lewin, R. 1975. "Starved Brains." *Psychology Today* 9 (4): 29–33.

Lewis, C. S. 1965. *Screwtape Proposes a Toast*. Glasgow: William Collins Sons.

Lewis, I. M. 1971. *Ecstatic Religion*. Baltimore: Penguin Books.

———. 1977. *Symbols and Sentiments: Cross-Cultural Studies in Symbolism*. New York: Academic Press.

Lex, B. 1979. "The Neurobiology of Ritual Trance." In *The Spectrum of Ritual*, eds. E. G. d'Aquili et al. New York: Columbia University Press.

Ley, R. G., and M. P. Bryden. 1979. "The Right Hemisphere and Emotion." *Brain and Language* 7:127–138.

Leyrer, P. M. 1978. "Psychophysiological Effects of Progressive Relaxation in Anxiety Neurotic Patients and of Progressive Relaxation and Alpha Feedback in Non-Patients." *Journal of Consulting and Clinical Psychology* 46:389–404.

Liedloff, J. 1975. *The Continuum Concept*. London: Future Publications.

Liley, A. W. 1972. "The Foetus as a Personality." *Australia and New Zealand Journal of Psychiatry* 6:99–105.

Lincoln, J. S. 1935. *The Dream in Primitive Culture*. London: The Cresset Press.

Linden, E. 1974. *Apes, Men, and Language*. New York: E.P. Dutton.

Loizos, C. 1966. "Play in Mammals." In *Play, Exploration and Territory in Mammals*, ed. P. A. Jewell and C. Loizos. New York: Academic Press.

———. 1967. "Play Behavior in Higher Primates: A Review." In *Primate Ethology*, ed. D. Morris. Chicago: Aldine.

Lonergan, B. J. F. 1958. *Insight: A Study of Human Understanding*. New York: Harper and Row.

Luce, G. G. 1971. *Biological Rhythms and Human and Animal Physiology*. New York: Dover.

Luckiesh, M. [1922] 1965. *Visual Illusions: Their Causes, Characteristics and Applications*. New York: Dover.

Luria, A. R. [1947] 1970. *Traumatic Aphasia*. English ed. The Hague: Mouton.

———. 1966. *Higher Cortical Functions in Man*. New York: Basic Books.

———. 1973a. "The Frontal Lobes and the Regulation of Behavior." In *Psychophysiology of the Frontal Lobes*, ed. K. H. Pribram and A. R. Luria. New York: Academic Press.

———. 1973b. *The Working Brain*. New York: Basic Books.

Lyons, W. 1986. *The Disappearance of Introspection*. Cambridge: MIT Press.

McCall, R. J. 1983. *Phenomenological Psychology*. Madison, Wis.: University of Wisconsin Press.

MacCormack, C. P., and M. Strathern. 1980. *Nature, Culture and Gender*. Cambridge: Cambridge University Press.

McCulloch, W. S. 1965. *Embodiments of Mind*. Cambridge: MIT Press.

MacDonald, G. F. n.d. "Prehistoric Art of the North Coast." Manuscript.

MacDonald, G. F., J. Cove, C. D. Laughlin, and J. McManus. 1989. "Mirrors, Portals and Multiple Realities." *Zygon* 23 (4): 39–64.

MacDonald, J. L. 1981. "Theoretical Continuities in Transpersonal Anthropology." *Phoenix: The Journal of Transpersonal Anthropology* 5 (1): 31–47.

McKenna, W., R. M. Harlan, and L. E. Winters, eds. 1981. *Apriori and World: European Contributions to Husserlian Phenomenology*. The Hague: Martinus Nijhoff.

MacLean, P. D. 1958. "Contrasting Function of Limbic and Neocortical Systems of the Brain and their Relevance to Psychophysiological Aspects of Medicine." *American Journal of Medicine* 25:611–626.

———. 1973. *A Triune Concept of the Brain and Behavior*. Toronto: University of Toronto Press.

———. 1978. "The Evolution of Three Mentalities." In *Human Evolution: Biosocial Perspectives*, eds. S. L. Washburn and E. R. McCowan. Menlo Park, Calif.: Benjamine-Cummings.

McManus, J. 1979. "Ritual and Ontogenic Development." In *The Spectrum of Ritual*, eds. E. G. d'Aquili, C. D. Laughlin, and J. McManus. New York: Columbia University Press.

Mahasi Sayadaw. 1978. *The Progress of Insight: A Treatise on Buddhist Satipatthana Meditation*. Kandy, Sri Lanka: Buddhist Publication Society.

Malmo, R. B. 1975. *On Emotions, Needs and Our Archaic Brain*. New York: Holt, Rinehart and Winston.

Malraux, A. 1971. *Felled Oaks: Conversation with DeGaulle*. New York: Holt, Rinehart and Winston.

Mandler, G. 1984. *Mind and Body: Psychology of Emotion and Stress*. New York: Norton.

Marshack, A. 1972. "Cognitive Aspects of Upper Paleolithic Engraving." *Current Anthropology* 13 (3–4): 445–477.

———. 1976. "Some Implications for the Paleolithic Symbolic Evidence for the Origin of Language." *Current Anthropology* 17 (2): 274–282.

Mascaro, J. 1965. *The Upanishads*. Baltimore: Penguin Books.

Maslow, A. H. 1968. *Toward a Psychology of Being*. 2nd ed. Princeton, N.J.: Van Nostrand.

———. 1969. "Theory Z." *Journal of Transpersonal Psychology* 1 (2): 31–47.

———. 1971. *The Farther Reaches of Human Nature*. New York: Viking.

Maturana, H. R., and F. J. Varela. 1987. *The Tree of Knowledge: The Biological Roots of Human Understanding*. Boston: Shambhala.

Maury, A. 1848. "Des hallucinations hypnagogiques ou du erreurs du sens dans l'état intermediare entre la veille et le sommeil." *Annales Medico-Psychologiques du System Nerveux* 11:26–40.

Mauss, M. 1969. *The Gift*. London: Cohen and West.

Mead, G. H. [1934] 1962. *Mind, Self, and Society*. Vol. 1. Chicago: University of Chicago Press.

Meltzoff, A., and M. K. Moore. 1977. "Imitation of Facial and Manual Gestures by Human Neonates." *Science* (Oct. 7): 75–78.

Menzel, E. W. 1963. "The Effects of Cumulative Experience on Responses to Novel Objects in Young Isolation-Reared Chimpanzees." *Behavior* 23:14–26.

————. 1966. "Responsiveness to Objects in Free-Ranging Japanese Monkeys." *Behavior* 26:130–150.

————. 1967. "Naturalistic and Experimental Research on Primates." *Human Development* 10:170–186.

————. 1968. "Primate Naturalistic Research and Problems of Early Experience." *Developmental Psychobiology* 1:175–184.

————. 1972. "Protocultural Aspects of Chimpanzee's Responsiveness to Novel Objects." *Folia Primatologica* 17:161–170.

Menzel, E. W., et al. 1963. "Effects of Environmental Restriction upon the Chimpanzee's Responsiveness in Novel Situations." *Journal of Comparative and Physiobiological Psychology* 56:329–334.

Menzel, E. W., et al. 1970. "The Development of Tool Using in Wild-Born and Restriction-Reared Chimpanzees." *Folia Primatologica* 12:273–283.

Merchant, C. 1980. *The Death of Nature*. New York: Harper and Row.

Merleau-Ponty, M. 1962. *Phenomenology of Perception*. London: Routledge and Kegan Paul.

————. 1964. *The Primacy of Perception*. Evanston, Ill.: Northwestern University Press.

————. 1968. *The Visible and the Invisible*. Evanston, Ill.: Northwestern University Press.

Merrell-Wolff, F. 1973a. *The Philosophy of Consciousness Without an Object*. New York: The Julian Press.

————. 1973b. *Pathways Through to Space: An Experiential Journal*. New York: The Julian Press.

Miller, G. A., E. H. Galanter, and K. H. Pribram. 1960. *Plans and the Structure of Behavior*. New York: Holt, Rinehart and Winston.

Miller, G. A., and D. McNeil. 1969. "Psycholinguistics." In *The Handbook of Social Psychology*, eds. G. Linzey and E. Arson. Vol. 3. Reading, Mass.: Addison-Wesley.

Miller, I. 1984. *Husserl, Perception, and Temporal Awareness*. Cambridge: MIT Press.

Miller, J. G. 1978. *Living Systems*. New York: McGraw-Hill.

Miller, N. 1969. "Learning of Visceral and Glandular Responses." *Science* 163:439–445.

Miller, S. 1973. "Ends, Means and Galumphing: Some Leitmotifs of Play." *American Anthropologist* 75:87–98.

Mills, L., and G. B. Rollman. 1980. "Hemispheric Asymmetry for Auditory Perception of Temporal Order." *Neuropsychologia* 18:41–47.

Milosz, C. 1953. *The Captive Mind*. New York: Vintage Books.

Mindell, A. 1982. *Dreambody: The Body's Role in Revealing the Self*. Santa Monica, Calif.: Sigo Press.

Mishkin, M., et al. 1977. "Kinesthetic Discrimination after Prefrontal Lesions in Monkeys." *Brain Research* 130:163–168.

Mitchell, R. C. 1977. *African Primal Religions*. Niles, Ill.: Argus Communications.

Mizuki, Y., et al. 1980. "Periodic Appearance of Theta Rhythm in the Frontal Midline Area During Performance of a Mental Task." *Electroencephalography and Clinical Neurophysiology* 49:345–351.

————. 1983. "The Relationship Between the Appearance of Frontal Midline

Theta Activity (Fm) and Memory Function." *Electroencephalography and Clinical Neurophysiology: Japan EEG/EMG Society Proceedings* 56 (5): 56.

Moerman, D. E. 1979. "Anthropology of Symbolic Healing." *Current Anthropology* 20 (1): 59–80.

Mohanty, J. N. 1972. *The Concept of Intentionality*. St. Louis, Mo.: Warren H. Green.

Molfese, D. L. 1976. "Cerebral Asymmetry: Changes in Factors Affecting its Development." In *The Origins and Evolution of Language and Speech*, eds. S. Harnad et al. Annals of the New York Academy of Sciences 280.

Montagu, A. 1975. *The Practice of Love*. Englewood Cliffs, N.J.: Prentice-Hall.

Mookerjee, A. 1982. *Kundalini: The Arousal of the Inner Energy*. New York: Destiny Books.

Moran, H. A., and D. H. Kelley. 1969. *The Alphabet and the Ancient Calendar Signs*. Palo Alto, Calif.: Dailey Press.

Morgenson, G. J., and E. R. Calaresu, eds. 1975. *Neural Integration of Physiological Mechanisms and Behavior*. Toronto: University of Toronto Press.

Morris, D. 1964. "The Response of Animals to a Restricted Environment." *Symposium of the Zoological Society* 13:99–118.

Motoyama, H., and R. Brown. 1978. *Science and the Evolution of Consciousness*. Brookline, Mass.: Autumn Press.

Mountcastle, V. B. 1957. "Modality and Topographic Properties of Single Neurons of Cat's Somatic Sensory Cortex." *Journal of Neurophysiology* 20:408–434.

Mountcastle, V. B., et al. 1975. "Posterior Parietal Association Cortex of the Monkey: Command Functions for Operations within Extrapersonal Space." *Journal of Neurophysiology* 38:871–908.

Movromatis, A. 1987. *Hypnagogia: The Unique State of Consciousness Between Wakefulness and Sleep*. New York: Routledge and Kegan Paul.

Munn, N. 1973a. "The Spatial Presentation of Cosmic Order in Walbiri Iconography." In *Primitive Art and Society*, ed. A. Forge. London: Oxford University Press.

———. 1973b. *Walbiri Iconography*. Ithaca, N.Y.: Cornell University Press.

Murphy, M., and S. Donovan. 1983. "A Bibliography of Meditation Theory and Research: 1931–1983." *Journal of Transpersonal Psychology* 15 (2): 181–228.

Myers, J. W. H. 1904. *Human Personality and Its Survival of Bodily Death*. London: Longmans Green.

Nanananda, B. 1976. *Concept and Reality in Early Buddhist Thought*. Kandy, Sri Lanka: Buddhist Publication Society.

Nanaroma Mahathera, M. S. 1983. *The Seven Stages of Purification and the Insight Knowledges*. Kandy, Sri Lanka: Buddhist Publication Society.

Narada Maha Thera. 1975. *A Manual of Abhidharma*. Kandy, Sri Lanka: Buddhist Publication Society.

Naranjo, C., and R. E. Ornstein. 1971. *On the Psychology of Meditation*. New York: Viking.

Nauta, W. J. H. 1971. "The Problem of the Frontal Lobe: A Reinterpretation." *Journal of Psychiatric Research* 8:167–187.

———. 1973. "Connections of the Frontal Lobes with the Limbic System." In

Surgical Approaches in Psychiatry, eds. L. V. Leitinen and K. E. Livingston. Baltimore: University Park Press.

Nebes, R. D., and R. W. Sperry. 1971. "Hemispheric Disconnection Syndrome with Cerebral Birth Injury in the Dominant Arm Area." *Neuropsychologia* 9:247–259.

Needham, R. 1973. *Right and Left: Essays on Dual Symbolic Classification.* Chicago: University of Chicago Press.

Neisser, U. 1976. *Cognition and Reality: Principles and Implications of Cognitive Psychology.* San Francisco: Freeman.

Neumann, E. 1954. *The Origin and History of Consciousness.* Princeton, N.J.: Princeton University Press.

———. 1963. *The Great Mother.* Princeton, N.J.: Princeton University Press.

Niedermeyer, E. 1982. "Maturation of the EEG: Development of Waking and Sleep Patterns." In *Electroencephalography*, eds. E. Niedermeyer and F. L. da Silva. Baltimore: Urban and Schwarzenberg.

Nishitani, K. 1982. *Religion and Nothingness.* Berkeley, Calif.: University of California Press.

Noll, R. 1985. "Mental Imagery Cultivation as a Cultural Phenomenon: The Role of Visions in Shamanism." *Current Anthropology* 26 (4): 443–461.

Norback, C. R. 1967. *The Human Nervous System.* New York: McGraw-Hill.

Norbeck, E. 1974. "The Development of Peer-Mate Relationships in Japanese Macaque Infants." *Primates* 15:39–46.

Norman, D. A., and T. Shallice. 1986. "Attention to Action: Willed and Automatic Control of Behavior." In *Consciousness and Self-Regulation*, eds. R. J. Davidson et al. Vol. 4. New York: Plenum.

Obrador, S. 1964. "Nervous Integration after Hemispherectomy in Man." In *Cerebral Localization and Organization*, eds. G. Schaltenbrand and C. N. Woolsey. Madison, Wis.: University of Wisconsin Press.

O'Nell, C. W. 1976. *Dreams, Culture and the Individual.* San Francisco: Chandler and Sharp.

Ornstein, R. E. 1973. *The Nature of Human Consciousness.* San Francisco: W. H. Freeman.

Ortner, S. B. 1973. "On Key Symbols." *American Anthropologist* 75 (5): 1338–1346.

———. 1974. "Is Female to Male as Nature is to Culture?" In *Woman, Culture and Society*, eds. M. Z. Rosaldo and L. Lamphere. Stanford, Calif.: Stanford University Press.

Owens, N. W. 1975. "Social Play Behavior in Free-Living Baboons, Papio anubis." *Animal Behavior* 23:387–408.

Pagano, R. R., and S. Warrenburg. 1983. "Meditation: In Search of a Unique Effect." In *Consciousness and Self-Regulation*, eds. R. J. Davidson, G. E. Schwartz, and D. Shapiro. Vol. 3. New York: Plenum.

Pagels, H. R. 1982. *The Cosmic Code.* New York: Bantam Books.

Passingham, R. E. 1973. "Anatomical Differences Between the Neocortex of Man and Other Primates." *Brain Behavior Evolution* 7:337–359.

Paul, R. A. 1982. *The Tibetan Symbolic World.* Chicago: University of Chicago Press.

Peacock, J. L. 1975. *Consciousness and Change*. Oxford: Basil Blackwell.

Peckham, M. 1965. *Man's Rage for Chaos*. Philadelphia: Clifton Books.

Penfield, W. 1952. "Epileptic Automatism and the Centrencephalic Integrating System." *Association Research Nervous Mental Disease* 30:513–528.

——. 1975. *The Mystery of the Mind*. Princeton, N.J.: Princeton University Press.

Pepper, R. L., and P. A. Beach. 1972. "Preliminary Investigation of Tactile Reinforcement in the Dolphin." *Cetology* 7:1–8.

Perinbanayagam, R. S. 1982. *The Karmic Theater: Self, Society, and Astrology in Jaffna*. Amherst, Mass.: The University of Massachusetts Press.

Peterson, A. C. 1980. "Biopsychosocial Processes in the Development of Sex-Related Differences." In *The Psychobiology of Sex Differences*, ed. J. E. Parsons. New York: Hemisphere.

Pfeiffer, J. E. 1982. *The Creative Explosion*. New York: Harper and Row.

Piaget, J. 1952. *The Origins of Intelligence in Children*. New York: International Universities Press.

——. 1962. *Play, Dreams and Imitation in Childhood*. New York: Norton.

——. 1966. "Response to Brian Sutton-Smith." *Psychological Review* 73:111–112.

——. 1970. *Structuralism*. New York: Harper and Row.

——. 1971a. *Biology and Knowledge*. Chicago: University of Chicago Press.

——. 1971b. *Mental Imagery in the Child*. London: Routledge and Kegan Paul.

——. 1973. *Main Trends in Psychology*. London: Allen.

——. 1975. *The Child's Conception of the World*. Totowa, N.J.: Littlefield, Adams and Co.

——. 1976. *The Grasp of Consciousness*. Cambridge: Harvard University Press.

——. 1977. *The Development of Thought*. New York: Viking Press.

——. 1980. *Adaptation and Intelligence*. Chicago: University of Chicago Press.

Piaget, J., and B. Inhelder. 1969. *The Psychology of the Child*. New York: Basic Books.

——. 1975. *The Origin of the Idea of Chance in Children*. New York: Norton.

Pick, A. D. 1979. *Perception and Its Development*. New York: John Wiley.

Piddocke, S. 1965. "The Potlatch System of the Southern Kwakiutl: A New Perspective." *Southwestern Journal of Anthropology* 21:244–264.

Pigeau, R. A. 1985. "Psychophysiology and Cognition." Ph.D. diss., Department of Psychology, Carleton University, Ottawa, Ont.

Ploye, P. M. 1973. "Does Prenatal Mental Life Exist?" *International Journal of Psycho-Analysis* 54:241–246.

Pohl, W. 1973. "Dissociation of Spatial Discrimination Deficits Following Frontal and Parietal Lesions in Monkeys." *Journal of Comparative Physiological Psychology* 82:227–239.

Poirier, F. E. 1979. "Nilgiri Langur Ecology and Social Behavior." In *Primate Behavior*, ed. L. A. Rosenblum. New York: Academic Press.

Poirier, F. E., and E. O. Smith. 1974. "Socializing Functions of Primate Play." *American Zoologist* 14:275–287.

Polanyi, M. 1958. *Personal Knowledge*. Chicago: University of Chicago Press.

——. 1965. "The Structure of Consciousness." *Brain* 88:799–810.

Popper, K. R. 1972. *Objective Knowledge: An Evolutionary Approach*. Oxford: Oxford University Press.

Popper, K. R., and J. C. Eccles. 1977. *The Self and Its Brain*. New York: Springer International.

Powers, W. K. 1977. *Oglala Religion*. Lincoln, Neb.: University of Nebraska Press.

Powers, W. T. 1973. *Behavior: The Control of Perception*. Chicago: Aldine.

Premack, D. 1976. *Intelligence in Ape and Man*. Hillsdale, N.J.: Lawrence Erlbaum.

Presley, C. F. 1967. *The Identity Theory of Mind*. Brisbane: Blackie.

Preston, R. 1975. "Cree Narrative: Expressing the Personal Meanings of Events." *Canadian Ethnology Service Paper* 30. Ottawa: National Museum of Man.

Pribram, K. H. 1971. *Languages of the Brain*. Englewood Cliffs, N.J.: Prentice-Hall.

———. 1976. "Self-Consciousness and Intentionality." In *Consciousness and Self-Regulation*, eds. G. E. Schwartz and D. Shapiro. Vol. 1. New York: Plenum.

———. 1977. "Observations on the Organization of Studies of Mind, Brain, and Behavior." In *Alternate States of Consciousness*, ed. N. Zinbert. New York: Free Press.

———. 1978. "On Behalf of the Neurosciences." *The Behavioral and Brain Sciences* 1:113.

———. 1981. "Emotions." In *Handbook of Clinical Neuropsychology*, eds. S. K. Filskov and T. J. Boll. New York: Wiley.

Pribram, K. H., and A. R. Luria. 1973. *Psychophysiology of the Frontal Lobes*. New York: Academic Press.

Pribram, K. H., and D. McGuinness. 1975. "Arousal, Activation, and Effort in the Control of Attention." *Psychological Review* 82:116–149.

Price-Williams, D. 1987. "The Waking Dream in Ethnographic Perspective." In *Dreaming: Anthropological and Psychological Interpretations*, ed. B. Tedlock. Cambridge: Cambridge University Press.

Prigogine, I. 1980. *From Being to Becoming*. San Francisco: Freeman.

Prigogine, I., and I. Stengers. 1984. *Order Out of Chaos: Man's New Dialogue with Nature*. New York: Bantam Books.

Puccetti, R. 1973. "Brain Bisection and Personal Identity." *British Journal of the Philosophy of Science* 24:339–355.

Qualls, P., and P. Sheehan. 1981. "Imagery Encouragement, Absorption Capacity, and Relaxation During Electromyograph Biofeedback." *Journal of Personality and Social Psychology* 4 (2): 370–377.

Radhakrishnan, S., and C. A. Moore. 1957. *A Source Book in Indian Philosophy*. Princeton, N.J.: Princeton University Press.

Radin, P. 1927. *Primitive Man as Philosopher*. New York: Dover.

Raikov, V. L. 1980. "Age Regression to Infancy by Adult Subjects in Deep Hypnosis." *American Journal of Clinical Hypnosis* 22 (3): 156–163.

Rakic, P. 1976. *Local Circuit Neurons*. Cambridge: MIT Press.

Randhawa, B. S. 1978. *Visual Learning, Thinking and Communication*. New York: Academic Press.

Rappaport, R. A. 1968. *Pigs for the Ancestors*. New Haven, Conn.: Yale University Press.

Rasmussen, D. M. 1971. *Mythic-Symbolic Language and Philosophical Anthropology*. The Hague: Martinus Nijhoff.

Ratcliff, G. 1979. "Spatial Thought, Mental Rotation and the Right Cerebral Hemisphere." *Neuropsychologia* 17:49–54.

Reagan, C. E., and D. Stewart, eds. 1978. *The Philosophy of Paul Ricoeur.* Boston: Beacon Press.

Redican, W. K., and G. Mitchell. 1974. "Play Between Adult Male and Infant Rhesus Monkeys." *American Zoologist* 14:295–302.

Reed, H. 1973. "Learning to Remember Dreams." *Journal of Humanistic Psychology* 13 (3): 33–48.

———. 1976. "Dream Incubation: A Reconstruction of a Ritual in Contemporary Form." *Journal of Humanistic Psychology* 16 (4).

Reichel-Dolmatoff, G. 1971. *Amazonian Cosmos.* Chicago: University of Chicago Press.

Renner, M. J., and M. R. Rosenzweig. 1987. *Enriched and Impoverished Environments.* New York: Springer-Verlag.

Richards, J., and E. von Glasersfeld. 1979. "The Control of Perception and the Construction of Reality." *Dialectica* 33 (1): 37–58.

Richmond, J. B., and S. L. Lustman. 1955. "Autonomic Function in the Neonate: Implications for Psychosomatic Theory." *Psychosomatic Medicine* 17:269ff.

Ricoeur, P. 1962. "The Hermeneutics of Symbols and Philosophical Reflection." *International Philosophical Quarterly* 2 (2): 191–218.

———. 1967a. *Husserl: An Analysis of His Phenomenology.* Evanston, Ill.: Northwestern University Press.

———. 1967b. "New Developments in Phenomenology in France: The Phenomenology of Language." *Social Research* 34:1–30.

———. 1967c. *The Symbolism of Evil.* New York: Harper and Row.

———. 1968. "Structure, Word, Event." *Philosophy Today* 12 (2–4): 14–38.

Ridington, R., and T. Ridington. 1970. "The Inner Eye of Shamanism and Totemism." *History of Religions* 10 (1): 49–61.

Rieber, R. W., ed. 1976. *The Neuropsychology of Language.* New York: Plenum.

Ring, K. 1974. "A Transpersonal View of Consciousness: A Mapping of Farther Regions of Inner Space." *Journal of Transpersonal Psychology* 6 (2): 125–155.

———. 1976. "Mapping the Regions of Consciousness: A Conceptual Reformulation." *Journal of Transpersonal Psychology* 8 (2): 77–88.

Roe, Peter G. 1982. *The Cosmic Zygote: Cosmology in the Amazon Basin.* New Brunswick, N.J.: Rutgers University Press.

Roffwarg, H. P., et al. 1962. "Dream Imagery: Relationship to Rapid Eye Movements of Sleep." *Archives of General Psychiatry* 7:235–258.

Roland, P. E. 1982. "Cortical Regulation of Selective Attention in Man: A Regional Cerebral Blood Flow Study." *Journal of Neurophysiology* 48 (5): 1059–1078.

Rosch, E. 1977. "Human Categorization." In *Studies in Cross-Cultural Psychology,* ed. N. Warren. Vol. 1. New York: Academic Press.

Rose, J. E., and C. N. Woolsey. 1949. "The Relations of Thalamic Connections, Cellular Structure and Evocable Electrical Activity in the Auditory Region of the Cat." *Journal of Comparative Neurology* 91:441–466.

Rosenzweig, M. R., et al. 1962. "Effects of Environmental Complexity and Training on Brain Chemistry and Anatomy: A Replication and Extension." *Journal of Comparative and Physiological Psychology* 55:429–437.

———. 1972. "Brain Changes in Response to Experience." *Scientific American* (March): 22–29.

Rouch, J. 1960. *La religion et la Magie Songhay*. Paris: Presses Universitaires de France.

Rouget, G. 1985. *Music and Trance: A Theory of the Relations Between Music and Possession*. Chicago: University of Chicago Press.

Rubinstein, R. A. 1983. "Structuralism and the Study of Cognitive Process." In *The Future of Structuralism*, eds. J. Oosten and A. DeRuijter. Gottingen-Geismar, West Germany: Edition Herodot.

Rubinstein, R. A., and C. D. Laughlin. 1977. "Bridging Levels of Systemic Organization." *Current Anthropology* 18:459–481.

Rubinstein, R. A., C. D. Laughlin, and J. McManus. 1984. *Science as Cognitive Process*. Philadelphia: University of Pennsylvania Press.

Ruppenthal, G. C., et al. 1974. "Development of Peer Interactions of Monkeys Reared in a Nuclear-Family Environment." *Child Development* 45:670–682.

Ryle, G. 1949. *The Concept of Mind*. New York: Barnes and Noble.

Sade, D. S. n.d. "Latent Processes and the Biological Bases of Social Organization." Manuscript.

———. 1973. "An Ethogram for Rhesus Monkeys: I. Antithetical Contrasts in Posture and Movement." *American Journal of Physical Anthropology* 38:537–542.

———. 1974. "The Vertebrate Ego." Paper presented at the annual meeting of the American Anthropological Association, Mexico City.

Sahlins, M. 1965. "On the Sociology of Primitive Exchange." In *The Relevance of Models for Social Anthropology*, ed. M. Banton. London: Tavistock.

Salk, L. 1973. "The Role of the Heartbeat in the Relations Between Mother and Infant." *Scientific American* 228 (5): 24–29.

Sargant, W. 1974. *The Mind Possessed*. New York: Lippincott.

Sarnat, H. B., and M. G. Netsky. 1974. *Evolution of the Nervous System*. New York: Oxford University Press.

Sawaguchi, T., and K. Kubota. 1986. "A Hypothesis on the Primate Neocortex Evolution: Column-Multiplication Hypothesis." *International Journal of Neuroscience* 30:57–64.

Schacter, D. L. 1977. "EEG Theta Waves and Psychological Phenomena: A Review and Analysis." *Biological Psychology* 5:47–82.

Schacter, D. L., and J. E. Singer. 1962. "Cognitive, Social and Physiological Determinants of Emotional State." *Psychological Review* 69:379–399.

Schaller, G. B. 1963. *The Mountain Gorilla*. Chicago: University of Chicago Press.

Schatzman, M. 1980. *The Story of Ruth*. Don Mills, Ont.: General Publishing Co.

Schechner, R. 1985. *Between Theater and Anthropology*. Philadelphia: University of Pennsylvania Press.

Schell, L. M. 1981. "Environmental Noise and Human Prenatal Growth." *American Journal of Physical Anthropology* 56:63–70.

Schmidt, S. J. 1976. *Texttheorie*. Munich: Wilhelm Fink.

Schneider, D. M. 1968. *American Kinship: A Cultural Account*. Englewood Cliffs, N.J.: Prentice-Hall.

Schneider, D. M., et al., eds. 1977. *Symbolic Anthropology*. New York: Columbia University Press.

Schreiber, F. R. 1974. *Sybil*. New York: Warner Books.

Schroder, H. M., M. Driver, and S. Streufert. 1967. *Human Information Processing*. New York: Holt, Rinehart and Winston.

Schumacher, J. A. n.d. "The Quantum Mechanics of Vision." Typescript.

Schuman, M. 1980. "The Psychophysiological Model of Meditation and Altered States of Consciousness: A Critical Review." In *The Psychobiology of Consciousness*, eds. J. M. Davidson and R. J. Davidson. New York: Plenum.

Schussler, G. C., and J. Orlando. 1978. "Fasting Decreases Triiodothyronine Receptor Capacity." *Science* 199:686–688.

Schutz, A. 1945. "On Multiple Realities." *Philosophical and Phenomenological Research* 5:533–576.

———. 1964. "Symbol, Reality and Society." In *Symbols and Society*, eds. L. Bryson et al. New York: Cooper Square.

Schutz, A., and T. Luckman. 1973. *The Structures of the Life-World*. London: Heinemann.

Schwartz, G. E., R. J. Davidson, and D. Goleman. 1978. "Patterning of Cognitive and Somatic Processes in the Self-Regulation of Anxiety: Effects of Meditation Versus Exercise." *Psychosomatic Medicine* 40 (4): 321–328.

Schwartz, G. E. and D. Shapiro. 1978. *Consciousness and Self-Regulation*. New York: Plenum.

Searle, J. R. 1983. *Intentionality: An Essay in the Philosophy of Mind*. Cambridge: Cambridge University Press.

Sebeok, T. A., and A. Ramsay. 1969. *Approaches to Animal Communication*. The Hague: Mouton.

Secord, P. F., ed. 1982. *Explaining Human Behavior: Consciousness, Human Action and Social Structure*. Beverly Hills, Calif.: Sage Publications.

Seligman, M. 1971. "Phobias and Preparedness." *Behavior Therapy* 2:307–320.

———. 1979. "On the Generality of the Laws of Learning." *Psychological Review* 77:406–418.

Seligman, M., and J. Hager. 1972. *Biological Boundaries of Learning*. New York: Appleton-Century-Crofts.

Seligman, M. E. 1975. *Helplessness: On Development, Depression and Death*. San Francisco: Freeman.

Selye, H. 1956. *The Stress of Life*. New York: McGraw-Hill.

Shankweiler, D., and M. Studdert-Kennedy. 1967. "Identification of Consonants and Vowels Presented to Left and Right Ears." *Quarterly Journal of Experimental Psychology* 19:59–63.

Shapiro, D. H. 1983. "Meditation As an Altered State of Consciousness: Contributions of Western Behavioral Science." *Journal of Transpersonal Psychology* 15 (1): 61–81.

Sharon, D. 1978. *Wizard of the Four Winds*. New York: Free Press.

Shearer, J., et al. 1979. "Waking, Sleeping and Cross-Phase Transference." Paper presented at the annual meeting of the Canadian Ethnological Society, Banff, Alberta.

Sheldrake, R. 1981. *A New Science of Life: The Hypothesis of Formative Causation*. Los Angeles: J. P. Tarcher.

Shepard, R. N., and L. A. Cooper. 1982. *Mental Images and Their Transformations*. Cambridge: MIT Press.

Sherburne, D. W. [1966] 1981. *A Key to Whitehead's Process and Reality*. Chicago: University of Chicago Press.

Sherif, M. 1977. "Crisis in Social Psychology: Some Remarks Towards Breaking Through the Crisis." *Personality and Social Psychology Bulletin* 3:368–382.

Shneour, E. A. 1974. *The Malnourished Mind*. Garden City, N.Y.: Doubleday.

Siegel, R. K. 1977. "Hallucinations." *Scientific American* 237 (4): 132–140.

Silber, H. [1917] 1971. *Hidden Symbolism of Alchemy and the Occult Arts*. New York: Dover.

Silver, J., and M. Y. Ogawa. 1983. "Postnatally Induced Formation of the Corpus Callosum in Acallosal Mice on Glia-Coated Cellulose Bridges." *Science* 220:1067–1069.

Simon, H. A. 1980. "The Behavioral and Social Sciences." *Science* 209:72–78.

———. 1981. *The Sciences of the Artificial*. Cambridge: MIT Press.

Skinner, B. F. 1974. *About Behaviorism*. New York: Knopf.

Slade, P. D., and R. P. Bentall. 1988. *Sensory Deception: A Scientific Analysis of Hallucination*. Baltimore, Johns Hopkins University Press.

Snellgrove, D., and H. E. Richardson. 1968. *The Cultural History of Tibet*. New York: Praeger.

Sontag, L. W. 1941. "The Significance of Fetal Environmental Differences." *American Journal of Obstetrics and Gynecology* 42:996–1003.

Sorokin, P. A. 1941. *The Crisis of Our Age*. New York: E.P. Dutton.

Sperber, D. 1975. *Rethinking Symbolism*. Cambridge: Cambridge University Press.

Sperry, R. W. 1974. "Lateral Specialization in Surgically Separated Hemispheres." In *The Neurosciences: Third Study Program*, eds. P. J. Vinken and G. W. Bruyn. Cambridge: MIT Press.

———. 1982. "Some Effects of Disconnecting the Cerebral Hemispheres." *Science* 217:1223–1226.

Sperry, R. W., et al. 1979. "Self Recognition and Social Awareness in the Deconnected Minor Hemisphere." *Neuropsychologia* 17:153–166.

Spiro, M. 1969. "Discussion." In *Forms of Symbolic Action*, ed. R. F. Spencer. Proceedings of the American Ethnological Society. Seattle: University of Washington Press.

Stace, W. T. 1960. *Mysticism and Philosophy*. New York: Lippincott.

Stave, U. 1978. "Maturation, Adaptation, and Tolerance." In *Perinatal Physiology*, ed. U. Stave. New York: Plenum.

Stein, D. G., J. J. Rosen, and N. Butters. 1974. *Plasticity and Recovery of Function in the Central Nervous System*. New York: Academic Press.

Stein, R. A. 1972. *Tibetan Civilization*. Stanford, Calif.: Stanford University Press.

Steltzer, U. 1984. *Children of the Good People: A Haida Potlatch*. Vancouver, B.C.: Douglas and McIntyre.

Steptoe, A. 1978. "New Approaches to the Management of Essential Hypertension with Psychological Techniques." *Journal of Psychosomatic Research* 22:339–354.

Stierli, J. 1957. *Heart and Savior*. Freiberg, West Germany: Herder and Herder.

Stone, L. J., et al. 1973. *The Competent Infant*. New York: Basic Books.

Stroebel, C. F., and B. C. Glueck. 1978. "Passive Meditation: Subjective, Clinical, and Electrographic Comparison with Biofeedback." In *Consciousness and Self-Regulation*, eds. G. E. Schwartz and D. Shapiro. New York: Plenum.

Sturgeon, T. 1975. *More than Human*. New York: Garland Publishing Co.

Stuss, D. T., and D. F. Benson. 1986. *The Frontal Lobes*. New York: Raven.

Suberi, M., and W. McKeever. 1977. "Differential Right Hemispheric Memory Storage of Emotional and Non-Emotional Faces." *Neuropsychologia* 15:757–768.

Sugarman, M. 1977. "Perinatal Influences on Maternal-Infant Attachment." *American Journal of Orthopsychiatry* 48:407–421.

Sugiyama, Y. 1967. "Social Organization of Langurs." In *Social Communication Among Primates*, ed. S. Altman. Chicago: University of Chicago Press.

Sullivan, E. V., et al. 1970. "A Developmental Study of the Relation Between Conceptual, Ego and Moral Development." *Child Development* 41:399–412.

Suppe, F., ed. 1977. *The Structure of Scientific Theories*. 2nd ed. Urbana, Ill.: University of Illinois Press.

Sutich, A. J. 1968. "Transpersonal Psychology: An Emerging Force." *Journal of Humanistic Psychology* 8:77–79.

Suzuki, D. T. 1967. "An Interpretation of Zen Experience." In *The Japanese Mind*, ed. C. A. Moore. Honolulu: East-West Center Press.

Suzuki, S. 1970. *Zen Mind, Beginner's Mind*. New York: Weatherhill.

Swisher, L., and I. Hirsch. 1971. "Brain Damage and the Ordering of Two Temporally Successive Stimuli." *Neuropsychologia* 10:137–152.

Talbot, S. A., and U. H. Marshall. 1941. "Physiological Studies on Neural Mechanisms of Visual Localization and Discrimination." *American Journal of Ophthalmology* 24:1255–1264.

Tart, C. 1975a. *States of Consciousness*. New York: Dutton.

————, ed. 1975b. *Transpersonal Psychologies*. New York: Harper.

Tavolga, M. C. 1966. "Behavior of the Bottlenose Dolphin (tursiops truncatus): Social Interaction in a Captive Colony." In *Whales, Dolphins, And Porpoises*, ed. K. S. Norris. Berkeley, Calif.: University of California Press.

Tedlock. B. 1987. "Dreaming and Dream Research." In *Dreaming: Anthropological and Psychological Interpretations*, ed. B. Tedlock. Cambridge: Cambridge University Press.

Teilhard de Chardin, P. 1959. *The Phenomenon of Man*. New York: Harper and Row.

Teleki, G. 1973. *The Predatory Behavior of Wild Chimpanzees*. Lewisburg, Penn.: Bucknell University Press.

Tellegan, A., and G. Atkinson. 1974. "Openness to Absorbing and Self-Altering Experiences ('Absorption'), A Trait Related to Hypnotic Susceptability." *Journal of Abnormal Psychology* 83:268–277.

TenHouten, W. 1978–79. "Hemispheric Interaction in the Brain and the Propositional, Compositional, and the Dialectical Modes of Thought." *Journal of Altered States of Consciousness* 4 (2): 129–140.

Teszner, D., et al. 1972. "L'asymmetrie droite-gauche du planum temporale." *Revue Neurologique* 126:444–449.

Teuber, H. L. 1972. "Unity and Diversity of Frontal Lobe Function." *Acta Neurobiologie Exp. (Warsz.)* 32:615–656.

Thigpen, C. H., and H. M. Checkley. 1957. *The Three Faces of Eve*. New York: McGraw-Hill.

Thom, R. 1975. *Structural Stability and Morphogenesis.* Reading, Mass.: W.A. Benjamine.

Thomas, C. C. 1968. *Early Experience and Behavior.* New York: Norton.

Thompson, A. H. 1935. *Bede: His Life, Times, and Writings.* Oxford: Oxford University Press.

Thorpe, W. H. 1966. "Ritualization in Ontogeny: I. Animal Play." *Philosophical Transactions of the Royal Society of London,* series B, 251:311–319.

Tickell, G. 1869. *The Life of Blessed Margaret Mary With Some Account of the Devotion to the Sacred Heart.* London: Burns, Oates and Co.

Tillich, P. 1963. *Systematic Theology.* Chicago: University of Chicago Press.

Timiras, P. S., and A. Vernadakis. 1968. "Brain Plasticity: Hormones and Stress." In *Endocrine Aspects of Disease Processes,* ed. G. Jasmin. St. Louis: Green.

Tobias, P. V. 1971. *The Brain in Hominid Evolution.* New York: Columbia University Press.

Trevarthen, C. 1969. "Brain Bisymmetry and the Role of the Corpus Callosum in Behavior and Conscious Experience." International Colloquium on Interhemispheric Relations, Czechoslovakia, June 10–13.

———. 1983. "Development of the Cerebral Mechanisms for Language." In *Neuropsychology of Language, Reading and Spelling,* ed. U. Kirk. New York: Academic Press.

Trungpa, C. 1981. *Journey Without Goal.* Boulder, Colo.: Prajna Press.

Tucci, G. 1961. *The Theory and Practice of the Mandala.* London: Rider and Co.

Tucker, D. M., and P. A. Williamson. 1984. "Asymmetric Neural Control Systems in Human Self-Regulation." *Psychological Review* 91 (2): 185–215.

Turiel, E. 1966. "An Experimental Test of the Sequentiality of Developmental Stages in the Child's Moral Judgements." *Journal of Personality and Social Psychology* 3:611–613.

Turkewitz, G., and P. A. Kenny. 1982. "Limitations on Input as a Basis for Neural Organization and Perceptual Development: A Preliminary Theoretical Statement." *Developmental Psychobiology* 15 (4): 357–368.

Turnbull, C. M. 1972. *The Mountain People.* New York: Simon and Schuster.

———. 1978. "Rethinking the Ik: A Functional Non-Social System." In *Extinction and Survival in Human Populations,* eds. C. D. Laughlin and I. A. Brady. New York: Columbia University Press.

Turner, V. 1967. *The Forest of Symbols.* Ithaca, N.Y.: Cornell University Press.

———. 1969. *The Ritual Process: Structure and Anti-Structure.* Chicago: Aldine.

———. 1974. *Dramas, Fields, and Metaphors.* Ithaca, N.Y.: Cornell University Press.

———. 1975. "Symbolic Studies." *Annual Review of Anthropology* 4:145–161.

———. 1979. *Process, Performance and Pilgrimage.* New Delhi: Concept Publishing House.

———. 1982. *From Ritual to Theatre.* New York: Performing Arts Journal Publications.

———. 1983. "Body, Brain, and Culture." *Zygon* 18 (3): 221–245.

Turner, V., and E. M. Bruner. 1986. *The Anthropology of Experience.* Urbana, Ill.: University of Illinois Press.

Tylor, E. B. [1881] 1960. *Anthropology.* abr. ed. Ann Arbor: University of Michigan Press.

Uexkull, J. V. 1909. *Umwelt und Innewelt der Tierre*. Berlin: Julius Springer.

Umiker-Sebeok, D. J. 1977. "Semiotics of Culture: Great Britain and North America." *Annual Review of Anthropology* 6:121–135.

Underhill, R. B. 1936. *The Autobiography of a Papago Woman*. Memoirs of the American Anthropological Association, 46. Menasha, Wis.

Uttley, A. M. 1966. "The Transmission of Information and the Effect of Local Feedback in Theoretical and Neural Networks." *Brain Research* 2:21–50.

Vajiranana, P. 1962. *Buddhist Meditation in Theory and Practice*. Kuala Lumpur, Malaysia: Buddhist Missionary Society.

Van Lawick-Goodall, J. 1968. "The Behavior of Free-Living Chimpanzees in the Gombe Stream Reserve." *Animal Behavior Monographs* 1:161–311.

———. 1971. *In the Shadow of Man*. Boston: Houghton Mifflin.

Van Vogt, A. E. 1970. *The Players of Null-A*. London: Dobson.

Varela, F. J. 1979. *Principles of Biological Autonomy*. New York: Elsevier North Holland.

Varela, F. J., et al. 1981. "Perceptual Framing and Cortical Alpha Rhythm." *Neuropsychologia* 19 (5): 675–686.

Vernon, P. E. 1969. *Intelligence and Cultural Environment*. London: Methuen.

Verny, T. 1982. *The Secret Life of the Unborn Child*. New York: Dell.

Vivekananda, Swami. [1956] 1982. *Raja-Yoga*. New York: Ramakrishna-Vivekananda Center.

Vycinas, V. 1961. *Earth and Gods*. The Hague: Nijhoff.

Wachterhauser, B. R. 1986. *Hermeneutics and Modern Philosophy*. Albany: State University of New York Press.

Waddell, L. A. [1895] 1972. *The Buddhism of Tibet, or Lamaism*. London: A. H. Allen, Dover.

Waddington, C. H. 1957. *The Strategy of the Genes*. London: Unwin Hyman.

———. 1972. "Determinism and Life." In *The Nature of Mind*. The Gifford Lectures 1971–72. Edinburgh: Edinburgh University Press.

Walens, S. 1981. *Feasting with Cannibals*. Princeton, N.J.: Princeton University Press.

Walker, B. 1982. *Tantrism: Its Secret Principles and Practices*. Wellingborough, Northamptonshire: Aquarian Press.

Walker, K. 1972. *Venture with Ideas*. New York: Samuel Weiser.

Wallace, A. F. C. 1956. "Revitalization Movements." *American Anthropologist* 58:264–281.

———. 1959a. "Cultural Determinants of Response to Hallucinatory Experience." *A.M.A. Archives of General Psychiatry* 1:58–59.

———. 1959b. "The Institutionalization of Cathartic and Control Strategies in Iroquois Religious Psychotherapy." In *Culture and Mental Health*, ed. Marvin K. Opler. New York: Harper.

———. 1966. *Religion: An Anthropological View*. New York: Random House.

———. 1969. *The Death and Rebirth of the Seneca*. New York: Random House.

Walsh, R. 1977. "Initial Meditative Experiences: Part I." *Journal of Transpersonal Psychology* 9 (2): 151–192.

———. 1978. "Initial Meditative Experiences: Part II." *Journal of Transpersonal Psychology* 10 (1): 1–28.

Walsh, R., and F. Vaughan. 1980. *Beyond Ego: Transpersonal Dimensions in Psychology*. Los Angeles: J. P. Tarcher.

Wambach, H. 1978. *Reliving Past Lives: The Evidence Under Hypnosis*. New York: Harper and Row.

Wang-ch'ug, Dorje. 1978. *The Mahamudra: Eliminating the Darkness of Ignorance*. Dharamsala, India: Library of Tibetan Works and Archives.

Warren, J. M., and K. Akert. 1964. *The Frontal Granular Cortex and Behavior*. New York: McGraw-Hill.

Webber, M. 1980. "Ritual: A Model of Symbolic Penetration." Master's thesis, Carleton University, Ottawa, Ont.

Webber, M., and C. D. Laughlin. 1979. "The Mechanism of Symbolic Penetration." Working Paper 79-8, Department of Sociology and Anthropology, Carleton University, Ottawa, Ont.

Webber, M., C. Stephens, and C. D. Laughlin. 1979. "The Cerebral Mask: The Logic by Which the Brain and Symbol are Connected." Paper presented at the International Congress of Americanists, Vancouver, B.C.

———. 1983. "Masks: A Reexamination, or 'Masks? You Mean They Affect the Brain?'." In *The Power of Symbols*, eds. N. R. Crumrine and M. Halpin. Vancouver, B.C.: University of British Columbia Press.

Weiss, J. M. 1972. "Psychological Factors in Stress and Disease." *Scientific American* 226:104–113.

Weissman, D. 1987. *Intuition and Reality*. Albany: State University of New York Press.

Wenger, M. A. 1941. "The Measurement of Individual Differences in Autonomic Balance." *Psychosomatic Medicine* 3:427.

Wenger, M. A., and B. K. Bagchi. 1961. "Studies of Autonomic Functions in Practitioners of Yoga in India." *Behavioral Science* 6:312–323.

Werner, G. 1970. "The Topology of the Body Representation on the Somatic Afferent Pathway." In *The Neurosciences*, eds. H. G. S. Quarton et al. New York: Rockefeller University Press.

Werntz, D. A., et al. 1982. "Alternating Cerebral Hemisphere Activity and the Lateralization of Autonomic Nervous Function." *Human Neurobiology* 1:225–229.

Westheimer, G. 1972. "Visual Acuity and Spatial Modulation Thresholds." *Handbook of Sensory Physiology* 7 (4).

Wheeler, J. A. 1982. "Bohr, Einstein, and the Strange Lesson of the Quantum." In *Mind in Nature*, ed. R. Q. Elvee. San Francisco: Harper and Row.

———. 1983. "Law Without Law." In *Quantum Theory and Measurement*, ed. J. A. Wheeler and W. H. Zurek. Princeton, N.J.: Princeton University Press.

Whitaker, H. A. 1971. *On the Representation of Language in the Human Brain*. Edmonton, Alta.: Linguistics Research Inc.

White, R. 1959. "Motivation Reconsidered: The Concept of Competence." *Psychological Review* 66:297–333.

Whitehead, A. N. 1927. *Symbolism*. New York: Capricorn Books.

———. 1929. *The Function of Reason*. Boston: Beacon Press.

———. 1964. *Concept of Nature*. Cambridge: Cambridge University Press.

———. 1978. *Process and Reality: An Essay in Cosmology*, rev. ed., D. R. Griffin and D. W. Sherburne. New York: Free Press.

Wilber, K. 1980. *The Atman Project: A Transpersonal View of Human Development*. Wheaton, Ill.: Theosophical Publishing House.

————. 1982. *The Holographic Paradigm and Other Paradoxes*. Boston: Shambhala.

————. 1983. *Up From Eden*. Boston: Shambhala.

————. 1984. *A Sociable God: Toward a New Understanding of Religion*. Boston: Shambhala.

Wilden, A. 1974. "Structuralism as Epistemology of Closed Systems." In *The Unconscious in Culture*, ed. I. Rossi. New York: Dutton.

Wilhelm, R. 1962. *The Secret of the Golden Flower: A Chinese Book of Life*. New York: Harcourt Brace Jovanovich.

Willis, J. D. 1972. *The Diamond Light*. New York: Simon and Schuster.

Wilson, C. 1972. *New Pathways in Psychology*. New York: Taplinger.

————. 1972a. "Discussion" of paper by Charles Savage in *The Pschoanalytic Forum*, ed. J. A. Lindon. Vol. 3.

Wilson, E. O. 1975. *Sociobiology: The New Synthesis*. Cambridge: Harvard University Press.

————. 1978. *On Human Nature*. Cambridge: Harvard University Press.

Wimsatt, W. 1980. "Reductionistic Research Strategies and Their Biases in the Units of Selection Controversy." In *Scientific Discovery*. Vol. 2, *Historical and Scientific Case Studies*, ed. T. Nickles. Norwell, Mass.: Kluwer Academic.

Winkelman, M. 1986. "Trance States: A Theoretical Model and Cross-Cultural Analysis." *Ethos* 14:174–203.

Witkin, H. A. 1971. "Social Influences in the Development of Cognitive Style." In *Handbook of Socialization Theory and Research*, ed. D. Goslin. Chicago: Rand McNally.

Witkin, H. A., et al. 1973. "Social Conformity and Psychological Differentiation." *Research Bulletin* (Educational Testing Service).

Wittgenstein, L. [1921] 1961. *Tractatus Logico-Philosophicus*. London: Routledge and Kegan Paul.

Wojciechowski, J. A. 1986. "Social Psychiatry in the Man-Made World." *American Journal of Social Psychiatry* 6 (3): 167–174.

Wolff, P. H. 1963. "Developmental and Motivational Concepts in Piaget's Sensorimotor Theory of Intelligence." *Journal of the American Academy of Child Psychiatry* 2:225–243.

Wolkove, N., et al. 1984. "Effect of Transcendental Meditation on Breathing and Respiratory Flow." *Journal of Applied Physiology* 56 (3): 607–612.

Woodroffe, J. [1919] 1974. *The Serpent Power*. New York: Dover.

Woolfolk, R. L. 1975. "Psychophysiological Correlates of Meditation." *Archives of General Psychiatry* 32:1326–1333.

Woolsey, C. N., and E. M. Walzl. 1942. "Topical Projection of Nerve Fibers from Local Regions of the Cochlea to the Cerebral Cortex of the Cat." *Johns Hopkins Hospital Bulletin* 8:315–344.

Wurtz, R. H., et al. 1982. "Brain Mechanisms of Visual Attention." *Scientific American* 246 (6): 124–135.

Yates, J. 1985. "The Content of Awareness is a Model of the World." *Psychological Review* 92 (2): 249–284.

Yin, R. 1970. "Face Recognition by Brain Injured Patients: A Dissociable Ability?" *Neuropsychologia* 8:395–402.

Yoshiba, K. 1968. "Local and Intertroop Variability in Ecology and Social Behavior of Common Indian Langurs." In *Primates*, ed. P. C. Jay. New York: Holt, Rinehart and Winston.

Young, A. 1982. "The Anthropologies of Illness and Sickness." *Annual Review of Anthropology* 11:257–285.

Young, J. Z. 1978. *Programs of the Brain*. Oxford: Oxford University Press.

———. 1987. *Philosophy and the Brain*. Oxford: Oxford University Press.

Young-Laughlin, J., and C. D. Laughlin. 1988. "How Masks Work." *Journal of Ritual Studies* 2 (1): 59–86.

Zinberg, N. E. 1977. *Alternate States of Consciousness*. New York: Free Press.

Zubek, J. P. 1969. *Sensory Deprivation: Fifteen Years of Research*. New York: Appleton-Century-Crofts.

INDEX

drugs, psychotropic, 156, 331; related experiences, 205
Dryopithecus, 123
dualism, 10

Eccles, Sir John, 102
ego, empirical, 32, 134, 241–266; as adaptive surface, 243; aliment of, 245; assimilation and accommodation, 249–252; average functioning of, 249; *décalages* in, 247–248; definition, 89, 243–244; development of, 246, 252–259; dreaming and, 267; ego-awareness, 90; ego-consciousness, loss of, 91; experience of, 243–246; formal operational, 259; operational, 255–259; preoperational, 253–255; primary adaptive structure of, 246; relegation and, 261–263; relevation and, 263–266; retrogression and transcendence of, 259–266; self-constructing, 252–253; sensorimotor, 253; systemic nature of, 246–247; unconscious and, 261–266. *See also* adaptation
eidetic image, 201, 203, 312; Tibetan visualization practice, 208; training to produce, 351, chap. 7 n. 5
eidetic intuition, Husserl's concept of, 29
electroencephalography (EEG); ergotropic-trophotropic tuning, 314; meditation, 310–311; prefrontal cortex, 116; sleeping and dreaming, 283–284
Eliade, Mircea, 215, 276
Ellul, Jacques, 174
empirical modification cycle (EMC): assimilation and accommodation, 252; definition, 59; development, 60; drawing of, 60; ontogenesis, 175; semiosis, 174
encephalization, 72, 124–125
enculturation, 66; pre-scientific, 10; social change and, 69
endorphins, 93
entrainment: actual and potential, 147–148; canalization of, 133; complexity of, 102; conscious network, 95; definition, 52–53; neural systems, 56; reentrainment, 151, 241

epigenetic landscape, 53–56, 60; drawings of, 54–55
epiphenomenalism, 10
epistemic process, 336–338; evolution of, 346
epistemology, 10, 344
epoche. *See* reduction
equilibration, 56; dynamic, 258
ergotropic system, 57
ergotropic-trophotropic system, 313–318; complementarity of subsystems, 315–316; pre- and perinatal entrainment, 318; retuning, 317; structural invariants, 322–323; tuning, 316–318
Erikson, Milton, 191, 279
Erlebnis, 108
eustress, 146
evolution: cortex, 125–128; neurognosis, 73; nervous system, 121; symbol, 181–187; unfoldment of, 6
exemplars, Kuhn's concept of, 342
experience: absorption states, 91, 118, 204; belief, understanding, and realization, 227–228; birth, 211; cortex and, 245; cthonic, 325; definition, 16–17, 108; desire and, 324; dreaming, 285; drug related, 331; ecstasy, 302, 312; empirical ego, 243–246; entrainment of, 106; ergotropic-trophotropic tuning, 319–320; flow and psychic energy, 299–300; higher psychic energy, 319–321; human, as extension of biological, 242; interpretation of, 152, 275; *!Kia*, among the Bushmen, 303; meditation, 203, 329; multiple realities, 274; as construct of the nervous system, 6; peak, 320–321; phases of, 140–141; portal, 273, 278, 326–328, 330; pre- and perinatal, 50, 214; psychic energy, 297–307, 319–321; shamanic ecstasy, 277; shamanic initiation, 232; symbolic, 245; symbols order, 188; transpersonal, 152, 227, 327; transpersonal, defined, 18–19; "two hands clapping" model, drawing of, 29; types of, 19; unfolding reality, 188; union, 209. *See also* consciousness

transductive logic, Piaget's concept of, 194, 255

transference, shamanic, 231

transformation of consciousness: cross-phasing, 154; stages of, 148–149; types of, 147–148

transpersonal anthropology. *See* anthropology

transpersonal experience. *See* experience

transpersonalism, 18–21; phenomenology and, xii

Tree of Life, 226

triune brain, MacLean's concept of, 70–72

trophotropic system, 57. *See also* ergotropic-trophotropic system

Tukano cosmology, 217–219

tuning the autonomic nervous system, definition of, 146–147

Turner, Victor, 161, 347; discovery of biogenetic structuralism, 351–352 chap. 8 n. 1; flow experience, 299–300; ritual as theater, 213–214

"two hands clapping" model of consciousness, 28–29, 106

U-curve hypothesis, 277

unconscious. *See* consciousness

understanding, 227, 242

unified field theory, 15

unpreparedness, Seligman's concept of, 63

vajra, 78

Varela, Francisco, 56, 337–338

vinnana, 351 chap. 7 n. 8

vipassana bhavana, 28

visions: Christian mystical, 306–307; in contemplation, 324; shamanic, 271

visualization: Buddhist practice of, 154; Tibetan meditation, 135; nine steps of Tibetan meditation, 199–200; Tibetan *yab-yum*, 207–211

Visuddhimagga, 351 chap. 7 n. 6

Vogt, A. E. van, 84

Void Consciousness. *See* consciousness

Waddington, C. H., 53

wang, 199, 208

warps of consciousness. *See* consciousness

Webber, Mark, 197, 203

Wheeler, John Archibald, 235–236

Whitehead, Alfred North, 57, 122, 189, 233–234; actual entity, 109

wholeness, drive of biological systems toward, 150

Wilber, Ken, 269–270, 340

will, 96

Winter Ceremony, Kwakiutl, 213

wisdom, in insight practice, 208

wolf ritual, Makah Indian, 197

womb symbolism. *See* symbol

yab-yum, Tibetan symbol of, 206–211

yidam, 207

yin-yang, 209

Also in NEW SCIENCE LIBRARY

Awakening the Heart: East/West Approaches to Psychotherapy and the Healing Relationship, edited by John Welwood.
Between Time and Eternity, by Ilya Prigogine and Isabelle Stengers. (*Forthcoming*)
The Holographic Paradigm and Other Paradoxes: Exploring the Leading Edge of Science, edited by Ken Wilber.
Imagery in Healing: Shamanism and Modern Medicine, by Jeanne Achterberg.
The Second Medical Revolution: From Biomedicine to Infomedicine, by Laurence Foss and Kenneth Rothenberg.
Space, Time, and Medicine, by Larry Dossey, M.D.
Waking Up: Overcoming the Obstacles to Human Potential, by Charles T. Tart.

COGNITIVE SCIENCE

Ritual and the Socialized Mind, by Henry M. Vyner. (*Forthcoming*)
Transformations of Consciousness: Conventional and Contemplative Perspectives on Development, by Ken Wilber, Jack Engler, and Daniel P. Brown.

SCIENCE AND SPIRITUALITY

Choosing Reality: A Contemplative View of Physics and the Mind, by B. Alan Wallace.
Perceiving Ordinary Magic: Science and Intuitive Wisdom, by Jeremy W. Hayward.
Quantum Questions: Mystical Writings of the World's Great Physicists, edited by Ken Wilber.
Science and Creation: The Search for Understanding, by John Polkinghorne.
Science and Providence: God's Interaction with the World, by John Polkinghorne.
The Tao of Physics: An Exploration of the Parallels between Modern Physics and Eastern Mysticism, second edition, revised and updated, by Fritjof Capra.
Up from Eden: A Transpersonal View of Human Evolution, by Ken Wilber.

ECOLOGY AND GLOBAL CONCERNS

Earth Conference One: Sharing a Vision for Our Planet, by Anuradha Vittachi.
The New Biology: Discovering the Wisdom in Nature, by Robert Augros and George Stanciu.
Staying Alive: The Psychology of Human Survival, by Roger Walsh, M.D.